Washington, DC

timeout.com/washingtondc

Published by Time Out Guides Ltd, a wholly owned subsidiary of Time Out Group Ltd.
Time Out and the Time Out logo are trademarks of Time Out Group Ltd.

© Time Out Group Ltd 2007
Previous editions 1999, 2001, 2004.

10 9 8 7 6 5 4 3 2 1

This edition first published in Great Britain in 2007 by Ebury Publishing
Ebury Publishing is a division of The Random House Group Ltd,
20 Vauxhall Bridge Road, London SW1V 2SA

Random House Australia Pty Limited 20 Alfred Street, Milsons Point, Sydney, New South Wales 2061, Australia
Random House New Zealand Limited 18 Poland Road, Glenfield, Auckland 10, New Zealand
Random House South Africa (Pty) Limited Isle of Houghton, Corner Boundary
Road & Carse O'Gowrie, Houghton 2198, South Africa

Random House UK Limited Reg. No. 954009

Distributed in USA by Publishers Group West
1700 Fourth Street, Berkeley, California 94710

Distributed in Canada by Publishers Group Canada
250A Carlton Street, Toronto, Ontario M5A 2L1

For further distribution details, see www.timeout.com

ISBN 10: 1-84670-000-0
ISBN 13: 978184670 0002

A CIP catalogue record for this book is available from the British Library

Colour reprographics by Wyndeham Icon, 3 & 4 Maverton Road, London E3 2JE

Printed and bound in Germany by Appl

Papers used by Ebury Publishing are natural, recyclable products made from wood grown in sustainable forests

Time Out Guides Limited
Universal House
251 Tottenham Court Road
London W1T 7AB
Tel + 44 (0)20 7813 3000
Fax + 44 (0)20 7813 6001
Email guides@timeout.com
www.timeout.com

Editorial

Editor Ros Sales
Deputy Editor Edoardo Albert
Consultant Editors Mark Jenkins, Brad McKee
Listings Editors Patrick Foster, Paula Wasley
Proofreader Gill Harvey
Indexer Anna Norman

Editorial/Managing Director Peter Fiennes
Series Editor Ruth Jarvis
Deputy Series Editor Lesley McCave
Business Manager Gareth Garner
Guides Co-ordinator Holly Pick
Accountant Kemi Olufuwa

Design

Art Director Scott Moore
Art Editor Pinelope Kourmouzoglou
Senior Designer Josephine Spencer
Graphic Designer Henry Elphick
Digital Imaging Dan Conway
Ad Make-up Jenni Prichard

Picture Desk

Picture Editor Jael Marschner
Deputy Picture Editor Tracey Kerrigan
Picture Researcher Helen McFarland

Advertising

Sales Director Mark Phillips
International Sales Manager Ross Canadé
International Sales Executive Simon Davies
Advertising Sales (Washington) Clint Tanner
Advertising Assistant Kate Staddon

Marketing

Group Marketing Director John Luck
Marketing Manager Yvonne Poon
Marketing & Publicity Manager, US Rosella Albanese

Production

Group Production Director Mark Lamond
Production Manager Brendan McKeown
Production Coordinator Caroline Bradford

Time Out Group

Chairman Tony Elliott
Managing Director Mike Hardwick
Financial Director Richard Waterlow
TO Magazine Ltd MD David Pepper
Group General Manager/Director Nichola Coulthard
TO Communications Ltd MD David Pepper
Group Art Director John Oakey
Group IT Director Simon Chappell

Contributors

Introduction Ros Sales. **History** Mark Jenkins. **Washington Today** Brad McKee. **Declared Unconstitutional** Mark Jenkins. **Architecture** Mark Jenkins. **Where to Stay** Denise Kersten. **Sightseeing** Steve Ackerman, Jessica Dawson (*A Mall with meaning, Walk: The road to the White House, Adolf Cluss's capital, J Edgar Hoover's Washington, From slave to freedman, Walk: Georgetown, Greening the city, H Street comes of age* Steve Ackerman; *The Smithsonian, Treasure rooms, Donald W Reynolds Center* Jessica Dawson). **Restaurants & Cafés** Denise Kersten, Kim O'Donnel, Caroline Schweiter (*Upscale but not uptight, Power playgrounds, The Ethiopian Connection* Caroline Schweiter). **Bars** Cathy Alter. **Shops & Services** Brad McKee. **Festivals & Events** Trey Graham. **Children** Patrick Foster. **Film** Mark Jenkins. **Galleries** Jessica Dawson. **Gay & Lesbian** Steve Gdula. **Music** Christopher Porter (*DC sounds: go go* Glenn Dixon; *DC sounds: indie* Mark Jenkins). **Nightlife** Kelly Potchak. **Sport & Fitness** Kimberly Forrest. **Theatre & Dance** Trey Graham. **Day Trips** Eric Wills. **Directory** Patrick Foster.

Maps john@jsgraphics.co.uk, except p256.

All photography by Elan Fleisher, except: page 12 Corbis; page 18 AP Photo / Empics; pages 19, 93 Bettmann / Corbis; page 27 Time Life Pictures / Getty Images; pages 64 (top right), 70, 79, 140 Alys Tomlinson; page 95 Courtesy Peabody Room, Georgetown Branch, District of Columbia Public Library; page 162 Jeff Tinsley; page 163 Trish Reynolds; page 167 Historic Tours of America; page 181 Ward Morrison; page 184 Tina Korhonen / Repfoto; page 204 (top right) Julia Heine / McInturff Architects; page 204 (bottom) Stan Barouh.

The following images were provided by the featured establishments/artists: pages 178, 182.

The Editor would like to thank all contributors to previous editions of *Time Out Washington*, whose work forms the basis for parts of this book.

Contents

Introduction

Everyone thinks they know Washington, DC. From the Capitol at one end of the Mall to the Lincoln Memorial at the other, with the White House off to the North and the Washington Monument somewhere in the middle, its structures are instantly recognisable. Neo-classical and sometimes rather sepulchral, the city's monumental core has provided a backdrop for world events from presidential inaugurations to anti-Vietnam War demonstrations. As a symbol of world power, Washington's historic heart has a power all of its own.

But what of the rest of the city? Around 582,000 people live within the District, according to the 2005 census. For DC Mayor Anthony Williams this figure was evidence of the end of a decades-long population drain to the suburbs. Washington today is changing fast. Gentrification is the city buzzword. Construction work is everywhere, particularly in areas east of 14th Street, NW, and property prices have risen dramatically (they've tripled or quadrupled in some areas). This has created tensions as residents of former low-income neighbourhoods have found themselves pushed out. Meanwhile, lucky new residents are flocking in. Like visitors, they can take advantage of free world-class museums, a clean and safe Metro service (Washington is easy to manage without a car), and enjoy spacious, leafy streets. These are getting even greener: several years ago the city received a private gift of $50 million to begin restoring the city's street trees; about 8,000 were planted in 2005 alone. Crime is down too. It's a complicated issue in DC, but it's safe to say that – in common with other American cities – crime rates have fallen dramatically.

With the influx of people with disposable incomes have come businesses to serve them. Washington now has glamorous bars (in addition to hallowed haunts of the political deal-makers; we list both), and eclectic restaurants and cafés. Straight-laced political staffers who live to work, heading home only to sleep ready for another dawn start in the corridors of power, probably still exist. But there are plenty more people for whom the city's burgeoning cultural life is an attraction. Washington is home to vibrant and creative art, music and theatre, and lively nightlife. This is a city on the move, with a direction very much its own. It's not New York. But then – as Washingtonians won't hesitate to point out – it doesn't want to be.

ABOUT TIME OUT CITY GUIDES

The fourth edition of *Time Out Washington, DC* is one of an expanding series of around Time Out guides produced by the people behind the successful listings magazines in London, New York, Chicago and other cities around the glob. Our guides are all written by resident experts who have striven to provide you with all the most up-to-date information you'll need to explore the city or read up on its background, whether you're a local or a first-time visitor.

THE LOWDOWN ON THE LISTINGS

Above all, we've tried to make this book as useful as possible. Websites, telephone numbers, transport information, opening times, admission prices and credit card details are all included in our listings, as are details of selected facilities, services and events. All were checked and correct at time of going to press. However, owners and managers can change their arrangements at any time. Before you go out of your way, we'd strongly advise you to phone to check opening times, dates of exhibitions and other particulars about the place you want to visit. While every effort has been made to ensure the accuracy of the information contained in this guide, the publishers cannot accept responsibility for any errors it may contain.

ESSENTIAL INFORMATION

For all the practical information you might need for visiting the area – including visa and customs information, details of local transport, a listing of emergency numbers, information on local weather and a selection of useful websites – turn to the Directory at the back of this guide (*pp220-236*).

THE LIE OF THE LAND

We have broken down the city into its best-known sections, and many of our chapters are divided according to these areas. We've included cross streets in all our addresses, so you can find your way about more easily; we've also included zip codes for any venue you might want to write to.

PRICES AND PAYMENT

We have noted where venues such as shops, hotels, restaurants and theatres accept the following credit cards: American Express (AmEx), Diners Club (DC), Discover (Disc), MasterCard (MC) and Visa (V). Many will also accept travellers' cheques, and/or other cards such as Carte Blanche.

The prices we've listed in this guide should be treated as guidelines, not gospel. If prices vary wildly from those we've quoted, ask whether there's a good reason. If not, go elsewhere. Then please let us know. We aim to give the best and most up-to-date advice, so we want to know if you've been badly treated or overcharged.

TELEPHONE NUMBERS

The area code for Washington, DC is 202. Maryland and Virginia use a variety of different area codes. We've included these codes in all telephone numbers printed in the guide.

Numbers preceded by 1-800 can be called free of charge from within the US, and some of them can be dialled (though not all free of charge), from the UK.

To dial numbers as given in this book from abroad, use your country's exit code (00 in the UK), followed by the country code of the United States. For more details of phone codes and charges, *see p233*.

MAPS

We've included a series of fully indexed colour street maps to the city at the back of this guide – they start on page 248. Where possible, we've printed a grid reference for each address that appears on the maps. There is also an overview map of the surrounding countryside, and a Metro transport map at the back of the guide on page 256.

LET US KNOW WHAT YOU THINK

We hope you enjoy *Time Out Washington, DC*, and we'd like to know what you think of it. We welcome tips for places that you consider we should include in future editions and take note of your criticism of our choices. You can email us at guides@timeout.com.

There is an online version of this book, along with guides to over 100 international cities, at **www.timeout.com**.

NEW TIME OUT
SHORTLIST GUIDES 2007

Time Out SHORTLIST — 'The slickest city guide publisher' The Times
Barcelona 2007
WHAT'S NEW | WHAT'S ON | WHAT'S NEXT

Time Out SHORTLIST — 'The slickest city guide publisher' The Times
London 2007
WHAT'S NEW | WHAT'S ON | WHAT'S NEXT

Time Out SHORTLIST — 'The slickest city guide publisher' The Times
New York 2007
WHAT'S NEW | WHAT'S ON | WHAT'S NEXT

Time Out SHORTLIST — 'The slickest city guide publisher' The Times
Paris 2007
WHAT'S NEW | WHAT'S ON | WHAT'S NEXT

Time Out SHORTLIST — 'The slickest city guide publisher' The Times
Prague 2007
WHAT'S NEW | WHAT'S ON | WHAT'S NEXT

Time Out SHORTLIST — 'The slickest city guide publisher' The Times
Rome 2007
WHAT'S NEW | WHAT'S ON | WHAT'S NEXT

The MOST up-to-date guides to the world's greatest cities

UPDATED ANNUALLY

WRITTEN BY LOCAL EXPERTS

Available at all major bookshops at only
£6.99 and from timeout.com/shop

Time Out SHORTLIST

In Context

US Capitol. *See p76.*

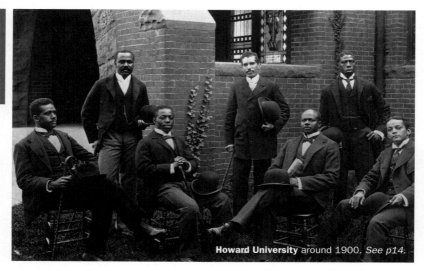

Howard University around 1900. *See p14.*

History

It began with a plan.

Symbolically, Washington is the heart of American democracy. More than 200 years after its founding, however, democracy for its own residents is only partial: DC's citizens can participate in presidential elections, but have no voting representation in the US Congress. This awkward circumstance is rooted in the city's founding, which was a political compromise between Northern and Southern states.

The Revolutionary War left the North with substantial debts that it pressed the new federal government to assume. In exchange, the Northerners abandoned their hopes of locating the government in a large Northern city such as New York or Philadelphia, each of which served as capital for a time. Instead, they agreed to construct a new city on the border between North and South. The actual choice was left to President George Washington, who chose a spot less than 20 miles from his Virginia plantation, Mount Vernon (*see p212* **Presidential seats**).

THE NEW CAPITAL

The first president was not the first person to recognise that the confluence of the Potomac and Anacostia rivers was a natural crossroads.

The area was an Indian meeting place a millennium before the Federal City was conceived. ('Potomac' may mean 'place where people trade' in the Algonquin language.) Still, the people who lived in the area when Europeans first arrived in the early 17th century left little besides place names.

Within the new city were two port towns that had been founded around 1750: Georgetown on the Maryland side and Alexandria in Virginia. Both were incorporated into the new District of Columbia, a diamond-shaped 100-square mile precinct that took 70 square miles from Maryland and 30 from Virginia.

But the new capital, which came to be known as Washington, would be built from scratch on land that was originally mostly farmland or forest – contrary to the popular belief that the city is built on a swamp. Washington hired a former member of his army staff, Pierre-Charles L'Enfant, to design the new city.

Construction of the White House and Capitol began in 1792-93, but neither was finished when John Adams, the country's second president, arrived in 1800. Adams and other members of the new government were but the first to notice the gap between the grandeur of L'Enfant's baroque street plan and the reality: a muddy frontier town of a mere 14,000 inhabitants, most of them living in Georgetown and Alexandria.

After 1801, residents of the District of Columbia lost their right to vote in Maryland or Virginia. The Constitution specified that Congress alone would control 'the federal district', although it's unclear that the document's drafters actually intended to disenfranchise the District's residents. The city of Washington was incorporated, with an elected city council and mayor appointed by the President. In 1820, the city's residents were allowed to elect the mayor as well. This was the first of the many tinkerings with the local form of government that were to follow.

'Washington was hardly a safe haven for former slaves.'

What progress had been made in creating the new capital was largely undone during the War of 1812. In 1814, after defeating local resistance at the battle of Bladensburg, British troops marched unopposed into the city and burned most of the significant buildings. President Madison fled the White House for the Octagon (*see p85*), the nearby home of Colonel John Tayloe. It was there that he ratified the Treaty of Ghent, which ended the war. Among the things destroyed by the British was the original collection of the Library of Congress, which didn't yet have its own building; former president Thomas Jefferson had sold the nation his library as the basis for a new collection.

After the War of 1812 established American sovereignty, European guests began to arrive to inspect the new capital. They were unimpressed. Visiting in 1842, Charles Dickens provided the most withering sobriquet for pre-Civil War Washington: 'the city of magnificent intentions'. It was another Englishman, however, who made the greatest impact on the city in this period. In 1829, James Smithson, a professor of chemistry at Oxford who had never even visited the United States, left his estate to the new nation for the founding of an educational institution. Congress was so bewildered by this bequest that it didn't act on it for more than a decade, but the Smithsonian Institution was finally founded in 1846. Its original building opened in 1855.

While the Smithsonian laid one of the earliest foundations for Washington's contemporary position as an information hub, the city showed

few signs of becoming a centre of commerce. In an attempt to increase trade, the Chesapeake & Ohio Canal was built, paralleling the Potomac River for 185 miles to Cumberland, Maryland. Ground was broken in 1828, and the canal's Georgetown terminus opened in 1840. The canal continued to operate into the early 20th century, but its importance was soon diminished by the Baltimore & Ohio Railroad, the country's first railway, which began operation in 1830 and arrived in Washington in 1835.

The other event of this period that had long-term significance for Washington was the 1846 retrocession to Virginia of the southern third of the District; this area now encompasses Arlington County and part of the city of Alexandria. Among the grievances of the area's residents was Congress's refusal to loan money to construct a Virginia-side canal connecting Alexandria to the west. The Virginia state government was more inclined to support the project than Congress, which has always been reluctant to spend money on people without any voting representatives in the Capitol. (The canal project was ultimately reduced to an aqueduct connecting Alexandria to the C&O Canal.) An underlying issue, however, was some Virginians' anticipation that Congress would soon restrict the slave trade in the District.

AFRICAN-AMERICAN CITY

From its founding, Washington had a large African-American population. By 1800, approximately one-quarter of the city's population was African-American, and most of those were slaves. By 1840, the ratio of white to black was similar, but there were almost twice as many free blacks as slaves. Free blacks and runaway slaves arrived in Washington to escape the horrors of life on Southern plantations, and quickly set up institutions to help their compatriots. Washington became a more attractive destination in 1850, when Congress did ban slave-trading (but not slavery itself). A year before Abraham Lincoln's 1863 Emancipation Proclamation, Congress abolished slavery in the District.

Despite the presence of some relatively prosperous free blacks, Washington was hardly a safe haven for former slaves. African-Americans were sometimes kidnapped off the city's streets and sold into slavery, the papers certifying their free status having been destroyed by their captors. Those who escaped this fate still had to live under the onerous 'black codes' adopted by Congress from the laws of Virginia and Maryland. These restricted African-Americans' property ownership, employment and trades, public meetings and even use of profane language. Being arrested for an infraction of these laws could result in a permanent loss of liberty, since jail wardens were authorised to sell their black prisoners to pay the cost of their incarceration.

CIVIL WAR CONSEQUENCES

The Civil War transformed Washington from a sleepy part-time capital into the command centre of an energised country – the first (but not the last) time that a national crisis actually benefited the city. New residents flooded into town, and such DC inhabitants as photographer Matthew Brady became nationally known for their war work. Among the new Washingtonians was poet Walt Whitman, who initially came to care for his wounded brother and then became a volunteer at the makeshift hospitals in the converted Patent Office and Washington Armory. (Whitman remained in the city for 12 years, working as a clerk at various federal agencies; he was fired from the Bureau of Indian Affairs when the new Secretary of Interior deemed *Leaves of Grass* to violate 'the rules of decorum & propriety prescribed by a Christian Civilization'.)

Several Civil War battles were fought near Washington, notably the two engagements at Manassas, now a local commuter-rail stop. A string of forts was built to protect the District, but only one saw action: Fort Stevens, site of an 1864 skirmish. The city's most significant war-related incident, the 1865 assassination of President Lincoln at Ford's Theatre, actually occurred five days after the South surrendered.

Following the end of the war, a Congress dominated by 'radical Republicans' made some efforts to atone for the sins of slavery. The Freedman's Bureau was established to help former slaves make the transition to freedom and in 1867 Howard University was chartered for African-American students. And all adult male residents of Washington were granted local suffrage in 1866, and 9,800 white and 8,200 'colored' men registered to vote.

Yet Congress did not address Washingtonians' lack of Congressional representation. In 1871, it reclassified the city as a territory, but quieted the latest round of rumours that it intended to move the capital west by authorising the construction of the massive State, War & Navy Departments Building directly west of the White House. A prominent local real-estate developer, Alexander Shepherd, was appointed to the territory's Board of Public Works, which he soon dominated. 'Boss' Shepherd began an ambitious programme of street grading and paving, sewer building and tree planting, transforming the city but also unfortunately quickly bankrupting it.

Only three years after establishing the territorial government, Congress abandoned it, putting the city under the control of three presidentially appointed commissioners. Local voting rights were eliminated, a move that one local newspaper welcomed as ending the 'curse' of African-American suffrage. President Grant, still a Shepherd supporter, nominated the 'Boss' to be one of the three new commissioners, but the Senate wouldn't confirm him. In 1876, Shepherd moved to Mexico, leaving behind a city that was beginning to look something like modern Washington.

The next major round of civic improvements was inspired in 1881 by severe flooding. A land-reclamation and flood-control project built Hains Point and West Potomac Park, quite literally creating the ground that would become the home of such Washington landmarks as the Lincoln and Jefferson Memorials. That same year, President Garfield was shot at the Baltimore & Potomac Railroad station (now the site of the National Gallery of Art) by a disgruntled job-seeker. Garfield died two months later in New Jersey, where he had been taken for the supposedly rehabilitative effect of the sea air.

'Federal government agencies were rigidly segregated.'

Following Shepherd's modernisation of the city, many improvement projects were undertaken. The Washington Monument was finally finished in 1885, and electric streetcars began operation in 1888, opening the areas beyond Boundary Street (now Florida Avenue) to development. In 1889, the National Zoological Park was founded in Rock Creek Park, which was officially established the following year.

NEW CENTURY AND THE NEW DEAL

Washington's 1900 centennial brought major plans to remake the city. Under the influence of the City Beautiful movement, the congressionally chartered McMillan Commission proposed restoring the primacy of the oft-ignored L'Enfant Plan and developing the neglected Mall and nearby areas along the river. Some of the city's poorest and most dangerous neighbourhoods were to be removed to create a grand greensward, and such unseemly intrusions as the Baltimore & Potomac station were to be banished from the Mall. The result of the latter dictum was Union Station, which upon its 1908 opening consolidated the city's several downtown railroad stations on a site north of the Capitol.

Covert Washington

Washington may not seem as exotic as Istanbul and Shanghai, or as ominous as Cold War-era Moscow and Berlin. Yet a former chief of the FBI's Washington Field Office, Ray Mislock, recently claimed that 'there are more foreign spies in Washington, DC than in any other city in the world'.

In 1917 Herbert O Yardley became a cryptologic officer with the American Expeditionary Forces in France. After the war, he was hired to create the first US peacetime code-breaking office, MI-8, also known as the Black Chamber. Its operations were very successful, but MI-8 was eliminated in 1929 by Secretary of State Henry Stimson, who supposedly announced, 'Gentlemen do not read each other's mail'. The impoverished Yardley wrote a controversial 1931 exposé, *The American Black Chamber*, and a lot of countries quickly changed their codes.

During the next World War, avoiding a potential spy scandal may have furthered John F Kennedy's presidential ambitions. As a young Naval Intelligence officer, JFK fervently romanced the glamorous Inga Arvad, a suspected Nazi operative. While FBI chief (and Kennedy nemesis) J Edgar Hoover kept the couple under surveillance, the future president's alarmed father, Joseph Kennedy Sr, pulled some strings to have his son transferred to active duty in the Pacific. There, his PT boat was sunk by the Japanese, an event that gave Kennedy war-hero status.

His affair with Arvad wasn't the only time the famously libidinous Kennedy entangled eros and intrigue. In 1964 one of the recently assassinated president's former lovers, Mary Pinchot Meyer, was mysteriously murdered on the C&O Canal towpath in Georgetown. While the slaying was never solved, two top CIA officials quickly arrived at Meyer's house to seize her diary. They were Cord Meyer, the victim's ex-husband, and James Angleton, the CIA counterintelligence chief .

Georgetown figures in more than a few Washington spy stories, even though the USA's own spies all operate from suburbs: the CIA is based in nearby McLean, Virginia; the Defense Intelligence Agency is headquartered at the Pentagon; and the National Security Agency snoops from Fort Meade, Maryland, which is near Baltimore-Washington International Airport. But Georgetown has been a frequent meeting place for spies and handlers, from Soviet courier Elizabeth Bentley in the '30s to US Navy analyst Jonathan Pollard, who a half-century later met his Israeli contact at Dumbarton Oaks. In 1985, CIA agent Aldrich Ames divulged the names of 20 agency informants in the Soviet bloc to a KGB man at Chadwick's, a K Street restaurant. The same year, the highest-ranking KGB agent ever to defect to the US, Vitaly Yurchenko, took leave of his CIA escort, slipped out through the kitchen and hailed a cab to the Soviet Embassy, where he de-defected.

The largest setback to American intelligence in recent years was the work of Robert Philip Hanssen, an FBI agent arrested in 2001 for supplying secret documents to the KGB. Hanssen spent much of his illegal income on stripper Priscilla Sue Galey, who worked at Joanna's 1819 Club, near Dupont Circle. It's still there, a reminder of the diverse activities that occur behind Washington's closed doors.

In 1910, the Fine Arts Commission was established to ensure the aesthetic worthiness of new federal structures, and an act was passed to limit the height of buildings.

A practical challenge to the McMillan Plan came with World War I, which prompted another Washington building boom. Dozens of 'temporary' structures were erected, including some built on the western part of the Mall. Many of these buildings were used not only during that war but for World War II as well. The last of them was torn down in 1971 and part of the space they occupied became Constitution Gardens, which opened in 1976.

The large numbers of sailors and soldiers demobilised in Washington after World War I are often cited as one of the root causes of the terrible race riots that convulsed the city in the summer of 1919. Nine people were killed in the worst disturbance, which began after false rumours spread that a black man had raped a white woman. Much of the violence spread from the Navy Yard into the predominantly African-American neighbourhoods nearby in Southwest.

Race relations were strained by the riots, but they were precarious even before them. Most of the advances for African-Americans in the post-Civil War era had been turned back by the early 20th century; President Woodrow Wilson, hailed as a visionary in foreign policy, was a reactionary on matters of race. Federal government agencies were rigidly segregated, as were most of the capital's public facilities – although its libraries, trolleys and buses, and baseball stadium (but not the teams that played there) were integrated.

In 1922, when the Lincoln Memorial (*see p65*) opened, the man who freed the slaves was commemorated by a racially segregated crowd; Tuskegee Institute President Robert Moten, an official invitee, was ushered to the negro section. Three years later, 25,000 hooded Ku Klux Klansmen marched down Pennsylvania Avenue, although the founding of a local Klan chapter drew little support. In 1926, the local superior court upheld the legality of voluntary covenants that were designed to prevent black people from buying property in predominantly white neighbourhoods.

Women won the vote in 1920, although not if they were DC residents. Meanwhile, separate and unequal African-American Washington

boomed, with the Harlem Renaissance mirrored on U Street, known as the Great Black Way. The Howard and other theatres frequently presented such performers as Ella Fitzgerald, Eubie Blake and Washington native Duke Ellington. The city's African-American neighbourhoods were swelled by dispossessed Cotton Belt agricultural workers, and the Depression was soon to send more Southern blacks to town.

In central Washington, the work begun by the McMillan Commission continued. Beginning in 1926, the construction of the Federal Triangle displaced the city's Chinatown and one of its roughest neighbourhoods, 'Murder Bay', while creating an area of monumental federal office buildings unified by their Beaux Arts style. Other events boosted the capital's national prestige: in 1924 and 1925, the Washington Senators baseball team made the first two of three trips to the World Series. (They won only

DC's model Metro

The first urban underground rail segment in the United States opened in Boston in 1897, when a few blocks of congested streetcar track were relocated below the street. Washington's Metro system could have begun the same way: several pieces of the city's trolley system were moved below ground, and one of those sections is still there – under Dupont Circle, and unused since 1961. But all of DC's streetcars ground to a halt shortly afterwards, when the US Congress, which then had absolute power over the District of Columbia, decided that they were old-fashioned, and banned them in 1962.

Like the authorities in other American cities, Congress had been subject to lobbying from

business interests determined to destroy public transport to make way for the car. However, it wasn't the end of the line for transit in DC. At almost the same time, Congress funded a study for a heavy-rail underground system.

The plan released in 1965 called for a 25-mile system, less than a quarter of the size of today's Metrorail network. The concept grew over time, and became entwined with a bitter fight over building freeways through the city centre. Eventually local protests managed to stop the decimation of the city by freeways, and the money earmarked for roads was transferred to Metro. This provided $2.2 billion of the eventual $9.7 billion cost of what was long called 'the 101-mile system'. (Today there are 106 miles of track.) The long-delayed groundbreaking came in December 1969, with the first short section – from Farragut North to Rhode Island Avenue – inaugurated in March 1976. The most recent additions, Largo Town Center and Morgan Boulevard on the Blue Line, opened in 2004.

Today, Metrorail carries almost 800,000 passengers on a typical weekday, making it the second busiest urban rail system in the

in 1924, and disappeared altogether in 1973.)
In 1927, the first Cherry Blossom Festival
was held, calling attention to the city's new
ornamental riverfront.

The Depression soon ended the major civic
improvement projects and made Washington
the focus for a different sort of national
attention. In 1931, a group called the Hunger
Marchers arrived in the city; they were followed
by some 20,000 jobless World War I veterans
who became known as the Bonus Army. They
encamped at various places around the city,
sometimes with their families, waiting for
Congress to pass legislation awarding them
back pay. Eventually troops under the
command of General Douglas MacArthur
dispersed the camps with bayonets and tear
gas. During this action four people were
killed, two of them young children.

In 1932, Franklin D Roosevelt was elected
president. When his New Deal created new

programmes and jobs, Washington again
benefited from national adversity. Local
construction crews began to work once more,
erecting the National Archives (*see p81*) and
the Supreme Court (*see p77*), both finished in
1935. Meanwhile, some of the president's
cabinet members and top advisers discovered
Georgetown, which fitted the 1930s vogue for
the colonial style; the old port town, which then
had a large African-American population,
became the first Washington neighbourhood
to go down the road towards gentrification.

The New Dealers took a more liberal stand
on racial issues. Although Roosevelt was
reluctant to antagonise segregationists with
major changes, he did sometimes invite black
leaders to receptions – and black musicians to
perform – at the White House. In 1939, when the
Daughters of the American Revolution refused
to let famed African-American contralto Marian
Anderson perform at the group's Constitution

country, after New York's. The connection is
somewhat ironic, since Metrorail was planned
from the beginning to be the antithesis of
New York's subway, which had a reputation
for being dirty, noisy, unreliable and crime-
ridden. Even the name 'Metro' was chosen
to avoid scary New York subway connotations
and evoke Paris or Montreal instead.

When Metro was being planned, only
four US cities had heavy-rail lines: New York,
Chicago, Philadelphia and Cleveland. New
York's was the best known, but all had similar
reputations – and they weren't good. So
Metro's planners decided to build a system
that would appear – and be – clean, airy, and
safe. They enlisted Chicago architect Harry
Weese, who designed vaulted stations to
combine the utility of poured-concrete forms
with a suggestion of Washington's iconic
domes. Clear sightlines were emphasised,
and places for potential attackers to hide
were minimised; video surveillance added
to the sense that Metro was wide open,
without the secret crannies of older systems.

Not every aspect of Weese's design was
hailed. He intentionally kept the stations dim,
saying that he wanted people to know they
were underground; some passengers who
tried to read complained that the ambience
was altogether too cave-like. And the heavy
reliance on escalators became a problem as
the system aged and mechanical systems
began to fail more frequently. (Built after

much underground infrastructure was already
in place, Metro had to go deep, requiring
some of the world's longest escalators.
The Wheaton station's escalator, taking
passengers to a depth of 230 feet, is the
deepest in the Western hemisphere.)

Overall, though, Weese's design has proved
both elegant and functional. Metro's crime
rate remains low, with most infractions
committed not in stations or on trains but
in parking lots and garages. There may even
be unanticipated potential benefits. Recent
forecasts of a possible terrorist poison-gas
attack on a US rail system suggest that
Metro, with its high ceilings, is less vulnerable
than others; much of the gas would rise, and
thus would not be diffused through the
tunnels by the gusts created by trains.

Recently, plans to expand Metrorail
have foundered due to cost. Maryland's
current governor is hostile to public transit,
and DC's government, which argues that it
pays too much of Metro's operating cost, is
discussing light-rail projects instead. Yet one
expansion is well into the planning stages: a
branch from the West Falls Church station to
Dulles International Airport, via the bustling
suburban office districts of Tysons Corner
and Reston. If all goes well, the first section
will open in 2011, with the final piece
completed in 2015 – making Metrorail a
129-mile system a mere 50 years after the
original 25-mile blueprint was announced.

Aftermath of 1968 riots. *See p19.*

Hall, Secretary of the Interior Harold Ickes immediately approved a concert at the Lincoln Memorial. Anderson performed there for an integrated crowd of 75,000.

World War II added to the city's bustle, as thousands of workers and volunteers arrived to further the war effort. National Airport opened in 1941, and the Pentagon (*see p109*), still the nation's largest federal office building, was rapidly constructed for the military command. (The Pentagon was built with separate bathrooms for white and black employees, but after FDR protested, signs distinguishing the facilities were never added to the doors.) Also opening in this period were two less martial structures, the Jefferson Memorial (*see p65*) and the National Gallery of Art (*see p67*). The arts kept a low profile for the remainder of the war, however, as such institutions as Dumbarton Oaks were requisitioned by wartime agencies.

Despite fears of a post-war depression, the city continued to boom in the late 1940s. As the Korean War began, the 1950 census put the District's population at 800,000, its highest point. Washington's new position as an imperial capital was emphasised by a series of controversial hearings on alleged Communist infiltration of the federal government. There were also two attacks by Puerto Rican nationalists: gunmen tried to shoot their way into Blair House to kill President Truman (he was living at the property, normally used for visiting dignitaries, during renovations to the White House). And then, soon after, attackers wounded five Congressmen on the floor of the House of Representatives.

In the 1950s, suburbanisation began to transform the land around Washington, most of it farms or woodland. Aided by new highways and federally guaranteed home mortgages, residential developments grew rapidly in the inner suburbs, followed by commercial development. Congress authorised the Interstate Highway System and supported plans for an extensive system of urban freeways for Washington that would destroy neighbourhoods and overwhelm the proportions of L'Enfant's plan.

The automobile, petroleum and rubber interests that worked quietly to destroy public transit systems in other American cities had no need for such subtlety in DC, which still had no elected local government. Corporate envoys influenced law makers to eliminate trolleys in favour of 'modern' cars and buses. Under Congressional pressure, streetcar lines were abandoned throughout the decade, with the final routes cut in 1962.

While the suburbs grew, Congress turned again to remaking embarrassing examples of poverty in the vicinity of the Capitol. Thousands of working-class inhabitants were displaced from Southwest Washington in a process called 'urban renewal'. (Critics called it 'urban removal'.) Southwest also became a focus for federal development, with massive new headquarters buildings erected near the new L'Enfant Plaza.

RIGHTS AND RIOTS

The city's white population began to decline precipitously in 1954, after the Supreme Court outlawed racial segregation. While many jurisdictions resisted the ruling, Washington quickly came into compliance. It was soon a majority black city, with a poverty rate that mortified federal officials. Under Presidents John F Kennedy and Lyndon Johnson, the capital became both the symbolic focus and a conspicuous test case of the civil rights movement and the 'war on poverty'.

In 1963, Martin Luther King Jr led a 200,000-person March for Jobs and Freedom to Washington, and delivered his 'I have a dream' speech at the Lincoln Memorial. Neither race relations nor inner-city economies improved significantly in the mid 1960s, and some feared the capital would soon experience the same sort of riots that had already scarred other major cities. Upon the 1968 assassination of Martin Luther King Jr, Washington and other cities erupted in flames. Twelve people were killed as rioters burned many small businesses in predominantly black sections of the city.

'In 1990 Mayor Barry was arrested after being videotaped smoking crack.'

Congress had already made tentative steps toward enfranchising Washington residents. In 1961, a Constitutional amendment gave Washington residents the right to vote in presidential elections, and in 1967, Congress restored the mayor and council system of government, but with all officials appointed by the president. Despite post-1968 fears that Washington would explode again, progress in establishing an elected local government was slow. Finally, in 1975, Walter Washington became the city's first elected mayor of the 20th century and its first African-American one.

The 'Free DC' battle for local voting rights was rooted in, and interconnected with, the larger civil rights movement. Many of the city's first elected officials – notably Marion Barry, who began the first of four terms as mayor in 1979 – were civil rights veterans. Almost as important,

however, was the anti-freeway campaign. An ad hoc citizens' group managed to stop most of the proposed highways through the city. Protests halted a planned freeway bridge across the Potomac River, and the slogan 'white men's roads through black men's homes' halted an eight-lane thoroughfare through Upper Northeast.

Local activists preferred a mostly underground rapid-rail system, which had already been discussed for half a century. Congress funded the system that would become the Metro, but influential Congressmen held up financing until residents also accepted the freeway system. They never did, and the Metro finally opened its first section in 1976. *See also p16* **DC's model metro**.

In the 1970s, Washington served as a backdrop for several national struggles, notably the one over the Vietnam war. President Richard Nixon, who recognised his local unpopularity, stressed 'law and order' – considered code words for racial fears – and painted the majority-black city as the nation's 'crime capital'. Then five burglars working indirectly for Nixon were arrested during a break-in at the Democratic National Committee campaign headquarters in the Watergate office building, and 'Watergate' gradually became synonymous with Washington and the corruption of the political system. Nixon resigned the presidency in 1974.

The city's reputation was supposed to be bolstered by the 1976 celebration of the nation's bicentennial, but most people skipped the party, perhaps frightened by reports of crowds that never materialised. Still, the year saw the opening of the National Air & Space Museum (*see p65*), which soon became the country's most popular museum.

Richard Nixon bids farewell after his resignation.

The following year, members of a small black Islamic group, the Hanafi Muslims, seized the District Building, the B'Nai Brith Building and the Washington Islamic Center in a protest against an obscure film depicting the prophet Mohammed. In the attack on the District Building, the headquarters of the mayor and the city council, a journalist was killed and councilman Marion Barry was wounded.

Faced with pressure from the DC statehood movement, in 1978 Congress passed a constitutional amendment that would have given the District voting representation in both the House and the Senate. The amendment was ratified by only 16 of the necessary 35 states, however, and expired in 1985.

In 1981, Ronald Reagan became president and, that same year, survived an assassination attempt outside the Washington Hilton Hotel. Reagan was ideologically opposed to big government and temperamentally averse to Washington. Nonetheless, after surviving the major recession of Reagan's first term, the region enjoyed a building boom, as new office buildings rose in both the city and its suburbs, especially Virginia. Tenants of the latter were known as 'Beltway bandits', after their proximity to the circumferential highway completed in 1964, which has become the main street of Washington's suburbs; many of them were government contractors who enjoyed the Reagan administration's large military build-up.

Although the city benefited from the tax revenues flowing from the new developments, Barry spent much of the money on assuring his political invulnerability. Years of rumours about the mayor's nocturnal activities were validated in 1990 when Barry was arrested after being videotaped smoking crack. Many Barry supporters were angered by the FBI sting,

however, charging entrapment. When brought to trial, Barry was convicted of only a misdemeanour, making him eligible for office at the end of his jail term.

DC IN THE 1990S AND 2000S

The city's white population has grown slightly in recent years, while middle-class blacks have departed in large numbers. The 2005 census put DC's population at 582,000, a figure that surely undercounts the illegal immigrants, many of whom fled Central America in the 1980s. Among Washington's foreign-born recent arrivals, Latinos are the fastest-growing group. The tension between these new residents and the city's predominantly black police force erupted in 1991, with two days of anti-police rioting in the largely Latino Mount Pleasant, Adams Morgan and Columbia Heights neighbourhoods.

Barry did indeed run again in 1994, winning re-election in a vote polarised along racial and class lines. He showed little interest in the job, however, and Congress had no patience for the notorious mayor. With revenues diminished by the early 1990s real-estate slump, the city was at great fiscal risk. Congress took advantage of the crisis to seize control of the city, putting a financial control board in charge of most municipal business.

When Barry was replaced by the sober, low-key Anthony Williams in 1999, Congressional leaders backed off. The pro-business Williams antagonised many residents, but his administration met the requirement to produce three years of balanced budgets, thus causing the financial control board to disappear in 2001.

On September 11 of that year, a hijacked airliner smashed into the Pentagon in nearby Virginia, killing 184. Although overshadowed by the much greater death toll in New York, the

Vietnam Memorial. *See p19.*

The making of a murder capital

The idea that Washington, gleaming marble capital of the American empire, is secretly a violent jungle has long had its appeal. *Newsweek* magazine first dubbed DC the country's 'murder capital' in 1941, and recently Republican supporters of the Iraq War have even crowed that the city is more dangerous than Baghdad.

Statistically, the latter claim is easily dismissed. And the 'murder capital' case is at best ambiguous. Homicides surged in Washington, beginning in the late 1980s, just as they did in most other large American cities, when an increase in crack cocaine use led to violent robberies and drug-gang wars. By the early 1990s, the label of murder capital of the United States was widely applied to DC. But since then, the number of murders has more than halved – from a peak of 489 to a low of 195 in 2005. (As of mid 2006, the trend is down further, if only slightly.) Clearly, something was very wrong then, and something is much better now. But there's little agreement about what either of those somethings are.

Real improvements shouldn't obscure the fact that it was demographic anomalies that sent Washington to the top of the per capita murder chart in the early '90s, rather than actual differences in its situation. The US Census Bureau concedes that it undercounts minority and immigrant residents, so the 'per capita' basis for calculating DC's 1990s crime rate was dubious. When the census released the 2000 numbers, it increased its estimate of Washington's population by 50,000 to 572,059; in mid 2006 it boosted it to 582,049. Even more significant is the fact that DC's population nearly doubles every weekday. A recent analysis of 2000 census data indicates that the city population grows daily to 982,853 – a 71.8 per cent increase, the largest in the US. (This is well ahead of second-place Boston, which expands by 41.1 per cent.) And that's not including the tourists, diners and clubbers who swell the city's body count seven days a week. Yet when two drunken suburbanites get into a fight in DC, that's tallied against the city's residential population to arrive at the 'per capita' assault rate.

Demographics aside, the fact remains that the actual number of murders has decreased dramatically, and no one really knows why. There are several identifiable factors, but calculating their exact effects is impossible. Crack cocaine burned its way through American inner cities, ultimately flaming out. The national and local economies improved in the 1990s, and unemployment declined. Rapid gentrification shoved some of the city's poorest and most desperate residents into the suburbs – especially Prince Georges County, Maryland, which has seen a major increase in crime, including murder. So perhaps DC's crime rate just isn't DC's anymore.

Washington's police department has attempted to take credit for declining felony numbers, but there's little evidence that the local cops are anything other than observers of crime trends. In the 1970s, the DC police had one of the country's best rates for solving murders, but that declined dramatically under Mayor Marion Barry, and has barely improved in the years since. Several highly publicised recent cases of violent attacks by felons who could have already been in custody for previous crimes illustrate the police department's continuing ineptitude.

Overall crime continues to decline in 2006, but at the time of writing there has been a spike in armed robberies, including a few that have escalated to murder. Some alarmed observers suggest that a diversion of funding and interest to 'homeland security' has undermined crime-fighting efforts. It would be comforting to think that crime increases can be explained that readily. Washington's 20-year journey to 'murder capital' and back shows that there are no easy explanations.

Pentagon attack – and the likelihood that a fourth plane was supposed to hit the Capitol or the White House – put the federal government on high alert, where it essentially remains. Security was tightened, barriers went up around federal buildings, and permanent new crowd-control methods were hastily planned. Tourism fell dramatically, but has since rebounded to former levels.

If the monumental core has never looked less welcoming, many inner-city neighbourhoods are rapidly gentrifying; prices of existing houses are soaring, and new buildings rising in many areas. Williams, who announced in 2006 that he won't seek a third term, did not deliver on some of his promises, but he did fulfill one 30-year-old dream: in 2005, the city was granted a new professional baseball team, the Washington Nationals.

Key events

700 Indians use the confluence of the Potomac and Anacostia Rivers as a meeting place.
1608 Captain John Smith is the first known European to explore the Potomac, although he was apparently preceded by fur traders.
1749 Alexandria founded by Scottish settlers.
1751 Georgetown chartered by the Maryland Assembly.
1790 The US Congress votes to establish a Federal City and to move the capital there from Philadelphia.
1791-92 Pierre-Charles L'Enfant plans the new city, but is soon fired.
1800 President John Adams moves to the District of Columbia, the new capital.
1802 The city of Washington is incorporated, with local government by an elected council and a mayor appointed by the president.
1814 British troops invade Washington.
1820 Congress allows Washington's 30,000 residents to elect the city's mayor.
1829 Englishman James Smithson leaves his estate to the new nation for the founding of an educational institution.
1846 The portion of the District south of the Potomac is ceded back to Virginia.
1850 Congress abolishes slave trade in Washington, but not slave ownership.
1861-65 The Civil War greatly expands Washington's influence and size.
1862 Congress bans slavery in the District.
1865 President Lincoln is assassinated at Ford's Theatre.
1871 Congress converts Washington to a territorial government.
1874 Congress abandons territorial government, eliminates local voting rights and gives control of the city to three presidentially appointed commissioners.
1881 President Garfield assassinated. Flood-control project creates Hains Point and West Potomac Park.
1902 The McMillan Commission begins to restore the L'Enfant Plan.
1912 The first of 2,000 cherry trees, a gift from Japan, are planted near the Tidal Basin.
1917 America's entry into World War I spurs another population and building boom.
1919 Inflamed by false rumours of a black man's rape of a white woman, white rioters attack black neighbourhoods. Nine die.
1922 In the city's worst natural disaster,

97 people are killed when the roof of the Knickerbocker Theater collapses during a 26-inch snowfall.
1924 The Washington Senators baseball team wins the World Series for the first and last time.
1928 The first licensed TV station in the US opens in Washington.
1932 The federal government grows dramatically under Franklin D Roosevelt's New Deal. Jobless World War I veterans camp in Washington and are eventually dispersed by troops, killing four.
1950 During the Korean War, the population grows to 800,000, its highest point.
1954 DC schools and recreation facilities desegregated.
1961 A Constitutional amendment gives Washington residents the right to vote in presidential elections.
1962 The last lines of the local trolley system close, shut down by Congressional edict.
1963 Martin Luther King Jr delivers his 'I have a dream' speech at the Lincoln Memorial.
1964 The Capital Beltway is completed.
1967 Congress re-establishes the mayor and council system of government for the city, but with all officials appointed by the president.
1968 Riots follow Martin Luther King Jr's assassination. Twelve people are killed.
1972 Burglars working indirectly for President Richard Nixon are arrested during a break-in at the Watergate Office Building.
1975 Walter Washington becomes the city's first elected mayor of the 20th century and its first African-American one.
1976 The first segment of the Metro rapid-rail system opens.
1981 President Reagan is wounded by a would-be assassin outside the Washington Hilton Hotel.
1990 Mayor Marion Barry is arrested after being videotaped smoking crack.
1994 After serving prison time, Marion Barry is re-elected mayor.
1995 Congress appoints a control board to run most of the city government.
1999 Anthony Williams becomes mayor.
2001 The final segment of the planned 103-mile Metro system opens; the control board closes. A hijacked plane hits the Pentagon, killing 184.
2005 Washington gets a new professional baseball team, after a 32-year absence.

Lincoln Memorial. *See p65.*

Washington Today

Washington seems to wake up to a new version of itself every day, though some people prefer the old one.

So many clichés and caricatures have been applied to Washington over the years that it would be hard for a visitor to know where to find an honest thread and pull towards the truth. To some people, DC is the capital of the free world; to others, it's a plantation. It's one big amusement park, or just the shooting gallery. A place you go to discover or a place you're merely sent by the electorate to deride. A magnet for the well-educated or, as one fresh-mouthed blogger put it, 'like high school with nuclear weapons'.

ASPIRATIONS AND REALITY: BUILDING THE NEW CITY

To people living here, Washington can be all those things in the course of a day. The truth is that the city has a way to go before it can reconcile its aspirations with the grimmer reality of its modern life. In a city that sat largely moribund for almost three decades (except, notably, for the start of Metrorail construction in the 1970s), a recent rush of building has astounded even the lifers. Some areas of the city have come to look like crane gardens, or Berlin in the late '90s, as the earth moves and dust swirls on block after block for ambitious new projects to build offices and housing, and even a new museum or two.

In the late 1990s, bullish developers began to transform the downtown area with a new sports arena and gigantic convention centre before fanning out towards the neighbourhoods to claim any tiny piece of leftover property, usually for condominiums and shops. Since 2001, there has been about $18 billion worth of new construction in the District. The most

Green and pleasant **Dupont Circle** (*see p92*), the heart of a wealthy neighbourhood.

surprising difference is seen in a large swath of the city's midsection that was burned during the riots of 1968, particularly from 14th Street, NW heading east. This area is once again burgeoning with the things that make a good city – a lot of new residents, and businesses to serve them. A nationwide real estate boom has seemed acutely magnified here: property values in much of the city doubled between 1995 and 2005, and in places like the Logan Circle section of town, they tripled and quadrupled. The number of permits issued to build new houses and apartments reached a 30-year high in 2005. The mayor, Anthony Williams, announced a campaign in 2000 to bring 100,000 new residents into the city by the decade's end, though between 2000 and 2005 the city lost about 57,000 people, according to census estimates.

The city owes whatever confidence it has recovered largely to Williams. Though he is not a very interesting person, he cuts a far more establishmentarian profile than did Marion Barry, his populist predecessor, who likes to wear a dashiki and was, in the end, concerned with little other than himself. Barry's mayoral career almost ended with his arrest by the FBI for smoking crack cocaine in a downtown hotel in 1990. Once he got out of jail, voters returned him to office in the belief he'd been framed. Barry stepped down for good in 1998 and made way for Williams, who had been

running the city while he was head of a special control board set up by Congress – which by constitutional writ has the last word on most District affairs. The board had been set up in 1995 as a hedge against the city's impending bankruptcy and a rebuke to Barry's second rule. Williams's somewhat stiff performance satisfied Congress, persuaded Wall Street to restore a decent rating to DC's municipal bonds, and came as a relief to voters, who kept him in office for a second term in 2002.

For years, residents had been fleeing Washington for the suburbs, unnerved by Barry's inept administration and a brutal crime rate that spiked in the early '90s with a crack cocaine epidemic. Four thousand people were murdered in Washington between 1988 and 1997 (*see p21* **The making of a murder capital**). Yet the city's affluent minority, who come in all colours and live mainly on the left-hand side of Northwest, seemed barely to register the hectic desperation of the poorer neighbourhoods that lie not at all far from them.

WHITE FLIGHT – BACK TO THE CITY
Historically, these poor neighbourhoods have been black, but perhaps not forever. These days, the buzzword in Washington is gentrification – a barely veiled code word for whitening.

People who have a choice are setting up home in DC again in droves. A lot though not all of them are white people who are moving into long-established black neighbourhoods, such as Shaw, LeDroit Park, Columbia Heights and Petworth in Northwest and sections of Northeast and Southeast as well. Between 2000 and 2004, census estimates charted the first increase for generations in the District's white population, which rose by 7.5 per cent to about 30 per cent of the head count. At the same time, the city's longstanding black majority continued to shrink, to about 57 per cent in 2004 from 60 per cent in 2000. Many of the District's African Americans have moved to the suburbs of Prince George's and Charles counties.

'DC's worst problem is surely the disgraceful state of the city's public schools.'

The conflicts that arise alongside these colour shifts are not solely racial, but for some people, race dovetails too neatly with the sharp inflation of property values. Many black residents with low or fixed incomes find themselves facing higher rents and property taxes that threaten their ability to stay on affordably, and they see the growing presence of white faces as no coincidence. Yet the changing makeup of the middle section of Washington has not been the binary black/white affair so often expressed in shorthand. Well ahead of the white influx came immigrants from Central America, Southeast Asia, the Caribbean and East Africa, often settling into enclaves of black Washington.

About 13 per cent of the city's population is foreign-born, a figure that has risen in recent years, albeit slightly – immigrants in the metropolitan region now number more than one million. Many have raised families in the District and are as vulnerable as anyone to the often shockingly high cost of living here. A fair number of these households wind up moving to the suburbs for cheaper housing. But members of DC's large Central American phalanx in particular have proved adept at forming cooperatives and buying entire apartment buildings rather than be pushed out of the city completely.

THE GOOD LIFE

For those who make a go of living in DC, the rewards are somewhat mixed. Residents gain the amenity of the city's parks, museums and countless other free or inexpensive attractions – for most of which they share the cost with the millions or other US taxpayers. The Metrorail and Metrobus systems are as clean, efficient,

comprehensive and affordable as any transit system in the United States. For motorists, many of DC's streets have been resurfaced, and 52 of the 214 bridges in town have been repaired or replaced. A bicycle master plan has put 25 miles of bike lanes on streets where there were almost none. Several years ago, the city received a private gift of $50 million to begin restoring the city's street trees; about 8,000 were planted in 2005 alone (*see p101* **Greening the city**). Municipal services such as motor vehicle registration, recreation centres, trash collection, and snow removal have improved considerably since Williams became mayor and began to infuse the practically foreign notion of customer service into the ranks of the city's civil employees. He even set up an all-purpose hotline (1-202 727 1000) for people to call when they have a problem that involves the city government.

Hart Senate Office Building.

EDUCATION, EDUCATION, EDUCATION

Yet a phone call cannot solve DC's most vexing problems, the worst of which is surely the disgraceful state of the city's public schools. Between the mayor's office, the DC Council, and a feckless school board, no one has seemed to be able to take firm control of the District's schools and put them on a track towards even mere adequacy. The voters have long made clear their exasperation with the system, but there has not been any potent effort made to hold public officials to account for its deficiencies.

The city runs 167 public schools with 58,000 students, and their performance consistently ranks among the worst in the nation. Certain public schools in the richer parts of town manage to remove themselves from this demoralising scenario, mainly through private fund raising by parents. And about 17,000 students are attending around 50 'charter' schools as part of a shadow school system that Republicans in Congress imposed on DC in 1996. The charter schools are run outside the official system but receive public funds nonetheless – about $140 million a year that would otherwise go towards funding conventional public schools, a galling number of which are housed in buildings that barely meet safety codes.

Many middle-class parents who cannot afford DC's extremely costly private schools see the charter schools as a haven and as a way to continue living in DC, though a lot of families have moved just outside the District's boundaries so they can send their kids to public schools in Maryland or Virginia. As badly as Mayor Williams has wanted to expand the District's population, he seems not to have understood that he can pursue all the forward-looking urban developments he wants, but that no city can truly flourish as a decent place to live without providing a decent public education system for all its young people.

Public libraries generally play a crucial supporting role in that cause. But in DC, where the museums are world class, the libraries are execrable. While dozens of major cities in the US have erected big, proud new libraries in the past decade, the District government has dithered over whether to repair or replace its outmoded central library downtown. The library building itself (*see p87*) is an architectural touchstone designed by Ludwig Mies van der Rohe and named after Martin Luther King Jr, but years of neglect have left it barely serviceable.

In a city whose cultural vibrancy seems generally on the upswing, the District's failings in providing these most basic intellectual batteries contribute to an overriding

ambivalence towards day-to-day life here. When residents' fears become manifest of a rise in crimes committed by juveniles, as has happened in recent months, the solution has been for the police chief, Charles Ramsey, to declare a 'crime emergency', assign more police officers to the streets, and install surveillance cameras at troubled spots around town. Those tactics may make people feel temporarily better (or not), but they do nothing to address the corrosive absence of places for DC's kids to learn.

A TALE OF TWO CITIES

The public school situation is part of a larger pattern that has persisted in Washington ever since its latest supposed renaissance began several years ago. Life in DC has been a cabaret for people who have benefitted from an excellent education, who have well-paying jobs and, ideally, no children to worry about. For them, the only way is up. But for residents who have (or are) kids, or who are poor, old, dependent, disabled, unhealthy, mentally ill, or are in any other way at the mercy of the rest of the world – well, here's the panic button. It's been pushed a million times before.

House Un-American Activities Committee. *See p31.*

Declared Unconstitutional

The US Constitution is America's gold standard for civil liberties, but like most things, it's open to interpretation.

In June 2006, the US Supreme Court ruled that the Bush administration could not deny Geneva Convention protection to the Guantanamo Bay prisoners it calls 'enemy combatants' (as opposed to 'prisoners of war'). Despite the level of controversy surrounding Guantanamo since its inception, this was not the first – and probably won't be the last – interpretation of the US Constitution to go against George W Bush. And controversial as Bush II is, he's hardly the first president to defy fundamental US law. Indeed, the Constitution has been a battleground ever since it took effect on 4 March 1789.

The more famous date is 4 July 1776, when the Continental Congress adopted the **Declaration of Independence**. Largely written by Thomas Jefferson, the document affirmed that 'all men are created equal' and possess 'certain unalienable rights', including 'life, liberty, and the pursuit of happiness'. This was intended as a rebuke to Britain's King George III, but it also foreshadowed more than 200 years of struggle over the legitimacy of American government.

During the War of Independence the 13 former colonies devised a loose alliance under the Articles of Confederation that featured no executive at all. That had proved unworkable, and so the Constitution was drafted. It promised to safeguard 'the blessings of liberty to ourselves and our posterity', as well as 'domestic tranquility', 'the common defence', and 'the general welfare'.

SECOND CITY?

Yeah. Whatever.

If you're not reading us, what are you doing in Chicago?

The main body of the Constitution primarily establishes the workings of the new government. It was left to the first 10 amendments – known as the Bill of Rights – to guarantee rights of free speech, the press, public assembly, and religion, among others. Most of these have proved controversial at one time or another, and many have been infringed over the years. Among the provisions that are still employed by interest groups to fight their causes are 'the right of the people to keep and bear arms', which has been used by the gun lobby to justify restricting gun control, and the ban on 'cruel and unusual punishment,' cited by opponents of the death penalty.

Of course, it's important to remember that when the Constitution was ratified, the Bill of Rights did not apply to *all* the residents of the newly minted country. For much of American history, 'unalienable rights' were denied, or given only grudgingly, to anyone who was not a male of northern European heritage. Slavery was not abolished nationwide until 1865 (13th Amendment), African-American men weren't guaranteed the right to vote until 1870 (15th) and women achieved suffrage only in 1920 (19th).

ENTER THE SUPREME COURT

Today, it's widely accepted that the US Supreme Court can rule local, state or federal laws 'unconstitutional', and thus invalid. Yet this process is not explicitly outlined in the Constitution. The Court took the power for itself in 1803, in the case of Marbury v Madison, a modest issue of a man who had been appointed to be a Justice of the Peace, but never got the job. The court's response to this case established the principle of **judicial review** over the Congress and the president. By the time Marbury v Madison was decided, a potentially major test case for judicial review had already been and gone. In 1798, under President John Adams, the Congress passed four Alien and Sedition Acts, conceived in anticipation of a war with France that never happened. The most controversial of the laws outlawed publishing 'false, scandalous, and malicious writing' against the government or its officials. The act was passed with an expiration date, and so vanished when Adams left office in 1801. It was never reviewed by the Supreme Court, but it is widely considered to have been unconstitutional.

John Marshall, Chief Justice of the Supreme Court during Marbury v Madison, still held the post in 1831-32, when the Court notably failed to assert itself against a president. Faced with expulsion by the state of Georgia, the Cherokee tribe sought the court's protection. While rejecting the Cherokees' case that they constituted an independent nation, the court's majority did rule that Georgia's anti-Cherokee laws were unconstitutional. But President Andrew Jackson, a veteran Indian-fighter, refused to enforce the court's decision. Ultimately, thousands of Cherokees were killed and the rest driven from their land, undertaking a forced march to the west that became known as the Trail of Tears.

'In 1857 the Supreme Court ruled that a slave could never become a free man.'

In 1857, it was the Supreme Court itself that trampled on minority rights in the case of Dred Scott. Born a slave, Scott argued that he should be free upon the death of his master, who had taken Scott into a non-slave area of the Louisiana Territory. The court ruled that Scott had no standing to sue, which would have been enough to end his case. But the court, then led by pro-slavery Chief Justice Roger Brooke Taney, went further to rule that a slave could never become a free man. The decision outraged many in the Northern states, and helped spark the Civil War. Four years later, when 11 Southern states seceded from the union and formed the Confederacy, slavery was among the central issues. But the Southerners also made a case that went to the heart of the American system: the Compact Theory, more recently known as 'states' rights' – the idea that individual states had joined the country by choice, and so have the power to nullify actions by the federal government that they consider to violate the Constitution or other agreements.

HABEUS CORPUS

In what was left of the country after secession, President Abraham Lincoln quickly acted without Congressional approval to make preparations for war. He suspended habeas corpus, which allows for the immediate release of a prisoner if his imprisonment is found inconsistent with the law. Among the people arrested in this period was Marylander John Merryman, who had criticised Lincoln's actions and recruited soldiers for the Confederate Army. Chief Justice Taney issued a writ for Merryman's release, on the grounds that only Congress can suspend habeas corpus, but it was ignored. Two years later, Lincoln finally got Congressional approval for his waiving of constitutional rights. In recent years, the precedent set by Lincoln has been cited by administration supporters in favour of President Bush's Iraq War policies.

WHO IS CREATED EQUAL?

The period after the Civil War was one of rapid expansion, both in terms of territory and population. Immigration was generally encouraged, but there was still evidence that Americans did not really believe that 'all men are created equal'. Large numbers of Chinese workers arrived to build the first transcontinental railroad, but when the project was completed in 1869, the new residents were deemed a nuisance. In 1882, Congress passed the Chinese Exclusion Act, the first US law to bar a particular nationality from entering the country. The act was not repealed until 1943, and Chinese immigration remained subject to a tight quota up to 1965.

EXPERIMENTING WITH EMPIRE

The US began to acquire overseas territories in late 19th century, picking up Puerto Rico and the Philippines in the 1898 Spanish-American War. Among the period's most imperial actions was President Theodore Roosevelt's acquisition of Panama, then part of Colombia. Following a French company's failure to complete a canal across the isthmus separating the Atlantic and Pacific, Roosevelt tried to purchase the land, and was rebuked. So he supported a local uprising organised by the New Panama Canal Company, and bought the land from the rebels. All this was done without the consent of Congress, although the Constitution stipulates that Congress must authorise all acts of war and ratify foreign treaties – but Roosevelt said he didn't mind being accused of acting unconstitutionally, 'provided that we can go on with the canal'. During World War I, an Espionage Act and a new Sedition Act were passed, outlawing negative comments about the US flag, military and – ironically – Constitution.

RED DREAD

When the war ended in 1918, the law was turned against a new perceived threat: communists, who had become an American obsession after the Russian Revolution. President Woodrow Wilson appointed a attorney general, A Mitchell Palmer, who began monitoring 'subversives'. A series of 'Palmer raids' in 1919-20 led to the arrest of some 6,000 suspects, many of whom were illicitly held for long stretches without being charged. More than 200 mavericks who did not hold US citizenship, including Russian-born anarchist Emma Goldman, were deported. Palmer's influence faded when his prediction of a US Communist uprising on May Day 1920 turned out to be baseless. By 1923, all the people held under the Espionage and Sedition Acts had been released from prison. Subsequently, they

were granted amnesty, as a postwar nation recognised that unpopular opinions are protected by the Constitution.

JUDICIAL REVIEW HITS THE NEW DEAL

This period of domestic tranquility soon ended, however, with the upheaval of the Depression, which was followed by the widely unpopular possibility of being pulled into a second world war. Franklin Delano Roosevelt, who served as president from 1933 to 1945, dealt forcefully with both crises, sometimes showing little regard for constitutional limits to his power. In the mid 1930s, Roosevelt's ambitious proposals to revive the US economy were often thwarted by the Supreme Court, which overturned such laws as the National Industrial Recovery Act on the grounds that government had infringed on states' authority. Most of the president's antagonists on the court were over 70, so in 1937 Roosevelt proposed a bill calling for all federal judges to retire by that age. If any of them didn't, a new judge could be appointed to serve in tandem with the older one. This scheme, which could have expanded the Supreme Court to as many as 15 members, was denounced as an attack on basic constitutional principles, and was soundly defeated.

WORLD WAR II AND ITS AFTERMATH: GLOBAL POWER

Soon after the US entered World War II in 1941, rumours spread through the western states that Japanese-Americans were spying or plotting sabotage. In early 1942, for reasons that had more to do with domestic politics than wartime strategy, Roosevelt issued an executive order to detain most US residents of Japanese descent. About 120,000 people, two-thirds of them American citizens, were held in camps in remote areas of the western states. No such blanket approach was taken toward residents of German or Italian extraction.

At the conclusion of previous international wars, the US had withdrawn from the world stage, but this time America adopted a radically different policy. World War II ended with the US government shifting its emphasis from fascism to communism. To fight the new threat meant remaining firmly on the world stage, fighting the Cold War through permanent worldwide intelligence and covert-action agencies that frequently flouted American law.

At home, a second anti-Red panic erupted, as the House Un-American Activities Committee and Senator Joe McCarthy pursued supposed subversives. Some actual spies were caught, but many people had their careers (and sometimes their lives) destroyed simply for having been members of the US Communist Party, an affiliation that should have been fully protected by the Bill of Rights. Veteran Red-baiter Richard Nixon became president in 1969, and was soon using secret, legally unauthorised tactics both in South-east Asia and in the US. He became the first American president to resign, after it was determined that he had sanctioned hush-money payments to the 'Watergate burglars', who had broken into the Democratic National Committee's offices in the Watergate complex.

In the 1980s President Ronald Reagan presided over a complex and illegal plot to sell arms to Iran, officially a US enemy. The scheme's goals included persuading Iran to help free hostages, but also to get money to fund a congressionally forbidden campaign to overthrow the elected government of Nicaragua. Ten members of Reagan's administration were convicted of various crimes associated with the Iran-contra scandal, and the president finally conceded some responsibility. Admitting that he had previously denied trading arms for hostages, he explained that 'my heart and my best intentions still tell me that's true, but the facts and the evidence tell me it is not'.

AND WHAT ABOUT GEORGE W BUSH?
History has yet to fully unravel many of the legally suspect actions of the federal government and its leaders since World War II, including those of George W Bush. What is certain about the younger Bush is that, like others before him, he has asserted his prerogative as a 'wartime president' to ignore constitutional limits on his power – whether by denying due process to 'enemy combatants' or authorising surveillance of American citizens. This despite the fact that the US is not 'legally' at war in this case (war can be declared only by Congress).

The president has issued more than 750 'signing statements', which specify his interpretation of legislation he has signed into law. Critics say this amounts to him picking which provisions he will ignore, as when he reserved the right to waive the torture ban in a law passed to protect 'war on terror' detainees. Although the Bush administration officially maintains it doesn't sanction torture, the president exempted his government from the provisions of what is often called the 'McCain torture ban' (after Senator John McCain, a principal sponsor), declaring that he will view interrogation limits in the context of his wider powers to protect national security. In mid 2006, a task force of the American Bar Association declared Bush's use of signing statements 'contrary to the rule of law and our constitutional system of separation of powers'.

At a glance

1831-2 President Jackson refused to implement a Supreme Court ruling that Georgia's anti-Cherokee laws were unconstitutional. Ultimately thousands of Cherokees were killed, the rest driven from their land.
1857 In the Dred Scott case, the Supreme Court ruled that a slave could never be a free man.
1862 During the Civil War, President Lincoln suspended habeus corpus without permission of Congress.
1882 Congress passed the Chinese Exclusion Act, banning Chinese from entering the country.
1903 President Theodore Roosevelt supported a local uprising in Panama, without the consent of Congress, to gain land for the Panama Canal.
1919-20 Arrest of some 6,000 suspected communists, many of whom were held for long periods without charge.
1942 World War II: Japanese-Americans incarcerated in camps.
1947 Senator Joe McCarthy pursued subversives in the House Un-American Activities Committee.
1974 Nixon resigned after it was determined he had sanctioned hush-money payments to the Watergate burglars.
1980s President Reagan presided over the Iran-contra scandal.
2001 President Bush's post-9/11 policies are said by many to ignore constitutional limitations on the power of the president.

Typical Washington rowhouses:
12th Street, NW.

Architecture

The city on the hill.

Despite some forays into modernism, the
practice of architecture in Washington
remains an ongoing debate about neo-
classicism. DC's two best-known buildings,
the Capitol and the White House, symbolise
American government and, specifically,
Congress and the President. They also
exemplify the city's dedication to a formal, low-
rise style at odds with most American cities.

Although Washington was the first major
Western capital designed from scratch, it never
occurred to its creators to build a city free of
classical precedents. Such founding fathers as
Thomas Jefferson (an avid, if self-educated,
architect) insisted on architectural styles that
recalled democratic Athens and republican
Rome. George Washington hired Pierre-Charles
L'Enfant to design a baroque street plan. He
also mandated that the new capital's structures
be built of brick, marble and stone, thus giving
a sense of permanence to a city – and a country
– that in its early days seemed a bit wobbly.

FIRST BUILDINGS

The city's oldest buildings actually precede
Washington's founding. The river ports of
Georgetown and Alexandria existed prior
to their incorporation into the District of
Columbia, and they contain most of the area's
examples of 18th-century architecture. The
city's only surviving pre-Revolutionary War
structure is Georgetown's **Old Stone House**
(3051 M Street, NW, 1-202 426 6851), a modest
1765 cottage with a pleasant garden.

Georgetown may have the feel of a colonial-
era village, but most of its structures date from
the 19th and early 20th centuries. Many are
Victorian, but some are in the Federal style, a
common early 19th-century American mode
that adds classical elements like columns,
pediments and porticoes to vernacular
structures usually made of brick or wood.

Across the river in the Old Town district
of Alexandria, which was once but is no
longer part of DC, there are some larger

In Context

pre-Revolutionary structures, including **Carlyle House** (*see p108*) and **Christ Church** (*see p108*), a Georgian-style edifice where George Washington was a vestryman. Like Georgetown, however, most of Old Town is of 19th- and 20th-century vintage.

Further south is George Washington's plantation, **Mount Vernon** (*see p213*), now a museum about Washington and the life of colonial-era gentry. This Georgian estate (including a dozen outbuildings) is one of the finest extant examples of an 18th-century American plantation. Next to Arlington National Cemetery is **Arlington House** (also known as the Lee-Custis House), a neo-classical mansion that was once the home of another Virginia aristocrat, Confederate general Robert E Lee.

Washington's two most metonymic structures, the White House and the Capitol, were both first occupied in 1800 and have been substantially remodelled and expanded since. James Hoban was the original architect of the **White House** (*see p71*), but Thomas Jefferson, who lost the competition to design what was originally called simply the President's House, tinkered with the plans while in residence during 1801-09; the most significant additions were new monumental north and south porticoes, designed in 1807 by Benjamin Latrobe but not built until the 1820s. Many additions followed, with some of the more

recent ones (for offices and security equipment) out of sight. The structure apparently got its current name after it was whitewashed to cover the damage that resulted from being burned in 1814 by British troops, although the sandstone façade was first whitewashed in 1797 while still under construction.

The **US Capitol** (*see p76*), at the centre of the city's grid, has grown dramatically from William Thornton's modest original design. Since the cornerstone was laid in 1793, virtually every visible part of the structure has been replaced, from the dome to the east and west façades. The last major renovation of the exterior was done in 1987, and a controversial and long-delayed underground visitor's centre is still under construction, now promised for mid 2007. Despite its grander scale, the Capitol remains true to the original neo-classical conception, with Corinthian columns making the case that the building is a temple to democracy.

Other buildings that survive from the Federal period are less august, although one of them takes a singular form. Built in 1800 as the city home of the prosperous Tayloe family, the **Octagon** (*see p85*) gives a distinctive shape to the Federal style. Actually a hexagon with a semi-circular portico, the house was designed by Capitol architect Thornton. Both the **Sewall-Belmont House** (144 Constitution

A neo-classical temple to democracy: the **US Capitol**.

Avenue, NE) and **Dumbarton Oaks** (*see p99*) are fine examples of the Federal style, although they've been much altered since they were built in, respectively, 1790 and 1801. (The earliest part of Sewall-Belmont House dates to about 1750.) Dumbarton Oaks is most notable for its elegant gardens and its scenic location on the edge of Rock Creek Park. All three structures are now museums.

Washington's first business district developed around the intersection of Pennsylvania Avenue and Seventh Street, NW, and there are still some examples of pre-Civil War vernacular architecture in this area. The buildings near the intersections of Seventh Street with Indiana Avenue, E Street and H Street in nearby Chinatown all offer examples of the period. Also noteworthy is the 500 block of Tenth Street, NW, whose most imposing structure is the 1863 **Ford's Theatre** (*see p201*), site of Abraham Lincoln's assassination.

The government buildings erected in the first half of the 19th century generally adhered to the Greek Revival style, which modelled itself on such Athenian edifices as the Parthenon, rediscovered by European architects in the mid 18th century. Two of these structures, the **Patent Office** and the **Tariff Commission Building** (part of which also functioned as the General Post Office), face each other at Seventh and F Streets, NW. Both are early examples of the city's official style – also known in the US and especially in DC as neo-Grec – and both were designed at least in part by Robert Mills, best known for the Washington Monument. In 2002, the long-neglected Tariff Building became the Hotel Monaco. The Patent Office, home to the National Portrait Gallery and the Smithsonian American Art Museum, reopened in July 2006 after extensive renovations.

Mills also designed the **US Treasury Building** (15th Street and Pennsylvania Avenue, NW), with its 466-foot Ionic colonnade along 15th Street. In the first major divergence from the L'Enfant Plan, this edifice was placed directly east of the White House, thus blocking the symbolic vista between the building and the Capitol. Construction began in 1836 and wasn't completed until 1871, but that's speedy compared to the progress of Mills's **Washington Monument** (*see p71*). Started in 1845, it was completed (after a 20-year break due to lack of funds) in 1884. The highest structure in the world at its completion, the 600-foot monument is unusually stark by the standards of 19th-century Washington architecture. That's because the colonnaded base of Mills's plan was never built, leaving only a tower modelled on an Egyptian obelisk. Other notable examples of the pre-Civil War

era are **St John's Church** (1525 H Street, NW, 1-202 347 8766), designed in 1816 by Benjamin Latrobe, the architect of the Capitol's first expansion, but subsequently much altered; **Old City Hall** (now occupied by Superior District Court offices, Fourth and F Streets, NW); and the modest but elegant Georgetown **Custom House & Post Office** (1221 31st Street, NW), derived from Italian Renaissance palazzos and typical of small US government buildings of the period.

AFTER THE CIVIL WAR

The more exuberant styles that came after the Civil War are presaged by the first **Smithsonian Institution** building (1000 Jefferson Drive, SW), designed by James Renwick in 1846. Its red sandstone suits the turreted neo-medieval style, which has earned it the nickname the Castle. Fifteen years later, Renwick designed the original building of the **Corcoran Gallery** (now the Renwick Gallery, *see p73*). Modelled on the Louvre, it is the first major French-inspired building in the US. The Renwick is a compatible neighbour to a more extravagant Second Empire structure, the **Eisenhower Office Building** (17th Street & Pennsylvania Avenue, NW, 1-202 395 5895). The lavish interior of the structure, originally the State, War and Navy Building, is open to tours by appointment on Saturdays.

'Second Empire, Romanesque Revival and other ornate styles are well represented.'

The Civil War led directly to the construction of the **Pension Building** (Fifth & F Streets, NW), designed by Montgomery Meigs in 1882 to house the agency that paid stipends to veterans and their families. Now the National Building Museum (*see p92*), the structure was based on Rome's Palazzo Farnese, but is twice the size. Outside is a frieze that depicts advancing Union Army troops; inside is an impressive courtyard, featuring the world's largest Corinthian columns. The atrium was once essential to one of the building's marvels, its highly efficient passive ventilation system, now supplanted by air-conditioning.

The Eisenhower Building and the Pension Building were disparaged by both classicists and modernists, who often proposed razing them. Equally unpopular was the **Old Post Office** (1100 Pennsylvania Avenue, NW, 1-202 289 4224), which now houses shops, restaurants and offices. The 1899 building is an example of the Romanesque Revival, which adapted the

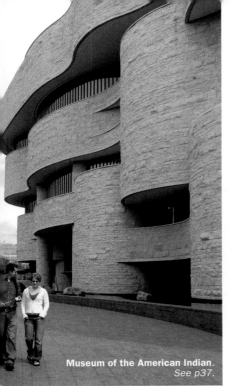

Museum of the American Indian.
See p37.

mausoleum at Halicarnassus, one of the seven
wonders of the ancient world. It was designed
by John Russell Pope, later the architect of
some of the city's most prominent buildings.
His work includes the **National Archives**
(*see p81*), the neo-classical temple that holds
the country's most fundamental documents.

The Archives is the tallest structure erected
during Washington's first large urban renewal
project, which during the 1920s converted one
of the city's most notorious precincts into the
government office district known as the Federal
Triangle. The Triangle's massive structures
provided the headquarters for most of the
executive-branch departments, and reiterated
the federal government's preference for
classicism. The project, which stretches from
Sixth to 15th Streets between Pennsylvania and
Constitution Avenues, NW, was interrupted by
the Depression, and its completion was then
debated for 50 years. Finally the government
committed to a design for the final structure,
the **Ronald Reagan Building** (14th Street
& Pennsylvania Avenue, NW), a hulking
mediocrity that opened in 1998. It too is in
classical drag, albeit with some tricky angles
to show that it's the work of the prominent
architectural firm of Pei Cobb Freed.

Pope went on to design several more neo-
classical temples, including the 1941 original
(now called West) building of the **National
Gallery of Art** (*see p66*) and the 1943
Jefferson Memorial (*see p65*). The latter is
partially derived from Rome's Pantheon, while
its 1922 predecessor, the **Lincoln Memorial**
(*see p65*), is modelled on Athens' Parthenon.

These contemplative edifices' bustling cousin
is **Union Station** (*see p80*), the 1908 structure
whose Daniel Burnham design borrows from
two Roman landmarks, the Arch of Constantine
and the Baths of Diocletian. Dramatically
remodelled before reopening in 1988, the
building's interior still features many of its
original architectural details – including
statues of centurions whose nudity is hidden
only by shields – but now incorporates shops,
eateries and a cinema. Most of the train-related
functions have been moved to an
undistinguished new hall to the rear.

Other notable neo-classical structures of
the period are the 1928 **Freer Gallery of Art**
(*see p63*) and the 1932 **Folger Shakespeare
Library** (*see p76*), an example of Paul Cret's
art deco-influenced 'stripped classicism'.

THE ARRIVAL OF MODERNISM

Modernism reached Washington after
World War II, but couldn't get comfortable.
One dilemma was (and is) the city's Height
Limitation Act, which bans skyscrapers.

rounded arches, dramatic massing and grand
vaults of 11th- and 12th-century Northern
European cathedrals. The structure contrasts
strongly with its Federal Triangle neighbours,
all built in a more sedate style in the 1920s,
and was threatened with demolition in the
1920s and again in the 1960s.

Second Empire, Romanesque Revival and
other ornate styles are still well represented in
the Logan Circle, Dupont Circle, Sheridan Circle
and Kalorama Triangle areas. Many palatial
homes were built in these areas in the late 19th
and early 20th centuries, and some survive as
embassies, museums and private clubs. Among
those open to the public are the **Phillips
Collection** (*see p95*) and **Anderson House**
(2118 Massachusetts Avenue, NW, 1-202 785
2040), home to the Society of the Cincinnati, a
group founded by Revolutionary War veterans.
The survival of the **Heurich Mansion** (1307
New Hampshire Avenue, NW, 1-202 429 1894), a
Victorian house museum that was once home to
a German-born beer mogul, is now in question.

One of the city's most remarkable
architectural fantasies is the **Scottish Rite
Temple** (1733 16th Street, NW, 1-202 232
3579), finished in 1915 and modelled on the

Washington-Dulles International Airport. One of modernism's few successes.

Various subterfuges have been employed to get an extra storey here or there, but no 'inhabitable' space is allowed to go above the 150-foot limit.

In the 1950s, modernist notions of design and planning were applied to an urban-renewal project, the New Southwest, with awkward results. Modernism also guided the nearby **L'Enfant Plaza**, a mammoth office, hotel and retail complex (bordered by Independence Avenue, Ninth Street and various freeway approaches); its masterplan was the first of several bad Washington designs by IM Pei, later one of the namesakes of Pei Cobb Freed. This ironically named assault on the L'Enfant Plan was followed by many stark, bleak buildings in Southwest, most of which were rented to the federal government.

'Modernist architects designed some of the city's least popular structures.'

In the 1960s and '70s, modernist architects designed some of the city's least popular structures, including the **J Edgar Hoover FBI Building** (*see p91*), a brutalist concrete fortress finished in 1972. Perhaps more damaging to the style's reputation, however, was the profusion of mediocre office buildings

in the 'New Downtown' along K Street and Connecticut Avenue, NW. Built with little consideration for Washington's distinctive street plan and without strategies for adapting the Bauhaus-derived American skyscraper style to the city's height limitation rules, these blank-walled knock-offs look like New York office blocks inexplicably stunted at the 12th floor.

Most of these buildings were designed by local architects, but nationally renowned modernists and post-modernists have also done lacklustre work in Washington, including Marcel Breuer's 1976 precast concrete **Hubert H Humphrey Building** (Second Street and Independence Avenue, SW). Adapting or abandoning Mies van der Rohe's 1972 black-box **Martin Luther King Jr Memorial Library** (901 G Street, NW) has recently been under discussion.

One of modernism's local successes is actually far from the District: **Washington-Dulles International Airport**, designed by Eero Saarinen in 1962 and now being expanded in accord with his widely imitated gull-wing scheme. Others include IM Pei's 1978 **National Gallery of Art East Building** (*see p66*) and Harry Weese's **Metro** system, which applies the same architectural motifs to all its stations. The latter two designs succeed in part because they're sensitive to their Washington context: the East Building's overlapping triangles play off the trapezoidal plot created by the L'Enfant street plan, while Metro's coffered vaults are simply an extreme example of stripped classicism. For more on the history of the Metro, *see p16* **DC's model Metro**.

The city's response to modernism is rooted in Georgetown, with its Federal-style structures, which became a fashionable neighbourhood when it began to be gentrified in the '30s, and **Lafayette Square**, which is surrounded by Federal-period houses. In the '60s, when demand for federal office space grew dramatically, replacing these houses with new office buildings was proposed. The eventual compromise was to erect two large structures just off the square, John Carl Warneke's 1969 **New Executive Office Building** (722 Jackson Place, NW) and **Court of Claims Building** (717 Madison Place, NW), which would defer to their older neighbours in form and material, if not in size.

These 'background buildings' set a precedent for design in the city's older districts; several local firms came to specialise in contextual postmodern structures that often incorporated façades of existing buildings. Examples include Shalom Baranes's remake of the **Army-Navy Club** (901 17th Street, NW) and Hartman-Cox's **1001 Pennsylvania Avenue, NW**, both

Washington Monument. *See p34.*

finished in 1987. Such 'façadomies' were widely criticised, especially when the new construction dwarfed the historic component; one conspicuous example of this is **Red Lion Row** (2000 Pennsylvania Avenue, NW). Yet the technique continues to be employed, with new examples along Seventh, Tenth and F Streets, NW.

The city's historicist architects are still influential, but no one style currently dominates. An updated, less dogmatic modernism is showcased in such structures as Kohn Pederson Fox's asymmetrical, vaguely industrial 1997 **World Bank** headquarters (1818 H Street, NW, 1-202 473 1806, tours by appointment), and Mikko Heikkinen and Markku Komonen's 1994 **Embassy of Finland** (3301 Massachusetts Avenue, NW, 1-202 298 5824, tours by appointment), which features a trellis façade, dramatic atrium and glass-wall overlook of Rock Creek Park. Such glass curtains are back in favour, notably in the sail-shaped exterior of Graham Gund Architects' near-triangular 2004 headquarters for the **National Association of Realtors** (500 New Jersey Avenue, NW).

On the Mall, 2004 brought a new example of neo-classicism, as well as a novel piece of contextual architecture. Friedrich St Florian's **World War II Memorial** (17th Street & Independence Avenue, SW) is an imperial-style shrine with a circular array of pillars and arches tucked into the vista between the Washington Monument and the Lincoln Memorial. The **Museum of the American Indian** (3rd Street & Independence Avenue, SW), adapted from a design by Douglas Cardinal, is clad in multi-hued limestone with a rough façade to suggest South-western mesas.

Many of today's architectural stars are not represented in Washington, and may never be; the Kennedy Center postponed plans for a Rafael Vinoly-designed expansion, and the Corcoran Gallery scrapped a Frank Gehry addition. The celebrity designer who's been busiest is Michael Graves. In addition to his 1997 **International Finance Corporation** building (2121 Pennsylvania Avenue, NW), he designed the **E Barrett Prettyman Courthouse annex** (3rd Street & Pennsylvania Avenue, NW) and is working on a Department of Transportation headquarters. British architect Norman Foster also has multiple projects, designing a trapezoidal addition for Capitol Hill's Acacia Building and a glass canopy for the Patent Office Building's courtyard. The canopy was supposed to be finished for the building's 2006 reopening, but was delayed when it had to be redesigned. Local architectural review boards decided that the initial scheme was insufficiently deferential to the historic structure.

Where to Stay

Ritz-Carlton, Georgetown. *See p54.*

Where to Stay

Where the Presidential Suite really is.

Finding a hotel in Washington used to be a pretty straightforward business: either you booked into a moderately priced generic chain hotel, or you dug deep into the company's expense account and stayed at the kind of lavishly expensive place where senators smoke cigars in wood-panelled lounges.

Those categories are still going strong but today there are more options: trendy boutiques, modern luxury properties, cosy B&Bs and even dirt-cheap hotels for the budget traveller.

Hotel Palomar (*see p48*), which opened in summer 2006, is one noteworthy newcomer to the capital. The 335-room high-end hotel just off Dupont Circle is run by the Kimpton Group, which owns six other unique hotels in the city. Its theme is 'art in motion' and true to that idea, works by local artists fill the lobby.

The **Beacon Hotel** (*see p49*), in Dupont Circle, is also a new addition to the hotel scene; it has a modern boutique atmosphere and a roof-top Martini bar. And then there's the **Park Hyatt** (*see p45*), which underwent a $24 million renovation, going from pink marble and gilding to wood, glass and steel.

Hay-Adams Hotel. See p41.

RATES AND SERVICES

Except in the smallest hotels, there is no such thing as a fixed rate in DC. Because many visitors swoop into town on business and leave by the weekend, rooms cost much more from Monday to Friday. And although prices are displayed in the rooms, almost no one pays the figure posted. All in all, rates vary according to the time of year, the day of the week and what discounts you can wangle.

The price categories below are for the cheapest rooms, and may not be available at all times. Rates decrease during summer – when locals flee the humidity – and late autumn, and are rock-bottom around Christmas. They are at their highest in spring, when DC sees a flux of school groups and cherry-blossom gazers. Bear in mind that taxes are added to prices quoted. In DC this is sales tax of 5.75 per cent, plus hotel tax of 14.5 per cent; in Maryland, sales tax is five per cent, with a seven per cent hotel or 'occupancy' tax. In Virginia, it's a combined local/state tax totalling 10.25 per cent.

When booking your room, ask about a corporate rate even if your company has no formal arrangement with the hotel. If relevant, inquire about senior rates too: some hotels offer 10 to 15 per cent off for guests over 65. Also mention any and all associations or frequent-flyer schemes you belong to, or – especially at quiet times – just ask straight out if there are any discounts available.

You can find lower rates at just about any DC hotel through web sites such as www.expedia.com, www.travelocity.com and www.orbitz.com. Internet wholesalers such as www.priceline.com offer hotel rooms at short notice or to the highest bidder. You can also reserve during office hours through Capitol Reservations (1-202 452 1270) or Washington, DC Accommodations (1-202 289 2220), which can sometimes get discounts and find a room even when the city's bursting with conferences.

In a town where the term 'presidential suite' might mean just that, there are only a handful of really low-budget options. DC has no campsites or RV/caravan sites. There is only one official youth hostel in town (**Hostelling International Washington, DC**, *see p48*), but thankfully it's a very good one.

A last word of warning: hotels change hands and names often in Washington, so double-check the name and address when you book.

The White House & around

Very expensive (over $250)

Hay-Adams Hotel

One Lafayette Square, NW, at 16th & H Streets, DC 20006 (1-202 638 6600/fax 1-202 638 2716/ www.hayadams.com). Farragut North or McPherson Square Metro. **Rates** $500-$800 single/double; $1,100-$5,500 junior suite/suite. **Credit** AmEx, DC, Disc, MC, V. **Map** p252 H5 ➊

A recent $19 million renovation only enhanced the already considerable grandeur of one of Washington's most elegant hotels. Its location on Lafayette Square provides great people-watching opportunities, as various anti-presidential protests take place in the park. The hotel unwittingly played a central role in the infamous Iran-Contra scandal in the 1980s, when millions of dollars of 'fundraising' changed hands in its leathery lounges. The roof deck has a great view of the White House and the basement bar oozes class. **Photo** *p40*.

Bar. Business centre. Concierge. Disabled-adapted rooms. Gym. Internet (free wireless). Parking ($30/night). Restaurant. Room service. TV (pay movies, DVD players).

Sofitel Lafayette Square

806 15th Street, NW, at H Street, DC 20005 (1-202 730 8800/fax 1-202 730 8500/www.sofitel.com). McPherson Square Metro. **Rates** $250-$600 single/ double; $350-$900 suite. **Credit** AmEx, Disc, MC, V. **Map** p250 H5 ➋

A relative newcomer close to the White House, Sofitel matches the standards of Washington's finest luxury hotels and adds a European flair. The contemporary design in its 220 rooms and 17 suites is worthy of a posh boutique hotel, and the French/ American cuisine at Café 15 draws diners who aren't staying here. Visitors love the soft down comforters, luxurious bathrooms and gracious staff.

Bar. Business centre. Concierge. Gym. Disabled-adapted rooms. Internet (wired high-speed in rooms $9.95/day; free wireless in public areas). Parking ($26/night). Restaurant. Room service. TV (pay movies).

The Capitol & around

Expensive ($160-$250)

Residence Inn by Marriott Capitol

333 E Street, SW, between 3rd and 4th streets, DC 20024 (reservations 1-800 228 9290/hotel direct 1-202 484 8280/fax 1-202 484 7340/www.capitol marriott.com). Federal Center SW Metro. **Rates** (incl breakfast) $159-$450 suites. **Credit** AmEx, DC, Disc, MC, V ➌

Opened in January 2005, the first Native American-owned Marriott is located four blocks south of the new National Museum of the American Indian and was built with the same limestone exterior. Inside, you'll find large suites with full kitchens (but uninspired decor) and good service. The hotel is especially family friendly; staff can configure four-bedroom suites and there are books and games available in the lobby. Ask for a room on one of the upper floors to escape the noise from nearby train tracks and construction. The surrounding area has few restaurants, so unless you plan to cook, you'll want to eat before returning to the hotel.

Business centre. Disabled-adapted rooms. Gym. Parking ($30/night). Swimming pool (indoor). Internet (complimentary wireless and wired high-speed). TV (pay movies, Nintendo game systems).

Moderate ($100-$159)

Holiday Inn on the Hill

415 New Jersey Avenue, NW, between D & E Streets, DC 20001 (reservations 1-800 638 1116/hotel direct 1-202 638 1616/fax 1-202 638 0707/www.hionthe hilldc.com). Union Station Metro. **Rates** $129-$329 single/double. **Credit** AmEx, DC, Disc, MC, V. **Map** p253 K6 ➍

The Holiday Inn on the Hill is quite possibly Washington's most family-friendly hotel. Under-19s stay free in a parent's room and under-12s don't pay to eat in the restaurant. The hotel also provides 10,000sq ft (930sq m) of meeting space as well as plenty of amenities for the business traveller. Rooms and bathrooms are not huge, but neither will you bump into the walls. It's near the Mall and all major tourist attractions (except great nightlife), as well as the Metro. Overall; you'll be hard pressed to find more for your money. Ask for a room far from the nearby fire station to avoid the occasional siren.

The best Hotels

For claustrophobics
Omni Shoreham (*see p52*) and **Hotel Palomar** (*see p48*).

For post-business relaxation
Park Hyatt (*see p45*), **Tabard Inn** (*see p51*) and **Fairmont** (*see p45*).

For seeing the sights on a shoestring
Hampton Inn Washington, DC-Convention Center (*see p48*).

For swinging singles
Jurys Washington Hotel (*see p51*), **Hotel Madera** (*see p49*) and **Hotel Helix** (*see p53*).

For White House views
Hay-Adams Hotel (*see p41*) and **Willard InterContinental** (*see p42*).

Bar. Business centre. Disabled-adapted rooms. Gym. Internet (free wired high-speed in rooms and wireless in public areas). Parking ($25/night). Restaurant. Room service. Swimming pool (outdoor). TV (pay movies, video games).

Union Station & around

Expensive ($160-$250)

Hotel George

15 E Street, NW, between New Jersey Avenue and North Capitol Street, Judiciary Square area, DC 20001 (reservations 1-800 576 8331/hotel direct 1-202 347 4200/fax 1-202 347 4213/www.hotel george.com). Union Station Metro. **Rates** $149-$429; $750-$1,200 suite. **Credit** AmEx, DC, Disc, MC, V. **Map** p253 K6 ⑤

The first Kimpton Group property in DC, the George sets the bar high. From the sleek, white lobby with grand piano to the hip, buzzy bar and excellent restaurant-bistro Bis, it generally hits the spot. Rooms vary, but are quite generously sized and decorated with refreshing restraint and style – not a floral in sight, and the only flourish is a Warhol-like print of a dollar bill. The newly renovated gym features high-tech equipment and steam rooms.
Bar. Business centre. Concierge. Disabled: adapted rooms. Internet (free wired high-speed). Parking ($26/ night). Restaurant. Room service. TV (pay movies).

Moderate ($100-$159)

Phoenix Park Hotel

520 North Capitol Street, NW, at Massachusetts Avenue, DC 20001 (reservations 1-800 824 5419/ hotel direct 1-202 638 6900/fax 1-202 393 3236/ www.phoenixparkhotel.com). Union Station Metro. **Rates** $139-$429 single; $169-$459 double. **Credit** AmEx, DC, Disc, MC, V. **Map** p253 K6 ⑥

A couple of blocks from the Capitol and across from Union Station, the Phoenix recently underwent a complete renovation, which means new furniture, linens, flat-screen TVs and fitness equipment. The Dubliner pub, which has an outdoor patio, is a gathering spot for local Hill workers and college students.
Bar. Disabled-adapted rooms. Gym. Internet (wireless and wired high-speed in rooms $9.95/day). Parking ($30/night). Restaurant. Room service. TV (pay movies).

Federal Triangle

Willard InterContinental

1401 Pennsylvania Avenue, NW, at 14th Street, DC 20004 (reservations 1-800 327 0200/hotel direct 1-202 628 9100/fax 1-202 637 7326/www. washington.interconti.com). Metro Center Metro. **Rates** $269-$610 single/double; $500-$4,200 suite. **Credit** AmEx, DC, Disc, MC, V. **Map** p252 H6 ⑦

As one of the very best hotels in DC, the Willard has hosted scores of figures of historical note, from Lincoln to Martin Luther King; since 1853 practically every US president has stayed here. The 341

oversized rooms and suites, all of which were renovated at the end of 2000, are stocked with modern amenities like wireless internet and CD players, while antique mirrors and four-poster beds maintain an old-fashioned sense of dignity. Some rooms have partial views of the White House or Capitol, and the hotel recently added a luxurious spa.
Bar. Business centre. Disabled: adapted rooms. Gym. Internet (free wireless in public areas; in-room wireless $10/day). Parking ($28/night). Restaurants (2). Room service. Spa. TV (pay movies).

South of the Mall

Very expensive (over $250)

L'Enfant Plaza Hotel

480 L'Enfant Plaza, SW, DC 20024 (reservations 1-800 635 5065/hotel direct 1-202 484 1000/fax 1-202 646 4456/www.lenfantplazahotel.com). L'Enfant Plaza Metro. **Rates** $259-$389 single/ double; $375-$795 suite. **Credit** AmEx, DC, Disc, MC, V. **Map** p253 J7 ⑧

A large opulent hotel located near the Mall and the Capitol. There are great views from the balconies but the business-heavy area largely shuts down at night. That said, the hotel goes out of its way to welcome families: children under 18 stay in parents' rooms for free, and pets are allowed. Business travellers are also very well catered for, and the rooftop swimming pool is perfect for downtime.
Bars (2). Business centre. Concierge. Disabled-adapted rooms. Gym. Internet (wireless $9.95/day). Parking ($26/night). Restaurants (2). Room service. Swimming pool (outdoor). TV (pay movies).

Mandarin Oriental

1330 Maryland Avenue, SW, at 12th Street, DC 20004 (reservations 1-888 888 1778/hotel direct 1-202 554 8588/fax 1-202 554 8999/www.mandarin oriental.com/washington). Smithsonian or L'Enfant Plaza Metro. **Rates** $350-$695 single/double; $900-$8,000 suite. **Credit** AmEx, DC, Disc, MC, V. **Map** p252 H7 ⑨

Many Washingtonians raised an eyebrow when the Mandarin chose a spot surrounded by government office buildings and a seafood market for its new 400-room hotel. But the international chain saw potential in the site – which, in fairness, is only a few blocks from the Mall and two Metro stations – and went about proving that location isn't everything. The hotel is sumptuous in every detail, from the gorgeous spa, indoor pool and top-notch restaurant to the bed linens and bathroom toiletries. It gives the Willard InterContinental, long the undisputed 'best' hotel in DC, a run for its money. Some rooms have views of monuments and the Tidal Basin.
Bars (2). Business centre. Concierge. Disabled-adapted rooms. Gym. Internet (free wireless in public areas; wired high-speed in rooms $12/day; web TV $6.95/day). Parking ($35/night). Restaurants (2). Room service. Spa. Swimming pool (indoor). TV (pay movies, DVD players).

Money's no object

Four Seasons.

It's a special occasion, and you're ready to break the bank. But where's the best place to go for a truly decadent splurge – the kind that might make you feel guilty if it weren't so amazing? Here are some suggestions.

The **Mandarin Oriental** (*see p42*) is one possibility. The large spa, fitness centre and indoor pool are spectacular – and spectacularly expensive to use if you're not actually staying at the hotel. Many rooms have dramatic river views and huge marble baths, and CityZen has got to be the best hotel restaurant in town.

If you prefer to stay in Georgetown, then check into a suite at the **Four Seasons** (pictured, *see p54*). The hotel was recently renovated in sumptuous detail, and the staff has mastered the art of pampering. And then unwind at the spa, one of DC's best.

Nearby is another luxurious choice, the **Ritz-Carlton Georgetown** (*see p54*). Housed in a restored industrial building on the Potomac River waterfront, the boutique Ritz is a see-and-be-seen kind of place for visiting celebrities and resident power-brokers.

Lavish and elegant, the **Hay-Adams** (*see p41*) exudes luxury with its ornate chandeliers, fine woodwork, soft linens and staff who will do just about anything to keep you happy. It's also close to the White House if you need to pop in to see the president.

Another landmark, the **Willard InterContinental** (*see p42*), is Washington's grande dame. Its huge lobby, afternoon tea service and traditional furnishings will transport you back in time. In the romantic Jenny Lind suite, a window above the jacuzzi frames the Washington Monument.

Less formal (but more fun) are the Kimpton Group's two high-end properties: **Hotel Monaco** (*see p47*) and **Hotel Palomar** (*see p48*). The Monaco, which occupies the stately, all-marble former General Post Office, is located in the vibrant Penn Quarter neighbourhood and has an excellent bar/restaurant, Poste. Dupont Circle's Palomar, which opened in summer 2006, features special 'relaxation suites' and an outdoor pool with cabanas. Both hotels offer in-room spa treatments.

Foggy Bottom/West End

Very expensive (over $250)

Park Hyatt

1201 24th Street, NW, at M Street, DC 20037 (reservations 1-800 233 1234/hotel direct 1-202 789 1234/fax 1-202 419 6795/www.parkwashington. hyatt.com). Foggy Bottom-GWU Metro. **Rates** $350-$695 single/double; $750-$995 suite. **Credit** AmEx, DC, Disc, MC, V. **Map** p252 F5 ⑩

A recent top-to-bottom overhaul has transformed this somewhat stodgy hotel into a modern luxury palace. You'll love the custom-designed furniture and soothing decor, limestone bathrooms with rain showers and deep tubs, and the new tea cellar, which features more than 50 rare brews from the east. The Blue Duck Tavern, a new restaurant, serves fine contemporary American fare.

Bar. Business centre. Concierge. Disabled-adapted rooms. Gym. Internet (wired high-speed $10/day). Parking ($35/night). Restaurant. Room service. Swimming pool (indoor). TV (satellite television with international channels).

Ritz-Carlton, Washington, DC

1150 22nd Street, NW, at M Street, DC 20037 (reservations 1-800 241 3333/hotel direct 1-202 835 0500/fax 1-202 835 1588/www.ritzcarlton.com/ hotels/washington_dc). Foggy Bottom-GWU Metro. **Rates** $329-$499 single/double; $579-$4,500 suite. **Credit** AmEx, DC, Disc, MC, V. **Map** p252 G5 ⑪

Something is always happening at the Ritz-Carlton. Various local celebs have joined the state-of-the-art fitness centre, Sports Club LA, to which guests have access. You'll see Secret Service men and beautiful people mingling in the lobby and in the intimate, luxurious lounges. Even the lowliest of rooms are labelled deluxe (they, like all other rooms, boast marble baths and high-speed internet access). If your company's paying, go for the Club experience, which offers a private lounge and 24-hour concierge service. The immediate neighbourhood is slightly dull, but the Ritz is its very own island of chic.

Bar. Business centre. Concierge. Disabled-adapted rooms. Gym. Internet (wired high-speed in rooms $9.95/day; wireless in public areas $10/day). Parking ($35/night). Restaurant. Room service. Spa. Swimming pool (indoor). TV (pay movies, DVD players and game systems available for rent).

Expensive ($160-$250)

Embassy Suites Hotel

1250 22nd Street, NW, at N Street, DC 20037 (reservations 1-800 362 2779/hotel direct 1-202 857 3388/fax 1-202 785 2411/www.embassysuites.com). Dupont Circle or Foggy Bottom Metro. **Rates** (incl breakfast) $169-$389 suite. **Credit** AmEx, DC, Disc, MC, V. Map p250 G4 ⑫

Yes, it's a generic chain hotel with identical twins in other cities. But the large, reasonably priced suites make this a good choice for families and business

Sofitel Lafayette Square. *See p41.*

travellers who need room to spread out. The complimentary breakfast is cooked to order, and there's a daily cocktail reception. New plasma-screen TVs and the swimming pool and sauna will help you relax after a day of sightseeing or board meetings.

Bar. Business centre. Concierge. Disabled-adapted rooms. Gym. Internet (wireless and wired high-speed $9.95/day). Parking ($19.95/night). Restaurant. Room service. Swimming pool (indoor).

Fairmont

2401 M Street, NW, at 24th Street, DC 20037 (reservations 1-866 540 4508/hotel direct 1-202 429 2400/fax 1-202 457 5010/www.fairmont.com/ washington). Foggy Bottom-GWU Metro. **Rates** (incl breakfast) $159-$619 single/double; $289-$789 Fairmont Gold single/double; $1,099-$4,500 suite. **Credit** AmEx, DC, Disc, MC, V. **Map** p252 F5 ⑬

The Fairmont's sunny, marble-floored lobby, so full of plants it looks like a greenhouse, instantly lifts the spirits. The pool, garden patio and 415 vast, bright rooms do the rest. The renovated fitness centre offers brand-new machines, a lap pool, squash and racquetball courts, aerobics classes and massages. Everyone, staff and guests alike, seem happy to find themselves here. The Fairmont Gold, a 'hotel within a hotel', is a club floor with separate check-in, and free continental breakfast, afternoon tea and evening cocktails in the private lounge. **Photo** *p46.*

Business centre. Disabled-adapted rooms. Gym. Internet (wireless $14.95/day; free for Fairmont Gold guests). Parking ($27/night). Restaurant. Room service. Spa. Swimming pool (indoor). TV (pay movies).

Hotel Lombardy

2019 Pennsylvania Avenue, NW, at I Street, DC 20006 (reservations 1-800 424 5486/hotel direct 1-202 828 2600/fax 1-202 872 0503/

Fairmont. *See p45.*

www.hotellombardy.com). Foggy Bottom-GWU or Farragut West Metro. **Rates** $175-$289 single/double; $249-$389 suite. **Credit** AmEx, DC, Disc, MC, V. **Map** p252 G5

Formerly a grand apartment building, this 134-unit boutique hotel retains some of that charm, with old-fashioned touches such as brass fixtures and crystal doorknobs, and a Middle Eastern-style bar. The views over Pennsylvania Avenue are good, but try not to get stuck in a room at the back of the building. There's also an attendant-operated lift – when was the last time you saw that in a hotel? Access to the pool at the nearby Washington Plaza Hotel is included.

Bar. Gym. Internet (free wired high-speed). Parking ($24/night). Restaurant. Room service. TV.

River Inn

924 25th Street, NW, between I & K Streets, Foggy Bottom, DC 20037 (reservations 1-888 874 0100/ hotel direct 1-202 337 7600/fax 1-202 337 6520/ www.theriverinn.com). Foggy Bottom-GWU Metro. **Rates** $169-$225 suite. **Credit** AmEx, DC, Disc, MC, V. **Map** p252 F5 ⓰

Once a family-friendly lodging that drew primarily government and university types, the River Inn became a boutique hotel when it was reinvented by Washington's hottest design firm. The new look exudes modern elegance, with dark wood and clean lines. The hotel pampers guests with plush robes, a video/CD library and in-room coffee makers; and its restaurant, Dish, serves up nostalgic American food.

Bar. Disabled-adapted rooms. Internet (free wireless first floor; free wired high-speed other floors). Parking ($20/night). Restaurant. Room service. TV (pay movies, game systems; DVD players in some rooms).

Moderate ($100-$159)

St Gregory Luxury Hotel & Suites

2033 M Street, NW, at 21st Street, DC 20036 (reservations 1-800 829 5034/hotel direct 1-202 530 3600/fax 1-202 466 6770/www.stgregory hotelwdc.com). Dupont Circle or Foggy Bottom-GWU Metro. **Rates** $139-$309 single/double; $159-$339 suite. **Credit** AmEx, DC, Disc, MC, V. **Map** p252 G5 ⑯

A whimsically stylish hotel – there's a life-sized statue of Marilyn in the lobby, skirt up – where each of the 154 rooms and suites look as if they were decorated by a pro. No expense has been spared with the floral displays and high-quality furniture. Many rooms also have full kitchens and some have balconies. The staff more than match the decor, treating everyone like VIPs. Stop by the hotel bar for a Mojito during happy hour.

Bar. Business centre. Disabled-adapted rooms. Gym. Internet (wired high-speed $9.95/day). Parking ($18.50 Fri, Sat nights; $25 weeknights). Room service. TV (pay movies; DVD players on request).

Downtown

Very expensive (over $250)

Madison

1177 15th Street, at M Street, NW, DC 20005 (reservations 1-800 424 8577/hotel direct 1-202 862 1600/fax 1-202 587 2705/www.loewshotels.com). McPherson Square Metro. **Rates** $229-$499 single/double; $429-$3,800 suite. **Credit** AmEx, DC, Disc, MC, V. **Map** p250 H5 ⑰

A downtown hotel whose luxurious and very traditional feel – just as founding father James Madison would have wanted – make it popular with visiting foreign dignitaries. One of its two restaurants, Palette, is sleek and modern – a departure from the rest of the hotel. The surrounding area is dominated by office buildings and is a little dull after dark, but you can easily walk to the livelier Dupont and Logan Circle neighbourhoods.

Bars (2). Business centre. Concierge. Disabled-adapted rooms. Gym. Internet (wired high-speed and wireless $10.95/day). Parking ($28/night). Restaurants (2). Room service. TV (pay movies and Sony PlayStations).

Expensive ($160-$250)

Hotel Monaco

700 F Street, NW, at 7th Street, DC 20004 (1-800 649 1202/1-202 628 7177/fax 1-202 628 7277/ www.monaco-dc.com). Gallery Place-Chinatown Metro. **Rates** from $169-$429 single/double; $469-$1,200 suite. **Credit** AmEx, DC, Disc, MC, V. **Map** p253 J6 ⑱

The transformation of the landmark General Post Office building into a high-end hotel (with equally top-notch restaurant, Poste) was a colossal undertaking for the Kimpton Group. The result, however, is remarkable – vivid colours and modern furniture in a classical building. The surrounding neighbourhood is vivid too, with the MCI Center, International Spy Museum and Mall all close by. The hotel's signature touch is the goldfish it lends to guests who could use the company.

Bar. Business centre. Concierge. Disabled-adapted rooms. Gym. Internet (free wired high-speed). Parking ($28/night). Restaurant. Room service. TV (pay movies).

Renaissance Mayflower Hotel

1127 Connecticut Avenue, NW, between L & M Streets, DC 20036 (reservations 1-800 228 9290/ hotel direct 1-202 347 3000/fax 1-202 776 9182/ www.renaissancehotels.com). Farragut North or West Metro. **Rates** $199-$459 single/double; $299-$529 suite. **Credit** AmEx, DC, Disc, MC, V. **Map** p252 G5 ⑲

With its grand floral displays, excellent food and professional, warm staff, the Mayflower epitomises Southern hospitality. Both Kennedy and Eisenhower stayed here before they moved to the White House, and FDR, Winston Churchill, Charles de Gaulle, Queen Elizabeth and Jimmy Stewart have all enjoyed the hotel's shimmering hospitality over the years. The property recently underwent a $9 million renovation, which means updated rooms and the addition of a VIP club floor. High tea, served every day from 3pm to 5pm, is a tradition. **Photo** *p49*.

Bars (2). Business centre. Concierge. Disabled-adapted rooms. Gym. Internet (wired high-speed in rooms for $9.95/day; free in suites). Parking ($26/night). Restaurants (2). Room service. TV (pay movies).

Moderate ($100-$159)

Comfort Inn Downtown/ Convention Center

1201 13th Street, NW, at M Street, DC 20005 (hotel direct 1-202 682 5300/reservations 1-877 424 6423/fax 1-202 408 0830/www.choicehotels.com). Mt Vernon Square/7th Street/Convention Center or McPherson Square Metro. **Rates** (incl breakfast) $129-$289 single/double. **Credit** AmEx, DC, Disc, MC, V. **Map** p252 H5 ⑳

A well-appointed hotel, Comfort Inn provides 100 surprisingly decent and, of course, comfortable rooms in an up-and-coming neighbourhood three blocks from the convention centre. The cheerful staff serve a free continental breakfast every morning.

Business centre. Concierge. Disabled-adapted rooms. Gym. Internet (free wired high-speed in rooms). Parking ($27/night). TV.

Hamilton Crowne Plaza

1001 14th Street, at K Street, NW, DC 20005 (reservations 1-800 227 6963/hotel direct 1-202 682 0111/fax 1-202 682 9525/www.hamiltoncrowne plazawashingtondc.com). McPherson Square Metro. **Rates** $150-$325 single/double; $300-$600 suite. **Credit** AmEx, DC, Disc, MC, V. **Map** p252 H5 ㉑

The gorgeous Beaux Arts architecture of the Hamilton dates from the 1920s, the elegant exterior on Franklin Square complementing the 318 small but elegantly appointed rooms and suites inside. Some of the rooms boast skyline views. 'Club level' guests get a private elevator, plus free breakfast and use of the club lounge, and there's a secure floor for female business travellers.

Bar. Business centre. Concierge. Disabled-adapted rooms. Gym. Internet (wireless $9.95/day in rooms, free in public areas). Parking ($28/night). Restaurant. Room service. TV (pay movies, game systems).

Budget ($99 or under)

Hostelling International Washington, DC

1009 11th Street, NW, at K Street, DC 20001 (hotel direct 1-202 737 2333/fax 1-202 737 1508/www. hiwashingtondc.org). Metro Center Metro. **Rates** (incl breakfast) $29-$32 per person. **Credit** MC, V. **Map** p252 J5 ㉒

A top-notch, dirt-cheap hostel close to the Metro and downtown Washington. Just two blocks from the Metro, it's convenient for sightseeing. You won't need the Metro to get to great dining and shopping, though; the immediate area has exploded with new restaurants and shops. The 228 guestrooms are unremarkable, but why spend time in your room?
Business centre. Disabled-adapted rooms. Gym. Internet (free wired high-speed in rooms and wireless in public areas). Parking ($22/night). Swimming pool (indoor). TV (pay movies).

Penn Quarter

Moderate ($100-$159)

Hampton Inn Washington, DC-Convention Center

901 6th Street, NW, at Massachusetts Avenue, DC 20001 (hotel direct 1-202 842 2500/fax 1-202 842 4100/www.hamptoninn.com). Gallery Place/ Chinatown Metro. **Rates** (incl breakfast) $119-$249 single/double; $179-$279 suites. **Credit** AmEx, DC, Disc, MC, V ㉓

Affordable, convenient and sparklingly clean, this chain hotel, opened in March 2005, has earned praise from visitors to Washington. Just two blocks from the Metro, it's convenient for sightseeing. You won't need the Metro to get to great dining and shopping, though; the immediate area has exploded with new restaurants and shops. The 228 guestrooms are unremarkable, but why spend time in your room?
Business centre. Disabled-adapted rooms. Gym. Internet (free wired high-speed in rooms and wireless in public areas). Parking ($22/night). Swimming pool (indoor). TV (pay movies).

Budget ($99 and under)

Hotel Harrington

436 11th Street, NW, at E Street, DC 20004 (reservations 1-800 424 8532/hotel direct 1-202 628 8140/fax 1-202 347 3924/www.hotel-harrington. com). Metro Center Metro. **Rates** $99-$109 single/ double; $125-$169 family room. **Credit** AmEx, DC, Disc, MC, V. **Map** p252 J6 ㉔

The Hotel Harrington is a budget hotel, plain and simple. The lobby and rooms are clean but outdated, the staff welcoming and helpful. People choose to stay here for two reasons: price and location. The hotel is surrounded by a neighbourhood where you'll never get bored, and the Smithsonian museums and the Mall are also within easy reach. Family rooms sleep up to six people, and the hotel has a self-service laundry.
Bar. Disabled-adapted rooms. Internet (free wireless). Parking ($10/night). Restaurants (2). Room service. TV.

Dupont Circle

Very expensive (over $250)

Hotel Palomar

2121 P Street, NW, DC 20037 (reservations 1-877 866 3070/hotel direct 1-202 448 1800/fax 1-202 448 1801/www.hotelpalomar-dc.com). Dupont Circle Metro. **Rates** $169-$575 single/double; $450-$2,100 suite. **Credit** AmEx, DC, Disc, MC, V ㉕

Formerly the Radisson Barcello, the Palomar is the Kimpton group's latest creation. Judging from the success of the company's other hotels – the Monaco, Madera, Topaz, George, Rouge and Helix – it's bound to be a hit. The Palomar shows the same playful spirit that has made the other hotels so popular; it has an outside water bar for dogs, a nightly wine hour, iPod docking stations on the clock radios and faux fur throws on the beds. There is also an outdoor swimming pool with cabanas and a northern Italian restaurant with pizza bar. The Palomar's theme is 'art in motion', and the hotel's collection includes pieces by local artists.
Bar. Business centre. Concierge. Disabled-adapted rooms. Gym. Internet (free wireless and wired high-speed). Restaurant. Room service. Parking ($32/night). Swimming pool (outdoor). TV (pay movies).

Mansion on O Street

2020 O Street, NW, between 20th & 21st Streets, DC 20036 (hotel direct 1-202 496 2000/fax 1-202 833 8333/www.omansion.com). Dupont Circle Metro. **Rates** (incl breakfast) $350-$2,000 suite. **Credit** AmEx, DC, Disc, MC, V. **Map** p250 G4 ㉖

Discretion exemplified, the 23-room B&B Mansion is hidden on a residential side street, with no sign to announce its presence. Each room in the three interconnected townhouses has a different theme: the Log Cabin suite, for example, has huge log beams, cowhide rugs and three Frederic Remington sculptures.

The complex also serves as a private club and non-profit museum, and everything you see, from the furniture to the wall hangings, is for sale. Some visitors love staying in a private mansion with 30 secret doors; others miss the better (and more accessible) service offered at conventional hotels.

Bar (self-service). Business centre. Internet (free wireless and wired high-speed). Parking ($25/night). Room service. Swimming pool (outdoor). TV.

Expensive ($160-$250)

Beacon Hotel

1615 Rhode Island Avenue, NW, at 17th Street, DC 20036 (reservations 1-800 821 4367/hotel direct 1-202 296 2100/fax 1-202 331 0227/www.beacon hotelwdc.com). Dupont Circle or Farragut North Metro. **Rates** $189-$259 single/double; $229-$259 suite. **Credit** AmEx, DC, Disc, MC, V. **Map** p250 G/H4 ㉗

Formerly the stodgy Governor's House Hotel, the Beacon has been completely remade into a boutique-style lodging befitting the trendy Logan Circle neighbourhood. Four nights a week, you can head to the rooftop for great views, designer Martinis and appetisers (weather permitting). The Beacon is convenient for Connecticut Avenue shopping and a short stroll to the White House. Passes to the YMCA are available on request. Some suites resemble small apartments, complete with kitchens. **Photo** *p53*.

Bar. Business centre. Disabled-adapted rooms. Parking ($15/night on weekends/$24 weeknights). Room service. Internet (wired high-speed and wireless $10.95/day). TV (pay movies; DVD players in some rooms).

Dupont at the Circle

1604 19th Street, NW, between Q & Corcoran Streets, DC 20009 (reservations 1-888 412 0100/hotel direct 1-202 332 5251/fax 1-202 332 3244/www.dupontatthecircle.com). Dupont Circle Metro. **Rates** (incl breakfast) $170-$240 single/double; $280-$450 suite. **Credit** AmEx, DC, Disc, MC, V. **Map** p250 G4 ㉘

Just off bustling Dupont Circle, this elegant B&B is housed in two connected townhouses dating from 1883. Thickly blanketed beds, a luxurious parlour and a charming family-style dining room make the place feel ritzy but comfy. The owner is friendly and helpful, and guests receive free passes to a nearby fitness centre and tickets to baseball games featuring the Washington Nationals, DC's new team. Smoking is prohibited throughout the inn.

Internet (free wireless). Parking ($15/night; reserve in advance). TV (certain rooms; some have DVD players).

Hotel Madera

1310 New Hampshire Avenue, NW, between N & 20th Streets, DC 20036 (reservations 1-800 430 1202/hotel direct 1-202 296 7600/fax 1-202 293 2476/www.hotelmadera.com). Dupont Circle Metro. **Rates** $139-$429 single/double. **Credit** AmEx, DC, Disc, MC, V. **Map** p250 G4 ㉙

More muted than the other Kimpton properties – for example, the flamboyant Hotel Rouge or whimsical Hotel Monaco – Madera plays with natural hues and

Renaissance Mayflower Hotel. *See p47.*

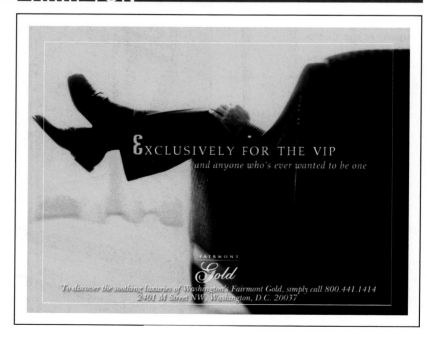

materials so as to create a soothing and sophisticated ambience. Unlike the other hotels in the group, though, the guest rooms here are prone to look rather, well, ordinary. Still, the location is hard to beat, the restaurant/bar Firefly is highly rated, and the speciality rooms include extras such as exercise equipment and kitchenette. The hotel offers a free wine hour and in-room yoga equipment.

Bar. Business centre. Disabled-adapted rooms. Internet (free wired high-speed in rooms). Parking ($28/night). Restaurant. Room service. TV (pay movies).

Moderate ($100-$159)

Swann House
1808 New Hampshire Avenue, NW, at 18th Street, DC 20009 (1-202 265 4414/fax 1-202 265 6755/ www.swannhouse.com). Dupont Circle Metro. **Rates** (incl breakfast) $150-$365 single/double; $35 per additional person. **Credit** AmEx, Disc, MC, V. **Map** p250 G4 ➌⓪

Unlike Washington's townhouse B&Bs, the Swann House, built in 1883, is a freestanding mansion, which means the hallways aren't cramped and the lighting is good throughout. The pleasant rooms, which vary in their colour schemes, are romantic without being twee and some have working fireplaces and jacuzzis. A small swimming pool nestles in a brick courtyard at the back. Although it's a four-block walk to the nearest Metro station, you are rewarded with a beautiful tree-lined neighbourhood within an easy stroll of the trendy bars on U Street and the hip strip of 17th Street. Swann House is no-smoking throughout, but there are plenty of decks and porches. Room prices include breakfast, afternoon nibbles and an evening sherry. Note: children under 12 are not allowed. A two-night stay is usually required at weekends.

Internet (free wireless). Parking ($14/night; reserve in advance). Swimming pool (outdoor). TV.

Tabard Inn
1739 N Street, NW, between Connecticut Avenue and 17th Street, DC 20036 (1-202 785 1277/fax 1-202 785 6173/www.tabardinn.com). Dupont Circle Metro. **Rates** (incl breakfast) $103-$133 single/double (shared bath); $148-$208 single/double (private bath). **Credit** AmEx, Disc, MC, V. **Map** p250 G4 ➌①

Each of the Tabard's 40 rooms is decorated in brilliant colours with a hotchpotch of slightly chipped antiques. Unique and classy, the hotel draws locals, who come to enjoy its excellent restaurant, garden courtyard in summer and roaring fire in winter. It's made up of three 19th-century townhouses and is the oldest continuously operated hotel in DC – the floors and doors squeak and there's no lift. Guests can use the nearby YMCA. All rooms are no-smoking.

Bar. Internet (free wireless). Parking ($29/night). Restaurant. TV (on request).

Topaz Hotel
1733 N Street, NW, between Connecticut Avenue and 17th Street, DC 20036 (reservations 1-800 775 1202/hotel direct 1-202 393 3000/fax 1-202 785

9581/www.topazhotel.com). Dupont Circle Metro. **Rates** $139-$399 double. **Credit** AmEx, DC, Disc, MC, V. **Map** p250 G4 ➌②

Topaz bills itself as DC's 'most enlightened boutique hotel', a theme that plays out with daily proverbs, morning energy drinks and speciality rooms (on request), which come furnished with exercise equipment and bottled water. There's also complimentary yoga equipment, or (for a fee) in-room spa treatments. It's not just for health nuts, though: in the evening, the small Topaz Bar comes to life with a complimentary wine hour, exotic cocktails, Asian-influenced fare and dance music.

Bar (with food service). Business centre. Concierge. Disabled-adapted rooms. Parking ($26/night). Internet (free wired high-speed). Room service. TV (pay movies).

Budget ($99 or under)

Jurys Washington Hotel
1500 New Hampshire Avenue, NW, at Dupont Circle, DC 20036 (reservations 1-800 423 6953/hotel direct 1-202 483 6000/fax 1-202 328 3265/www. jurysdoyle.com). Dupont Circle Metro. **Rates** $99-$355 single/double. **Credit** AmEx, DC, Disc, MC, V. **Map** p250 G4 ➌③

You'll not find a better view of Dupont Circle than from this hip hotel perched right in the middle of the action. It's owned by the Irish hotel chain, but this is no shamrock-and-claddagh affair; instead, sleek furnishings adorn the lobby. The sunny rooms are modern and fully equipped; most were recently renovated and include 32-inch flat-screen TVs. Dupont Grille, the hotel's striking restaurant, complete with floor-to-ceiling windows, serves an interesting mix of cuisines. Biddy Mulligans, a popular Irish bar, is the place to go for the perfect pint of Guinness.

Bar. Business centre. Disabled-adapted rooms. Gym. Internet (free wired high-speed). Parking ($20/night). Restaurant. Room service. TV (pay movies).

Adams Morgan/ Woodley Park

Very expensive (over $250)

Marriott Wardman Park
2660 Woodley Road, NW, at Connecticut Avenue, DC 20008 (reservations 1-800 228 9290/hotel direct 1-202 328 2000/fax 1-202 234 0015/www.marriott. com). Woodley Park-Zoo/Adams Morgan Metro. **Rates** $339-$459 single/double; $500-$3,200 suite. **Credit** AmEx, DC, Disc, MC, V. **Map** p249 F2 ➌④

A huge (more than 1,300 rooms) and labyrinthine hotel perched on a hill near the Woodley Park-Zoo/Adams Morgan Metro stop. If you get lost (as you inevitably will), ask the friendly staff, who seem to be everywhere. Although the 1918 building is gorgeous and surrounded by luscious greenery, the larger wing of the complex is monolithic and lacks character. On the plus side, the rooms have been upgraded with new bathrooms and beds, and the hotel has a large new fitness centre. Expect to see weddings or conferences here; the hotel has extensive facilities for the latter.

Bar (1). Business centre. Disabled-adapted rooms. Gym. Parking ($23-$28/night). Restaurants (2). Swimming pool (outdoor). Internet (free wireless in public areas; $9.95/day high-speed wired in rooms). TV (pay movies).

Expensive ($160-$250)

Omni Shoreham

2500 Calvert Street, NW, at Connecticut Avenue, DC 20008 (reservations 1-888 444 6664/hotel direct 1-202 234 0700/fax 1-202 265 7972/www.omni shorehamhotel.com). Woodley Park-Zoo/Adams Morgan Metro. **Rates** $179-$329 single/double; $350-$3,500 suite. **Credit** AmEx, DC, Disc, MC, V. **Map** p250 F2 ⑮

One of Washington's largest and grandest hotels, the Omni Shoreham is located on 11 acres in the pleasant Woodley Park neighbourhood, thus allowing the space for beautiful, formal gardens. The National Zoo, Rock Creek Park, Adams Morgan and the Metro are all within easy walking distance. The lobby and restaurant are quite posh, though the

hotel is showing its age (75 years) in some places. Many of the bedrooms are former apartments, which means they're among the largest in town.

Bar. Business centre. Concierge. Disabled-adapted rooms. Gym. Internet (free wireless; wired high-speed in rooms $9.95/day). Parking ($28). Restaurant. Room service. Spa. Swimming pool (outdoor). TV (pay movies).

Budget ($99 or under)

Adam's Inn

1746 Lanier Place, NW, at 18th Street, DC 20009 (reservations 1-800 578 6807/hotel direct 1-202 745 3600/fax 1-202 319 7958/www.adamsinn.com). Woodley Park-Zoo/Adams Morgan Metro then 90, 92, 93, bus. **Rates** (incl breakfast) $89 single with shared bath; $99 single with private bath; $10 per extra person. Two-night minimum stay for Sat reservations. **Credit** AmEx, DC, Disc, MC, V. **Map** p250 G2 ⑯

Clean, sunny rooms fill the inn's three 100-year-old townhouses on a quiet and pretty street in Adams Morgan. The welcoming staff and old-fashioned furnishings and fireplaces make for a cosy stay. While the rooms don't have phones or TVs (invaluable for those seeking peace and quiet), there is a common

More for less

Washington hotels aren't cheap, but that's not to say you can't find a good deal. Two of the best bargains are **Adam's Inn** (*see p52*) and the **Kalorama Guest House** (*see p53*), both B&Bs in Adams Morgan, where you can snag a clean room in a great neighbourhood for under $100. The city's most vibrant nightlife is within walking distance – just think of the money you'll save on cab fares.

Jurys Washington Hotel (*see p51*) – in what just might be the city's best location, right on Dupont Circle – is also great value. The hotel is clean, modern and recently renovated, and the Irish staff run a tight ship. Rooms start at $99, but you'll feel as though you're staying somewhere much more expensive.

Frequent visitors love the **Tabard Inn** (*see p51*), a cosy establishment close to both Dupont Circle and the business district. The rooms are filled with charming antiques, the restaurant is top notch, and there's a fireplace in the library where you can sip sherry or philosophise over a glass of fine wine. Prices (which start at $103 and include an excellent breakfast) are shockingly low for such a nice place.

The **Hampton Inn Washington** (*see p48*), near the Gallery Place/Chinatown Metro and the convention centre, has none of the Tabard's character, but it's a hit with business travellers and sightseers. Everything is brand new and the staff are worthy of a five-star hotel. For the price (the rooms start at $119), extras like complimentary internet access, a swimming pool and hot tub, refrigerators and microwaves in bedrooms seem like true luxuries.

Cocktail hour at the **Beacon Hotel**. *See p49*.

lounge, kitchen and garden patio if you crave company, and nearby 18th Street offers enough bars and restaurants for a week. One of the best deals in town. *Internet (free high-speed on shared terminal; wireless in some areas). Parking ($10/night; reserve in advance). Payphone.*

Jurys Normandy

2118 Wyoming Avenue, NW, at Connecticut Avenue, DC 20008 (reservations 1-800 423 6953/hotel direct 1-202 483 1350/fax 1-202 387 8241/www.jurys doyle.com). Dupont Circle Metro then L1 bus. **Rates** $89-$225 single/double. **Credit** AmEx, DC, Disc, MC, V. **Map** p250 G3 ㊲

Tucked along a quiet street amid some of Washington's most expensive homes, this small, well-run hotel has gracious touches: the garden patio and glass conservatory are just a couple of the unexpected pleasures. Though the 75 rooms are on the small side and none have views to speak of, they were recently renovated and feature contemporary mahogany furniture. *Disabled-adapted rooms. Internet (free wired high-speed in rooms and wireless in public areas). Parking ($20/night). TV (pay movies).*

Kalorama Guest House

2700 Cathedral Avenue, NW, at 27th Street, DC 20008 (1-202 328 0860/fax 1-202 328 8730/www.kaloramaguesthouse.com). Woodley Park-Zoo/Adams Morgan Metro. **Rates** (incl breakfast) $65-85 single/double (shared bath); $75-$95 single/double (private bath); $95-$135 suite. **Credit** AmEx, DC, Disc, MC, V. **Map** p249 F2 ㊳

Kalorama B&B is successful because it's such a good deal. The 47-unit property is in prime real estate, close enough to nightlife but far enough for peace and quiet. There's a garden patio and in winter guests gather in the afternoon for a glass of sherry around the fireplace. Suites are the only rooms with private phones and TVs. The Cathedral Avenue location is two blocks from the Metro. *Internet (free wireless in some areas). Parking ($10/night).*

Other locations: 1854 Mintwood Place, NW, at Columbia Road, DC 20009 (hotel direct 1-202 667 6369/fax 1-202 319 1262).

Logan Circle

Moderate ($100-$159)

Hotel Helix

1430 Rhode Island Avenue, NW, between 14th & 15th Streets, DC 20005 (reservations 1-800 706 1202/hotel direct 1-202 462 9001/fax 1-202 332 3519/www.hotelhelix.com). McPherson Square Metro. **Rates** $139-$399 single/double; suites $100 extra. **Credit** AmEx, DC, Disc, MC, V. **Map** p250 H5 ㊴

Pop culture is the theme at this fun and funky hotel – which pays homage to Andy Warhol – in the hip Logan Circle neighbourhood. Expect bright colours, mod furniture, oversized photos, lots of plastic and great design. Catering to a twenty- and thirtysomething clientele, the hotel has wisely placed flat-screen TVs and Nintendo video game systems in all the rooms. At the nightly 'Hour of Bubbles', staff serve complimentary champagne and wine in the lounge, which has an outdoor patio. The Metro is a bit of a hike, but the neighbourhood is vibrant. **Photo** *p54*. *Bar (with food service). Business centre. Disabled-adapted rooms. Gym. Parking ($26/night). Room service. Internet (free wireless). TV (pay movies).*

Hotel Rouge

1315 16th Street, NW, at Massachusetts Avenue & Scott Circle, DC 20036 (reservations 1-800 738 1202/hotel direct 1-202 232 8000/fax 1-202 667 9827/www.rougehotel.com). Dupont Circle or McPherson Square Metro. **Rates** $139-$399 single/double. **Credit** AmEx, DC, Disc, MC, V. **Map** p250 G4 ㊵

There's nothing refined about Rouge, which prides itself on being brash and playful, but chances are you won't mind. Decor is retro chic verging on the camp – with ten white Venus statues outside and

white leather chairs inside. The hotel offers a complimentary wine hour on weekdays and Bloody Marys on weekend mornings, plus free in-room yoga equipment. The immediate surroundings are lacklustre, but Dupont Circle is nearby.

Bar (with food service). Business centre. Disabled-adapted rooms. Gym. Parking ($26/night). Room service. Internet (free wireless). TV (pay movies).

Georgetown

Very expensive (over $250)

Four Seasons

2800 Pennsylvania Avenue, NW, between 28th & 29th Streets, DC 20007 (reservations 1-800 819 5053/hotel direct 1-202 342 0444/fax 1-202 944 2076/www.fourseasons.com/washington). Foggy Bottom-GWU Metro then 30, 32, 34, 35, 36 bus or Georgetown Metro Connection bus. **Rates** $375-$725 single/double; $495-$5,755 suite. **Credit** AmEx, DC, Disc, MC, V. **Map** p249 F5 ④

One of DC's most comfortable hotels, the Four Seasons has long attracted VIP guests. The health spa is both serious and sybaritic, and good art is displayed throughout. Even if you're not lucky enough to be staying here, you can at least treat yourself to afternoon tea on the Garden Terrace. If you can stump up the money for a reservation, ask to stay in the east wing, where a recent $40 million renovation enlarged the rooms and updated the decor. **Photo** *p43.*

Bar. Business centre. Concierge. Disabled-adapted rooms. Gym. Internet (wireless $10.95/day; web TV $12.95/day). Parking ($35/night). Spa. Swimming pool (indoor). Restaurant. Room service. TV (pay movies).

Ritz-Carlton, Georgetown

3100 South Street, NW, at 31st Street, DC 20007 (reservations 1-800 241 3333/hotel direct 1-202 912 4100/fax 1-202 912 4199/www.ritzcarlton.com/ hotels/georgetown). Foggy Bottom-GWU Metro then 30, 32, 34, 35, 36 bus or Georgetown Metro Connection bus. **Rates** $475-$500 single/double; $895-$5,000 suite. **Credit** AmEx, DC, Disc, MC, V. **Map** p249 E5 ④

With just 86 guest rooms – about a third of which are executive suites – the Ritz's new Georgetown property is more intimate than its Foggy Bottom sister (*see p45*). Located near the Potomac River waterfront, the hotel is housed in a renovated red-brick building with a 130ft smokestack. The industrial architecture makes a striking backdrop for the chic modern furnishings. Some rooms have views of downtown and the river. The building also houses a cinema, spa and coffee shop, plus a restaurant (Fahrenheit) and Martini lounge (Degrees). The upmarket neighbourhood is not near the Metro, but there's plenty here to keep you entertained. **Photo** *p45.*

Bar. Business centre. Concierge. Disabled-adapted rooms. Gym. Internet (wired high-speed in rooms $9.95/day). Parking ($30/night). Restaurant. Room service. Spa. TV (pay movies; DVD players and game systems available for rent).

Hotel Helix. *See p53.*

Expensive ($160-$250)

Georgetown Suites

1111 30th Street, NW, between K and M streets, & 1000 29th Street, NW, at K Street, DC 20007 (reservations 1-800 348 7203/hotel direct 1-202 298 7800/fax 1-202 333 5792/www.georgetown suites.com). Foggy Bottom-GWU Metro then 30, 32, 34, 35, 36 bus or Georgetown Metro Connection bus. **Rates** (incl breakfast) $170-$600 suite. **Credit** AmEx, DC, Disc, MC, V. **Map** p249 F5 ㊸

This 217-suite hotel, divided into two buildings, is on a quiet street off the main drag of M Street. Formerly condominiums, each suite is well equipped with full kitchens and some units have patios. It's also well situated for forays into Georgetown and along the Potomac river. The rooms are bright and spacious – some are absolutely huge – and the bathrooms have been newly renovated.
Business centre. Concierge. Disabled-adapted rooms. Gym. Internet (free wireless). Parking ($18/night). TV.

Hotel Monticello

1075 Thomas Jefferson Street, NW, between M & K Streets, DC 20007 (reservations 1-800 388 2410/hotel direct 1-202 337 0900/fax 1-202 333 6526/www.monticellohotel.com). Foggy Bottom-GWU Metro then 30, 32, 34, 35, 36 bus or Georgetown Metro Connection bus. **Rates** (incl breakfast) $169-$350 single/double. **Credit** AmEx, DC, Disc, MC, V. **Map** p249 F5 ㊹

Formerly the Georgetown Dutch Inn, the charming Hotel Monticello, named after Thomas Jefferson's country estate (the man himself once lived on this street), offers quiet rooms amid the hubbub of Georgetown. All 47 suites have roomy living areas, complete with microwave and mini-fridge, and big, modern bathrooms with upmarket toiletries and fluffy robes. Get a room with a view of M Street and indulge in some people-watching from your window.
Business centre. Disabled-adapted rooms. Internet (free wireless). Parking ($25/night). TV.

Arlington, VA

Expensive ($160-$250)

Key Bridge Marriott

1401 Lee Highway, at Wilson Street, VA 22209 (reservations 1-800 228 9290/hotel direct 1-703 524 6400/fax 1-703 524 8964/www.marriott.com). Rosslyn Metro. **Rates** $299-$369 single/double; $375-$575 suite. **Credit** AmEx, DC, Disc, MC, V.

You won't find a better view of the Washington skyline at night than from the top of the Key Bridge Marriott. A large and luxurious hotel built for conventions (it has 17 meeting rooms), it's about a mile from Arlington National Cemetery and a quick walk across the bridge to Georgetown. The Metro, too, is nearby. A recent $13 million renovation included an expanded 24-hour gym and an improved business centre. Be sure to request a room with a city view.

Bar. Business services. Gym. Concierge. Disabled-adapted rooms. Parking ($12/night). Restaurant. Swimming pool (indoor/outdoor). Room service. Internet (free wireless in lobby; wired high-speed in rooms $9.95/day). TV (pay movies, game systems).

Budget ($99 or under)

Days Inn

2201 Arlington Boulevard, at Route 50 & North Pershing Drive, Arlington, VA 22201 (1-703 525 0300/fax 1-703 525 5671/www.daysinn.com). Rosslyn Metro then hotel shuttle. **Rates** $90-$150 single/double. **Credit** AmEx, DC, Disc, MC, V.

Days Inn is undergoing a makeover, which should be finished by 2007. Still, don't expect frills – just a good deal. There's free parking and a shuttle to the Rosslyn Metro station, under-17s stay free in a parent's room and the staff members are friendly.
Bar. Gym. Internet (free wireless). Parking (free). Restaurant. Swimming pool (outdoor). Telephone. TV.

Bethesda, MD

Moderate ($100-$159)

Hyatt Regency Bethesda

One Bethesda Metro Center, Wisconsin Avenue at Old Georgetown Road, MD 20814 (1-301 657 1234/fax 1-301 657 6453/www.bethesda.hyatt.com). Bethesda Metro. **Rates** $129-$409 single/double; suites $150 extra. **Credit** AmEx, DC, Disc, MC, V.

Children will adore this luxurious hotel for its rooftop pool, thrilling 11-storey atrium lobby and three speedy glass elevators. Each of the 389 rooms has huge desks and black-and-white photographs of the city's monuments – the best hotel art in the DC area. Another perk: the hotel recently upgraded all of its beds with top-of-the-line mattresses.
Bar. Business centre. Concierge. Disabled-adapted rooms. Gym. Internet (wireless in rooms $9.95/day). Parking ($12-$20/night). Restaurant (2). Room service. Swimming pool (indoor). TV (pay movies).

Budget ($99 or under)

Clarion Hotel Bethesda Park

8400 Wisconsin Avenue, at Woodmont Avenue, Bethesda, MD 20814 (1-301 654 1000/fax 1-301 654 0751/www.choicehotels.com). Bethesda or Medical Center Metro, then free hotel shuttle at half past every hour. **Rates** $79-$264 single/double. **Credit** AmEx, DC, Disc, MC, V.

A few blocks from the Metro station, this large and rather mediocre chain hotel has 155 rooms. It's a real bargain, provided you can get one of the lower rates, which vary depending on the time of year. The Olympic-sized outdoor pool is a plus, but avoid Chatter's sports bar.
Bar. Business centre. Disabled-adapted rooms. Gym. Internet (free wired high-speed; wireless $9.95/day). Parking ($11/night). Restaurant. Room service. Swimming pool (outdoor). TV (pay movies).

Pierre-Auguste
Luncheon of the Boating Party (detail),

Experience art in a setting unlike any other in Washington.

Linger in our intimate galleries to experience
one of the most exquisite collections of impressionist and
modern American and European art in the world.

21st at Q Street, NW | Dupont Circle Metro
Open Tuesday–Sunday and Thursday evenings
(202) 387-2151 · www.phillipscollection.org

THE PHILLIPS
COLLECTION

Sightseeing

National Air & Space Museum.
See p65.

Introduction

Keys to the city.

It's hard now to picture those halcyon days when visitors could stroll freely into the White House, and – who knows – maybe even meet the president. World War II brought the first major security step-up at the White House, and five years after 9/11, security remains tight.

Unpredictable security crackdowns aren't the only variables faced by visitors. Demonstrations, marathons, even food festivals can shut down important buildings and major thoroughfares. Museums may be fully or partially closed at short notice for press conferences and special events – it's always best to phone to check before you turn up. Wise is the visitor who consults the tourist website (www.washington. org), the morning paper or the TV news to check their plans aren't going to be disrupted.

It's worth the effort. Major government buildings and museums are free, although of late some privately funded attractions have started to charge admission fees. And more recently visitors have begun to look beyond the traditional attractions of the National Mall into the life of the city itself.

On the Mall itself security measures are quirky and inconsistent: some museums sport airport-style metal detectors, others don't. It's a good idea to keep your keys, change and other heavy metal in a small bag to breeze through the monitors. More than ever, visitors must make reservations, often weeks in advance, for public tours or over-subscribed events and exhibitions. For some bookings (including tours of the White House and Capitol), Americans find aid in their

congressional representatives; foreigners may find their embassies can help (foreign passport holders can only see the White House by arranging a tour through their embassy). For a list of local embassies, *see p226*, or go to www.embassy.org. Ask the Convention & Tourism Corporation (*see p234*) for a copy of its calendar, which details forthcoming events as far as a year ahead, and book straight away.

For further museum listings, including temporary exhibitions, consult the *Washington Post* and the free *Washington City Paper*.

Note that on federal holidays, certain museums are closed (though the Smithsonian's buildings shut only on Christmas Day). During busy periods you should also consider booking tickets in advance. Disabled visitors or those with special needs are advised to phone individual museums about facilities. Also, though the US is generally extremely child-friendly, a few museums do not allow children under a certain age. Museums that are part of the Smithsonian Institution are marked (S).

ORIENTATION AND NEIGHBOURHOODS

DC's logical street-naming system makes finding your destination easy – if you master a couple of basic rules (which are explained in full on p221).

The National Mall and its attendant institutions are on a walkable scale (if you like a lot of walking, that is – pack some comfy shoes) and forays further afield are not a problem given the efficient Metro system and relatively low cab fares. The must-see monuments and museums situated on and around the Mall are covered in our **Monumental Centre** chapter, starting on p61.

DC Neighbourhoods, on pp83-106, covers the rest of the District, including the corporate downtown zone and Dupont Circle, a residential area with an urban feel and buzzing street scene. Further north are Adams Morgan (lively and ethnically diverse) and the U Street/14th Street Corridor in Shaw – the hip, historic hub of DC's African-American culture. West of Rock Creek sits Georgetown, long on elegance but short on Metro stations.

The federal centre extends into Virginia and Maryland. We cover **Arlington** and **Alexandria**, both in Virginia, on pp107-110.

Our street maps, starting on p248, show these area divisions.

Lincoln Memorial. See p65.

Guided tours

DC has more than its fair share of tour companies, which between them offer a huge variety of guided (and self-guided tours). A great place to start is the **Cultural Tourism DC** website (www.culturaltourismdc.org), which has a full list of tours (including links to some of those listed below).

The following tours are also recommended. Where only one tour is provided we have given the cost; for others you're advised to call or check the website. Booking is advised for all. For bicycle tours, see p197.

Anecdotal History Walks
1-301 294 9514/www.dcsightseeing.com.
Cost $100/hr (3hr minimum, plus transportation costs).
Anthony Pitch, British journalist turned DC historian, does private, custom group tours by appointment and occasional public tours – check website for times and prices.

Bike the Sites
1-202 842 2452/www.bikethesites.com.
Guided tours by various types of bike (or even electronic scooters, aka 'personal convenience vehicles' – great for the mobility-impaired). Tours leave from the Old Post Office Pavilion (12th Street & Pennsylvania Avenue, NW).

C&O Canal Barge Rides
1057 Thomas Jefferson Street, NW, at M Street, Georgetown (1-202 653 5190).
Cost $8; $5-$6 concessions.
Leisurely, mule-drawn canal boat rides on the C&O Canal between Georgetown and Great Falls, Maryland. Runs daily April to October.

Duck Tours
1-202 832 9800/www.trolleytours.com.
Cost $32; $16 concessions; free under-4s.
A narrated tour of the monuments in a World War II amphibious vehicle, which navigates the streets, then floats on the Potomac. The 90-minute tour leaves from the front of Union Station every hour on the hour from 10am to 3pm daily (mid-March-late November).

Nina's Dandy Cruises
Zero Prince Street, between King & Duke Streets, Alexandria, VA (1-703 683 6076/ www.dandydinnerboat.com).
Dinner, lunch or brunch cruises past the major monuments, sailing out of Old Town Alexandria year-round.

Old Town Trolley Tours
1-202 832 9800/www.trolleytours.com.
Cost $32; $16 concessions; free under-4s.
Trolleys – actually buses in twee disguise – run every half hour from 9am to 4.30pm daily, and until 5.30pm in the spring and summer. Stops aren't marked, but you can hop on at will (though you can only make the full circle once).

Potomac Riverboat Company
1-703 548 9000/www.potomacriver boatco.com.
One-way or round-trip narrated boat tours of Alexandria, Mount Vernon or DC. Trips run six days a week, from mid March to October, and most leave from Alexandria Docks.

Scandal Tour
1-202 783 7212/www.gnpcomedy.com.
Cost $30.
This 90-minute tour features costumed performers acting out different scandals that took place in DC, such as the Watergate break-in. It kicks off at 1pm on Saturdays in spring and summer at the Old Post Office Pavilion (12th Street & Pennsylvania Avenue, NW).

Spies of Washington Tour
1-703 273 2381/www.spytour.com.
Cost $45.
Periodic explorations of the haunts of espionage under the auspices of Francis Gary Powers, Jr, son of the U-2 spy plane pilot shot down over the USSR in 1959.

Tour DC
1-301 588 8999/www.tourdc.com.
A range of tours (Georgetown, Embassy Row, Dupont Circle) run by happily downshifted attorney Mary Kay Ricks.

Tourmobile
1-202 544 5100/www.tourmobile.com.
Guided bus tours around the major sights (including Arlington National Cemetery), with options to get off and reboard at any point on the circuit. Twilight tours are also available.

Washington Photo Safari
1-202 537 0937/1-877 512 5969/ www.washingtonphotosafari.com.
Sick of blurry holiday photos? Combine sightseeing with snapping by booking one of the tours offered by experienced photographer E David Luria. Elaborate equipment not necessary: even a disposable camera will do.

Sightseeing

The Monumental Centre

The neo-classical core: monuments, museums and open space.

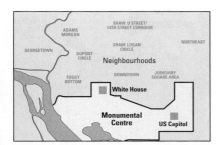

The Mall & Tidal Basin

Map p252-p253

The Mall is the nexus of picture-postcard Washington, an axial greenway of impressive museums crowned by the Capitol.

That experience was in part inspired by George Washington's wish that his new nation have a suitably imposing capital. To that end he hired Pierre-Charles L'Enfant to design the fledgling city, and the L'Enfant Plan was the result. And given that the one thing a government is good at doing is producing plans, sure enough in 1902 another scheme – the McMillan Plan – reinterpreted L'Enfant's original vision. Now, a century later, the National Capital Planning Commission referees continual development debates over this quasi-sacred space.

The Mall from west to east

The western boundary of the mall centres on the **Lincoln Memorial**, in front of the long Reflecting Pool. Beyond rises the needle of the Washington Monument and, finally, at the eastern end of the Mall, the Capitol, two miles away. The previously uncluttered vista between the Lincoln and Washington monuments was interrupted controversially in 2004 by the new **National World War II Memorial**.

Starting south-east of the Lincoln Memorial, across the Tidal Basin, the circular **Jefferson Memorial** commemorates the brainy third US president and author of the *Declaration of Independence*. Tucked just south is a new monument to Jefferson's friend, local Revolutionary-era thinker **George Mason**, relaxing on a bench with his ever-present books.

Washington Monument. *See p71.*

National Air & Space Museum. *See p65.*

The **Franklin Delano Roosevelt Memorial** enlivens West Potomac Park, across the cherry tree-rimmed Tidal Basin, which has paddleboats for rent. Nearby is the site designated for a memorial to civil rights leader Martin Luther King, slated to involve a relief bust and excerpts from his speeches. It was from from the Lincoln Memorial that King delivered his famous 'I have a dream' speech four decades ago.

Two war monuments flank Lincoln's. To the north-east is the V-shaped black wedge of the **Vietnam Veterans Memorial**, with a nearby underground visitor centre in the works; to the south-east is the evocative **Korean War Veterans Memorial**. Walking east past Constitution Gardens on the Mall's northern border, you first encounter the new, controversially sited **National World War II Memorial**. Next is the starkly impressive **Washington Monument**, honouring the 'father of his country', who selected this site for its capital.

To the north spreads the Ellipse, formally the President's Park South. It contains the **Boy Scout Memorial**, which recalls the Socialist Realist style of the former USSR, and the **First Division Memorial**, an 80-foot monument to the soldiers of the First Division of the US Army. Atop is a gilded bronze Victory. On the north of the Ellipse is the **Zero Milestone**, from which distances from the capital are measured.

The Washington Monument overlooks museumland. The turreted red fortress, guarded by a carousel, is the **Smithsonian Castle**, which houses an information centre and the crypt for Smithsonian benefactor, Englishman James Smithson.

Clustered about are the palazzo-like **Freer Gallery** (Asian art); its younger sibling, the subterranean **Arthur M Sackler Gallery**; the Sackler's twin, the **National Museum of African Art**; and the old **Arts & Industries Building**, now slowly being demolished by neglect. Further along are the doughnut-shaped **Hirshhorn Museum & Sculpture Garden**, the modernist, glass and marble of the **National Air & Space Museum** – the world's most visited museum – and the **National Museum of the American Indian**.

On the north side, the grounds between 14th and 15th streets are designated for an African-American museum, now raising construction funds, while the **National Museum of American History** (closed in 2006 for lengthy renovations) and the **National Museum of Natural History** are between 14th and Ninth Streets. An adjacent sculpture garden's pool becomes an ice rink in winter. Next in line, the neo-classical **National Gallery of Art** connects to the angular geometry of its **East Building**.

On the far side of the Capitol Reflecting Pool, at the foot of Capitol Hill, stands a sprawling sculptural group that features an equestrian statue of Ulysses S Grant, the triumphant Union general, modelled after the Victor Emmanuel memorial in Rome. Crowning the hill is the United States **Capitol**, whose dome Lincoln insisted be finished during the Civil War as a symbol of the Union's durability.

Arthur M Sackler Gallery (S)

1050 Independence Avenue, SW, between 11th &
12th Streets, The Mall & Tidal Basin (1-202 633
4880/www.asia.si.edu). Smithsonian Metro. **Open**
July-mid Aug 10am-5.30pm Mon-Wed, Fri-Sun; 10am-
8pm Thur. *Mid Aug-June* 10am-5.30pm daily.
Admission free. **Map** p252 J7.

Opened in 1987, the Sackler has more flexibility than
its neighbour, the Freer Gallery, whose mandate for-
bids the exhibition of anything from outside its collection. The Sackler does international loan
exhibitions of Asian art, from ancient to contemporary. Connected to the Freer by an underground pas-
sageway and sharing its director and administration,
the Sackler was built up around a 1,000-piece Asian
art gift from Dr Arthur M Sackler.

Visitors enter through architects Shepley Bulfinch
Richardson and Abbott's first-floor granite pavilion
(a similar pavilion, by the same firm, is at the National
Museum of African Art). You then head below ground
into a maze of overlapping bridges and long pas-
sageways that give the feel of an ancient temple.
Artefacts on permanent display include pieces from
China – such as lacquered tropical hardwood Ming-
style furniture (1368-1644) and a late 17th-century
Qing dynasty rosewood armchair – and sculpture
from South and South-east Asia, including 12th-cen-
tury Hindu temple sculpture and fifth-century BC
Jainist religious figures. The museum recently invigorated its contemporary art programme with an
installation by Chinese artist Cai Guo-Qiang.

Franklin Delano Roosevelt Memorial

Off West Basin Drive, SW, at the Tidal Basin
(1-202 426 6841/www.nps.gov/fdrm). Smithsonian
Metro. **Map** p252 G7.

FDR, who led the country through the Great
Depression and World War II, was the only president to be elected four times. Despite Roosevelt's
preference for a simple desk-sized memorial slab
(still in place outside the National Archives), in 1997
designer Lawrence Halprin created an epic monument here. The four 'galleries' combine waterfalls,
giant stones engraved with memorable quotations
and sculptures (including a statue of Eleanor
Roosevelt, the first First Lady to be honoured in a
national memorial). Disabled advocates objected
that the original, somewhat dyspeptic statue of the
polio-stricken president only hinted that he used a
wheelchair. A second, jauntier FDR, with wheels in
full view, joined the display in 2000.

Freer Gallery of Art (S)

Jefferson Drive, SW, at 12th Street, The Mall &
Tidal Basin (1-202 633 4880/www.asia.si.edu).
Smithsonian Metro. **Open** *July-mid Aug* 10am-5.30pm
Mon-Wed, Fri-Sun; 10am-8pm Thur. *Mid Aug-June*
10am-5.30pm daily. **Admission** free. **Map** p252 J7.

When Detroit business magnate Charles Lang Freer
(1854-1919) began collecting the works of American
painter James McNeill Whistler in the 1880s, the
artist encouraged him to collect Asian art while on
his travels to the Middle and Far East. Freer did so,
amassing neolithic Chinese pottery, Japanese screens
and Hindu temple sculpture, along with works by
19th-century American painters. In 1904 he offered
his collection to the Smithsonian, which commissioned this dignified, grey granite, Renaissance
palazzo-style building from architect Charles Adam
Platt to house the collection; it opened in 1923. The
collection's mandate precludes any lending of its
26,500-piece holdings, which are rotated regularly on
display. Occasional special exhibitions are small

Jefferson Memorial. *See p65.*

but smart. An underground passage connects the Freer to the neighbouring Sackler Gallery.

Hirshhorn Museum & Sculpture Garden (S)

Independence Avenue, SW, at Seventh Street, The Mall & Tidal Basin (1-202 633 4674/http:// hirshhorn.si.edu). L'Enfant Plaza Metro. **Open** *July* 10am-5.30pm Mon-Wed, Fri-Sun; 10am-8pm Thur. *Aug-June* 10am-5.30pm daily. **Admission** free. **Map** p253 J7.

This spectacular, aggressively modern cylindrical building by Skidmore, Owings and Merrill enlivens the predominantly neo-classical architecture lining the Mall. The purpose of the structure, which was completed in 1974, was to house self-made Wall Street millionaire Joseph Hirshhorn's collection of 20th-century painting and sculpture. SOM's chief architect, Gordon Bunshaft, has created a three-storey hollow concrete drum supported on four curvilinear piers. In keeping with the modernist tradition, there is no ceremonial entrance, only a utilitarian revolving door (strictly speaking there are two, but usually only one is in use).

The third-floor and basement galleries host iterations of the museum's 'Gyroscope' exhibitions, which are non-chronological installations of works from the permanent collection. Particular strengths include a significant Giacometti collection, the largest public collection of works by Thomas Eakins outside the artist's native Philadelphia, and a pair of Willem de Kooning's rare 'door paintings' (the museum boasts the largest public collection of his work in the world).

The basement galleries also house large-scale installations like Rachel Whiteread's *Untitled (Library)* and rotating video programmes in the museum's 'Black Box'. Second-floor galleries host major travelling exhibitions, many of which are solos of great living artists; recent examples include Japanese-born Hiroshi Sugimoto and German Anselm Kiefer. The museum also offers the well-regarded Directions series, spotlighting unusual or cutting-edge artists; past shows have featured a performance by Oliver Herring and a Jim Lambie installation. On Thursday evenings during the summer, the museum extends its hours and offers outdoor performances.

Jefferson Memorial

Southern end of 15th Street, SW, at the Tidal Basin & East Basin Drive (1-202 426 6841/www.nps. gov/thje). Smithsonian Metro. **Map** p252 H8.

FDR promoted this 1942 shrine to the founder of his Democratic Party, balancing that to the Republicans' icon, Lincoln. Roosevelt liked it so much he had trees cleared so he could see it from the Oval Office. In 2006 the Park Service imposed a fee on commercial wedding-party photographers, whose newlywed clients covet the backdrop.

John Russell Pope designed an adaptation (sneered at by some as 'Jefferson's muffin') of the Roman Pantheon that the architect Jefferson so admired. It echoes the president's designs for his home, Monticello, and for his rotunda at the University of Virginia. The Georgia marble walls surrounding Jefferson's 19ft likeness are inscribed with his enduring words. Alas, the 92-word quote from the *Declaration of Independence* contains 11 spelling mistakes and other inaccuracies. **Photo** *p64*.

Korean War Veterans Memorial

The Mall, SW, just south of Reflecting Pool, at Daniel French Drive & Independence Avenue (1-202 426 6841/www.nps.gov/kwvm). Smithsonian Metro. **Map** p252 G7.

This monument, which honours the 12 million Americans who fought in the bloody 'police action' to prevent communist takeover of South Korea, features 19 battle-clad, seven-foot soldiers slogging across a V-shaped field towards a distant US flag. Their finely detailed faces reflect the fatigue and pain of battle, while bulky packs show beneath their ponchos. Reflected in the polished granite wall, these 19 become 38 – in reference to the 38th parallel separating North and South Korea. Unlike the wall at the Vietnam Veterans Memorial, this shows a subtle mural sandblasted into rock, a photo-montage of the support troops – drivers and medics, nurses and chaplains.

Lincoln Memorial

The Mall, 23rd Street, NW, between Henry Bacon Drive & Daniel French Drive (1-202 426 6841/ www.nps.gov/linc). Smithsonian or Foggy Bottom-GWU Metro. **Map** p252 F7.

Despite its appearance on the penny and the $5 bill, the Lincoln Memorial is perhaps most recognisable as the site of historic demonstrations. In 1939, when the Daughters of the American Revolution barred the African-American contralto Marian Anderson from singing in their Constitution Hall, she performed for more than 75,000 people from these steps. It was here that Martin Luther King Jr delivered his 'I have a dream' speech in 1963. Just a few months later, President Lyndon Johnson led candle-carrying crowds in ceremonies concluding national mourning for John F Kennedy. Half a century of debate followed Lincoln's assassination in 1865 before Henry Bacon's classical design was chosen in 1911 (over proposals ranging from a triumphal arch to a memorial highway from Washington to Gettysburg).

The 'cage' surrounding Lincoln has one Doric column representing each of the 36 states in the Union at the time of his death, their names inscribed above. The 19ft-high marble statue of Lincoln himself, by Daniel Chester French, peers out over the Reflecting Pool, his facial expression seeming to change at different times of day. Cut into the wall to the left of the entrance is Lincoln's *Gettysburg Address*; to the right is his second inaugural address.

National Air & Space Museum (S)

Sixth Street & Independence Avenue, SW, The Mall & Tidal Basin (1-202 633 1000/www.nasm.si.edu). L'Enfant Plaza Metro. **Open** *Sept-May* 10am-5.30pm

Sightseeing

daily. *June-Aug* 9am-5.30pm daily. **Admission** *Museum* free. *Planetarium* $8; $7-$7.50 concessions. **Credit** AmEx, MC, V. **Map** p253 J7.

Opened in 1976, Air & Space tops visitors' to-do list, year in, year out. Even the museum slump after 9/11 barely touched this crowd-pleaser, which still registers more than nine million visitors a year. The imposing Tennessee marble modernist block, by Hellmuth, Obata and Kassabaum, incorporates three skylit, double-height galleries, which house missiles, aircraft and space stations. In the central Milestones of Flight hall, towering US Pershing-II and Soviet SS-20 nuclear missiles stand next to the popular moon rock station, where visitors can stroke a lunar sample acquired on the 1972 Apollo 17 mission. The

1903 Wright Flyer – the first piloted craft to maintain controlled, sustained flight (if only for a few seconds) – and Charles Lindbergh's Spirit of St Louis are both suspended here.

Permanent exhibitions in the museum detail the history of jet aviation and satellite communications. Updates acknowledge contemporary information technology, but most of the collection's low-tech presentation maintains the quaint optimism of the early space age. A bevy of hands-on exhibits appeal to children, who line up to pilot a full-size Cessna aircraft in the How Things Fly exhibit or to walk through the research lab in the Skylab Space Station. The Albert Einstein Planetarium offers half-hour multimedia presentations about stars and outer

The Smithsonian

Founded by wealthy British chemist and mineralogist James Smithson (1765-1829), who conferred his fortune on the United States government, the Smithsonian Institution was created by an act of Congress in 1846. Smithson requested that it be an institution promoting research and the dispersal of academic knowledge. Nonetheless, his motives for founding it remain unclear: he had never set foot on American soil.

Architect James Renwick designed the first building, known as the Castle because its combination of late Romanesque and early Gothic styles included signature turrets, on a prime piece of national real estate on the verdant Mall. Completed in 1855, the Castle now serves as the Smithsonian Information Center and administrative hub – and should be the first port of call for any visitor. The Victorian red-brick Arts & Industries Building, designed as the Smithsonian's first hall devoted solely to exhibitions, was added in 1881 (until recently a venue for rotating exhibitions, the building is closed indefinitely for major renovations). Over the years, collections shown here became large enough to warrant their own buildings. After the creation of the National Zoo in 1890, Congress began the steady erection of museums lining the Mall, beginning with the Museum of Natural History in 1910. From 1923 to 1993, 11 new museums entered the Smithsonian portfolio, most of them holding fine art.

Today the Smithsonian owns more than 140 million objects (plus a further 128 million in its libraries and archive collections), covering everything from ancient Chinese

pottery to dinosaurs, Italian Renaissance painting to moon landings, so you're bound to find at least one collection that interests you.

Recently, cuts in federal funding have driven the Smithsonian management to seek alternatives sources of finance – such as naming-rights deals and exclusive-content deals – with sometimes controversial results. One big grant to the American History Museum was withdrawn after staff protested that the donor was trying to influence programming. And documentary filmmakers have taken exception to a deal that gives a cable channel exclusive rights to the Smithsonian's film and video footage.

INFORMATION

There is one central phone number – 1-202 357 2700 – where you can get information on all the Smithsonian's museums. The website – www.si.edu – is also useful and has links to the individual museums' homepages.

Smithsonian Access, a brochure detailing the disabled facilities at the museums, is available at each museum – or call 1-202 786 2942. If you need to arrange special facilities – such as a sign-language interpreter – call the museum two weeks in advance.

Smithsonian Institution museums are marked with an **(S)** in our listings.

Smithsonian Information Center

Smithsonian Institution Building (The Castle), 1000 Jefferson Drive, SW, between Seventh & 12th Streets, The Mall & Tidal Basin (1-202 357 2700/24hr recorded information 1-202 357 2020/www.si.edu). Smithsonian Metro. **Open** 8.30am-5.30pm daily. **Map** p252 J7. Opens an hour and a half before the museums to give you time to plan your visit.

space; the Langley Theater shows IMAX films on air and space flight. After an exhausting mission, pick up some freeze-dried space food in the gift shop. The museum's annex, the Steven F Udvar-Hazy Center, named after its major donor, opened in Chantilly, Virginia, in December 2003. Its hangar-like halls hold the restored Enola Gay, the shimmering B-29 that dropped the first atomic bomb, and the space shuttle Enterprise, among other large-scale treasures. A shuttle bus service makes a round trip between the two outposts several times a day (tickets cost $15 for the round trip, and you're strongly advised to book in advance by calling 1-202 633 4629). **Photo** *p62*.

National Gallery of Art

West Building: *Constitution Avenue, between Fourth & Seventh Streets, NW.*
East Building: *Constitution Avenue & Fourth Street, NW, The Mall & Tidal Basin (1-202 737 4215/www. nga.gov). Archives-Navy Memorial, Judiciary Square or Smithsonian Metro.* **Open** 10am-5pm Mon-Sat; 11am-6pm Sun. **Admission** free. **Map** p253 J6.
Pittsburgh investment banker and industrialist Andrew Mellon was born the son of a poor Irish immigrant but went on to serve as US Treasury Secretary from 1921-32. In 1941 he presented the National Gallery's West Building as a gift to the nation. Mellon's son, Paul, created the gallery's East Building in 1978. Mellon junior, who had donated over 900 artworks during his lifetime, bequeathed $75 million and 100 paintings – including works by Monet, Renoir and Cézanne – on his death in 1999.
In designing the Tennessee marble West Building, architect John Russell Pope borrowed motifs from the temple architecture of the Roman Pantheon. The white marble stairs at the Constitution Avenue entrance lead to the main-floor rotunda, with its impressive green Italian marble floors and columns around a bubbling fountain encircled by fragrant flora and greenery. On this level, galleries lead off the building's 782ft longitudinal spine. The ground level houses artificially lit galleries as well as a gift shop and garden court café. An underground concourse has a cafeteria (the gelato is renowned), another shop and a moving walkway that connects the West Building to the skylit, IM Pei-designed East Building.

The West Building's skylit main floor reads like an art history text: masterworks from the 14th to the 19th centuries pepper practically every gallery. Late medieval Flemish highlights include Jan Van Eyck's *Annunciation* and Rogier van der Weyden's tiny *St George and the Dragon*. Pre- through high-Renaissance Italian works represent a large pro-portion of the collection. Giotto's seminal *Madonna and Child* hangs here, as does Leonardo da Vinci's almond-eyed portrait of *Ginevra de' Benci* and Botticelli's *Adoration of the Magi*. Giovanni Bellini and Titian's *Feast of the Gods* commands Gallery 17, to the north of the West Garden Court.

Snaking westwards, galleries mainly devoted to Titian hold his luscious *Venus with a Mirror* and the terrifying *St John the Evangelist on Patmos*.

National Museum of the American Indian. *See p69.*

US Capitol.
See p78.

Rembrandt's 1659 self-portrait, with his intent gaze, hangs among 17th-century Dutch and Flemish works, which also include a solid selection of Van Dyck. Goya's portraits of Spanish notables, meanwhile, are showcased nearby. Downstairs, the West Wing sculpture galleries, which occupy the entire northwest quadrant of the building's ground floor, now register 24,000sq ft divided into 22 galleries, following a major expansion in 2002. More than 900 works are on view, including masterpieces from the Middle Ages to the early 20th century. Visitors entering from the museum's Sixth Street entrance encounter works by Auguste Rodin and Augustus Saint-Gaudens. From there, they move in reverse chronological order from the 19th century to the Middle Ages, with detours into a pair of galleries housing early modern sculpture. Highlights of the collection include Leone Battista Alberti's bronze *Self-Portrait* plaque (c1435); Honoré Daumier's entire bronze sculptural oeuvre, including all 36 of his caricatures of French government officials, and the world's largest collection of Edgar Degas original wax and mixed-media sculptures.

The East Building's triple-height, skylit atrium is dominated by Alexander Calder's 32ft by 81ft aluminum and steel mobile. The gallery's small but strong collection of 20th-century art includes several must-sees on view in the concourse-level galleries. Don't miss Barnett Newman's minimalist *Stations of the Cross*, a 15-panel installation of monochromatic paintings that ring the walls of a dedicated room. You'll also want to visit *Angel of History*, Anselm Kiefer's massive, elegiac lead sculpture of a fighter jet – the piece weighs 2,000lb.

The Micro Gallery, just inside the West Building's main-floor Mall entrance, has 15 individual cubicles with touch-screen colour monitors where visitors can learn more about individual works, movements, artists and the precise location of each work. Conservation techniques are also explained.

The gallery opened a sculpture garden in 1998 on a six-acre square across Seventh Street from the West Building. Designed by Philadelphia landscape architect Laurie Olin, the garden's circular fountain bubbles in summer, and is transformed into an ice-skating rink in winter. Nestled among the cedars of Lebanon and linden trees are Louise Bourgeois' 10ft bronze cast *Spider*, whose spindly legs span 24ft, Sol LeWitt's 15ft-high concrete *Four-Sided Pyramid*, and Tony Smith's stout *Moondog*.

National Museum of African Art (S)
950 Independence Avenue, SW, between Seventh & 12th Streets, The Mall & Tidal Basin (1-202 633 4600/www.nmafa.si.edu). Smithsonian Metro. **Open** 10am-5.30pm daily. **Admission** free. **Map** p252 J7.

This museum's entrance pavilion, designed by Shepley Bulfinch Richardson and Abbott, lies across the amazing Enid Haupt Garden from its twin, the Sackler. The primary focus of the collection, which opened in 1987, is ancient and contemporary work from sub-Saharan Africa, although it also collects arts from other African areas, including a particularly strong array of royal Benin art. The Point of View gallery is devoted to thematic explorations of objects in the collection, while temporary shows present a wide variety of African visual arts, including sculptures, textiles, ceramics and photos. Contemporary art surveys are also included in the museum's roster.

National Museum of the American Indian

Independence Avenue & Fourth Street, SW, The Mall & Tidal Basin (1-202 633 1000/www.nmai.si.edu). L'Enfant Plaza Metro. **Open** 10am-5.30pm daily. **Admission** free. **Map** p253 J7.

Dedicated to America's colonised and historically abused indigenous people, the National Museum of the American Indian marks the latest addition to the Mall's museum ring. Occupying a triangle of land across the Mall from the National Gallery and directly east of the Air & Space Museum, the structure was designed by a Native American team; the building is as much a part of the message as the exhibits. The details are extraordinary: dramatic, Kasota limestone-clad undulating walls resemble a wind-carved mesa; the museum's main entrance plaza plots the star configurations on 28 November 1989, the date that federal legislation was introduced to create the museum; fountains enliven outdoor walkways.

Visitors enter at the dramatic Potomac Hall rotunda, with its soaring 120ft dome. The museum's permanent collection, exhibited on the third and fourth floors, orbits around thousands of works assembled at the turn of the 20th century by wealthy New Yorker George Gustav Heye, including intricate wood and stone carvings, hides and 18th-century materials from the Great Lakes region. Collections also include a substantial array of items from the Caribbean, Central and South America. Kitschy permanent exhibitions, Our Universes, Our Peoples, and Our Lives, feature segments devoted to topics like cosmology, history and present-day life. Rotating temporary exhibitions

offer more sedate presentations. Interactive technology allows visitors to access in-depth information about each object; a resource centre is open seven days a week. Two theatres screen films and multimedia presentations. And as an alternative to the usual kind of food provided by museums, the café here features Native foods. **Photo** *p67*.

National Museum of Natural History (S)

Tenth Street & Constitution Avenue, NW, The Mall & Tidal Basin (1-202 633 1000/www.mnh.si.edu). Smithsonian Metro. **Open** *June-Aug* 10am-7.30pm daily. *Sept-May* 10am-5.30pm daily. **Admission** free. **Map** p252 J6.

The gem at the heart of the Museum of Natural History is a state-of-the-art IMAX cinema and an 80,000sq ft brushed-steel and granite Discovery Center housing a cafeteria and exhibition space. The rotunda, too, is an impressive structure, dominated by an eight-ton African elephant. A renovation in the late 1990s added chrome- and halogen-filled galleries; more recently, in late 2003, the museum's restored west wing opened its glistening, 25,000sq ft Kenneth E Behring Hall featuring interactive displays alongside 274 taxidermied critters striking dramatic poses. The gem and mineral collection attracts gawking spectators, who ring two-deep the very well-guarded 45.52-carat cut blue Hope Diamond. The museum is a real magnet for children: its Dinosaur Hall has an assortment of fierce-looking dinosaur skeletons and a 3.4-billion-year-old stromatolite; tarantulas and other live arthropods ripe for petting inhabit the Insect Zoo.

National World War II Memorial

The Mall, 17th Street, from Independence to Constitution Avenues (1-202 426 6841/www.wwii memorial.com). Smithsonian or Farragut West Metro. **Map** p252 G6/7.

Dedicated in 2004, the monument that honours America's 'Greatest Generation' is a grandiose affair on a 7.4-acre plot, featuring granite space dominated by the central Rainbow Pool between two 43ft triumphal arches, representing the Atlantic and Pacific theatres of war. Fifty-six wreath-crowned pillars represent the US states and territories (including the Philippines), while a bronze Freedom Wall displays 4,000 gold stars, each signifying 100 war dead. The ceremonial entrance, descending from 17th Street, passes bas-reliefs depicting events of the global conflict. A Circle of Remembrance garden off to the side fosters quiet reflection. A visitor kiosk and restrooms clutter the periphery.

The memorial attracted controversy right from the outset, partly due to its location (boggy enough to require pumping and breaking the sweep of the Mall), and partly its heavy neo-classical design, which prompted *Der Spiegel* to quip that it looked

A Mall with meaning

For most of the 19th century the area that is now the Mall was a swampy tract of land appropriated by stockyards, a railroad station and 'the most active and importune squatters'. But in 1902 the McMillan Commission revisited L'Enfant's vision of a grand *allée* stretching from the Capitol to the Washington Monument, then for good measure extended it on for an extra mile of land reclaimed from the Potomac to where the Lincoln Memorial now stands.

Over the decades the area took on a role not only as a space for public celebrations (like the Smithsonian Annual Kite Festival, *pictured*) but as the theatre for great national events. Here, at the Lincoln Memorial, Martin Luther King delivered his 'I have a dream' speech in 1963 (on the same site as Marian Anderson's dramatic Easter recital of 1939). In 1979 Pope John Paul II celebrated mass here. And in 1981 the site of the presidential inauguration was moved from the East Front of the Capitol to the West, adding further gravitas to the grounds.

And, of course, the Mall is famous as the site of demonstrations, among them the anti-Vietnam War protests of the 1960s and '70s, the 'tractorcades' of discontented farmers in the late 1970s, the Million Man marchers in the '90s and the anti-globalisation and anti-Iraq War protestors of the 2000s.

Its growing ceremonial status has put pressure on the Mall as groups vie for a share of the turf. Revolutionary War thinker George Mason nabbed a spot by the Jefferson Memorial, while a nearby swatch by the Tidal Basin awaits a Dr King monument. A memorial to the two presidents Adams and an African American Museum have also been approved. Conservative campaigners have pressed for a Ronald Reagan memorial square in the centre of the Mall, while partisans of other causes covet many surrounding patches of ground.

The National World War II memorial, opened in 2004, also proved controversial. Some criticised the design as backward-looking and grandiose, others deplored the interruption of the Mall's grand open sweep between the Capitol and the Lincoln Memorial.

The development of an underground information and education centre at the Vietnam Veterans' Memorial is the most recent big development on the Mall, but it's unlikely to be the last. Never was the phrase 'watch this space' more literally spoken.

as if Hitler had won. However, the memorial's apologia is engraved in granite at the 17th Street entrance, saying why those who defended freedom during World War II fully deserve their place between the heroes of the 18th (Washington) and 19th (Lincoln) centuries. To partly preserve the open vista, the memorial was sunk below street level.

Vietnam Veterans Memorial

West Potomac Park, just north of the Reflecting Pool at Henry Bacon Drive & Constitution Avenue, NW (1-202 462 6841/www.nps.gov/vive). Foggy Bottom or Smithsonian Metro. **Map** p252 G6.

Despite initial controversy, the sombre black granite walls of the Vietnam Veterans Memorial have become a shrine, with pilgrims coming to touch the more than 58,000 names, make pencil rubbings and leave flowers, letters and flags. In 1981, 21-year-old Yale University senior Maya Ying Lin won the nationwide competition with this striking abstract design – two walls, each just over 246ft long – angled to enfold the Washington Monument and the Lincoln Memorial in a symbolic embrace. Political pressures forced later additions: first, a flagpole, then a sculpture by Frederick Hart of three Vietnam GIs. In 1993 came the Vietnam Women's Memorial, a sculpture group inspired by Michelangelo's *Pietà*. Happily, these additions were placed harmoniously. A submerged education centre has been approved just to the west.

Names on the wall appear in the chronological order that they became casualties. To descend gradually past the thousands of names to the nadir, then slowly emerge, is to follow symbolically America's journey into an increasingly ferocious war, only to try to 'wind it down' over years. It can be a genuinely touching experience.

Washington Monument

The Mall, between 15th & 17th Streets, & Constitution & Independence Avenues (1-202 426 6841/www.nps.gov/wamo). Smithsonian Metro. **Open** 9am-5pm daily. **Map** p252 H7.

The Washington Monument was completed in 1884, 101 years after Congress authorised it. It rises in a straight line between the Capitol and the Lincoln Memorial, but is off-centre between the White House and the Jefferson Memorial because the original site was too marshy for its bulk. Private funding ran out in the 1850s, when only the stump of the obelisk had been erected. Building resumed in 1876, producing a slight change in the colour of the marble about a third of the way up. The 555ft monument – the tallest freestanding masonry structure in the world – was capped with solid aluminum, then a rare material.

Timed tickets up the Monument are available for free from the 15th Street kiosk, which opens at 8.30am from autumn through to spring. You can book in advance by calling National Park reservations on 1-800 967 2283 for an admin fee of $1.50 per ticket plus 50¢ per order.

South of the monument, a cast-iron plate near the light box conceals an underground 162in miniature of the monument, measuring the rate at which the big version is sinking into the ground: around a quarter-inch every 30 years. **Photo** *p61*.

The White House & around

Set above the Ellipse to the north of the Mall, the **White House** opens up the rectangular dynamic of the Mall with north–south sightlines to the Washington Monument and Jefferson Memorial. Directly north of it is the park named for the Marquis de Lafayette, hero of the American Revolution. Workers and tourists fill its benches at lunchtime; a round-the-clock anti-nuclear protest has camped here continuously since 1981. The stretch of Pennsylvania Avenue between the park and the White House is reserved for the use of pedestrians only due to security considerations.

Though the park is named after Lafayette, its most prominent statue – the hero on the horse in the middle – is Andrew Jackson at the Battle of New Orleans in 1815. This was the first equestrian statue cast in the US at the time of its unveiling in 1853. His four companions are European luminaries of the American Revolution: Lafayette, Comte de Rochambeau, General Kosciusko and Baron von Steuben.

Every president since James Madison has attended at least one service at the mellow yellow St John's Episcopal Church north of the park at 16th and H Streets. A brass plate at pew 54 marks the place reserved for them.

TV news-watchers might recognise the green awning across Jackson Place to the west of the square: this is **Blair House** (1660 Pennsylvania Avenue, NW), where visiting heads of state bunk. Next door, at Pennsylvania and 17th Street, is the **Renwick Gallery** – an 1859 building in the French Second Empire mode, named after its architect, James Renwick. Part of the Smithsonian, it commonly features 20th-century crafts. Lately its opulent Grand Salon has replicated period exhibits – like that of George Caitlin's Indian Gallery – of the kind local grandee William Wilson Corcoran built this place to display. These contrast with the contemporary American exhibits featured elsewhere. At the end of the 19th century, the original collection moved three blocks south into the purpose-built **Corcoran Museum of Art**, the Beaux Arts building on the south-west corner of 17th and E Streets. Just west of it, toward Foggy Bottom, is the **Octagon** (*see p85*).

Decatur House, at 748 Jackson Place, was home to naval hero Stephen Decatur, as well as French, British and Russian diplomats, and 19th-century statesmen Henry Clay and Martin Van Buren. Across the square, at H Street and Madison Place, is the Dolley Madison House

(closed to the public), home of the widowed but effervescent first lady until her death.

Bookending Lafayette Square are the New Executive Office Building on the west and the US Court of Claims opposite, tucked behind historic edifices. West of the White House is the **Dwight D Eisenhower Executive Office Building**, aka the Old Executive Office Building (OEOB). With its 900 Doric columns and French Empire bombast, this was the largest office building in the world in 1888, housing the entire State, War and Navy departments. Presidential aides posted here included George W Bush's 'Strategery Group', political operatives wryly named for their boss's linguistic lapses.

The Treasury, the third-oldest federal office building in Washington, interrupts Pennsylvania Avenue because the ornery President Jackson, exasperated at endless debate, declared, 'Put it there!' Symbolically close is a cluster of solid-looking banks and former banks, vestiges of the old financial district, once known as 'Washington's Wall Street', now the 15th Street Financial Historic District.

Corcoran Museum of Art

500 17th Street, NW, between New York Avenue & E Street, The White House & around (1-202 639 1700/www.corcoran.org). Farragut West Metro. **Open** 10am-5pm Mon, Wed, Fri-Sun; 10am-9pm Thur. **Admission** $8; $4-$6 concessions. Pay what you wish after 5pm Thur. **Credit** AmEx, MC, V. **Map** p252 G6.

When District financier William Wilson Corcoran's collection outgrew its original space (now the Renwick Gallery), gallery trustees engaged architect Ernest Flagg to design its current Beaux Arts building, which opened in 1897. (A public embarrassment followed a recently aborted Frank Gehry-designed addition.) Despite a handful of significant bequests that added the minor Renoirs and Pissarros that now grace the wood-panelled Clark Landing, the Corcoran's strength remains its 19th-century American painting collection, featuring landscapes of the American West by Albert Bierstadt, Frederick Church and Winslow Homer. Church's mammoth oil, *Niagara*, and Bierstadt's *Mount Corcoran* capture Americans' reverence for the natural world.

The museum's 6,000 pieces also include contemporary art, photography, prints, drawings and sculpture. Notable displays include the Evans-Tibbs collection of African-American art and drawings by John Singer Sargent. Visitors looking for contemporary work will find it on view in special exhibitions, including the museum's biannual surveys. The museum hired a new director in 2006 who promises to refocus the sometimes wayward institution.

Decatur House

748 Jackson Place, NW, at H Street (1-202 842 0920/www.decaturhouse.org). Farragut West Metro. **Open** 10am-5pm Tue-Sat; noon-4pm

Sun. *Guided tours* depart every hr, 15mins past the hr. **Admission** free; suggested donation. **Credit** AmEx, MC, V. **Map** p252 H5.

Admiral Nelson declared Stephen Decatur 'the greatest hero of the age' for his 1804 raids crippling the 'Barbary' pirates. Decatur uttered the famous toast, 'my country, right or wrong', but he died in a needless duel in 1820. The house was designed by architect Benjamin Henry Latrobe for Decatur in 1818. The permanent collection comprises furniture, textiles, art and ceramics of the period.

Renwick Gallery of the Smithsonian American Art Museum (S)

17th Street & Pennsylvania Avenue, NW, The White House & around (1-202 633 2850//http://american art.si.edu/renwick/renwick_about.cfm). Farragut North or Farragut West Metro. **Open** 10am-5.30pm daily. **Admission** free. **Map** p252 G5.

This mansarded building, modelled on the Louvre, was built across from the White House in 1859 by architect James Renwick to house the art collection of financier and philanthropist William Wilson Corcoran. The space soon became too small for the displays, and it changed hands several times before opening in 1972 as the Smithsonian's craft museum. The exhibition of 20th-century American crafts – defined as objects created from materials associated with trades and industries, such as clay, glass, metal and fibre – often showcases striking work. In the mansion's refurbished Grand Salon picture gallery, paintings that exemplify the taste of wealthy late 19th-century collectors hang in gilt frames stacked two and three high; works on view rotate regularly. Temporary exhibitions, which are held downstairs, survey artistic movements or artists.

The White House

1600 Pennsylvania Avenue, NW, between 15th & 17th Streets (1-202 456 7041/www.whitehouse.gov). McPherson Square Metro. **Open** *Tours* 7.30am-12.30pm Tue-Sat. Booking essential; see review below. *Visitors' centre* 7.30am-4pm daily. **Admission** free. **Map** p252 H6.

Part showplace, part workplace, the White House is sometimes called 'the people's house'. Indeed, until the 20th century the public could walk freely in and the grounds remained open until World War II. Today the Executive Mansion is open only to pre-arranged groups of ten or more, who simply get to peek at a scant eight rooms out of the house's 132, and with little time to linger. The public tour is self-guided (though highly regimented) and there's not much in the way of interpretation, but the nation proudly clings to keeping its leader's residence open to the public.

To arrange a tour, US citizens should contact their Senator or Representative; some may help by putting individuals together to make a group. Visitors with foreign passports should contact their nation's embassy. Tours may be scheduled up to six months in advance.

Finished in 1800, the White House has been home to every US president except George Washington. Early presidents lived and worked above the shop. In 1902 Teddy Roosevelt added the East Gallery and the West Wing, which grew to include today's renowned Oval Office.

Each new first lady can furnish the White House as she pleases: Jacqueline Kennedy, for example, replaced the B Altman department store furniture and frilly florals of her predecessors, the Trumans and Eisenhowers, with understated blues and whites. Her overall refurbishment of the White House restored many historic furnishings and artworks to the rooms. Her tour on national television

was a triumph. Each president, meanwhile, imposes his character on the Oval Office, bringing in favourite furniture and personal selections from the White House art collection.

There are also offices for around 200 executive branch staffers, and recreational facilities, including a cinema, tennis courts, putting green, bowling alley and, courtesy of the elder George Bush, a horseshoe pitch. All told, there are 32 bathrooms, 413 doors, three elevators, seven staircases and a staff of more than 100, including florists, carpenters and cooks.

On the tour, you may get a look in the China Room, the pantry for presidential crockery. Don't miss Nancy Reagan's $952-per-setting red-rimmed china,

Walk The road to the White House

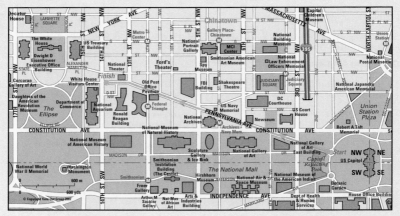

In 1977, new President Jimmy Carter walked the traditional inauguration parade route up Pennsylvania Avenue from the Capitol to the White House, and most of his successors have followed suit, popping out of the limo for at least a few token steps. It's an interesting route to follow, the core of old Washington.

Its nickname of 'America's Main Street' is not particularly apt: this ceremonial thoroughfare is anything but homey. Passing the ornate little **Peace Monument** at First Street and the Capitol reflecting pool, the walker encounters on his left IM Pei's angular **East Wing** of the National Gallery (*see p67*), with its neo-classical predecessor just beyond. To the right is the 'Watergate Courthouse' known from the Nixon-era scandals, now sporting a jazzy new east wing of its own.

Just beyond, the **Canadian Embassy** justifies its special location by architecturally echoing the city's monumental motifs. A gallery inside displays Canadian artworks. Adjoining rises the new **Newseum** (*see p93*) – an interactive museum dedicated to print and broadcast journalism, relocated from Virginia and due to open in autumn 2007.

At Sixth Street begins the Federal Triangle, a cluster of heavy neo-classical government offices begun in the 1920s. Some of the buildings here recycle an old look, with vintage store façades fronting pricey offices. The venerable National Council of Negro Women occupies what locals still call the Apex Building, once home to Apex Liquor store. The building's eastern extension takes in the one-time studio of Matthew Brady, photographer of Lincoln and Civil War scenes.

which sparked a controversy about conspicuous consumption – as had Mrs Lincoln's previously.

Up the marble stairs, visitors enter the cavernous East Room, which holds the sole item from the original White House: the 1797 portrait of George Washington that Dolley Madison rescued just before the British burned the place down on 24 August 1814. The East Room is the ceremonial room where seven presidents have lain in state – and where Abigail Adams, wife of the second president, John, hung her laundry. At 3,200sq ft, the space could hold the average American home.

Next is the Green Room, once Jefferson's dining room, and where James Madison did his politicking after Dolley had liquored up important guests in the Red Room, the tour's next stop, decorated as an American Empire parlour of 1810-30. It was here that Mary Todd Lincoln held a seance to contact her dead sons and where President Grant and his former generals refought the Civil War on the carpet using salt shakers and nut dishes as troops.

The colour naming scheme continues in the Blue Room – although it actually has yellow walls. The furnishings here, the traditional home of the White House Christmas tree, were ordered in 1817 by President Monroe. Last stop: the cream and gold State Dining Rooms, which can seat up to 140. Then you're out the door. If you want to glimpse the living

Sightseeing

Across Seventh Street and to the south looms the National Achives, with the Lone Sailor statue marking the **US Navy Memorial**. An equestrian statue of General WS Hancock, a combat hero who lost the presidential election of 1880 by about 1,000 votes, is grander than that of President Garfield (First & Maryland, SW), who beat him.

The sterility of the 900 block stems from FBI director J Edgar Hoover's vetoing of plans for shops at the front of the FBI building on security grounds. The avenue resumes its character at 11th Street, with the old *Washington Star* newspaper building. The **Old Post Office** tower disrupts the Federal Triangle façade with Romanesque impudence. Its tourist pavilion struggles along, but an ascent of the tower offers a truly impressive panorama. West lies the **Ronald Reagan Building**, a massive complex containing a food court and a tourist centre (where visitors must inhospitably pass through security). It engulfs the John A Wilson Building (1909), DC's city hall, usually called by its previous name, the District Building. The statue outside depicts Alexander 'Boss' Shepherd, who oversaw a large building programme after the Civil War to prevent the government moving to St Louis, spending $20 million when only $10 million had been approved. Shepherd then prudently relocated himself to Mexico.

Across is **Freedom Plaza**, with L'Enfant's city plan etched into the pavements, alongside sometimes arch comments by historic visitors like Charles Dickens. Polish-Americans ensured that the incongruous statue of Revolutionary hero Casimir Pulaski held its longtime ground. The **National Theatre** (see p201) has thrived here since 1835.

On to the legendary **Willard Hotel** (see p42), the grand 1902 incarnation of the hostelry where statesmen plotted and partied and Julia Ward Howe wrote 'The Battle Hymn of the Republic'. The beguiling view makes Hotel Washington's rooftop bar, the **Sky Terrace** (515 15th Street, NW, 1-2020 638 5900) a favourite rendezvous.

Featuring a popular ice rink in winter, **Pershing Park** to the south commemorates American campaigns of World War I. The Avenue doglegs around the Treasury, passing the **White House**, where we end our walk, then resuming for a pleasant mile to Georgetown.

Navy Memorial.

United States Botanic Garden. *See p78*.

quarters and you're not a heavy campaign contributor, rent a DVD, for Hollywood has created an authentic replica 'White House West' set repeatedly used in cinema and TV productions. Nowadays tourists repair to the White House Visitors' Center, in the dignified former search room of the Patent Office, at 15th and E Streets, NW, which has historical displays and even living history re-enactments. In some ways, the new arrangements tell visitors more than the old walk-throughs ever did.

Alternatively, you can stop at the White House Historical Association offices (740 Jackson Place, NW, on the west side of Lafayette Park, 1-202 737 8292, open 9am-4pm Mon-Fri) to pick up an extensive guide to the mansion, a CD-ROM, or the definitive books by official historian William Seale. **Photo** *p80*.

The Capitol & around

An angry senator once scolded President Lincoln that his administration was on the road to hell – in fact, just a mile from it. Lincoln shot back that that was almost exactly the distance from the White House to the Capitol. The Legislative Branch on the east end of Pennsylvania Avenue balances the Executive on the west.

Standing at the east end of the Mall is the commanding presence of the **United States Capitol**. Achieving both dignity and grace

from every angle – though the walk along the Mall via the Capitol Reflecting Pool and its ducks shouldn't be missed – the Capitol rises elegantly to the occasion.

The **United States Botanic Garden** at the foot of the Capitol employs high-tech climate controls to replicate the home climate of flora from around the globe. Its highlight is the central rainforest room, equipped with a catwalk affording palm tree-top views. This glass palace coddles tropical and subtropical plants, cacti, ferns, palm trees, shrubs and flowers, including its hallmark 500 varieties of orchid.

North of the Capitol, the grounds extend towards **Union Station**. Downhill is a carillon dedicated to conservative 'Mr Republican', Ohio Senator Robert A Taft, son of a president and perennial aspirant himself.

Around the Capitol throbs a civic city of Congressional office buildings (the Senate's to the north, the House's to the south). In its eastern lee are the decorous **Supreme Court** and the lavish **Library of Congress**. Beside the art deco Adams Building annex is the incomparable **Folger Shakespeare Library**. Books here are available only to scholars, but the Elizabethan Garden and the museum reward public visits. So far, the librarians have refrained from turning the outdoor statue of Puck, exclaiming 'What fools these mortals be!' around so as to glance at Congress.

Adjoining the Senate offices is the **Sewall-Belmont House** (144 Constitution Avenue, NE; *see p33*), a three-storey Federal Period mansion, with a museum detailing women's suffrage struggles.

Folger Shakespeare Library

201 East Capitol Street, SE, between Second & Third Streets (1-202 544 4600/www.folger.edu). Capitol South or Union Station Metro. **Open** *Great Hall* 10am-4pm Mon-Sat. *Library* 11am-4pm Mon-Sat. *Guided tours* 11am Mon-Fri; 11am, 1pm Sat. **Admission** free. **Map** p253 L7.
The marble façade sports bas-relief scenes from Shakespeare's plays. Inside is the world's largest collection of the playwright's works, including the 79-volume *First Folio* collection. Standard Oil chairman Henry Clay Folger, who fell in love with Shakespeare after hearing Ralph Waldo Emerson lecture on him, endowed the lot. Items include musical instruments, costumes and films, as well as 27,000 paintings, drawings and prints. Open during the library's annual celebration of Shakespeare's birthday in April, the Reading Room has a copy of a bust of the Bard from Stratford's Trinity Church and a stained-glass window of the Seven Ages of Man as described in *As You Like It*. The intimate theatre (*see p201*) is a replica of one from an Elizabethan inn.

Library of Congress

Visitors' Center, Jefferson Building, First Street & Independence Avenue, SE (1-202 707 8000/ www.loc.gov). Capitol South Metro. **Open** 10am-5.30pm Mon-Sat. *Guided tours* 10.30am, 11.30am, 1.30pm, 2.30pm, 3.30pm Mon-Fri; 10.30am, 11.30am, 1.30pm, 2.30pm Sat. **Admission** free. **Map** p252 L7.

The national library of the US, the Library of Congress is the world's largest. Its three buildings hold some 100 million items – including the papers of 23 US presidents – along 535 miles of bookshelves. Contrary to popular notion, the Library does not have a copy of every book ever printed, but its heaving shelves are still spectacular.

To get to grips with the place, it's best to start with the 20-minute film in the ground-floor visitors' centre, excerpted from a TV documentary, which provides a clear picture of the place's scope and size. An even better option is to join a guided tour (note that they are limited to 50 people). To use any of the specialised research rooms or enter the grand main reading room, you have to register as a reader.

The original Library was crammed into the Capitol. Ransacked by the British in 1814, it revived when president-scholar Thomas Jefferson offered his collection of 6,487 books. The Thomas Jefferson Building – the main one – was finished in 1897 and splendidly restored upon its centennial. Based on the Paris Opera House, the Library has granite walls supporting an octagonal dome, which rises to 160ft above the spectacular Main Reading Room. Gloriously gaudy mosaics, frescos and statues overwhelm the visitor with a gush of 19th-century high culture. A permanent rotating exhibition, American Treasures of the Library of Congress, displays significant items from America's past – from the contents of Lincoln's pockets on the night he died to film of a youngster frolicking in the Library's Neptune Fountain in 1906. The Bob Hope and American Variety gallery traces the life of the popular entertainer. A visitors' gallery overlooks the striking Great Hall – white marble with red and gold roof panels – adorned with brass zodiac symbols, neo-Greek mosaics, mermen, nymphs and Muses. The main reading room has classical marble archways and great plaster figures of disciplines (Philosophy, Religion, Art, History – all women) flanked by bronze images of their mortal instruments (Plato, Moses, Homer, Shakespeare – all men).

The James Madison Building, opened in 1980, encloses an area greater than 35 football fields. It houses the copyright office, manuscript room, film and TV viewing rooms and the incredible photography collections. Staff run frequent lunchtime 'language tables' where regulars, students and strangers drop in to converse in tongues ranging from Ukrainian to Swahili. Diagonally opposite is the 1939 John Adams Building, which contains the Science and Business reading rooms. On a mural near the ceiling, Chaucer's pilgrims trudge perpetually toward Canterbury.

Anyone with photo ID can obtain a research card within about ten minutes. You can't wander all the shelves yourself: a librarian will dig out your selected text. The Library catalogue is also available online at www.lcweb.loc.gov, though many of the old card-catalogue entries are found only in their original drawers. The Library also stages free concerts, poetry readings, films and lectures, *see p190.*

Supreme Court

First Street & Maryland Avenue, NW (1-202 479 3211/www.supremecourtus.gov). Capitol South or Union Station Metro. **Open** 9am-4.30pm Mon-Fri. **Map** p253 L6.

The ultimate judicial and constitutional authority, the United States Supreme Court pays homage in its architecture to the rule of law. Justices are appointed for life, and their temple reflects their eminence. Designed by Cass Gilbert in the 1930s, its classical façade incorporates Corinthian columns supporting a pediment decorated with bas-reliefs representing Liberty, Law, Order and a crew of historical lawgivers. The sober style conceals whimsy in the shape of sculpted turtles lurking to express the 'deliberate pace' of judicial deliberations. There are also ferocious lions – enough said.

United States Holocaust Memorial Museum. *See p82.*

Sightseeing

You can tour the building any time, entering from Maryland Avenue. The ground level has a cafeteria, an introductory video show, and a gift shop. The regular tour lacks heavy Law and Order theatrics, but the venue is awesome. The cathedral-like entrance hall daunts one into hushed tones. The sober courtroom, with its heavy burgundy velvet draperies and marble pillars, is where the nine judges hear around 120 of the more than 6,500 cases submitted each year. The black-robed figures appear as the Court Marshal announces 'Oyez! Oyez! Oyez!' and sit in seats of varying height, handcrafted to their personal preferences. Goose-quill pens still grace the lawyers' tables, for tradition's sake.

When the court is in session, from October to April, visitors can see cases argued on Mondays, Tuesdays and Wednesdays from 10am to 3pm. Two lines form in the plaza in front of the building: one for those who want to hear the whole argument (better be there by 8am), and the 'three-minute line', for those who just want a peek. In May and June, 'opinions' are handed down usually on Tuesdays and Wednesdays. Check the newspapers' Supreme Court calendars to see what cases are scheduled. Celebrated cases draw massive queues. When the court is out of session, there are regular lectures in the courtroom about court procedure and the building's architecture.

United States Botanic Garden

245 First Street, at Maryland Avenue (1-202 225 8333/www.usbg.gov). Federal Center SW Metro. **Open** 10am-5pm daily. **Admission** free. **Map** p253 K7.

In 1842 the Navy's Wilkes Expedition returned from exploring Fiji and South America, showering Congress with a cornucopia of exotic flora. The present conservatory was erected in 1930 and recently modernised with state-of-the-art climate controls and a coconut-level catwalk around the central rainforest.

The conservatory displays 4,000 plants, including endangered species. Themed displays feature the desert and the oasis, plant adaptations and the primeval garden. The orchid collection is a particular delight. Across Independence Avenue, Bartholdi Park displays plants thriving in Washington's climate, ranged around an alluring fountain created by Bartholdi, sculptor of the *Statue of Liberty*. The new National Garden aims to be a showcase for 'unusual, useful, and ornamental plants that grow well in the mid-Atlantic region'.

United States Capitol

Capitol Hill, between Constitution & Independence Avenues (recorded tour information 1-202 225 6827/www.aoc.gov). Capitol South or Union Station Metro. **Open** *Guided tours* 9am-4.30pm Mon-Sat (last ticket 3.30pm). **Admission** free. **Map** p253 K7.

French architect Major Pierre L'Enfant, hired by President Washington to plan the federal city, selected Capitol Hill – a plateau, actually – as 'a pedestal waiting for a monument'. Indeed it was. In 1793 George Washington and an entourage of local masons laid the building's long-lost cornerstone,

then celebrated by barbecuing a 500-pound ox. Thirty-one years later, despite a fire, a shortage of funds and the War of 1812, the structure was complete. But as the Union grew, so did the number of legislators. By 1850 architects projected the Capitol would have to double its size. In 1857 they added wings for the Senate (north) and the House of Representatives (south). An iron dome (a 600-gallon paint job each year makes it look like marble) replaced the wooden one in 1865. Abe Lincoln insisted it be finished during the Civil War as a symbol of the durability of the Union.

Today the Capitol – which has 540 rooms, 658 windows (108 in the dome alone) and 850 doorways – is a small city. As well as the 535 elected lawmakers, an estimated 20,000 workers toil daily among the six buildings (not including the Capitol itself) – all connected by tunnels – that make up the complex. Within this massive workforce is a 1,200-member police department, doctors, nurses, electricians, carpenters, day-care personnel and more. There are power plants, libraries, shops, restaurants, gyms and maintenance workshops. A US flag flies over the Senate and House wings when either is in session; at night a lantern glows in the Capitol dome.

There are now only two ways for visitors to enter the Capitol: with an official tour, or with a pass to the visitors' galleries that overlook the House and Senate floors. Both are free and available daily on a first-come, first-served basis. Tickets for the one-hour, 40-person tours are distributed between 9am and 3.30pm from a kiosk on the southwest corner of the Capitol grounds, near the Botanic Garden. For US citizens, gallery passes are available from the office of the visitor's Senator or Representative. Those with foreign passports may get passes from the South Screening Facility, a kiosk on the southeast side of the building. You will be asked to check in bags and follow guidelines to avoid disrupting proceedings (no pagers, mobile phones or cameras).

Before 9/11, a massive underground visitors' centre was planned. This controversial structure, which is currently under construction (and well over budget) on the Capitol's east side, was subsequently redefined and redesigned as an integral part of the building's security system. Visitors will enter through the centre upon its completion, currently set for spring 2007. **Photos** *p68*.

Union Station & around

Daniel Burnham's Beaux Arts-style **Union Station** is a monument to the railroad age. The Thurgood Marshall Judiciary Building east of Union Station complements the former City Post Office – now the **National Postal Museum** – also built by Burnham, to present an elegant urban vista. In front of the trio, the flags of all the US states and territories are ranged around the central Columbus Memorial Fountain (1912).

Treasure rooms

Peacock Room.

Sometimes the surroundings of an exhibitiion are as extraordinary as the paintings. Here we list must-see rooms in DC's finest museums that are an experience in themselves.

Salon Doré at the Corcoran Gallery of Art

The 18th-century neo-classical Salon Doré – transported from the Hôtel de Clermont in Paris, complete with gilded and mirrored panelling decorated with garlands, Corinthian pilasters and trophy panels – is a feast for the eyes. Given to the museum by industrialist and US Senator William A Clark (1839-1925), the room was removed from its original location in aristocratic Faubourg Saint-Germain and brought to New York, where it was installed in Clark's Fifth Avenue mansion. Upon his death, the Corcoran built a wing to accommodate Clark's sizeable bequest, which opened in 1928. Though the room served as a bedroom for its original occupant, the widow of the Marquis de Saissac, it wasn't outfitted to its current gaudy glory until its purchase by Pierre-Gaspard-Marie Grimod, Comte d'Orsay, in 1768. For Corcoran Gallery, *see p73*.

Music Room at the Phillips Collection

Duncan Phillips' luxuriant 1897 mansion, a welcome escape from the Mall melée, holds a special treat: a dark, enveloping Music Room with spectacular oak wainscoting and ceiling coffers. Commissioned by Duncan's parents as an addition to the house, the room originally functioned as Duncan and his brother James' recreation room – and a very sophisticated rec room indeed. Later, it was converted to a recital space, playing host to Sunday afternoon concerts, beginning in 1941. Emerging musical talents were often featured here; the room showcased early performances by the likes of Glenn Gould and Jessye Norman. Today, the room continues to host Sunday concerts from September to May. For the Phillips Collection, *see p95*.

Peacock Room at the Freer Gallery of Art

An immersive experience transported from the Gilded Age, Whistler's deep green and gilt Peacock Room was purchased by Detroit business magnate Charles Lang Freer in 1904. The museum's only permanent installation, this 1876-77 dining room was transported wholesale from British shipowner Frederick R Leyland's London townhouse. Whistler covered the ceiling with a gold leaf and peacock feather pattern, and added gilded shelving and painted wooden shutters with immense plumed peacocks. His Japanese-influenced canvas, *The Princess from the Land of Porcelain*, presides over the room. For Freer Gallery of Art, *see p63*.

Dining Room at Hillwood Museum and Gardens

This sumptuous room, covered in 18th-century French oak panels, hosted some of Washington's most lavish dinner parties. Presided over by cereal heiress Marjorie Merriweather Post, meals here honoured presidents, politicians, and visiting dignitaries. Though today the dining table is regularly set with spectacular displays of porcelain, silver and glassware, once a year these are removed and the gorgeous table uncovered. Spanning 28 feet long at its fullest length, the piece features around 70 types of minerals and marbles set into its surface in glorious stylised floral motifs. For Hillwood Museum and Gardens, *see p102*.

The most famous house in the world? The **White House**. *See p73.*

The neighbourhood around Union Station was once a shantytown of Irish railroad labourers, who christened their marshy abode 'Swampoodle' after its swamps and puddles.

National Postal Museum (S)

2 Massachusetts Avenue, NE, at First Street, Union Station & around (1-202 633 5555/www.si.edu/ postal). Union Station Metro. **Open** 10am-5.30pm daily. **Admission** free. **Map** p253 L6.
Audiovisual and interactive presentations in this family-friendly museum detail the invention and history of stamps, the postal service and stamp collecting. The frequent special exhibitions aren't likely to bowl over serious philatelists. For a bit of fun you can send your own postcard electronically from the museum. Serious scholars, on the other hand, should head to the museum's huge library and research centre.

Union Station

50 Massachusetts Avenue, NE (1-202 298-1908/ www.unionstationdc.com). Metro Union Station. **Open** *Station* 24hrs daily. *Shops* 10am-9pm Mon-Sat; noon-6pm Sun. **Map** p253 K/L 5/6.
Built in 1908, Union Station grandiosely reflects its inspiration – the Baths of Diocletian in Rome. Envisioning the most splendid terminal in the country, architect Daniel 'make no small plans' Burnham lavished the building with amenities, including a nursery, a swimming pool and even a mortuary for defunct out-of-towners. The Main Hall is a huge rectangular space, with a 96ft-high barrel-vaulted ceiling and a balcony with 36 sculptures of Roman legionnaires.

The station languished when rail travel declined. The President's Room, reserved for chief executives welcoming incoming dignitaries such as King George VI and Haile Selassie, is now a restaurant. In 1953 a decidedly non-stop express train bound for Eisenhower's inauguration smashed into the crowded concourse; incredibly, nobody was killed. Two

decades later, a deliberate but also disastrous hole was sunk in the Great Hall to make way for the multi-screen video set-up of an ill-conceived (and short-lived) visitors' centre. At this stage, despite its lingering grandeur, the station seemed doomed to the wrecking ball.

But in 1988 a painstaking $165-million restoration programme was begun, during which time entertainment came into play. There are now shops, amusements and eateries of all sorts, and even a multi-screen cinema. Rents are high and some of the shops have failed, but successors always seem to come along and more sales per square foot move through the shops here than any other DC mall. It's easy to forget that the marble and gilt palace's main function is still as a railway station – with lines to New York, Chicago, Miami and New Orleans, as well as the suburbs – though the crowds at rush hour will bring you back to your senses.

The Federal Triangle

The nine-block-long triangle of monolithic federal buildings wedged between Pennsylvania Avenue, NW, and the Mall is known as the Federal Triangle. The government bulldozed the whole district in the 1920s, claiming 'eminent domain' (the right of compulsory purchase), and today the Federal Triangle is the ballpark for the heavy hitters of the government machine, housing some 28,000 office workers. The triangle is both a labyrinth and a fortress. Security is tight, and visitors usually end up asking about six different people before finally making it to their destination. Wags call it the Bermuda Triangle.

All but three of the buildings in the Triangle were built between 1927 and 1938 as massive Beaux Arts limestone structures, complete with high-minded inscriptions, to house various federal agencies, such as the Departments of Commerce and Justice, and the **National Archives**. The Internal Revenue Service headquarters are inscribed with the words of former justice Oliver Wendell Holmes: 'Taxes are what we pay for a civilised society'. The three exceptions are the John Wilson (District) Building (the city hall, on the corner of 14th and E Streets), the Ronald Reagan Building, and the **Old Post Office**. Once sneered at as the 'old tooth' and slated for demolition, the latter now sports a tourist mall and a brilliant view from the top of its 315ft tower.

Built in the 1990s, the **Ronald Reagan Building & International Trade Center** (on 14th Street, opposite the Department of Commerce) is the most expensive building ever constructed in the US for federal use, at a cost of over $700 million. It was supposed to symbolise Reagan's passion for free enterprise and global trade, but it's really an embodiment of big government, with one-and-a-half times the floorspace of the Empire State Building.

The DC Chamber of Commerce Visitor Information Center is located here, along with a fast-food court. In the basement of the Commerce Department, an unexpected novelty is the National Aquarium of Washington, DC, an old-fashioned exhibit that affords a closer look at sea creatures than many more modern aquaria.

National Archives

Constitution Avenue, NW, between Seventh & Ninth Streets (1-866 272 6272/www.archives.gov). Archives-Navy Memorial Metro. **Open** *mid Mar-Sept* 10am-7pm daily. *Sept-mid Mar* 10am-5.30pm daily. **Admission** free. **Map** p253 J6.
The vast collection of the National Archive & Record Administration (NARA) represents the physical record of the birth and growth of a nation in original documents, maps, photos, recordings, films and a miscellany of objects. The catalogue resonates with national iconography and historical gravitas (and pathos): it includes the Louisiana Purchase, maps of Lewis and Clark's explorations, the Japanese World War II surrender document, the gun that shot JFK, the Watergate tapes and documents of national identity, among them the *Declaration of Independence*, *Constitution* and *Bill of Rights* (collectively known as the Charters of Freedom). Nearby is one of the original copies of the *Magna Carta*.

The building that houses them was opened in 1935 and designed to harmonise with existing DC landmarks – in other words, it's neo-classical in style. In a city of monumental architecture the most distinctive features are the bronze doors at the Constitution Avenue entrance. Each weighs six and a half tons and is 38ft high and 11in thick. Though security is their main function, they also remind the visitor of the importance of the contents. Unless you're a

history junkie, skip the rote tour, which basically consists of a guide displaying copies of the various documents held in the stacks, and cut straight to the main attraction. That's the Rotunda, where the original Charters of Freedom are mounted, triptych-like, in a glass case at the centre of a roped-off horseshoe containing other key documents. A renovation completed in 2003 protecting them with high-tech gizmos proved itself in 2006 when the building flooded. A semi-circular gallery running behind the Rotunda stages temporary exhibitions drawn from the vast collections. Research access (photo ID required) is via the door on Pennsylvania Avenue. A free shuttle bus connects to Archives II in College Park, Maryland for collections housed there, including all post World War II files.

Old Post Office

1100 Pennsylvania Avenue, NW, between 11th & 12th Streets (1-202 606 8691/www.nps.gov/opot). Federal Triangle Metro. **Open** *Sept-May* 9am-4.45pm Mon-Fri; 10am-5.45pm Sat, Sun. *June-Aug* 9am-7.45pm Mon-Fri; 10am-5.45pm Sat, Sun. **Admission** free. **Map** p252 J6.
Washington's best views may be from the Washington Monument, but from here you get to see the Monument itself. It's a 47-second ride to the ninth floor; you then change to another elevator bound for the 12th, and top, floor. The Pavilion below is a mix of souvenir shops and tourist eateries.

The Northwest Rectangle

The Northwest Rectangle is not an official appellation, but it's sometimes used to describe the rectangle of federal buildings west of the Ellipse and south of E Street that roughly mirrors the Federal Triangle to the east. It's really just part of Foggy Bottom (*see p83*), an industrial immigrant area in the 19th century, but any original character that the area has retained emerges only further north.

In this southern part, it's grandiose federal anonymity all the way. From west to east, the buildings of interest are the **State Department**, whose opulent reception rooms can be toured by arrangement; then, dropping down to Constitution Avenue, the American Pharmaceutical Association, the National Academy of Sciences, with its invitingly climbable statue of Einstein, the Federal Reserve Board and the Organisation of American States (OAS). Behind the OAS art-gallery annex is the **Department of the Interior**, housing in its museum examples of Native American arts, with authentic goods for sale in its craft shop. Attempting to improve its PR, the **IMFCenter** – scene of an annual siege by anti-globalisation protesters – offers displays explaining international finance.

Department of the Interior Museum

1849 C Street, NW, between 18th & 19th Streets,
The Northwest Rectangle (1-202 208 4743). Farragut
West Metro. **Open** 8.30am-4.30pm Mon-Fri & 3rd
Sat every mth. **Admission** free. **Map** p252 G6.
The Department of the Interior's exhibits are a hotchpotch of Indian arts and crafts: Pueblo drums; Apache
basketwork; Cheyenne arrows that a soldier plucked
from dying buffaloes at Fort Sill Indian Territory
(Oklahoma) in 1868. You can also see early land boun-
ties and exhibits about endangered species, complete
with shoes made from crocodile skin. The gift shop,
one of Washington's best-kept secrets, is over 60 years
old and contains wares from 40 Indian tribes, from
Navajo folk art to Alaskan ivory. Note that tours are
by reservation only and that photo ID is required.

IMF Center

720 19th Street, NW, between G & H Streets (1-202
623 6869/www.imf.org/center). Farragut West
Metro. **Open** 10am-4.30pm Mon-Fri. **Admission**
free. **Map** p252 G5.
A permanent display traces the development of
world monetary policies, while special exhibits follow the history of various countries, reflected in their
coins and currencies.

State Department Diplomatic Reception Rooms

C & 22nd Streets, NW (1-202 647 3241/www.state.
gov/www/about_state/diprooms/index.html). Foggy
Bottom-GWU Metro. **Guided tours** 9.30am, 10.30am,
2.45pm Mon-Fri. **Admission** free. **Map** p252 G6.
When the State Department was finished in 1951,
the wife of the Secretary of State wept when con-
fronted with the chrome, glass-and-concrete walls
and tasteless furniture. Today, the diplomatic reception rooms, fit to receive foreign dignitaries, are
dubbed Washington's best-kept secret – a delight
for serious arts and antiques lovers. They contain
national masterpieces from 1740 to 1825, valued at
some $90 million. Among the collection are
Chippendale pieces; the English Sheraton desk on
which the Treaty of Paris was signed in 1783, ending the Revolutionary War; and a table-desk used
by Thomas Jefferson. There are also some none-too-
exciting exhibits in the lobby on the history of the
State Department, which is the oldest of the cabinet
departments. Note that you can only visit by guided tour, for which reservations are required (call or
email 90 days ahead).

South of the Mall

To the south of the Mall lie mostly nondescript
federal buildings (Federal Aviation
Administration, Transportation Department
and so on). The principal exceptions are the
United States Holocaust Memorial
Museum and the **Bureau of Engraving**
& Printing, where the greenback is printed.
Both are to the west near the Tidal Basin.

To the east, L'Enfant Plaza is ironically
named, considering that it's supposed to honour
the man whose city plan made Washington so
stately – this barren expanse is set for a
makeover – with a National Children's Museum
planned to perk things up.

Bureau of Engraving & Printing

14th Street, SW, at C Street, (1-202 874 2330/
www.moneyfactory.com). Smithsonian Metro.
Tours 9-10.45 am, 12.30-2pm, every 15mins
Mon-Fri. *May-Aug* Extended summer hours 5-7pm.
Admission free. **Map** p252 H6.
As the sign says, 'The Buck Starts Here!'. The printing in the title refers to hard currency: this is where
the dollar bill is born. The 40-minute guided tour
provides a glimpse into the printing, cutting and
stacking of the 37 million banknotes produced daily.
It's all done behind the thickest of plate glass, with
scads of security. In the off-season (September to
April) you should be able to go in with a minimal
wait; in summer, you'll need a timed-tour ticket,
given out from 8am to 1.40pm (and also from 3.30-
6.40pm from June to August) from the booth just outside in Raoul Wallenberg Place (in summer you'll
probably have to queue). Go at 7.45am to be sure of
getting on a tour or, if you are a US citizen, ask your
Congressional representative to get you on one of
the 'VIP' tours in advance.

United States Holocaust Memorial Museum

100 Raoul Wallenberg Place, SW, at 14th Street,
South of the Mall (1-202 488 0400/www.ushmm.
org). Smithsonian Metro. **Open** *Apr-mid June* 10am-
5.30pm Mon, Wed, Fri-Sun; 10am-8pm Tue, Thur.
Mid June-Mar 10am-5.30pm daily. Closed Yom
Kippur. **Admission** free. **Map** p252 H7.
Since its opening in 1993, the Holocaust Museum has
attracted legions of visitors to its permanent exhibition, for which timed passes are required (call
ahead to reserve; most same-day passes are distributed by 10am). The three-floor exhibition presents
a chronological history of the Holocaust from the rise
of Hitler and Nazism in the mid 1930s, the forced
incarceration of Jews in ghettos and death camps in
the early 1940s, through to the Allied liberation and
subsequent war-crime trials. Visitors, assigned a
Holocaust victim's identity card and biography
referred to during their visit, are herded into a dimly
lit, steel-clad freight elevator that deposits them into
an environment of unparalleled sobriety. Photo- and
text-intensive accounts of atrocities unfold dispas-
sionately, but objects and symbols make powerful
impressions: thousands of camp victims' shoes piled
in a heap personalise the losses.
   The building (designed by Pei Cobb Freed) incorporates red brick and slate-grey steel girders and
catwalks, echoing death camp architecture; within
the permanent exhibition, skylit zones alternate with
claustrophobic darkness. Notable artworks include
a Richard Serra sculpture and graceful Ellsworth
Kelly and Sol LeWitt canvases. **Photo** *p77.*

DC Neighbourhoods

The other city.

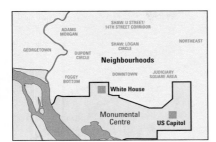

Beyond the monumental core of the Mall is a genuine, rather quirky city, populated by people rather than politicians and made more from brick than marble. DC's Cultural Tourism coalition has encouraged people to explore Washington's distinctive neighbourhoods through regular events and self-guided walking tour routes, facilitated by kiosks and free guide booklets.

The city is divided into quadrants, taking the Capitol – slightly east of centre – as its nexus, and we follow these divisions below.

Northwest

Northwest is the most affluent quadrant, with the majority of the city's residential hinterlands, streetlife and nightlife. It is roughly bisected from south to north by Rock Creek Park. The Northwest section of this chapter starts with the neighbourhoods nearest the Monumental Centre, heads north and then west to Rock Creek Park, Georgetown and further suburbs.

Foggy Bottom

Map p252

West and south-west of the White House down to the Potomac River, Foggy Bottom takes its name from its original, marshy riverside location. That the name is so well known in the US is due largely to the Department of State, which moved into the recently renamed Truman Building (2201 C Street, NW) in 1950. The immigrant settlers who once worked in the factories wouldn't recognise the area's current hauteur. A historic district on the National

K Street, Downtown.

Chinatown. See p87.

Registry since 1987 because of the design of its rowhouses, these days Foggy Bottom is home to highly transient foreign service workers, federal appointees, college students and performing artists – along with older long-term residents.

Near the dock where the US government first arrived in its muddy new capital in 1800, the white marble box of the John F Kennedy Center for the Performing Arts (known as the **Kennedy Center**, *see p200*) rises above the river. North of the Kennedy Center lie the swirling contours of the **Watergate complex** (at 26th Street & Virginia Avenue, NW), site of the eponymous 1972 burglary that unravelled Richard Nixon's presidency. Shops and delis line its courtyard. The humble Howard Johnson motel across the street, from where Tricky Dick's 'plumbers' monitored the break-in, is now a George Washington University dorm.

At Virginia and New Hampshire Avenues, a statue of valiant Mexican President Benito Juarez points symbolically towards the distant monument to George Washington, who inspired him. Above Virginia Avenue, Foggy Bottom seeps from monumental into urban Washington. Although many of the neighbourhood's characteristic tiny townhouses were bulldozed to make way for notoriously expansionist George Washington University (already sprawled over a score of blocks), some neat pockets – such as the area between New Hampshire Avenue and K Street – survive.

The **Octagon** was President James Madison's refuge for seven months after the British invaders torched the executive mansion in 1814. The **Arts Club of Washington** (2017 I Street, NW, 1-202 331 7282) was home to his successor, James Monroe, until the charred mansion was rebuilt.

Around Pennsylvania Avenue, Foggy Bottom frequently succumbs to 'façadism', token retention of the fronts of historic buildings to satisfy preservation rules, with massive modern structures ballooning behind. The blatant Mexican Chancery (1911 Pennsylvania Avenue, NW) and slightly subtler Red Lion Row (2000 Pennsylvania Avenue, NW) are prime examples. The Spanish Chancery on Washington Circle is subtler still, and more stylish.

North of Pennsylvania Avenue, the 'New Downtown' to the west of Farragut Square is the haunt of the 'K Street lawyer' lobbyists. Despite the fall of freespending lobbyist Jack Abramoff in 2006, spending limits on entertaining members of Congress remain pretty theoretical. Expense-account hangouts still aren't cheap.

A stroll down the block-long promenade of the **Renaissance Mayflower Hotel** (1127 Connecticut Avenue, NW; *see p47*), renovated to its pristine 1925 chic, may also yield a glimpse of celebrity clientele.

To keep K Street fit for Guccis to tread, the self-taxing Golden Triangle Business Improvement District, centred on Farragut Square, tidies streetscapes here. A corps of cheery, uniformed functionaries give directions and keep an eye on pesky panhandlers.

Kennedy Center

2700 F Street, NW, at New Hampshire Avenue & Rock Creek Parkway (1-800 444 1324/1-202 467 4600/www.kennedy-center.org). Foggy Bottom-GWU Metro. **Open** 10am-11pm daily. **Map** p252 F6.
Festooned with decorative gifts from many nations, 'Ken Cen' is as much a spectacle as the shows it presents, with its six theatres and concert halls, three rooftop restaurants and great views from the open-air terrace. Free concerts (6pm daily) liven up the Millennium Stage, and free 45-minute guided tours (10am-5pm Mon-Fri; 10am-1pm Sat, Sun, call 1-202 416 8340) leave from Parking Lobby A, opposite the gift shop. Parking is inadequate when several shows are playing at once – better to walk or take the free shuttle bus from the Foggy Bottom-GWU Metro stop. *See also p200*.

The Octagon

1799 New York Avenue, NW, at 18th Street (1-202 638 3221/recorded information 1-202 638 3105/ www.theoctagon.org). Farragut West or Farragut North Metro. **Open** 10am-4pm Tue-Sun.
Admission $5; $3 concessions; free under-6s.
No credit cards. **Map** p252 G6.
Designed for its odd-shaped lot by Dr William Thornton, first architect of the Capitol, this elegant brick mansion was completed in 1800. The aristocratic Tayloes offered it to a fellow Virginian, President Madison, when he was made homeless by the 1814 White House fire. More like a pregnant hexagon than an octagon, the house – reputedly haunted – is a gem of light and proportion. The related American Institute of Architects headquarters are next door; hence the Octagon hosts topical architectural exhibitions as well as Madison-era furnishings – including the desk where Madison signed the Treaty of Ghent in 1815, ending the war between the US and Britain. *See also p33*.

Downtown

Map p252-p253

DC's 'Old Downtown' east of the White House is now distinguished from 'New Downtown' north of Foggy Bottom. Once synonymous with F Street's theatres, restaurants and department stores, the area was bustling until the City decided to remake the area as an office district rather than a retail and entertainment one. In 1985 the Hecht Company opened at 12th and G Streets, the first freestanding department store built in an American downtown in four decades. Now it's been bought out by Macy's.

Recently, Old Downtown has rebounded emphatically. An influx of law firms spawned such power-lunch hangouts as DC Coast at K and 14th Streets and Oceanaire Seafood Room (for both, *see p115*) at F and 12th. At Franklin Square (14th & I Streets, NW), strip clubs long ago gave way to offices, which chip in to maintain the park. Even the statue facing 14th Street – of Irishman John Barry, Father of the US Navy – got its purloined sword restored.

National Theatre (1321 Pennsylvania Avenue, NW; *see p201*) flourishes afresh after years as a Ken Cen colony, while the **Warner Theatre** (at 13th & E Streets, NW; *see p190*) reflects a thorough restoration. At 511 Tenth Street, NW, is **Ford's Theatre** (*see p201*). Still a functioning theatre, its main claim to fame is as the site of Lincoln's assassination.

The National Press Club (14th & F Streets, NW), opened in 1924, still draws reporters, and sponsors speeches by newsmakers, foreign and domestic. The *Washington Post*, at 1150 15th Street, NW (1-202 334 6000), can be toured by arrangement. One block west is the home of the **National Geographic Society**.

Donald W Reynolds Center

After six long years under renovation, the former US Patent Office building, home to both the **National Portrait Gallery** and the **Smithsonian American Art Museum**, reopened its Greek Revival structure in summer 2006. One of Washington's oldest public buildings, the original, Robert Mills-designed south wing opened in 1840; on display were models for government patents and a cache of national artefacts (the third floor was home to the first 'National Gallery'). Three wings were added later, each facing a central courtyard. Today, two exceptional Smithsonian collections share space on all floors. Highlights of American painting and portraiture include Gilbert Stuart's seminal Lansdowne portrait of George Washington and Alfred Bierstadt's massive 1868 landscape *Among the Sierra Nevada, California*. Collections run from early Americana to contemporary art; sculpture, painting, installation and a small selection

of decorative arts are on view. Third-floor highlights include the extraordinary balconied Victorian revival Great Hall; the Luce Foundation Center for America Art, a visible storage and study centre where paintings and objects hang, salon-style, behind glass; and several glass-walled conservation studios. The second-floor Portico Café offers dramatic views down Eighth Street to the National Archives. The museum's inner courtyard will remain a forest of scaffolding until late 2007, when a Norman Foster-designed roof will cover what promises to be a dramatic public atrium.

Smithsonian American Art Museum & National Portrait Gallery

Eighth & F Street, NW, Downtown (1-202 633 1000/www.reynoldscenter.org). Gallery Place-Chinatown Metro. **Open** 11.30am-7pm daily. **Admission** free. **Map** p285 J6.

The **Russian Embassy** (1125 16th Street, NW, between L & M Streets) was a wedding gift for the daughter of sleeping-car tycoon George Pullman; the gushy palazzo became the embassy of Tsarist Russia in 1917. With US recognition in 1934, the USSR moved in, planting hammer-and-sickle motifs amid the gilt cherubs adorning the walls. The red flag finally came down in 1991. This Russian Embassy is now only the ceremonial appendage of the working compound on Wisconsin Avenue at Calvert Street. That US spies had burrowed a surveillance tunnel under the latter building came to light, embarrassingly, in 2001.

Sixteenth Street is also notable for its procession of handsome houses of worship, which line it all the way to Maryland, and its Renaissance-style Meridian Hill Park (aka Malcolm X Park), adorned with cascading waterfalls and a statue of Joan of Arc.

The former Greyhound bus terminal at 12th Street and New York Avenue used to be a wino magnet. Now its streamlined façade, treasured by Washington's ardent art deco devotees, fronts an office building complementing its lines. Street-level tenants include restaurants and bars. In 1987, the **National Museum of Women in the Arts** redeemed a dignified 80-year-old Renaissance Revival Masonic lodge that had become a cinema.

The gigantic new Convention Center north of Mount Vernon Square replaced a drab, punier predecessor at Ninth Street and New York Avenue. On the square itself, the old wedding-cake Carnegie Library housed the failed City Museum of Washington, DC. The successor **Martin Luther King Jr Memorial Library** sparks passionate debate as to whether it should be replaced as dysfunctional or venerated as a late design of Bauhaus guru Mies van der Rohe.

The **National Museum of American Art** and the **National Portrait Gallery**, which split the historic Patent Office building at Seventh and F Streets, reopened in 2006 to acclaim after six years' restoration – the building has been renamed the **Donald W Reynolds Center for American Art and Portraiture** (*see p86* Donald W Reynolds Center). Across Seventh Street looms the **Verizon Center**, a huge venue for basketball, hockey, concerts and horse shows. The arena triggered an explosive revival along Seventh Street, with escalating rents blowing some old Chinese businesses out of Chinatown. Although their names may be written in Chinese characters, chains like Legal Sea Foods and even Hooters don't quite pass chopstick muster. Gaudy chinoiserie still obscures some quite old house façades; Wok-'n'-Roll restaurant

(604 H Street, NW, 1-202 347 4656) occupies Mary Surratt's boarding house, where in 1865 John Wilkes Booth's co-conspirators plotted Abe Lincoln's doom. Texan barbecues and Irish bars now thrive within sight of the world's largest Chinese arch (over H Street, at Seventh Street), given by the People's Republic of China. When a hefty chunk of the arch broke away a few years ago, local Taiwanese rejoiced in a perceived omen. DC's Chinese population has largely dispersed through the suburbs, but Chinatown remains the community's spiritual centre and site of dragon dancing at Chinese New Year.

Nearby houses of worship testify to Washington's immigrant past, particularly St Mary's Mother of God (727 Fifth Street, NW), a downsized copy of Germany's Ulm Cathedral, ministering to German immigrants, now drawing nostalgic Catholics to its Tridentine Latin masses. St Patrick's Catholic Church (619 Tenth Street, NW) was established in 1794 to serve the Irish immigrants who came to build the White House; the present building rose a century later. Holy Rosary Church (595 Third Street, NW) has masses in Italian, plus cultural events at its Casa Italiana next door. In 2004 a cluster of Jewish congregations bought back the historic synagogue at Sixth and I Streets from the black Baptist congregation that had long occupied – then outgrown – it. Dating from 1876, Washington's first synagogue (on Third Street) now houses the **Jewish Historical Society** and its museum. In 2005, the revived congregation of Adolf Cluss's Calvary Baptist Church (8th & I Streets) regained its innovative steeple (*see p90* **Adolf Cluss's capital**).

The District's long-frustrated goal of a 'living downtown' is finally real, as recent urban deserts bloomed with costly condos. The hottest coming property is north-east of Mount Vernon Square, in an area known as NoMa, named (with envious eyes on Manhattan's SoHo) for NOrth of MAssachusetts Avenue).

Jewish Historical Society of Greater Washington

701 Third Street, NW, at G Street, Judiciary Square area (1-202 789 0900/www.jhsgw.org). Judiciary Square Metro. **Open** by appointment only. **Admission** suggested donation $3. **Credit** MC, V. **Map** p253 K6.

Exhibits of local Jewish history organised by the Jewish Historical Society occupy the ground floor of this now-landmarked former synagogue – the oldest in Washington. Built in 1876 of red brick, the structure was adopted by the Society in 1960; its sanctuary was restored in the 1970s, preserving the original ark, pine benches, and slender columns that support the women's balcony.

Sightseeing

Ford's Theatre & Lincoln Museum

511 Tenth Street, NW, between E & F Streets (box office 1-202 347 4833/Park Service 1-202 426 6924/ www.fordstheatre.org or www.nps.gov/foth). Metro Center or Gallery Place-Chinatown Metro. **Open** 9am-5pm daily. **Admission** free. **Map** p252 J6.

On Good Friday, 1865, President Lincoln was enjoying a comedy in Ford's Theatre when actor John Wilkes Booth entered the presidential box and shot him. Wounded in his dramatic leap to the stage, Booth escaped painfully on horseback, only to be killed by US troops 12 days later. Today's active theatre looks as it did that day, although rather less-punishing chairs offer a concession to tender modern derrières. Exhibits in the Lincoln Museum downstairs include Booth's Derringer pistol and Lincoln's bloodstained clothes. Cross the street to Petersen House (516 Tenth Street, NW, 1-202 426 6924), where Lincoln expired at 7.22am the next morning. *See also p201.*

Martin Luther King Jr Memorial Library

901 G Street, NW, between Ninth & Tenth Streets (general information 1-202 727 1111/www.dc library.org/mlk). Gallery Place-Chinatown Metro. **Open** 9.30am-9pm Mon-Thur; 9.30am-5.30pm Fri, Sat; 1-5pm Sun. **Map** p253 J6.

The centre of DC's public library system contains the third-floor Washingtoniana Room, where extraordinary reference librarians help sort through books, historical directories, maps and more than 13 million newspaper clippings concerning the District of Columbia and vicinity, fragile materials stored without climate control. Developers and City officials keen on a state-of-the-art replacement battle admirers of architect Mies van der Rohe's 1972 Bauhaus box.

National Museum of Women in the Arts

1250 New York Avenue, NW, at 13th Street, Downtown (1-202 783 5000/www.nmwa.org). Metro Center Metro. **Open** 10am-5pm Mon-Sat; noon-5pm Sun. **Admission** $8; $6 concessions; free members. **Credit** AmEx, MC, V. **Map** p252 H5.

Though it was founded in 1981 by Wallace and Wilhelmina Holladay to showcase important art by women, the museum didn't occupy its current 70,000sq ft Renaissance Revival building (by Waddy Butler Wood) until six years later. The museum provides a survey of art by women from the 1700s to the present. Highlights include Renaissance artist Lavinia Fontana's dynamic *Holy Family with St John* and Frida Kahlo's defiant 1937 self-portrait *Between the Curtains*. Artists Helen Frankenthaler, Camille Claudel and Elisabeth Vigee-LeBrun are also represented. Though it has sometimes been faulted for its touchy-feely programming, the museum offers sophisticated fare in its special exhibitions.

Verizon Center

601 F Street, NW, at Seventh Street (1-202 628 3200/www.verizoncenter.com). Gallery Place-Chinatown Metro. **Open** events only. **Map** p253 J6.

This huge arena hosts some 200 public events a year, including concerts, family entertainment, horse shows and college athletics, as well as pro games by the Washington Capitals NHL hockey team and the Washington Wizards NBA basketball team. It involves all the economic excesses now de rigueur in American professional sport: startling admission prices, 110 exorbitant sky-boxes for corporate entertaining, restaurants restricting admission to top-end ticketholders and other money- and class-based novelties. Still, it's well designed and conveniently atop a Metro station.

National Geographic Society

Gilbert H Grosvenor Auditorium *1600 M Street, NW, at 16th Street (1-202 857 7700/ www.nationalgeographic.com/explorer).*
Explorers Hall *1145 17th Street, NW, at M Street (1-202 857 7588/www.nationalgeographic. com/explorer).*
Both *Farragut North Metro.* **Open** 9am-5pm Mon-Sat; 10am-5pm Sun. **Admission** free. **Map** p252 H5.

Founded in 1890 by local patricians, the Geographic has funded nearly 6,000 exploration and research projects to destinations from China to Peru and pole to pole. It also publishes the *National Geographic Magazine*, the rather stodgy but iconic vehicle that brought the outside world to generations of

Sightseeing

Marian Koshland Science Museum.
See p91.

Americans. The Grosvenor Auditorium hosts traditional illustrated lectures by daring explorers, but also presents international concerts and videos, even beer tastings. Adjacent Explorers Hall is a free museum with changing exhibitions on subjects as diverse as dinosaurs of the Sahara, Lucy the oldest humanoid, even the sunny side of Judas Iscariot.

Penn Quarter

Map p252-p253

North of Federal Triangle, this developer-dubbed area is known simply as 'downtown' to residents, who recall it as the main shopping district. In recent years, it has blossomed with new restaurants, developments, displays and theatres.

Nineteenth-century District residents shopped along Pennsylvania Avenue and Seventh Street. But then the success of the fixed-price Woodward & Lothrop department store after 1882 made F Street the principal shopping mecca, while business on the Avenue declined. Distressed by the tawdriness of Pennsylvania Avenue as he rode in his 1961 inaugural procession, President Kennedy charged a commission to revamp 'America's Main

Street'. The Pennsylvania Avenue Development Corporation rose to the occasion.

The sinuous water crane perched on the quirky Temperance Fountain at Seventh Street and Pennsylvania Avenue punctuates the Seventh Street arts corridor of galleries and studios blooming behind Victorian cast-iron storefronts. The former Lansburgh's department store now houses posh apartments above the **Shakespeare Theatre** (450 Seventh Street, NW; *see p201*). The **US Navy Memorial** plaza nicely frames the Eighth Street axis between the **National Portrait Gallery** (*see p86*) and the National Archives (*see p81*). The **International Spy Museum** at Ninth and F has been a smash hit, despite its decidedly un-Washington admission fees. Nearby, the **Marian Koshland Science Museum** beckons more soberly.

In the vicinity of the White House, grand old hotels like the **Washington** (515 15th Street, NW) with its famous rooftop bar, and the lavish **Willard Inter-Continental** (1401 Pennsylvania Avenue, NW; *see p42*) have recovered their lost lustre. JFK would have been pleased.

Adolf Cluss's capital

Arts & Industries Building.

Architect Adolf Cluss (1825-1905) emerged from obscurity as a draughtsman at the Navy Yard to become the prime mover in redesigning the city in the wake of the Civil War. With a background in engineering, Cluss was able to move into architecture, favouring brick made from the city's clay soil and obsessing over light, ventilation and fire safety. His great opportunity came in 1871, when the Territory of the District of Columbia was formed under Alexander 'Boss' Shepherd, with a programme to turn the tawdry town into 'a capital worthy of a republic'. As the city's chief engineer, Cluss plunged into giving Washington what would become its characteristic look, planning 'tree boxes' of greenery between the streets and the sidewalks, ceding homeowners tax-free front yards, with freedom to extend bay windows into that space, and designing public and private buildings on a human scale.

Few would have realised that the makeover of the post-Civil War capital was actually in the hands of a communist. Born in Heilbrunn, Wurrtemberg, Cluss had led the Communist League of Mainz during the 1848 revolution, coming as Marx's personal agent to Washington, where he ran the Communist League, USA from his Navy Yard office. He prospered and married, experiencing social mobility unlikely in Europe, finally telling Marx that communism wouldn't work here. But his early social philosophy remained a major influence on his urban planning.

Even after the spendthrift Shepherd regime collapsed in scandal in 1874, Cluss continued to leave his mark through many churches, private homes, public buildings, and Washington's first apartment house. Most are gone, because they centred on old Downtown, where office blocks claimed the sites of Cluss's winsome, eclectic Rundbogenstil works. We list those that remain below.

The keeper of the Cluss legacy is the DC Goethe-Institut, which runs programmes and walking tours of the architect's 19th-century red-brick city (www.goethe.de/washington).

● **Sumner School** (1872) 17th & M Streets, NW (202 442-6060). The first public high school for African Americans, now the DC Public School Museum and Archives.

● **Masonic Temple** (1869) 910 F Street, NW. The building has thrived as a restaurant and offices. Across the street, the National Portrait Gallery reopened in 2006 drawing acclaim for its interiors, which Cluss redesigned after a fire. (He also restored the Smithsonian's Castle Building interiors after another conflagration.)

● **Calvary Baptist Church** (1864, 1869) 777 Eighth Street, NW. In 2004 Cluss's unique steeple, which had been blown down by a 1913 hurricane, was replaced with a replica.

● **Eastern Market** (1873) Seventh and C Streets, SE. A plaque extolling Cluss was installed in 2006, even as revisions were proposed to alter his design with skylights, massive wheelchair ramps and air-conditioning.

● **Alexandria, Virginia City Hall** (1873) 301 King Street. It retains the original Cluss look on the Cameron Street side only.

● **Franklin School** (1869) 13th and K Streets, NW. The building won contemporary design acclaim as far away as England and Argentina.

● **Arts & Industries Building** (1881, 900 Jefferson Drive, SW). Regarded as Cluss's mid-Mall masterpiece, it became the centre of controversy when the Smithsonian Institution left the premises, pleading that the handsome but deteriorating roof it had long neglected was too costly to fix. The building is now on the National Trust for Historic Preservation's list of top ten endangered buildings.

The **J Edgar Hoover FBI Building** (935 Pennsylvania Avenue, NW, between Ninth & Tenth Streets, 1-202 324 3447) presents a sterile streetscape because Hoover vetoed planned street-level shops and restaurants as potential security threats. *See also p93* **J Edgar Hoover's Washington**.

A locally popular pastime is the day-long Wednesday auction conducted at Weschler's (909 E Street, NW, 1-202 628 1281) for over a century. Treasures, trash and grab bags keep the bidders lively.

International Spy Museum

800 F Street, NW, between 8th & 9th Streets, Penn Quarter (1-202 393 7798/www.spymuseum.org). Gallery Place-Chinatown Metro. **Open** *Mid Apr-mid Aug* 9am-8pm daily. *Mid Aug-mid Oct* 10am-8pm daily. *Mid Nov-mid Mar* 10am-6pm daily. *Last admission* 2hrs before closing. **Admission** $15; $12-$14 concessions; free under-4s, members. **Credit** AmEx, Disc, MC, V. **Map** p253 J6.

If your idea of a fun museum experience includes adopting a cover and memorising your alias's vitals – age, provenance, travel plans and itinerary (you'll be asked questions later) – you've come to the right spot. Testing your sleuthing abilities, along with gawking at an array of funky spy gadgets, including KGB-issued poison pellet shooting umbrellas and Germany's Steineck ABC wristwatch camera, adds up to fun for some folks – many of them under 20. Be aware that this is an 'event' museum: expect to be herded in groups and subjected to overhead public addresses at the beginning of your tour.

Despite the racket, James Bond junkies will be in heaven – the groovy silver Aston Martin from 1964's *Goldfinger* assumes a central spot on the circuit. Recent special exhibitions boast more Hollywood spy memorabilia. Not surprisingly, the museum has proved a huge hit since it opened in 2002; consider booking tickets in advance.

Marian Koshland Science Museum of the National Academy of Sciences

Sixth Street & E Street, NW, Judiciary Square area (1-202 334 1201/www.koshland-science-museum. org). Gallery Place-Chinatown Metro. **Open** 10am-6pm Mon, Wed-Sun (last admission 5pm). **Admission** $5; $3 concessions. **Credit** MC, V. **Map** p253 J6.

Though modestly sized and featuring only three exhibitions (one permanent and two rotating), this museum, named after immunologist and molecular biologist Marian Koshland, proves something of an eye-opener. State-of-the-art, interactive displays teach visitors by doing, not just showing. **Photo** *p89*.

US Navy Memorial & Heritage Center

701 Pennsylvania Avenue, NW, between Seventh & Ninth Streets (1-202 737 2300/www.lonesailor.org). Archives-Navy Memorial Metro. **Open** *Mar-Oct* 9.30am-5pm Mon-Sat. *Nov-Feb* 9.30am-5pm Tue-Sat. **Admission** free. **Map** p253 J6.

Dedicated on the Navy's 212th birthday in 1987, this memorial features the world's biggest map of itself – a flat granite circular map 100ft across, with this very spot at its centre – compassed by an apron with 22 bas-reliefs depicting naval highlights like Teddy Roosevelt's globe-circling Great White Fleet of 1907,

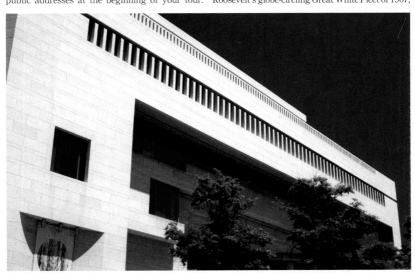

Canadian Embassy: home to a gallery highlighting the work of Canadian artists. *See p92.*

Sightseeing

Commodore Perry's 1854 expedition to Japan and the 'Silent Service' of submarines. Off-centre stands a statue of the Lone Sailor, stolid in his pea jacket. The subterranean visitor centre contains a cinema with a 52ft screen, showing authentically noisy depictions of navy life.

Judiciary Square

Map p253

Judiciary Square is the hub of the city's courts. The **National Building Museum** occupies the 1883 Pension Building, a Renaissance palace sporting an extraordinary frieze of Civil War troops perpetually patrolling the premises. Its atrium is spectacular and its gift shop imaginative. Across F Street, bronze lions flank the National Law Enforcement Officers Memorial to the nearly 15,000 cops killed in the line of duty since 1794 with an explanatory visitors' centre (605 E Street, NW, 1-202 737 3213).

The Court of Appeals building (Fifth & D Streets) was once Washington's city hall, a chaste 1820 Greek Revival design by British architect George Hadfield. Lincoln's statue at the front is significant as the first public memorial to the murdered president, sculpted by his acquaintance, Lot Flannery, who knew how he looked while orating, and dedicated in 1868 on the third anniversary of his death.

Down the stairs that constitute Fourth Street, beside the statue of Chief Justice John Marshall that once graced the Capitol grounds, the **Canadian Embassy** (501 Pennsylvania Avenue, NW, **photo** *p90*) – awarded its prominent site in honour of close bi-national relations – houses a gallery spotlighting Canadian artists. The new **Newseum**, a grander incarnation of the previous museum, rises adjacent on its west side.

Protected by statues of General Meade, victor at Gettysburg, and legal commentator Sir William Blackstone, the US Court House opposite the embassy is gradually losing its 'Watergate Courthouse' identity as subsequent scandals unfold before interminable grand juries, while a new wing to the east enlivens its appearance.

The Japanese-American Memorial at Louisiana and D, NW, honours Americans of Japanese descent interned during World War II, and the Nisei regiments of their sons who fought for the US. An eloquent sculpture depicts traditional Japanese cranes trapped in barbed wire.

National Building Museum

401 F Street, NW, between Fourth & Fifth Streets, Judiciary Square area (1-202 272 2448/www. nbm.org). Judiciary Square Metro. **Open** 10am-5pm Mon-Sat; 11am-5pm Sun. **Admission** suggested donation $5. **Credit** AmEx, MC, V. **Map** p253 J6.

A privately run collection, the National Building Museum produces smart, noteworthy exhibits focusing on architects and urban design concerns, both contemporary and historical. However, the main attraction is without doubt the building's Italian Renaissance-style Great Hall, with its central fountain and eight colossal 75ft-high Corinthian columns: visitors crane their necks for a vertiginous look at the ceiling 15 storeys above. The red-brick building, designed as the US Pension Building, was completed in 1887. One of the permanent exhibitions relates the history of the building; another documents changing architectural styles. The museum shop offers the quirkiest museum buys in town, with all manner of gadgets and gizmos up for grabs.

Newseum

Pennsylvania Avenue, at Sixth Street, NW (www.newseum.org). Archives-Navy Memorial Metro. **Map** p253 J6.

This interactive museum dedicated to print and broadcast journalism is shuttered until autumn 2007, when a brand-new building on Pennsylvania Avenue and Sixth Street, NW, is unveiled. The museum will feature 70,000 square feet of exhibition space, 15 theatres, and a Wolfgang Puck restaurant.

Dupont Circle

Map p250

Dupont Circle is perhaps the most cosmopolitan DC neighbourhood, its bars and bistros drawing a diverse public. The circle itself is a populous green space, with a collection of chess tables in constant use. A central marble fountain sprays into the air in honour of Civil War admiral Samuel Francis Dupont. In the late 19th century, mansions began sprouting in this recent backwater to accommodate arriviste millionaires, in time morphing into Embassy Row. The area was a countercultural hotbed in the 1960s, when anti-Vietnam War and black power activists claimed the circle for demonstrations; anti-globalists seek the old energy there today.

By and large, though, the neighbourhood has hit the mainstream. Chain stores have infiltrated Connecticut Avenue, but enough idiosyncratic bookstores and bistros and galleries (sporting open-house receptions every first-Friday evening) survive to reward a wander.

Large hotels and apartment buildings start to dominate the landscape about four blocks north, heading towards Adams Morgan (*see p96*). The pavement outside the Washington Hilton on the corner of Connecticut Avenue and T Street was the site of John Hinckley's attempted assassination of President Reagan in 1981.

Off Connecticut Avenue, the blocks north of the circle consist largely of well-kept Edwardian rowhouses, art galleries and

J Edgar Hoover's Washington

With his rapid-fire speech, J Edgar Hoover (1895-1972) didn't sound like a Washingtonian, but he lived his entire life here. As a boy, he learned to motormouth to overcome stuttering. At age 11, he took to carrying packages for customers at Eastern Market for dime tips, running back from each job. He thus earned the lifelong nickname 'Speed' among his few intimates. Hoover was born on New Year's Day at 413 Seward Square, SE to a civil-servant father prone to nervous disorders and a strong mother, who he lived with for 42 years. A magnificent stained-glass Hoover Memorial Window graces the church on the **Capitol Hill United Methodist Church** in Seward Square, though its label conveniently vanished when his reputation posthumously went south.

He was an ambitious child: at age ten, he had business cards printed reading 'John Edgar Hoover. Student'. Rather than attend his neighbourhood's Eastern High School – then two blocks from home – he journeyed several miles to study at the more prestigious Central High. To work his way through George Washington University he worked shifts at the Library of Congress, learning the art of cataloguing. He was to put this skill to good use in later life with his secret files about powerful people, which only he and his lifelong secretary could penetrate. These files were a major source of his power: Hoover used the files on public officials' sexual peccadillos to blackmail them. The files may have saved his job from the several presidents who considered firing him.

Hoover came to prominence as the deputy to Attorney General A Mitchell Palmer. In the 1920s, he earned a reputation as a dauntless G-man, reforming a corrupt, inept agency into the Federal Bureau of Investigation and bagging celebrity gangsters like John Dillinger and Baby-Face Nelson along the way. Gifted in public and press relations, Hoover was responsible for catchphrases like 'Public Enemy Number One' and 'America's ten most wanted'.

He began his law-enforcement career as an anti-communist, and this was a lifelong obsession. Accused of friendly relations with the Mafia, he preferred to target 'subversives' like Martin Luther King Jr. He was the architect of COINTELPRO, a programme that infiltrated and sometimes disrupted leftist and civil rights organisations – its campaign against the Black Panthers was particularly brutal.

The FBI headquarters occupied more and more of the Department of Justice Building at Ninth and Pennsylvania Streets, NW, which he shared with his ostensible superiors, the US attorneys general. Here he initiated the public FBI tours, celebrating his agency and always culminating with a devastating machine-gun demonstration. In time, the **FBI building** (see p91) named for him rose across the street. He vetoed plans for street-level shops that would have gone some way towards mitigating its brutalist façade on the grounds of security. The tours were suspended after 9/11 and have still not resumed; there are plans for them to begin again in 2007.

For decades, Hoover and Clyde Tolson, his assistant director, companion (and, some speculate, lover), lunched daily at the **Mayflower Hotel** (see p47), both seated with their backs to the wall and invariably ordering cottage cheese salad. After his mother's death, Hoover moved to 4936 30th Place, NW, as nondescript and suburban a residence as one could find within the District.

Hoover's desk and an exhibition on his career is a feature on the free guided tour of the **Masonic House of the Temple** (1733 16th Street NW, 1-202 232 3579). Housed here, the Hoover Memorial Foundation opens its holdings to researchers by appointment. And in the **Congressional Cemetery** (see p105), Hoover's burial place, is a bench reverentially crafted by his loyal agents.

Sightseeing

National Zoo. See p103.

gorgeous mansions now occupied by embassies or non-profit associations. If the weather is nice, amble northwards through the blocks west of Connecticut Avenue – known as Kalorama – to check out the impressive architecture and exhibitions. The galleries display contemporary, experimental and traditional art, from painting to sculpture to photography. At the heart of them all is the **Phillips Collection**, opened in 1921 as the first permanent museum of modern art in America. For more information on other galleries, *see pp171-6*.

Massachusetts Avenue, from Scott Circle, East of Dupont Circle, through to Upper Northwest (*see p99*) is known as 'Embassy Row'. For a cheap tour, catch any westbound 'N' Metrobus at Dupont Circle and cruise past the mosque established for diplomats in the 1950s (No.2551, at Belmont Road, Kalorama), the embassies of Turkey, the Netherlands, Brazil, the Vatican, and others. Further on, into Upper Northwest, the British Embassy (No.3100) sports a statue of Churchill, with one foot on British soil (all embassies are deemed their nations' territory) and the other on American, reflecting his ancestry. The US confiscated the former Iranian Embassy across the way following the seizure of the American Embassy in Tehran and the holding of its staff

hostage in 1979, only to rent it out for extremely expensive parties and wedding receptions.

Although for security reasons the US has encouraged embassies to move to new quarters in the International Drive enclave further north, many cling to the now cramped but elegant millionaires' mansions of yesteryear. Lots of embassies open their doors for concerts, art displays and charity events (see www. embassyseries.org).

Foreign heroes patrol this strand: there's a statue of Gandhi at 21st Street, near the Indian embassy; Czechoslovakian leader Masaryk adorns 22nd Street; and, further north, political martyr Robert Emmet gazes toward the Irish Embassy from the 2200 block. At the Norwegian embassy (2720 34th Street, NW), in 2005 King Harald V dedicated a statue of his mother, Crown Princess Märtha, who bunked at the White House with the Roosevelts after the Nazis overran her country in 1940.

Phillips Collection

1600 21st Street, NW, at Q Street, Dupont Circle (1-202 387 2151/www.phillipscollection.org). Dupont Circle Metro. **Open** 10am-5pm Tue, Wed, Fri, Sat; 10am-8.30pm Thur; 11am-6pm Sun. **Admission** Sat, Sun & special exhibitions $12; $10 concessions; free under-18s. Mon-Fri (permanent collection only) free; suggested donation equivalent to weekend prices. **Credit** AmEx, MC, V. **Map** p282 G4.

This mansion was opened as a gallery in the 1920s by Marjorie and Duncan Phillips as a memorial to his father. The building was remodelled in the 1960s and underwent further renovation in the '80s, when an extension increased its space by almost 20,000sq ft. In 2006, the museum unveiled its Sant Building, another expansion project that added airy galleries for modern art, an outdoor sculpture terrace and café, an art and technology laboratory and an auditorium. The museum's signature painting, Renoir's *Luncheon of the Boating Party*, enjoys pride of place in the permanent collection galleries. There, significant Van Gogh oils rub shoulders with Steiglitz prints and a solid selection of lesser-known works by Picasso, Bacon, Vuillard and Rothko – that is, if a travelling show hasn't deposed them temporarily. The historical surveys and one-person shows held here tend to be conservative crowd-pleasers – Impressionists and 20th-century photography, say – or scholarly efforts examining the likes of Hiroshige and Paul Klee.

Society of the Cincinnati at Anderson House

2118 Massachusetts Avenue, NW, at 21st Street, Dupont Circle (1-202 785 2040). Dupont Circle Metro. **Open** 1-4pm Tue-Sat. **Admission** free. **Map** p282 G4.

Practically unknown to most Washingtonians, this museum, the former residence of American diplomat Larz Anderson III and his wife Isabel, contains works acquired on the couple's many trips to Asia and Europe. Anderson, a direct descendant of a founding member of the Society of the Cincinnati, bequeathed his house to that organisation, which was formed just after the American Revolution with the aim of sharing wealth among bereft army veterans who had fought for independence (the group included Founding Father George Washington). In 1902 the Andersons hired Boston architectural firm Arthur Little and Herbert Browne to construct the limestone Beaux Arts mansion, and imported Italian artisans to carve and inlay wood and gilt floors and ceilings. Downstairs, a room devoted to rotating historical exhibitions about the American Revolution, and others hung with Japanese screens and wall frescoes, are open to the public. The upstairs rooms, which are only accessible on hourly guided tours, contain numerous bejewelled Chinese semiprecious stone and jade trees and Flemish Renaissance tapestries dating from the late 16th and early 17th centuries.

From slave to freedman

Yarrow Mamout had a remarkable life; unusually, his image remains.

Yarrow Mamout was an enslaved brick-maker, thought to be originally from Senegal. A well-known face about Georgetown by the late 1790s, Mamout's religious practices (he is said to have been Washington's first Muslim) caused some bemusement among the locals, but it seems he was generally viewed with affection as a local character.

Born around 1736, Yarrow was enslaved and sold to the Bealls, a family of Scottish ancestry, who apparently named him after the ballad 'Braes of Yarrow'. He bargained for his freedom by making enough bricks for their town house, which is still standing. Mr Beall died, but his wife honoured his promise. Despite financial reverses, Yarrow owned three houses at what is now 3330-3332 Dent Place, NW. He probably lies buried behind the easternmost.

He had his portrait painted twice, in 1819 by the eminent Charles Wilson Peale (who believed him to be 134 years old), and in 1822 by local artist James Alexander Simpson. Both were completed at a time when portraits of blacks were extremely unusual. Peale's has been lauded as 'perhaps the most sensitive portrait in early America' of a black person, but Simpson's (*above*) may be

more accurate, and it's in the Peabody Room of the Georgetown Neighborhood Library (3260 R Street, NW, at Wisconsin Avenue, 1-202 282 0214). Note that the room's hours are limited; phone in advance.

Textile Museum

2320 S Street, NW, between 23rd & 24th Streets, Dupont Circle (1-202 667 0441/www.textile museum.org). Dupont Circle Metro. **Open** 10am-5pm Mon-Sat; 1-5pm Sun. **Admission** suggested donation $5. **Credit** AmEx, MC, V. **Map** p282 F4.

A modest collection nestled amid regal townhouses, the Textile Museum has two permanent exhibitions: the Textile Learning Center describes the history and procedures of textile production, while the Collections Gallery rotates selections of historic rugs and textiles. Recent changing shows have been high-tech, with one about textiles made with digital technology. Every Saturday the museum hosts textile and rug appreciation programmes.

Adams Morgan

Map p250

To the east of Dupont Circle, 18th Street becomes the main strip of lively Adams Morgan some nine walkable blocks north, known for its ethnic restaurants and militant diversity. Streetlife started out as leisurely Latino, with Africans and others lately livening the mix. The pace picks up at night, though, when 18th Street (up to and including the spots along Columbia Road, which intersects 18th Street at the top of the hill) morphs into a big bar and dining scene. Nowhere else in the city can you hop from one joint to the next with better results. The bars range from flat-out frat-boy hangouts to salsa and reggae clubs, and on warm summer evenings outdoor cafés pack in customers while the streets pack automobiles in futile late-night quests for parking spaces.

Adams Morgan got its name in the 1950s, when progressive-minded residents opted to integrate the white Adams school with the black Morgan school. The area is still home to a wide range of nationalities and races. DC is home to the largest community of Ethiopians outside Ethiopia. One place in Adams Morgan that is always lively during the day is **Malcolm X Park** – officially Meridian Hill Park (bordered by 16th, Euclid, 15th and W Streets, NW).

Shaw

Map p250-p251

Bounded by North Capitol Street and 16th Street on the east and west, and by Irving Street and M Street to the north and south, Shaw

Walk Georgetown

Starting the walk where Rock Creek flows into the Potomac, note the new House of Sweden, a unique embassy/trade office/condo at 2900 K Street, NW. A detour north on 30th Street leads to the C&O Canal visitor centre, embarkation point for leisurely mule-drawn barge-rides evoking early trade. An inviting towpath parallels the Potomac, although beware how far you go: it runs 186 miles west to Cumberland, Maryland.

Back on K Street, a turn north on Thomas Jefferson Street leads to the **Old Stone House**, Georgetown's earliest, a modest working-class home that dates from 1768. A right turn down M Street leads past historically plaqued buildings to the Thomas Sim Lee corner, which was Georgetown's original boundary.

A block north is the 3000 block of N Street, NW. Jacqueline Kennedy lived in the 1794 mansion at 3017 for a year after her husband's assassination.

Crossing Georgetown's shopping and bar-hopping throughfare, Wisconsin Avenue, at N Street, one finds Martin's Tavern thriving as it did when Jack Kennedy (by some accounts) proposed to Jackie in Booth #3. They lived down the street at 3307 when he was elected president. (JFK junkies can obtain a self-guided tour called 'The Kennedys' Georgetown' at www.georgetowndc.com, or phone 1-202 944 5295.)

Ascending to O Street in search of other glam couples, one encounters antiquated embraces historic neighbourhoods, including Howard University, the U Street Corridor and Logan Circle. All were bastions of African American DC, fostering black businesses, churches and scholarship during the dismal decades of racial segregation. Today Shaw has bounced back from long decline, which culminated in the disastrous 1968 riots (*see p19*). And if U Street hasn't quite returned to its days as America's 'Black Broadway', it's getting there pretty fast.

U Street/14th Street Corridor

U Street has been reborn as a centre of trendy commerce and nightlife, surrounded by rowhouses that have become interracial magnets for the city's hipsters. The neighbourhood is bisected by 14th Street – which is experiencing its own revival, heralded by the reopening of the **Tivoli Theatre** (3333 14th Street, NW) in burgeoning Columbia Heights.

Anchored by **Howard University**, the neighbourhood became the hub of African American culture. Poet Langston Hughes and jazz great Duke Ellington matured here.

Along with Ella Fitzgerald, Nat King Cole and Redd Foxx, they made 'You' Street world-famous. During the 1930s, 'Black Broadway' was a cultural powerhouse. Recently, signs and photo displays in store windows have evoked those glory days. Yet the symbol of its rampant gentrification was the opening of a tanning parlour.

An enclave of the New You is restaurant, café and art space Busboys & Poets (1390 V Street, NW, *see p126*). Its old-school neighbour is Ben's Chili Bowl (*see p125*), on U Street between 12th and 13th Streets, a lunchcounter frequented by celebs such as Bill Cosby and ex-mayor Marion Barry, famous for its chilli dogs and energy. The **Lincoln Theatre** (*see p190*), next door, was once a grand stage for black performances in the age of segregation. At the U Street-Cardozo Metro station is an African-American Civil War Memorial. Born in U Street's heyday of the 1920s, the Republic Gardens bar/restaurant (1355 U Street, NW, *see p194*), remains Washington's upscale lounge for African Americans. Nearby, on 14th Street, aside from a couple of swanky lounges, the main attraction is music space the Black Cat (*see p183*).

cobblestones and streetcar tracks as well as the **Bodisco House** (3322 O Street, NW), home of the fiftysomething Russian ambassador who in 1840 married a local 16-year-old, the lovebirds being dubbed Beauty and the Beast. Now it is the home of sometime Democratic presidential candidate John Kerry, the wealthiest member of the US Senate through his ketchup-heiress spouse, Teresa Heinz Kerry.

Straight ahead looms **Georgetown University**, dominated by the distinctive neo-Gothic Healy Hall (1877). Founded in 1789, Georgetown is the nation's oldest Catholic and Jesuit college and one of America's hottest universities. If the gatehouse information booth isn't open, any student can point you to Loyola Hall, where Bill Clinton '68 once bunked.

A turn down 37th Street passes **Holy Trinity Church**, where JFK last attended mass before his assassination. A left turn down N Street passes the renowned Georgetown School of Foreign Service, its building betraying its origins as the original university hospital. Nearby you'll find Georgetown's most iconic image: a turn down 36th Street dead-ends at

Prospect Street, where a turn to the left in the 3500 block leads past the homes and the steep stairs immortalised on film in *The Exorcist*. Descend them if you dare. Note that the houses are considerably further from the steps than Hollywood magic placed them.

Passing the massive car-barn building, cross M Street at 34th Street to Francis Scott Key Park, flying a fifteen-star flag to honour the author of America's national anthem, 'The Star-Spangled Banner' (1814). Plaques here display Key's history, and that of the neighbourhood. Key's home was torn down to build the western access loop to the bridge named for him, which at least affords splendid views of the river.

A stroll east down M Street – Georgetown's other commercial corridor – approaches the area's heart, the intersection of Wisconsin and M Streets, NW. Dean & Deluca gourmet grocery (3276 M Street, NW) occupies the old **Georgetown Market House** (1865), which spanned the Canal until raised 15 feet to its present site by mule-power in 1871. Nearby, Georgetown Park has imaginatively transformed a sprawling transit facility into an inviting shopping mall.

Congressional Cemetery. *See p105.*

Howard University

2400 Sixth Street, NW, at Howard Place (1-202 806 6100/www.howard.edu). Shaw-Howard University Metro then 70, 71 bus. **Map** p283 J2.

With a hall of fame that includes former mayors and Supreme Court justices, Howard University has a legacy to brag about. It was chartered in 1867 as a theological seminary to train black ministers to teach slaves emancipated by the Civil War. By 1940 half of African Americans in college studied here, including much of the leadership that planned the legal assault on Jim Crow segregation. Ironically, their success in opening educational opportunities eventually forced Howard to compete for top African-American students, now lured by other prestigious universities. Howard holds some of the best collections on African history and art in the country at the Howard University Museum on the first floor of the Founders Library.

Georgetown

Map p248-p249

George, Maryland, was laid out in 1751 and variously tried to unite with Washington City (1857) and secede from the District (often). Losing its separate government in 1871, Georgetown drew the line at its proposed designation as 'West Washington'. Today's Georgetown is unlike the rest of the city, with tranquil residential streets lined with historic homes, and haughty boutiques. Its physical division from the rest of the District by Rock Creek enhances its insularity.

At the upriver limit of navigation for ocean vessels, the town started life as a colonial tobacco port. Oxen pulled huge cylinders of 'sot weed' down its 'rolling road', now Wisconsin Avenue. From the mid 1800s, black Georgetown thrived south of P Street between Rock Creek and 31st Street. Some 1,000 African-American families slept here at night, working by day as cooks, domestics and stable boys. Although it's hard to fathom now, Georgetown was dwindling into slumishness by the 1930s. Then, a 'colonial revival' made old homes fashionable again. Many of FDR's New Dealers moved in amid the multi-generation 'cave dwellers', turning Georgetown into a chic address; JFK's 'New Frontiersmen' finished the transformation. **Georgetown University** is an academically rigorous and media savvy institution; its students populate the nightlife throngs.

The intersecting shopping strips are M Street and Wisconsin Avenue. The sidewalks are crowded at weekends with people throwing money around at the chic clothing stores. Built by cabinet-maker Christopher Layman in 1765, the **Old Stone House** (3051 M Street, NW,

1-202 426 6851) is the oldest home in DC, its garden offering repose to the weary consumer. Stately **Tudor Place** (1644 31st Street, NW) rests serenely isolated on extensive grounds. **Dumbarton Oaks** is home to a first-class collection of Byzantine and pre-Columbian art. Landscape architect Beatrix Farrand designed its celebrated formal gardens.

At night Georgetown jumps with dozens of bars and restaurants filled with suburban twentysomethings and international glitterati. In the summer, garish **Washington Harbour**, at the southern end of Wisconsin Avenue on the Potomac River, is overrun with people looking to eat, drink and flirt. The restaurants are forgettable and the drinks overpriced, but breezes off the Potomac make the promenade a nice stroll. Just west of here, Jack's Boathouse (*see p195*) still rents canoes for aquatic sightseeing.

Georgetown University

37th & O Streets, NW (1-202 687 0100/www. georgetown.edu). Dupont Circle Metro then G2 bus, Foggy Bottom-GWU Metro then 30, 32, 34, 35, 36, 38B, Georgetown Metro Connection bus. **Map** p281 D4.

A Jesuit institution founded in 1789 by John Carroll, first Catholic bishop in the United States. Alumni fought on both sides in the Civil War, inspiring the school colours, blue and grey. Equally polarising alumni of more recent vintage include Bill Clinton and pundit Pat Buchanan. Georgetown Law School across town is highly ranked; the School of Foreign Service draws top geopolitical junkies.

Upper Northwest

Map p248-p249

The affluent sector north of Georgetown is often referred to as 'West of the Park', the park being the extensive, leafy landscape of Rock Creek Park. It is home to some of the city's wealthiest residents. Massive homes and posh boutiques stack up, one after another, on streets such as Foxhall Road and upper Wisconsin Avenue.

Washington National Cathedral is the the second-largest place of worship in the US. On the cathedral grounds are two selective prep schools favoured by the children of the elite: St Alban's and National Cathedral School. Beyond lies another, Sidwell Friends. Nearby are the **Khalil Gibran Peace Garden** and the **US Naval Observatory** (3450 Massachusetts Avenue, NW, 1-202 762 1467), housing the official residence of the vice-president. Its first occupant, multimillionaire Nelson Rockefeller, reportedly found the mansion too small.

Dumbarton Oaks Research Library & Collections

1703 32nd Street, NW, between R & S Streets, Georgetown (1-202 339 6401/www.doaks.org). Bus 30, 32, 34, 36. **Open** Museum and shop closed until 2007. *Garden* mid Mar-Oct 2-6pm Tue-Sun. Nov-mid Mar 2-5pm Tue-Sun. **Admission** *Garden* $7; $5 concessions. Free Nov-mid Mar. **No credit cards**. **Map** p281 E4.

Wealthy art connoisseurs Mildred and Robert Woods Bliss purchased the 19th-century Federal-style brick mansion Dumbarton Oaks in 1920. In 1940 they commissioned architects McKim, Mead and White to build an addition, which they filled with their modest-sized collection of Byzantine art. The array of portable, sumptuous Byzantine objects, including rare sixth-century ecclesiastical silver, is one of the world's finest. That same year the Blisses gave the property, collections and a newly endowed research library to Harvard University.

In 1963 the octagonal Philip Johnson-designed wing was completed; today it houses the pre-Columbian collection in galleries encircling a central fountain. Unmissable exhibits include a miraculously preserved Peruvian burial mantle from 400 BC and the grotesque 'Head of a Maize God', originally crafted in AD 775 for a Honduran temple. The 16 acres of flora-filled formal gardens skirting the mansion, the creation of Beatrix Farrand, are also open to the public and worth a wander.

Katzen Arts Center at American University

4400 Massachusetts Avenue, NW, at Nebraska Avenue, Upper Northwest (1-202 885 1300/www.american.edu/museum). Tenleytown-AU Metro then N2, N4 bus or Friendship Heights Metro then N3, N4, N6, N8 bus. **Open** *Museum* 11am-4pm Tue-Thur; 11am-7pm Fri, Sat; noon-4pm Sun. **Admission** free.

This 36,000sq ft public museum and sculpture garden is devoted to special exhibitions of contemporary art and student shows from the University's art department. Check the museum website for up-to-date listings.

Kreeger Museum

2401 Foxhall Road, NW, between Dexter & W Streets, Upper Northwest (1-202 337 3050 /reservations 1-202 338 3552/www.kreeger museum.com). D6 bus. **Open** 10am-4pm Sat. Closed Aug. *Guided tours* 10am-1.30pm Tue-Fri (reservations required); frequently Sat. **Admission** suggested donation $8; $5 concessions. **Credit** AmEx, MC, V. **Map** p280 C3.

This intimate museum, housed in a spectacular 1967 Philip Johnson-designed travertine home nestled in woods, is best visited on one of its small, 90-minute guided tours. Alternatively, visitors may stop in during the day on Saturday. Either way, it's worth it: The late insurance magnate David Lloyd Kreeger and his wife Carmen amassed a small but striking collection of 180 works by 19th- and 20th-century

heavyweights. The museum's scale allows visitors to savour the details of works by Kandinsky, Chagall, Stella and Braque; two rooms showcase Monet's cliffside landscapes. The Kreegers also collected African ceremonial art, and their outdoor sculpture terrace overlooking verdant woodland has bronzes by Henry Moore, Jean Arp and Aristide Maillol. An annual special exhibition augments permanent collection gems. Public transport doesn't take you very close to the museum; it's probably easier to take a cab. Note that children under 12 are only allowed to visit on Saturday afternoons. See the website for details of Open House events.

National Museum of Health & Medicine

6900 Georgia Avenue, NW, at Elder Street, Upper Northwest (1-202 782 2200/http://nmhm.washington dc.museum). Silver Spring Metro then 70, 71 bus/Takoma Park Metro then 52, 53, 54 or K2 bus. **Open** 10am-5.30pm daily. **Admission** free. Museum is scheduled to move sometime between 2006-2012 to Bethesda, Maryland, so check website for current information.

Highlights (if you can call them that) at this anatomical museum, which was founded as the Army Medical Museum in 1862, include an assortment of preserved organs, a coal miner's blackened lungs and live leeches bobbing about in a petri dish. The memorable exhibit on medicine during the Civil War includes the bullet that killed Abraham Lincoln, as well as a detailed account of Major General Daniel Sickles' annual visits to his formaldehyde-preserved amputated leg (lost during the Battle of Gettysburg). Among the more recent acquisitions are the latest clotting agents QuikClot and HemCon, both used by the US military during manoeuvres in Iraq and Afghanistan. Although a visit will prove more informative than stomach-churning, it's probably best not to head for dinner immediately afterwards.

Rock Creek Park

Upper Northwest (1-202 895 6070/www.nps.gov/ rocr). **Open** *Park* dawn-dusk daily. *Nature Center & Planetarium* 9am-5pm Wed-Sun. Closed some holidays. **Map** p281 F3.

Nestled between sprawling condo corridors and busy commercial strips lie 1,750 acres of forest called Rock Creek Park, following that stream all the way to the city line to join an extension into Maryland. One of the largest such preserves in the nation, its 29 miles of hiking trails and ten miles of bridle paths intersect a net of bicycle paths. At weekends, several park roads close to motor vehicles. Its central thoroughfare, Beach Drive, a major commuter cut during weekday rush hour, is a quiet route to picnic groves (some with barbecue facilities) and playing fields at other times.

The park is a magnet for wildlife, its deer population swollen to nuisance levels. The Nature Center just off Military Road details its history and ecology, offering daily nature walks and similar events.

Greening the city

Proud of their 'City of Trees', Washingtonians were shocked when a *Washington Post* article juxtaposed satellite photos from 1973 and 1999 showing that their cherished leafy cover was radically falling away.

Philanthropist Betty Brown Casey responded with a huge endowment to re-green the city. By 2002, students had walked 955 miles of DC, documenting the state and condition of over 100,000 street trees, each identified on an interactive map on a website (www.casey trees.org) Numerous citizens' groups have taken to planting more trees, and in addition to a new tree replacement law, the city's commemoration of 9/11 involved memorial groves in each of the city's eight wards, the first already shading the Congressional Cemetery (*see p105*).

But it's not only in silviculture that Washington has surprisingly green credentials; the District's environmental renaissance continues in other areas too. The healthy state of Rock Creek Park brings burgeoning wildlife populations – including some animals not usually associated with urban settings. Deer have romped out of the park and recently bears and coyotes have put in urban appearances. For years volunteers lifted fish over man-made barriers so they could reach their spawning grounds. Now Rock Creek has a new set of fish ladders

making the task redundant. Meanwhile, over on the Anacostia, Canada geese have gobbled aquatic vegetation recently planted in an attempt to revive the river's ecosystem.

Methods of living without destroying our environment are demonstrated at the National Building Museum (*see p92*). The Green House exhibition (until June 2007) includes a full-size furnished version of a modern, environmentally friendly prefab home, which uses materials such as recycled paper for worktops and bamboo for flooring, as well as energy-saving appliances. Also on display are models of 20 green homes from around the world.

As well as promoting rain barrels and rain gardens that aim to decrease the flow of water into the city's old sewer system (which can lead to wastewater being propelled into the Anacostia), DC Greenworks (www.dcgreen works.org) also introduced the concept of green roofs to the city. In 2004 the first installation atop 1425 K Street, NW – the headquarters of the Casey Trees Endowment Fund – was completed. Casey volunteers lead free twice-monthly tours of the site (phone 1-202 833 4010). Don't expect exotic hanging gardens of Babylon, but rather expanses of mostly low-growing sedums, succulent ground covers resistant to temperature extremes, sprouting from special mats. While initial setup costs look high, green roofs last far longer than conventional ones, require less maintenance, and provide insulation. They also reduce and clean stormwater run-off, cool the air and improve air quality.

The American Society of Landscape Architects has also felt the benefit of a roof planted with black-eyed susans, cactuses, grasses, succulents and other plants. Executive vice-president Nancy Somerville told the *Washington Post*: 'Landscape architects are leading many green roof projects across the US and abroad, so it was only fitting that ASLA provide a demonstration project on this sustainable technology that can cure so many ills.' Phone 1-202 898 2444 for information on tours of the garden, at 636 I Street, NW. Even government buildings are getting a toe-hold on the technology: the Department of Agriculture roof has 120 feet of pre-grown modules for demonstration purposes. Area contractors now even offer to install green roofs on private residences.

Sightseeing

Eastern Market. See p105.

The planetarium offers free star-gazing sessions from April to November. Staff also provide directions to the attractions concealed in the foliage, including a golf course, walking and biking trails, even the remains of Civil War fortifications. Birders flock to Picnic Groves 17 and 18 just south, prime perches from which to observe the warblers migrating during the spring and autumn, DC being fortuitously situated on the 'Eastern Flyway' migration route. The District's only public riding stable, sharing the Nature Center parking lot, offers guided trail rides through the hilly terrain. East lies Carter Barron Amphitheatre, which stages low-cost summertime shows, from free Shakespeare in the Park productions to R&B and gospel concerts. Nearby Fitzgerald centre hosts major tennis competitions. See also, p166. For more on the Rock Creek's sporting facilities, see pp195-8.

Washington National Cathedral

Massachusetts & Wisconsin Avenues, NW (1-202 537 6200/www.cathedral.org/cathedral). Bus 30, 32, 34, 35, 36, 90, 92, 93, N2, N3, N4, N6 bus. **Open** *Sept-May* 10am-5.30pm Mon-Fri; 10am-4.30pm Sat; 8am-6.30pm Sun. *June-Aug* 10am-8pm Mon-Fri; 10am-4.30pm Sat; 8am-6.30pm Sun. **Admission** free; suggested donation $3. **Credit** AmEx, Disc, MC, V. **Map** p281 E2.

Washington National Cathedral was built in 14th-century Gothic style, stone upon stone, without structural steel, an exercise that took most of the 20th century and was only finished in 1990. Its medievalism has been somewhat updated: there's a gargoyle of Darth Vader in the north-west corner, while the much-admired stained-glass Space Window contains a piece of lunar rock. The top of the tower is the highest point in DC; there are great views from the observation gallery. Afternoon tea can be taken here on Tuesdays and Wednesdays at 1.30pm (reservations required).

The cathedral offers self-paced CD-based audio tours ($5); alternatively, join one of various guided tours, which are held at regular intervals. Special events can often mean that certain parts of the cathedral are closed at short notice, so it's best to phone first to check (the same applies if you have a specific tour in mind).

The Episcopalian Washington National cathedral holds some 1,200 services a year, yet has no congregation of its own. It is meant to be a church for all. Every president since Theodore Roosevelt has visited, as have Martin Luther King Jr and the Dalai Lama. Funeral services of various distinguished national figures (including, in June 2004, Ronald Reagan) have been held here. Medieval gardens appropriately adorn the cathedral's spacious grounds, supporting a popular herb shop.

Woodley Park

East towards Connecticut Avenue before Rock Creek Park, Woodley Park is a small but bustling neighbourhood featuring upscale homes, varied restaurants and the **National Zoo**. Conventioneers throng the restaurants along the short strip by the Metro station on Connecticut Avenue, and the handful of outdoor cafés make the area a popular spot on summer nights.

North of Cleveland Park is **Hillwood Museum & Gardens**, with late socialite Marjorie Merriweather Post's remarkable collection of Russian objets d'art and serene Japanese landscaping.

Hillwood Museum & Gardens

4155 Linnean Avenue, NW, between Tilden & Upton Streets, Upper Northwest (1-202 686 8500/ reservations 1-202 686 5807/www.hillwood museum.org). Van Ness-UDC Metro. **Open** 10am-5pm Tue-Sat (reservations required). Closed Jan. **Admission** (reservation deposit) $12; $7-$10 concessions; $5 under-18s. **Credit** AmEx, MC, V.

It's not for nothing that it's known as a museum and a garden, the grounds are as much a reason as the collection of Russian art for making the trek from downtown to this quiet, residential neighbourhood. The house and garden were purchased by cereal heiress Marjorie Merriweather Post in 1955 to house her collection of French and Russian decorative art. Seduced by Russian culture after living there for 18 months in the 1930s, Post amassed the largest collection of imperial Russian art objects outside that country. Portraits of tsars and tsarinas, palace furnishings and a porcelain service commissioned by Catherine the Great are displayed in Hillwood's gilt and wood-panelled rooms. The French collection includes Sèvres porcelain, 18th-century furniture and Beauvais tapestries.

Visitors can also roam the 12-acre manicured grounds, including a Japanese-style garden with plunging waterfall. Guided evening tours, when offered, are not to be missed: the waning light makes for romantic strolls in the gardens. Note that you must book in advance for the museum, and that children under the age of six are only allowed in the gardens, not the museum. You can ask for the return of your deposit after your visit, or donate the sum to the museum.

National Zoo

3001 block of Connecticut Avenue, NW, at Rock Creek Park (1-202 357 2700/information 1-202 673 4800/www.natzoo.si.edu). Woodley Park-Zoo/Adams Morgan Metro. **Open** *Grounds* Nov-Mar 6am-6pm daily. Apr-Oct 6am-8pm daily. *Buildings* Nov-Mar 10am-4.30pm daily. Apr-Oct 10am-6pm daily. **Admission** free. **Map** p281 F2.

The free-admission National Zoo offers a diverting escape. Particularly during the off-season, when the paths are not cluttered by pushchairs, the zoo offers a perfect (albeit hilly) stroll, away from the bustle of Connecticut Avenue. Tree-shaded paths wind through the margins past the various animals. The stars had been two pandas, brought on ten-year loan from China in 2001, until they were overshadowed by the birth of insufferably cute cub Tai Shan in 2005 (destined to move to Asia in 2008). New is the Asia Trail, linking habitats for sloth bears and Japanese giant salamanders. The zoo's 2007 plan sends its pachyderms packing for three years, while the old Elephant House transforms into the Elephant Trails environment, part of its campaign to save the Asian branch of the species.

Cleveland Park

Further north is Cleveland Park, an affluent enclave sited on the farm where in 1886 President Cleveland and his gorgeous 21-year-old bride preferred to live rather than the White House. It boasts a mix of restaurants and the AMC Loews Uptown (*see p168*), a sometime premier venue with a gigantic screen and comfy seats.

Northeast

Map p251

Washington was never known for industry. Today, its minimal manufacturing and warehouse area, mostly along New York Avenue, NE, is sprouting high-tech businesses and edgy nightclubs.

A couple of blocks east of the Supreme Court is the **Frederick Douglass Museum** (316 A Street, NE, 1-202 547 4273), early residence of the famous abolitionist, now housing the Caring Foundation, celebrating worthy philanthropists but maintaining one room as it was in Douglass's time. Constantino Brumidi, the artist who painted the frescos in the Capitol, lived nearby, at 326 A Street. A development target abutting the Amtrak line north of Union Station is the degraded Washington Coliseum (Second

Sightseeing

and K Streets, NE), in 1964 the site of the Beatles' American concert debut.

To the north, the **Catholic University of America** (620 Michigan Avenue, NE) is a pontifical institution known for its drama department (its members perform at the university's **Hartke Theatre**). Adjoining the university is the **National Shrine of the Immaculate Conception** (400 Michigan Avenue, NE, 1-202 526 8300). Begun in 1914 in a Byzantine style rarely seen in US Catholic churches, it was only completed in 1959.

Across Harewood Road at No.4250 gleam the traditional golden domes of the **Ukrainian Catholic National Shrine of the Holy Family** (1-202 526 3737). Downhill is the ambitious **Pope John Paul II Cultural Center** (3900 Harewood Road, NE, 1-202 635 5400), displaying mementos of the late pontiff and interactive exhibits about his spiritual and worldly concerns.

Across North Capitol Street is the leafy campus of the Armed Forces Retirement Home, founded as Soldiers' Home with Mexican War tribute. The cottage that President Lincoln used as his retreat is to open to the public in September 2007. Check www.lincolncottage.org for details.

The **Franciscan Monastery** (1400 Quincy Street, NE, 1-202 526 6800) has a glorious mixture of influences: the church is modelled on Hagia Sophia in Istanbul, while beneath is a replica of the catacombs of Rome; the splendid garden's meandering paths connect replicas of religious sites.

Along the west bank of the Anacostia, DC's previously neglected river now enjoying ecological restoration, is the **United States National Arboretum**, a 440-acre enclave containing both local and exotic foliage. Near the arboretum is **Mount Olivet Cemetery** (1300 Bladensburg Road, NE, between Montana Avenue and Mount Olivet Road, 1-202 399 3000), final resting place of White House architect James Hoban and of Mary Suratt, who was hanged for her alleged role in Lincoln's assassination. On the New York Avenue side of the arboretum, one brick kiln stands as a reminder of the brickyards that constituted Northeast's first major industry. Anacostia Park follows the river's east bank and contains **Kenilworth Aquatic Gardens**. Although located near a highway that shares its name, the gardens are a quiet retreat full of aquatic plants, including lilies and lotuses. Now that

H Street comes of age

H Street, NE was an unremarkable neighbourhood shopping strip until the 1968 riots drove it into shabby decline. As 21st-century gentrification pressed relentlessly north and east of Union Station, the strip began a radical makeover.

Signs of revival in the commercial strip include **Reader's Lounge and Quieto Café** (421 H Street, NE, 1-202 544-7000) selling coffee and secondhand books. Then, from the junction with 12th Street, NE, onwards there begins a three-block entertainment zone, sparked largely by local bar-owner Joe Englert. Almost overnight in 2006, shabby storefronts and townhouses mushroomed into offbeat theme bars and restaurants. Even a frozen custard stand swirled into the newly minted 'Atlas District'.

New kids on the block include the Caribbean restaurant **Phish Tea** (1335 H Street, NE, 1-202 396-2345), music venue **The Red and the Black** (*see p185*), the **Argonaut Tavern** (1433 H Street, NE, 1-202 397 1461, www.argonautdc.com) and **H Street Martini Lounge** (1236 H Street, NE, 1-202 397 3333, www.hstreetlounge.com). Oddest of the lot is **The Palace of Wonders**,

which stages periodic vaudeville revues in a setting festooned with bizarre side-show kitsch like two-headed sheep skulls and mermaid skeletons (1210 H Street, NE, 1-202 398 7469, www.palaceofwonders. com). In the works are the **Pug** (1234 H, www.thepug.dc.com), a boxing theme bar, and **Rock and Roll Hotel** (1353 H Street, NE, www.rockandrolldc.com). To keep up with the all the newcomers, check the interactive map at www.atlasdistrict.com.

Combining a long-dark movie house with adjacent retail buildings, the ambitious **Atlas Performing Arts Center** (1333 H Street, NE, 1-202 399 7993, www.atlaslic.net) has four performance stages and is also the new home of the Joy of Motion Dance Center. Independent troupes can tread these boards for a fee, ensuring varied and interesting programming. The nearby **H Street Playhouse** is home to the forward-looking and creative Theater Alliance (*see p205*).

There is no Metro station along H Street east of Union Station, and the X-2 is the only full-time bus that runs the length of H Street, NE. There is also a plan for a trolley line to run from Union Station.

the Anacostia is getting cleaner, this area attracts all sorts of reptiles, amphibians and water-loving mammals.

Kenilworth Aquatic Gardens

Anacostia Avenue & Douglas Street, NE, at Quarles Street (1-202 426 6905/www.nps.gov/nace/keaq). Deanwood Metro. **Open** 7am-4pm daily. **Admission** free.

Kenilworth Aquatic Gardens is a 12-acre garden with a network of ponds displaying a variety of aquatic plants. A one-armed Civil War veteran started water gardening here as a hobby in 1880; then, in the 1920s, the public – and President Coolidge – began to visit for a stroll. On the northern boundary, a path leads to the Anacostia River. On the southern boundary, a boardwalk leads to vistas of the reviving wetlands. During the week you may have the place to yourself. It's off the beaten track, and shunned by some who assume the low-income neighbourhood at the approach is dangerous.

United States National Arboretum

3501 New York Avenue, NE, entrance at Bladensburg Road & R Street (1-202 245 2726/www.usna.usda. gov). Stadium-Armory Metro then B2 bus. **Open** *Grounds* 8am-5pm daily. *National Bonsai Collection* 10am-3.30pm daily. **Admission** free.

Technically a research division of the Agriculture Department, this haven always has many more trees than people, even on its busiest days during the spring azalea season. Highlights include a boxwood collection, dwarf conifers, an Asian collection, a herb garden and 'herbarium' of dried plants, as well as the National Bonsai Collection, which contains more than 200 trees donated by Japan and is said to be worth something in the order of $5 million. Also on display, somewhat incongruously, are 22 columns removed from the Capitol's East Front during its 1958 expansion. See the website for details of tours, talks and other events such as the (very popular) full-moon hikes.

Southeast

There's Southeast and then there's 'Southeast'. The latter usually refers not to the whole quadrant but to some of the city's rougher neighbourhoods, across the Anacostia River and far from the centre of town.

Capitol Hill

Map p253

Bounded to the west by the Capitol building and South and North Capitol Streets, to the south by the Southeast Freeway, to the north by H Street, NE and to the east by 11th Street, this genteel neighbourhood overlays two quadrants – Southeast and Northeast. Since more of it falls into the former, most of it is dealt with here.

East of the Capitol building, a working-class town developed around the Navy Yard, separated from the rest of the city by a 'desert', as a Swiss visitor noted in 1825. Today, its parochial small-town origins afford it a distinctively strollable ambience, although million-dollar home sales are no longer news. Businesses along Pennsylvania Avenue, SE, include bars and restaurants luring a youthful, politics-obsessed crowd. There are still vintage hangouts like the fabled Tune Inn (331 Pennsylvania Avenue, SE, *see p135*), little changed since VJ Day. The neighbourhood's heart is **Eastern Market**, now complemented by the revived Barracks Row on Eighth Street between Pennsylvania Avenue and M Street, SE, winner of a national Main Street revival award. Its growing restaurant roster dishes out two dozen cuisines, from Belgian and Cuban to Turkish and soul food – available without the congestion of Adams Morgan.

Aside from Pennsylvania Avenue itself, the Hill's principal shopping streets are the Seventh-Eighth Street dogleg from Eastern Market, featuring food stores, galleries and craft shops, supplemented by the market's weekend flea and craft marts.

The **US Marine Barracks** (Eighth and I Streets, SE) has been on this site since 1801 and its commandant's house is the second oldest federal residence after the White House. On Friday nights from May to September, an impressive Marine parade drill is held (reservations required; call 1-202 433 6060).

Capitol Hill's largest open space is Lincoln Park, which interrupts East Capitol Street between 11th and 13th Streets. Grateful freedmen chipped in for its Emancipation Monument (1876), depicting Abraham Lincoln and a newly freed slave, though the monument was criticised when it was unveiled because the bondsman seemed to be kneeling before the president. Nearby is a sculpture of African-American educator Mary McLeod Bethune, flanked by festive children.

Congressional Cemetery (1801 E Street, SE), the resting place of such eminent Washingtonians as photographer Matthew Brady, Choctaw chief Pushmataha and 'March King' John Philip Sousa, celebrates its 200th anniversary in 2007. Look for free guide pamphlets at the gatehouse. Plots are available if you care to stay permanently.

The once dodgy tract by the Washington Navy Yard suddenly sprouted contractors' office buildings when the Naval Sea Systems Command moved into brilliantly refitted industrial buildings. Ships are no longer built at the Navy Yard, but guns and weaponry were being manufactured there as recently as the 1991 Gulf War. A Navy museum displays the Yard's heritage.

Land just east at South Capitol Street was named as the site for a new baseball stadium in 2005, when Washington regained a major league baseball team after three dark decades (*see p196* **Go Nationals**).

Eastern Market
225 Seventh Street, SE, between C Street & North Carolina Avenue (1-202 544 0083/www.eastern market.net). Eastern Market Metro. **Open** dawn-late afternoon Sat, Sun. *Permanent inside stalls* 7am-6pm Tue-Sat; 9am-4pm Sat. **Map** p253 L7.
Built in 1873 on plans by Adolf Cluss, Washington's last remaining public food market has become the heart of the Capitol Hill community; its weekend flea and craft markets are a popular draw.

Washington Navy Yard
Eleventh & O Street, SE. Navy Yard Metro. **Map** p253 L8.
The US Navy's oldest shore facility produced the big guns for American ships in World War II. Post-9/11 restrictions were lifted – partly – in 2004, but visiting involves running a security gauntlet. Located on the base are the Navy Museum (Building 76, 901 M Street, SE, 1-202 433 4882), which has a permanent exhibition on US naval history spanning the period from the Revolutionary War to the present.

Anacostia

Anacostia Community Museum for African American History & Culture (S)
1901 Fort Place, SE, at Martin Luther King Jr Avenue, Anacostia, Southeast (1-202 287 3306/ www.si.edu/anacostia). Anacostia Metro then W2, W3 bus. **Open** 10am-5pm daily. **Admission** free.
Housed in an unprepossessing red-brick building at the top of a hill in the District's historically black Anacostia neighbourhood, this modest museum hosts changing thematic exhibitions spotlighting history, culture and creative expression from an African American perspective. Recent acquisitions include the 19th-century diary of one-time slave Adam Francis Plummer, who wrote of his foiled plan to escape on the Underground Railroad. The Center for African American History & Culture also presents exhibits in the Smithsonian's Arts & Industries Building on the Mall. Free events such as poetry slams help boost the museum's profile.

Frederick Douglass National Historic Site (Cedar Hill)
1411 W Street, SE, at 14th Street (1-202 426 5961/ www.nps.gov/frdo). Anacostia Metro then B2 bus. **Open** *Mid Oct-mid Apr* 9am-4pm daily. *Mid Apr-mid Oct* 9am-5pm daily. House closed for renovation until early 2007; visitor centre remains open. **Admission** $2. **Credit** MC, V.

Built in 1854, this Victorian country house was the home of black leader Frederick Douglass from 1877 until his death in 1895. Born a slave in Maryland, Douglass escaped to found an abolitionist newspaper, eventually advising Lincoln and other presidents. A proposal to restore the whitewashed landmark's original brown colour scheme distressed the neighbourhood during its closure for renovation, to end in 2007. The site's visitor centre and grounds remain open while the house is closed.

Southwest

Map p253
There's not much of Southwest DC, the reason being that Virginia took back its quadrangle in 1846. The sliver of territory east of the Potomac that remained was not helped by a massive 1950s 'urban renewal' project that obliterated neighbourhoods in favour of office space. Now the area is known mostly for containing the western elbow of the National Mall. Its primary draws are the museums and federal buildings to the south of the Mall, and the Tidal Basin, which are covered – down to the Eisenhower Freeway – in the Monumental Centre chapter (*see pp61-82*).

Fishing boats have hawked their catch near the Tidal Basin inlet since 1790, before there was a city. You can still get seafood at the **Fish & Seafood Market** (1-202 686 1068), just south of the Case Memorial Bridge; some vendors will even cook it up for you. The ponderous waterfront development, largely comprising oversized tour-bus restaurants, is set to be redeveloped, though the lively houseboat colony should stay anchored. The promenade climaxes at the willowy memorial to the gentlemen who gave ladies their seats on the *Titanic*'s lifeboats. Beyond, Fort McNair – the army's oldest post – has gone off-limits for security reasons.

Inland, **Wheat Row** (1315-21 Fourth Street, SW) is a curiosity of the 1950s urban renewal programme. Built in 1794, these distinguished residences were incorporated into a modern apartment complex. The area's theoretical juxtaposition of rich and poor populations did not uniformly foster the envisioned social harmony. Law House (1252 Sixth Street), dubbed 'Honeymoon House' in 1796 when its prominent owners moved in, kept the tag, despite their messy celebrity divorce a while later. Nearby, the pioneering theatre company **Arena Stage** (1101 Sixth Street, SW; *see p200*) continues its vital dramatic presence and in-the-round productions after flirting with relocation elsewhere. But the arrival of the Washington Nationals – DC's first major league baseball team for three decades – across South Capitol Street promises to have a major impact on the area.

Arlington & Alexandria

Virginia's suburban hot spots.

Northern Virginia is a comparatively liberal pocket of a famously conservative state, the 'Old Dominion', so called because it remained loyal to the Crown during the English Civil War. Arlington and part of Alexandria were part of the original District of Columbia diamond from 1800 to 1846, when they retroceded to Virginia, claiming federal neglect but covertly fearing that Congress might ban slavery in the capital. Beyond its military precinct along the river – with Arlington Cemetery and the Pentagon – Arlington is a low-key suburb recently enlivened by a restaurant and entertainment strip sprouting above Metro stations along Wilson Boulevard. Its Fashion Center mall at Pentagon City draws throngs of international visitors. Self-consciously quaint but vigorous 'Old Town' Alexandria, a restored riverport with a history that predates the capital by half a century, can make a welcome break from all that federal seriousness.

Alexandria

Downstream on the Potomac river, Alexandria was established in 1749 by Scots traders and laid out by a young surveyor named George Washington. Old Town's 18th-century charm started drawing crowds of sightseers and shoppers in the 1960s. Cobbled streets that had survived more from lethargy than historical sensibility were re-stoned at vast expense, neglected houses meticulously restored; the vacant warehouses along King Street sprouted bars, boutiques and antique shops. Commerce now extends 19 blocks from the river to King Street Metro station, with an atmosphere that is lively yet leisurely. Indeed, the town's promotional tag is 'the fun side of the Potomac'; for more information go to www.funside.com. In this environment, residents' and merchants' interests don't always coincide, as is demonstrated by an ongoing dispute between householders keen on parking and zoning limitations and merchants anxious to accommodate outsiders.

Old Town rewards random wanderings. For background and orientation arm yourself with some maps and pamphlets from the visitors' centre in historic **Ramsay House** (221 King Street, 1-703 838 4200) before setting out to discover the flounder houses, dwellings with

half-gable roofs descending asymmetrically, that are characteristic of 18th- and early 19th-century Alexandria dwellings. Forty originals survive, with dozens of neo-flounders marking recent developments.

The Civil War indelibly marked the town; some reminders include the Confederate Statue (1888), glowering in the middle of the intersection of South Washington and Prince Streets, its back defiantly turned on the nation's capital. A free map of significant local war sites is available at the nearby **Lyceum, Alexandria's History Museum**.

A few blocks east, at 121 N Fairfax Street, is the 18th-century **Carlyle House**. Next door, the old Bank of Virginia has been restored for use – as a bank, surprise, surprise. Across the street is **Gadsby's Tavern Museum**.

George Washington prayed as well as played in Alexandria, attending **Christ Church**. He was also a patron of the voluntary fire company that built the original **Friendship Fire House**, west on King Street.

From 1792 until 1933, Quaker druggist Edward Stabler's family made medicines for patrons including Washington and Lee. Today the **Stabler-Leadbeater Apothecary Shop**

Alexandria.

on Fairfax Street appears just as it did for generations. Further north are **Lee-Fendall House** and **Alexandria Black History Museum**.

Alexandria is not only a heritage town; at the **Torpedo Factory Art Center** local artists create new sculpture and painting, although the past can't be escaped even here: the site is a renovated factory that produced munitions for World War I.

Back towards King Street Metro station, Dulany Street is the new home of the **United States Patent & Trademark Museum**. To the west, on Callahan Drive you'll find the **George Washington Masonic National Memorial**.

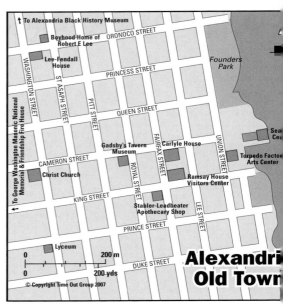

To Alexandria Black History Museum
ORONOCO STREET
Boyhood Home of Robert E Lee
Lee-Fendall House
PRINCESS STREET
Founders Park
WASHINGTON STREET
ST ASAPH STREET
PITT STREET
QUEEN STREET
To George Washington Masonic National Memorial & Friendship Fire House
Gadsby's Tavern Museum
Carlyle House
FAIRFAX STREET
UNION STREET
Sea Ce...
CAMERON STREET
Christ Church
ROYAL STREET
Ramsay House Visitors Center
Torpedo Factory Arts Center
KING STREET
Stabler-Leadbeater Apothecary Shop
LEE STREET
PRINCE STREET
Lyceum
0   200 m
0   200 yds
DUKE STREET
© Copyright Time Out Group 2007
Alexandri...
Old Town

Alexandria Black History Museum

902 Wythe Street, at Alford Street (1-703 838 4356/http://oha.ci. alexandria.va.us/bhrc). Braddock Road Metro. **Open** 10am-4pm Tue-Sat. **Admission** free.
This museum of Virginia's African-American heritage occupies a former Jim Crow library built in 1940 to escape racially integrating the Alexandria Public Library (717 Queen Street, 1-703 838 4555), now the city's historical repository.

Carlyle House

121 N Fairfax Street, between King & Cameron Streets (1-703 549 2997). King Street Metro then 29K bus or Dash bus AT2, AT3, AT5, AT7. **Open** 10am-4.30pm Tue-Sat; noon-4.30pm Sun. Guided tours every half hr. **Admission** $4; $2 concessions; free under-11s. **No credit cards.**
John Carlyle built his Scottish-Palladian stone palace here in 1751 and it was then used as the meeting place for British colonial governors to plan their campaign against the French forces squeezing the Crown's claims to the Ohio river valley. General Edward Braddock then marched down the eponymous road west, towards Pennsylvania – and disaster.

Christ Church

Cameron & N Washington Streets (1-703 549 1450/ www.historicchristchurch.org). King Street Metro then 29K bus or Dash bus AT2, AT3, AT5, AT7. **Open** 9am-4pm Mon-Sat; 2-4pm Sun. **Admission** free, $5 donation suggested for adults.
Dubbed 'The Church in the Woods' in 1773, this Episcopal (Anglican communion, though maybe not for much longer) house of worship has been in continuous service since. The pew assigned to George Washington, No.15, is preserved in its original high-backed eminence. In January 2004 Archbishop Desmond Tutu ordained his daughter here.

Friendship Fire House

107 S Alfred Street, between King & Prince Streets (1-703 838 3891/http://oha.ci.alexandria.va.us/ friendship). King Street Metro then 29K bus or Dash bus AT2, AT3, AT5, AT7. **Open** 10am-4pm Fri, Sat; 1-4pm Sun. **Admission** free.
The volunteer fire brigade, formed in 1774, built this snug station in 1855. The museum has a display of antique firefighting apparatus.

Gadsby's Tavern Museum

134 N Royal Street, between King & Cameron Streets (1-703 838 4242/http://oha.ci.alexandria. va.us/gadsby). King Street Metro then 29K bus or Dash bus AT2, AT3, AT5, AT7. **Open** *Nov-Mar* 11am-4pm Wed-Sat; 1-4pm Sun. *Apr-Oct* 10am-5pm Tue-Sat; 1-5pm Mon, Sun. Guided tours every 30mins. **Admission** $4; $2 concessions; free under-11s. **Credit** MC, V.
These buildings comprise a tavern dating from 1785 and a hotel built in 1792. Towards the end of the 18th century they were joined together by Englishman John Gadsby and quickly became a local meeting place for many significant 18th-century figures. In 1798 George Washington graced a ball here, the first of two occasions on which he attended the celebrations in honour of the birthday. The 18th-century hostelry is well preserved in the older building. The 'ordinary' – or tavern – next door serves colonial-style food and drink, to the tune of period entertainment. A rare specimen of primitive refrigeration, the ice cellar permitted the mint juleps that helped to make the steamy summers endurable.

George Washington Masonic National Memorial

101 Callahan Drive, between King & Duke Streets (1-703 683 2007/www.gwmemorial.org). King Street Metro. **Open** 9am-4pm daily. Guided tours 9.30am, 11am, 1pm, 2.30pm, 3.30pm daily. **Admission** free.
Sitting on a hill dominating low-lying Alexandria, in the imagined style of the ancient Pharos of Alexandria, the George Washington Masonic National Memorial is in striking contrast to the general's more famous tower across the river in DC. Masonic memorabilia related to US presidents who were Freemasons includes a reconstruction of the lodge hall Washington attended. The view from the top of the monument (only accessible as part of a guided tour) is impressive.

Lyceum, Alexandria's History Museum

201 S Washington Street, at Prince Street (1-703 838 4994/http://oha.ci.alexandria.va.us/lyceum). King Street Metro then 29K bus or Dash bus AT2, AT3, AT5, AT7. **Open** 10am-5pm Mon-Sat; 1-5pm Sun. **Admission** free.
In 1839 local culture-vultures built a Greek Revival library-auditorium for debates, concerts and literary soirées. Today it celebrates Alexandria's heritage with changing displays on local life and products.

Seaport Center

Zero Thompsons Alley, at the Potomac River, between Queen & Cameron Streets (1-703 549 7078). King Street Metro then 29K bus or Dash bus AT2, AT3, AT5, AT7. **Open** 9am-5pm daily. **Admission** free.
The Alexandria Seaport Foundation was formed in 1983 to recall the town's maritime origins, and to that end converted the Swedish schooner *Lindo* – rechristened *Alexandria* – into the city's flagship. Sadly, the ship sank off Cape Hatteras in 1996. The foundation rallied with its floating Seaport Center, with demonstrations of boat-building.

Stabler-Leadbeater Apothecary Shop

105-107 Fairfax Street, at King Street (1-703 836 3713/www.apothecarymuseum.org). King Street Metro then 29K bus or Dash bus AT2, AT3, AT5, AT7. **Open** 10am-4pm Mon-Sat; 1-5pm Sun. **Admission** phone for details. **Credit** AmEx, Disc, MC, V.
Stabler-Leadbeater Apothecary Shop is a time capsule of old-time medications, with modern pharmaceuticals alongside Native American herbal remedies in their original jars. The revival of alternative therapies puts some of these remedies into intriguing perspective. The gift shop sells odd, old collectibles.

Torpedo Factory Art Center

105 N Union Street, at King Street (1-703 838 4565/www.torpedofactory.org). King Street Metro then 29K bus or Dash bus AT2, AT3, AT5, AT7. **Open** 10am-5pm daily. *Guided tours* phone for details. **Admission** free.

A World War I munitions plant, the Torpedo Factory now spawns arts, not arms, with three storeys of studios and galleries. Exhibits of the old war work line the lobby, including a signature torpedo. Alexandria Archeology operates a small 'hands-on' museum upstairs, where volunteers and guests help clean and preserve cultural detritus excavated from colonial privies.

United States Patent & Trademark Museum

400 Dulany Street (1-571 272 0095/www.uspto.gov/ web/offices/ac/ahrpa/opa/museum/welcome.html). King Street Metro. **Open** 9am-5pm Mon-Fri; noon-5pm Sat. **Admission** free.
This paean to Yankee ingenuity wittily tells the tales of inventors and their devices since Samuel Hopkins received the first US patent, for making potash, in 1790. Here are charming early samples of everything from pop-up toasters (1919), the Birdseye frozen food process (1930) and the skateboard (1962) to disposable nappies. The gizmo champ is Thomas Edison, who took out 1,093 patents, for diverse items including the phonograph and the lightbulb.

Arlington

Stately **Memorial Bridge** (1932) formally connects Lincoln's memorial to the home of his Civil War nemesis, Robert E Lee, symbolically linking North and South. The bridge makes landfall at Lady Bird Johnson Park, which includes the discreet **Lyndon B Johnson Memorial Grove** (www.nps.gov/lyba). Ground was broken at the adjacent **Pentagon** in mid 2006 for a 1.93-acre maple grove, sheltering 184 cantilevered benches, one for each person killed on 9/11 when terrorists flew a hijacked jet into the building. The days of public tours around the Pentagon, the world's largest public building, are long gone, but it is planned that the memorial will be open to all. The newest feature in this martial terrain is the **Air Force Memorial** (1-703 247 5808, www.airforcememorial.org), three stainless steel spikes soaring 270 feet from a promontory south of **Arlington National Cemetery**. The memorial was dedicated in October 2006.

Arlington National Cemetery

1-703 695 3250/Tourmobile info 1-703 979 0690/ www.arlingtoncemetery.org. Arlington Cemetery Metro. **Open** Apr-Sept 8am-7pm daily. Oct-Mar 8am-5pm daily. **Admission** free.
It is the right of anyone killed in action in any branch of military service, or who served for 20 years, to be buried at Arlington along with their spouse. It's ironic, then, that the cemetery started almost as an act of Civil War vengeance: in 1861 Union forces seized the estate of Confederate General Robert E Lee and in 1864 they began burying soldiers close enough to Arlington House to make sure that Mr and Mrs Lee

could never take up residence again. However, time has worked its healing magic and transformed Arlington into a place of honour and memory.

Built in 1802-1816, Arlington House is now a museum (open 9.30am-4.30pm daily) and appears as it did in Lee's time. Entranced by the commanding view, President Kennedy was said to have murmured, 'I could stay here forever.' Shortly afterwards he took up residence in the cemetery, to be joined later by Robert F Kennedy and Jacqueline Kennedy Onassis.

By an imposing marble amphitheatre is the Tomb of the Unknowns, including unidentified casualties of US conflicts up to Vietnam. Today the Pentagon keeps DNA samples of all military personnel, making it unlikely that future remains will be unidentifiable. The changing of the guard on the hour (every hour between October and March, every half an hour from April to September) remains moving in its reverent precision. Horse-drawn caissons still bear the remains of troops qualified for burial, from the dwindling veterans of World War II to Iraq War victims.

Tombs range from unadorned white headstones, such as that of actor Lee Marvin, to sculpted personal memorials, like the one to the former world heavyweight boxing champion Joe Louis (both men were veterans of World War II), next to it. The Tourmobile route naturally features celebrity sites, but strollers can discover more obscure, but often just as interesting, memorials and tombs. Memorials include the mast of the battleship *Maine* (whose explosion in Havana harbour sparked the Spanish-American War), the monument to the Navajo Code Talkers (whose language baffled Japanese code-breakers during World War II), and commemorations of the Space Shuttle *Columbia* casualties.

At the north end is the Netherlands Carillon, a Dutch thank you for their liberation from the Nazis. Beyond is the US Marines' Iwo Jima Memorial, a giant recreation of the celebrated photo of the raising of the flag during the 1942 battle.

The Women in Military Service to America Memorial (1-800 222 2294) is inset behind the original Main Gate wall to create a light-flooded arch with 16 display niches. Three permanent photo displays survey woman at war from the earliest days to the present. Late in 2005, a special exhibit of Women in the Global War on Terror opened.

Arlington Cemetery's visitors' centre is just past the entrance on Memorial Avenue. Here you can locate particular graves or pick up maps to wander the cemetery on foot (note that some significant graves are a mile or more uphill). Alternatively, buy tickets for the Tourmobile coach circuit ($5.25; $2.50 concessions). The coach makes brief stops at each major point of interest, but to avoid that cattle-drive feeling, take your time and reboard the subsequent service (tickets are valid).

Drug Enforcement Agency Museum

700 Army Navy Drive, across from Pentagon City Mall (1-202 307 3463/www.deamuseum.org).
Pentagon City Metro. **Open** 10am-4pm Tue-Fri; also by appointment. **Admission** free.
The exhibits here trace the history of drugs and the law in America, primarily through the relics of 20th-century drug culture that have been collected by DEA agents. With the tours of the Pentagon, FBI and other security agencies currently curtailed for obvious security reasons, the displays of drug-smugglers' ingenuity and the narcs' persistence is the best law-and-order show in town.

Iwo Jima Memorial and headstones at **Arlington National Cemetery**.

Eat, Drink, Shop

Restaurants

Top tables in the seat of power.

Eat, Drink, Shop

Washington has always been a sophisticated city, with elegant venues for entertaining the prominent and powerful. And in recent years, with Americans' increased knowledge about food and the urban centre's economic revival, DC's dining culture has evolved. These days the names of local chefs, many of whom have been recognised nationally, are as familiar as those of local sports stars; on websites, chatters brag of restaurant visits like notches on their belts.

All of which means that in both quantity and quality, local eateries rival those of New York and San Francisco. Award-winning New American restaurants grace both downtown (**Equinox**, **Cashion's Eat Place**) and the suburbs (**Restaurant Eve**); carryouts give way to yuppy hangouts as the capital gentrifies. Highly personalised takes on ethnic cuisine (**Obelisk**, **Marcel's**) are the vehicle of choice for some of the city's star chefs, with Southern food in particular well represented (**Georgia Brown's**, **Vidalia**, the **Majestic Café**).

Of course, the action isn't all at the high end. Waves of immigration have long meant that DC's boasts of international character are at least partly true; you can eat your way around the world within the Beltway. Many a newcomer reared on chain Mexican has come to appreciate the gamut of authentic Latin American cuisines; many a visiting relative has been treated to an Ethiopian feast, difficult to find elsewhere in the country. The more affordable inner suburbs, where immigrant communities establish themselves, are hubs for Salvadorean, Vietnamese and Caribbean cuisine, although representative establishments can be found throughout the area.

Whatever your preference and budget, keep in mind that Washington is an expensive city and servers essentially earn their living from gratuities. Natives tend to tip 20 per cent or even higher; 15 per cent on the pretax bill is expected, even at the humblest of restaurants.

The best Restaurants

For a taste of the south
Capital Q (see p116); Georgia Brown's (see p117); Majestic Café (see p132); Market Lunch (see p130); Vidalia (see p115).

For crab
Equinox (see p113); Market Lunch (see p130); Oceanaire Seafood Room (see p115).

For dining al fresco
Lauriol Plaza (see p121); Perry's (see p125); Tabard Inn (see p120).

For late-night eating
Amsterdam Falafelshop (see p125); Ben's Chili Bowl (see p125); The Diner (see p121); Full Kee (see p118); LeftBank (see p123); Ugly Mug (see p131).

For nostalgia
Ben's Chili Bowl (see p125).

White House & around

Sandwich bar

Breadline
1751 Pennsylvania Avenue, NW, between 17th & 18th Streets (1-202 822 8900). Farragut West Metro. **Open** 7.30am-3.30pm Mon-Fri; 11am-3pm Sat. **Main courses** $6-$12. **Credit** AmEx, MC, V. **Map** p252 G5 ❶
On a downtown block with plenty of other quick breakfast and lunch options, Breadline is always packed. This counter-order eaterie has earned cult status among Washingtonians for its soups, salads and gargantuan sandwiches, made with artisanal loaves and quality fillings. The food isn't cheap, but the portions are large enough to keep the average person going all day. The turkey sandwich, for example, comes with so much meat that it is physically impossible to keep more than half between the slabs of fresh bread. If you've got room, add some boutique soda and Route 11 chips – Virginia-made potato crisps that come in a variety of novelty flavours.

Foggy Bottom

Asian

Café Asia
1721 I Street, NW, between 17th & 18th Streets (1-202 659 2696/www.cafeasia.com). Farragut West Metro. **Open** 11am-10pm Mon-Thur; 11am-11pm Fri, Sat; 5-10pm Sun. **Main courses** $8-$22. **Credit** AmEx, MC, V. **Map** p252 G5 ❷

If you like your sushi loud and upfront, then you'll thoroughly enjoy Café Asia. It's pretty hard to ignore the blaring music coming from the bar/lounge area, which always seems to be hopping with excited singles. The pan-Asian menu is far from inspiring, but its survey coverage of the region is above average and everything is well done. The new downtown location has two floors, each with a bar, and offers communal tables for larger groups.
Other locations: 1550 Wilson Boulevard, at Pierce Street, Rosslyn (1-703 741 0870).

Kaz Sushi Bistro
1915 I Street, NW, between 19th & 20th Streets (1-202 530 5500/www.kazsushibistro.com). Farragut West Metro. **Open** 11.30am-2pm, 6-10pm Mon-Fri; 6-10pm Sat. **Main courses** $10-$16 lunch; $12-$25 dinner. **Credit** AmEx, MC, V. **Map** p252 G5 ❸
Sushi king Kazuhiro Okochi made his mark at Sushi-Ko (*see p130*), successfully melding Asian and Western ingredients, before bringing the winning formula here. The sushi itself is top-notch, featuring fish that is is gorgeous and glistening, while the rice has a touch of sweetness unlike any you'll find elsewhere. But should your tastes not include raw fish, there's also a bounty of wonderfully cooked items on offer, including grilled baby octopus, coriander-crusted calamari and Asian-style short ribs.

Contemporary American

Equinox
818 Connecticut Avenue, NW, between H & I Streets (1-202 331 8118/www.equinoxrestaurant. com). Farragut West Metro. **Open** 11.30am-2pm, 5.30-10pm Mon-Thur; 11.30am-2pm, 5.30-10.30pm Fri; 5.30-10.30pm Sat; 5-9pm Sun. **Main courses** $30-$35. **Credit** AmEx, MC, V. **Map** p252 H5 ❹
Chef Todd Gray is known for his emphasis on the seasonal and regional; Equinox's three- to six-course tasting menu generally includes such delicacies as Chesapeake Bay crab, Carolina grouper and locally grown organic vegetables. The suited power brokers who frequent the place – conveniently located halfway between the White House and K Street – may or may not appreciate Gray's efforts to acquire sustainably farmed fish and humanely raised meat, but they surely appreciate the deceptively simple preparations in which such ingredients shine. Service in the understated dining room, presided over by Ellen Kassoff-Gray, is deft and friendly. Reservations are required.

Fish

Kinkead's
2000 Pennsylvania Avenue, NW, between 20th & 21st Streets (1-202 296 7700/www.kinkead.com). Foggy Bottom-GWU Metro. **Open** 11.30am-2.30pm, 5.30-10pm Mon-Thur, Sun; 11.30am-2.30pm, 5.30-10.30pm Fri; 5.30-10.30pm Sat. **Main courses** $15-$21 lunch; $24-$32 dinner. **Credit** AmEx, DC, Disc, MC, V. **Map** p252 G5 ❺

IndeBleu. *See p115*.

This upscale brasserie features some of the finest fish in the region and one of Washington's best wine lists. The bar area is lively, with nightly jazz piano/ bass, and roomy enough to accommodate bar-side nibbling. Although seafood is the menu's focus, the meaty items carry their weight. Oyster lovers, take note: the raw bar gets top marks.

French

Marcel's
2401 Pennsylvania Avenue, NW, between 24th & 25th Streets (1-202 296 1166/www.marcelsdc.com). Foggy Bottom-GWU Metro. **Open** 5.30-10pm Mon-Thur; 5.30-11pm Fri, Sat; 5.30-9.30pm Sun. **Main courses** $13-$28. **Credit** AmEx, DC, MC, V. **Map** p252 F5 ❻
Marcel's is the kind of restaurant that you'd expect to find on Pennsylvania Avenue: exquisite food, beautifully served in a sumptuous dining room by adept professionals. Chef Robert Wiedmaier's Flemish-inflected French fare manages the classical balance of taste and textures: subtle versus sharp-flavoured, savoury versus sweet, generous versus leaving you wanting more. Boudin blanc and rack of lamb are exemplary, and a gratin of mussels is an essay on the varieties of sensation contained within the words salty, rich and intense. The servers get extra points for friendliness: even if you're not one of the place's traditional, old-money clients, they'll still treat you as if you were.

Eat, Drink, Shop

FOR OFFICE USE ONLY

Indian

Bombay Club

815 Connecticut Avenue, NW, between H & I Streets (1-202 659 3727/www.bombayclubdc.com). Farragut West or Farragut North Metro. **Open** 11.30am-2.30pm, 6-10.30pm Mon-Thur; 11.30am-2.30pm, 6-11pm Fri; 6-11pm Sat; 11.30am-2.30pm, 5.30-9pm Sun. **Main courses** $13-$19. *Set brunch* $18.50. **Credit** AmEx, DC, MC, V. **Map** p252 H5 ❼

Bombay Club evokes not the multihued Mumbai of today but India in the time of the Raj, when English gentlemen could sit in restrained, masculine dining rooms and, presumably, cherry-pick the best of the subcontinent's cuisine. Decorous waiters in penguin suits warn against the supposed heat of a non-threatening lamb vindaloo (thali platters, tandoori meats and Goan curries are also on offer); the menu offers discreet explanations of the various regional styles. A favourite of the Clintons, the place wafts power and privilege along with the scent of samosas.

Nirvana

1810 K Street, NW, between 18th & 19th Streets (1-202 223 5043/www.dcnirvana.com). Farragut West Metro. **Open** 11.30am-3pm, 5-9pm Mon-Thur; 11.30am-3pm, 5-10pm Fri; noon-3pm, 5-10pm Sat. **Main courses** $8-$12. **Credit** AmEx, Disc, MC, V. **Map** p252 G5 ❽

You can eat in a hurry and on the cheap at Nirvana's lunchtime vegetarian buffet – a welcome option on expense-account K Street – but it's the variety and quality of the food that constitute the place's main attraction. Buffet themes change daily, showcasing many of India's regional cuisines in turn. The à la carte menu offers many atypical items – hot and cold street snacks, stuffed peppers, unusual breads – as well as the full complement of standards. The decor is festive multi-coloured tables plopped down in an otherwise austere setting; service is efficient.

Southern

Vidalia

1990 M Street, NW, between 19th & 20th Streets (1-202 659 1990/www.vidaliadc.com). Dupont Circle Metro. **Open** 11.30am-2.30pm, 5.30-10pm Mon-Thur; 11.30am-2.30pm, 5.30-10.30pm Fri; 5.30-10.30pm Sat; 5.30-10pm Sun. **Main courses** $12-$18 lunch; $18-$29 dinner. **Credit** AmEx, DC, Disc, MC, V. **Map** p250 G5 ❾

Onions are much in evidence in the hushed, golden dining room of Vidalia, which itself is named after the Southern sweet variety. You'll find them in a spread for the complimentary bread, in a rich hot soup made with duck broth and in the discreet artwork adorning the walls. But the restaurant's raison d'être is neither single-ingredient schtick nor even strictly Southern cooking; it proudly proclaims its cuisine to be 'American regional'. There are many dishes in which pork is the star player – a cassoulet boasts several varieties – and grits and oysters are likely suspects on winter menus.

American

DC Coast

Tower Building, 1401 K Street, NW, at 14th Street (1-202 216 5988/www.dccoast.com). McPherson Square Metro. **Open** 11.30am-2.30pm, 5.30-10.30pm Mon-Thur; 11.30am-2.30pm, 5.30-11pm Fri; 5.30-11pm Sat. **Main courses** $14-$19 lunch; $16-$28 dinner. **Credit** AmEx, MC, V. **Map** p252 H5 ❿

The 'coast' of the name refers not just to the Atlantic but also the West and Gulf Coasts. It's a pretty wide net to cast, but the brains behind DC Coast – and they are brains, the creators of several of Washington's hottest dining spots – have found a way to integrate Southern, Southwestern and even Pacific Rim influences on the menu in their cavernous, well-appointed dining room. Soy sauce and tabasco share space in the kitchen; bok choy and bacon both grace the tables. The busy, businessy crowd eats it all up with gusto.

Fish

Oceanaire Seafood Room

1201 F Street, NW, at 12th Street (1-202 347 2277/ www.oceanaireseafoodroom.com). Metro Center Metro. **Open** 11.30am-10pm Mon-Thur; 11.30am-11pm Fri, Sat; 5-9pm Sun. **Main courses** $13-$19. **Credit** AmEx, DC, Disc, MC, V. **Map** p252 H6 ⓫

Don't be surprised if you spot senators and lobbyists making back-room deals at this see-and-be-seen spot for Washington's power set. Seafood is given steakhouse treatment – in other words, served in huge portions – in this art deco-styled dining room that feels like an ocean liner. The menu changes daily, reflecting availability and seasonality of the goods. Ever tried Arctic char? Now's your chance. Or sample oysters, clams, crab and lobster at the raw bar. And for dessert? Go for the baked Alaska.

French/Indian fusion

IndeBleu

707 G Street, NW, at 7th Street (1-202 333 2538/ www.bleu.com/indebleu). Gallery Place-Chinatown Metro. **Open** 11.30am-1.15pm Mon-Fri; 5pm-2am Mon-Thur, Sun; 5pm-3am Fri-Sat. **Main courses** $25-$39. **Credit** AmEx, Disc, MC, V. **Map** p253 J5 ⓬

A newcomer to Washington's ultra-expensive dining scene, IndeBleu combines the flavours of India and France. For example: veal tenderloin with cardamom-flavoured sweetbreads and tandoori rack of lamb, served with a ragout of green lentils. The result, critics have declared, far surpasses most fusion restaurants. The stylish and sumptuous decor makes IndeBleu worth visiting; if you're not prepared to splurge out on a full dinner, then consider stopping by the lounge for a drink. **Photo** *p113.*

Eat, Drink, Shop

Latin/Caribbean

Ceiba

701 14th Street, NW, at G Street (1-202 393 3983/ www.ceibarestaurant.com). Metro Center Metro. **Open** 11.30am-2.30pm, 5.30-10.30pm Mon-Fri; 5.30-11pm Sat. **Main courses** $16-$27. **Credit** AmEx, DC, Disc, MC, V. **Map** p252 H5 ⓭

Brightly coloured murals, discreetly placed, are about the only whimsical touches in Ceiba's majestic space, much frequented by expense-account diners. Otherwise, the look is sleek, modern neutrals, with furniture from Brazil and stone and tiles from Yucatan. The cuisine, though, is an abundance of invention, with Latin-American and Caribbean food as inspiration. There's a lot of seafood – conch chowder, crab fritters, several variants on seviche – as well as Cuban pork sandwiches and black bean soup. It's hearty rather than homey food, as studied as its slick presentation.

Mediterranean

Zaytinya

Pepco Building, 701 Ninth Street, NW, at G Street (1-202 638 0800/www.zaytinya.com). Gallery Place-Chinatown Metro. **Open** 11.30am-10pm Mon, Sun; 11.30am-11.30pm Tue-Thur; 11.30am-midnight Fri, Sat. **Main courses** $4-$12. **Credit** AmEx, DC, Disc, MC, V. **Map** p253 J5 ⓮

With a stunning white-and-blue interior, this Penn Quarter hot-spot finds inspiration in Greece, Turkey and Lebanon. Trendy Zaytinya is one of Washington's most popular restaurants, and a no reservations policy keeps the spacious bar packed. Once parties are seated, cones of piping hot bread arrive, and the fun begins. The menu of 60-plus meze dishes is kind to both vegetarians and carnivores.

Our tips? Cabbage dolades or Santorini fava beans to start, followed by braised lamb shank with eggplant purée. Finish with Turkish Delight, an aptly named sundae of walnut ice-cream, yoghurt mousse, honey and orange-caramel sauce.

Pizza/American

Matchbox

713 H Street, NW, at 7th Street (1-202 289 4441/ www.matchboxdc.com). Gallery Place/Chinatown Metro. **Open** 11am-midnight Mon-Fri; noon-midnight Sat. **Main courses** $12-$25. **Credit** AmEx, Disc, MC, V. **Map** p253 J5 ⓯

Aptly named, this narrow, three-storey restaurant is always packed. Why? Three reasons: the thin-crust pizzas that come out of Matchbox's brick oven; the platters of mini-hamburgers, and the casual, fun atmosphere. In the mood for something a little fancier? Matchbox also serves traditional bistro dishes like pork tenderloin, rockfish and duck.

Southern

Capital Q

707 H Street, NW, at Seventh Street (1-202 347 8396/www.capitalqbbq.com). Gallery Place-Chinatown Metro. **Open** 11am-9pm Mon-Wed; 11am-midnight Thu-Sat. **Main courses** $8-$10. **Credit** ($15 minimum) AmEx, MC, V. **Map** p253 J5 ⓰

The down-home vibe of this Texas-style barbecue joint – with rustic walls, classic rock and the side dishes served out of big vats, like at a church picnic – makes it an appealing alternative in a neighbourhood clotted with chain restaurants. You decide on your meat – brisket or short ribs, sausage, pulled pork or chicken – pick sandwich or platter, and load up on sides. The Texas caviar (a black-eyed-pea salad) is a nice counterpoint to all the heat and meat.

Rasika. *See p117.*

Georgia Brown's

950 15th Street, NW, between I & K Streets (1-202 393 4499/www.gbrowns.com). McPherson Square Metro. **Open** 11.30am-10pm Mon-Thur; 11.30am-11pm Fri; 5pm-11pm Sat; 10am-2.30pm, 5.30-10pm Sun. **Main courses** $15-$22. **Set brunch** $32.95, $21.95 under-12s. **Credit** AmEx, DC, Disc, MC, V. **Map** p252 H5 **⑰**

One of DC's earliest and best attempts to upscale Low Country cooking, Georgia Brown's makes the case for saying that Washington is, in fact, a Southern city. Soul music plays softly in the warm-wood dining room; cornbread and dense, creamy biscuits, served with sweet butter, accompany the entrées. Fried green tomatoes, a showpiece of the restaurant, involve thin slices of the vegetable layered with herbed cream cheese, breaded, and laced with a spicy remoulade. In another twist on tradition, there are even a few decent vegetarian options. Beloved of local politicos, the restaurant serves power lunches, dinners, and a Sunday jazz brunch.

Tex-Mex

Austin Grill

750 E Street, NW, at 8th Street (1-202 393 3776/ www.austingrill.com). Gallery Place-Chinatown or Archives Navy-Memorial Metro. **Open** 11am-10pm Mon-Thur; 11am-11pm Fri, Sat; 11am-9pm Sun. **Main courses** $9-$18. **Credit** AmEx, DC, Disc, MC, V. **Map** p253 J6 **⑱**

The Tex-Mex cousin of Jaleo (*see below*), located next door, Austin Grill fills the gap between upscale dining and fast-food munching. It's popular with a variety of diners – families who don't want to deal with high-maintenance restaurants and singles who are looking for chow that doesn't interrupt meeting potential suitors. There are plenty of tequilas to sample and everything comes with chips and salsa. **Other locations**: throughout the city.

Penn Quarter

Cafés & coffeehouses

Footnotes

Olsson's Books & Records, 418 Seventh Street, NW, between D & E Streets (1-202 638 7610/www.foot notescafe.com). Archives-Navy Memorial or Gallery Place-Chinatown Metro. **Open** 9am-8pm Mon-Fri; 10am-8pm Sat; noon-7.30pm Sun. **Main courses** $5-$10. **Credit** AmEx, MC, V. **Map** p253 J6 **⑲**

A halfway point on the tourist march down Seventh Street from Gallery Place to the Mall, Footnotes often serves as much a refuge as a restaurant. Adjoining a branch of the Olsson's bookstore chain, the tiny café serves sandwiches, salads, coffee and tea, along with smoothies, beer and wine. A little preciousness in the naming of dishes is forgivable, if only because the couches are comfortable – and the staff seem disinclined to disturb lingerers. There's a nice selection of pastries, too.

Indian

Rasika

633 D Street, NW, between 6th & 7th Streets (1-202 637 1222/www.rasikarestaurant.com). Archives-Navy Memorial Metro. **Open** 11.30am-2.30pm, 5.30pm-10.30pm Mon-Thur; 11.30am-2.30pm, 5.30pm-11pm Fri; 5.30pm-11pm Sat. **Main courses** *Lunch* $7-$22; *Dinner* $8-$28. **Credit** AmEx, Disc, MC, V. **Map** p253 J6 **⑳**

When was the last time you dined at an Indian restaurant with a sommelier? Get ready for Rasika, one of the most exciting restaurants to open in Washington in years. The newest sibling to the Bardeo restaurant family (Ardeo, Bombay Club, *see p115*, Oval Room), Rasika is under the creative eye of Vikram Sunderam, who ran the kitchen at London's Bombay Brasserie for 14 years. Here, Sunderam is giving Washington its upscale Indian due. Grouped into categories including 'chaat', 'tawa', and 'tandoor', the menu covers much ground, with ample choices for both vegetarians and carnivores. Whatever you do, try the palak chaat, a signature dish of crispy baby spinach leaves dressed with yoghurt that melts on the tongue. **Photo** *p116*.

Latin

Café Atlántico

405 Eïghth Street, NW, at D Street (1-202 393 0812/www.cafeatlantico.com). Archives-Navy Memorial or Gallery Place-Chinatown Metro. **Open** 11.30am-2.30pm, 5-10pm Mon-Thur, Sun; 11.30am-2.30pm, 5-11pm Fri, Sat. **Main courses** $19-$25. **Credit** AmEx, Disc, MC, V. **Map** p253 J6 **㉑**

José Andrés' nuevo latino cuisine goes beyond the predictable upscaling of tacos, introducing innovative ingredients – *huitlacoche*, or corn fungus, and corn nut powder – and combinations thereof on a menu as whimsical as the decor of his three-level restaurant. The most well known and recognisable Latino of Café Atlántico's dishes is the popular guacamole, made to order tableside; toward the other end of the spectrum is shrimp with candied pumpkin seeds and 'lime air'. At the six-seat restaurant-within-a-restaurant Minibar – reservations well in advance are essential – diners are presented, sometimes spoon-fed, 30-odd courses of food essences and spritzes and foams. A slightly more down-to-earth experience is available at weekends, when the restaurant serves 'Latino dim sum'.

Spanish

Jaleo

480 Seventh Street, NW, at E Street (1-202 628 7949/www.jaleo.com). Gallery Place-Chinatown or Archives Navy-Memorial Metro. **Open** 11.30am-10pm Mon, Sun; 11.30am-11.30pm Tue-Thur; 11.30am-midnight Fri, Sat. **Tapas** $3-$8. **Main courses** $10-$15. **Credit** AmEx, DC, Disc, MC, V. **Map** p253 J6 **㉒**

Eat, Drink, Shop

With Jose Andres (Café Atlántico, see p117;Zaytinya, see p116) at the helm, Jaleo focuses on tapas: garlic shrimp, chorizo with garlic mash, salads of apple and manchego cheese and marinated mushrooms – to name just a few. Don't miss the date and bacon fritters or the patatas bravas, a steaming hot bowl of potatoes with a spicy sauce. **Other locations**: 7271 Woodmont Avenue, Bethesda, MD (1-301 913 0003); 2250A Crystal Drive, Arlington, VA (1-703 413 8181).

Judiciary Square area

Asian

Full Kee
509 H Street, NW, between Fifth & Sixth Streets (1-202 371 2233). Gallery Place-Chinatown Metro. **Open** 11am-1am Mon-Thur, Sun; 11am-2am Fri, Sat. **Main courses** $5-$16. **No credit cards**. **Map** p253 J5 **㉓**
One of several old-school joints still hanging on in an increasingly gentrified Chinatown, Full Kee meets all the criteria for a Chinese-food snob: poultry hanging in the window, menu additions posted on the walls on brightly coloured paper, a largely Asian clientele. Short on luxury, the place is long on food options, with plenty of choices for adventurous eaters of both meat and vegetables. DC foodies rave about Full Kee's noodle soups. The place now serves beer, but it has yet to change another longstanding policy: no credit cards.

Fish

DC's seafood lovers are looking forward to the return of **Johnny's Half Shell**, which was in the process of moving to a new address (400 North Capitol Street, NW, at Louisiana Avenue) at the time of writing. Johnny's is known for its super high-grade ingredients, from oysters on the half shell to grilled sea scallops, prepared to simple, gimmick-free perfection.

French

Bistro Bis
Hotel George, 15 E Street, NW, between North Capitol Street & New Jersey Avenue (1-202 661 2700/www.bistrobis.com). Union Station or Judiciary Square Metro. **Open** 7-10am, 11.30am-2.30pm, 5.30-10.30pm daily. **Main courses** $7-$18 brunch; $13-$15 lunch; $17-$22 dinner. **Credit** AmEx, DC, Disc, MC, V. **Map** p253 K6 **㉔**
A soigné hotel restaurant within walking distance of the Capitol and Union Station, Bistro Bis serves the gamut of French food, from mussels and *pommes frites* to complicated preparations and composed plates. Tourists rub elbows with the occasional celebrity, onion soup with beef bourguignon. Of-the-moment design firm Adamstein & Demetriou created the decor, a riff on the classic brasserie: the

dining room features warm woods, tile floors and frosted glass; and the front room, which opens on to a patio with more tables, boasts a zinc-topped bar. Weekend brunch, which adds egg dishes and beef-based bloody Marys to the mix, is justly popular.

Dupont Circle

Asian

Raku
1900 Q Street, NW, at 19th Street (1-202 265 7258). Dupont Circle Metro. **Open** 11.30am-10pm Mon-Thur, Sun; 11.30am-11pm Fri, Sat. **Main courses** $10-$13.50. **Credit** AmEx, MC, V. **Map** p250 G4 **㉕**
Choosing between Thai, Japanese, Korean or Chinese restaurants can be a bit difficult. But at Raku, you don't have to. The menu includes staples from all four national cuisines, including fried egg rolls, sushi (try the crunchy tuna roll), and pad Thai. If you feel like trying something new, go for the tamarind guava BBQ ribs or the golden chicken crêpe salad. Raku bills itself as an 'Asian diner'. The atmosphere inside is appropriately frenetic, while the food is simple and satisfying. **Other locations**: 7240 Woodmont Avenue, at Elm Street, Bethesda (1-301 718 8680).

Sushi Taro
1503 17th Street, NW, at P Street (1-202 462 8999/ www.sushitaro.com). Dupont Circle Metro. **Open** 11.30am-2pm, 5.30-10pm Mon-Thur; 11.30am-2pm, 5.30-10.30pm Fri; 5.30-10.30pm Sat. **Main courses** $7-$45. **Credit** AmEx, DC, Disc, MC, V. **Map** p250 H4 **㉖**
Located above a drugstore on the strip of 17th Street NW that is the centre of gay life in DC, Sushi Taro is large, informal and fun. There are low tables for traditional Japanese dining, but only a few; most of the diners seem to come for big platters of sushi and sashimi, delivered from the long bar by servers in Hawaiian shirts. There are relatively few exotic fish on offer – though of course the daily sampler changes according to what's available – but there are also refreshingly few novelty rolls. Tables are close together, and the restaurant can get loud when it's crowded – which is often; the place is popular.

Thaiphoon
2011 S Street, NW, between 20th Street & Connecticut Avenue (1-202 667 3505/www. thaiphoon.com). Dupont Circle Metro. **Open** 11.30am-10.30pm Mon-Thur, Sun; 11.30am-11pm Fri, Sat. **Main courses** $9-$12. **Credit** MC, V. **Map** p250 G4 **㉗**
Shiny stainless steel and a striking front window invite you to be part of the buzz at this bright, bustling place. The menu is lengthy, covering many Thai classics, from papaya salad to fish steamed in banana leaves; the presentation is pretty and the flavours freshly assertive. Try the Thai iced coffee for dessert. Vegetarians are well fed here.

Cafés & coffeehouses

Teaism

*2009 R Street, NW, at Connecticut Avenue (1-202
667 3827/www.teaism.com). Dupont Circle Metro.*
Open 8am-10pm Mon-Thur; 8am-11pm Fri; 9am-
11pm Sat; 9am-10pm Sun. **Credit** AmEx, MC, V.
Map p250 G4 ㉓
Freshly baked nan, salty oat cookies and Thai chick-
en curry are on offer at this café-style oasis from the
bustle of urban living. Whether you stop off for a
cup of chai or a bento box, you'll feel ready to pound
the pavement once again. In warm weather, try the
iced Moroccan mint tea; there's nothing more
refreshing. The spacious Eighth Street branch, with
its downstairs hideout, has a calmer vibe.
Other locations: 800 Connecticut Avenue,
NW, at H Street, Downtown (1-202 835 2233);
400 Eighth Street, NW, at D Street, Penn Quarter
(1-202 638 6010).

Contemporary American

Afterwords Cafe

*1517 Connecticut Avenue, NW, at Q Street (1-202
387 1462/www.kramers.com). Dupont Circle Metro.*
Open 7.30am-1am Mon-Thur; 7.30am Fri-1am Mon
continuously. **Main courses** $9-$15. **Credit** AmEx,
Disc, MC, V. **Map** p250 G4 ㉔
The best place in DC for a first date – you meet in
the adjoining Kramerbooks and rejoice or despair at
your new friend's taste in literature – Afterwords
Café tries to be all things to all people. Bustling and
capacious, the glass-enclosed dining room serves
food from morning until late night, including
'sharezies' – make-your-own appetiser platters,
ambitious New American dinners with suggested
wine or beer pairings, and decadent desserts. You
and your date are sure to find common ground somewhere on the menu. And when you've got to know
each other better, you can return for Afterwords'
hearty weekend brunch.

Komi

*1509 17th Street, NW, between P & Q Streets
(1-202 332 9200). Dupont Circle Metro.* **Open**
11.30am-3pm, 5.30-10pm Mon-Thur; 11.30am-3pm,
5.30-11pm Fri, Sat. **Main courses** $10-$17. **Credit**
AmEx, MC, V. **Map** p250 H4 ㉚
Johnny Monis is gathering quite a following for himself in his tiny Dupont Circle restaurant. Komi's low-
key dining room, a straight shot from front window
to kitchen window, is home to some of the most
adventurous eating in the city; the twentysomething
chef is essaying New American cuisine with nods to
his Mediterranean heritage and whatever else
strikes his fancy. But neither he nor his staff of per-
sonable, fashionable servers is lacking in discipline;
just as his talent is for showcasing unusual ingredients without showboating, theirs is for putting
guests at ease with the ever-changing menu. Foodies
will be talking about Monis's suckling pig for years.

Hank's Oyster Bar. See p120.

Eat, Drink, Shop

LeftBank. *See p123.*

Tabard Inn

1739 N Street, NW, between 17th & 18th Streets (1-202 833 2668/www.tabardinn.com). Dupont Circle Metro. **Open** 7-10am, 11.30am-2.30pm, 6-10pm Mon-Thur; 7-10am, 11.30am-2.30pm, 6-10.30pm Fri; 8-10am, 11am-2.30pm, 6-10.30pm Sat; 8-9.30am, 10.30am-2.30pm, 6-10pm Sun. **Main courses** $3-$8 breakfast; $5-$15 brunch; $9-$15 lunch; $18-$28 dinner. **Credit** AmEx, DC, MC, V. **Map** p250 G4 ③①

Tucked at the back of a 19th-century brownstone, home to a family-run hotel (*see p51*), the Tabard is an eclectic and shamelessly romantic destination. Dine in the lounge in front of the fireplace, in the garden under the shade of a silk parachute, or in the private dining room. The menu favours crisp and local ingredients: fried oysters top a salad of corn and baby spinach. Salmon and trout, both housesmoked, are an excellent standby. Sunday's crowds (seriously, make reservations far in advance) brunch on just-made doughnuts and eggs Benedict.

Fish

Hank's Oyster Bar

1624 Q Street, NW, between Church and 16th Streets, Dupont Circle (1-202 462 4265/www.hanksdc.com). Dupont Circle Metro. **Open** 5.30-10pm Mon, Tue; 5.30-11pm Wed-Fri; 11am-3pm, 5.30-11pm Sat; 11am-3pm Sun. **Main courses** $6-$18. **Credit** AmEx, Disc, MC, V. **Map** p250 H4 ③②

The east side of Dupont Circle has long needed an injection of new restaurant life, so when chef Jamie Leeds opened Hank's Oyster Bar in an old pizza joint that had seen better days, there was a sound of welcomed relief from local gourmets. Offering a daily rotation of oysters on the half shell, Hank's has become a serious contender among Washington raw bar destinations. For this reason alone, a visit is worthwhile. But there are lots of other reasons to hit this popular neighbourhood spot with a café feel. Here, you can make a meal of small plates (garlic steamed mussels, popcorn shrimp and calamari, peel

'n' eat shrimp) or dive right into a larger plate, surf or turf. To wit, Leeds serves up a daily 'Meat and Two' specials, the 'two' meaning side dishes (including seasonal veg, macaroni and cheese, buttermilk onion rings). The only thing that's missing is dessert, the reason for the parting gift of dark chocolate chunks delivered with the bill. **Photo** *p119.*

Indian

Heritage India

1337 Connecticut Avenue, NW, between N Street & Dupont Circle, Dupont Circle (1-202 331 1414/www.heritageindia.biz). Dupont Circle Metro. **Open** 11.30am-2.30pm, 5.30-10.30pm Mon-Fri; 5.30-11pm Sat; 5.30-10.30pm Sun. **Main courses** $8-$22. **Credit** AmEx, Disc, MC, V. **Map** p250 G4 ③③

Top-quality, complex-flavoured Indian food (the chef once plied his trade at Bombay Club) and an interesting wine list, without the worry of getting overly dressed up. Vegetarians love this place, where meatless dishes make up about a third of the menu – including the fabulous begumi khazana, a feast served on a silver platter.

Other locations: 2400 Wisconsin Avenue, NW, at Calvert Street, Glover Park (1-202 333 3120).

Italian

Obelisk

2029 P Street, NW, between 20th & 21st Streets (1-202 872 1180). Dupont Circle Metro. **Open** 6-10pm Tue-Sat. **Set dinner** $60. **Credit** DC, MC, V. **Map** p250 G4 ③④

The menu changes constantly at Peter Pastan's prix-fixe-only, reservations-required townhouse, depending on what's fresh and what catches the chef's fancy. But you can always count on an array of antipasti; pasta, meat, cheese and dessert courses; and exemplary service. Squab makes regular appearances – it's worth the awkwardness of dealing with the tiny bones – as do seasonal vegetables and fish thats come right from the water. Nominally Italian, the cooking is both catholic and classical. The wine list is extensive, the breads house-made, the atmosphere unpretentious.

Pizzeria Paradiso

2029 P Street, NW, between 20th & 21st Streets (1-202 223 1245/www.eatyourpizza.com). Dupont Circle Metro. **Open** 11.30am-11pm Mon-Thur; 11.30am-midnight Fri; 11am-midnight Sat; noon-10pm Sun. **Main courses** $9-$17. **Credit** DC, MC, V. **Map** p250 G4 ㉟

Good quality, wood-oven pizza that keeps locals coming back for more. Expect to wait for a table, even at the larger Georgetown location. The salad of white beans and tuna, plus the antipasto plate of salami and Italian cheeses, are worth considering if pizza is not your thing. But do try the effervescent lemonade. All in all, a fun excursion.
Other locations: 3282 M Street, NW, between Potomac & 33rd Streets, Georgetown (1-202 337 1245).

Sette Osteria

1666 Connecticut Avenue, NW, at R Street (1-202 483 3070/www.setteosteria.com). Dupont Circle Metro. **Open** 11.30am-1am Mon-Thur; 11.30am-2am Fri, Sat; 11.30am-midnight Sun. **Main courses** $10-$19. **Credit** AmEx, Disc, MC, Visa. **Map** p250 G4 ㊱

From wood-fired pizzas to roasted veal with herbs, this stylish Dupont Circle restaurant serves excellent (and affordable) Neapolitan fare. The pastas are especially good; try gnocchi alla Sorrentina (with tomato, mozzarella and basil) or baked lasagna. In warm weather, Sette's large outdoor seating area comes into its own as an arena for people-watching, while in winter, the indoors is cosy.

Tex-Mex

Lauriol Plaza

1835 18th Street, NW, at T Street (1-202 387 0035/www.lauriolplaza.com). Dupont Circle Metro. **Open** 11.30am-11pm Mon-Thur, Sun; 11.30am-midnight Fri, Sat. **Main courses** $7.50-$17.95 brunch; $7-$19 dinner. **Credit** AmEx, DC, Disc, MC, V. **Map** p250 G3 ㊲

This has to be DC's most popular restaurant: even with a capacity for up to 350 diners in its two storeys (plus rooftop), the line for a table often spills over on to the sidewalk. Food is reasonably priced Tex-Mex fare. From Margaritas and salsa, to Mexican staples like enchiladas and fajitas, to specialties from Peru, Cuba and elsewhere, there's a little of everything for the Latin food fan, and the scene is always jumping.

Thai

The Regent

1910 18th Street, NW, between Florida Avenue and T Street (1-202 232 1781/www.regentthai.com). Dupont Circle Metro. **Open** 11.30am-3pm, 5-10pm Mon-Thur; 11.30am-3pm, 5-11pm Fri; noon-3pm, 5-11pm Sat; 5pm-10pm Sun. **Main courses** $11-$16. **Credit** AmEx, Disc, MC, V. **Map** p250 G3 ㊳

This newcomer is slightly dressier and more refined (and also somewhat more expensive) than most of DC's other Thai restaurants. The flavours – lots of coconut milk, green and red curry, lemongrass and chilli paste – are perfectly balanced, and the setting is oh-so-serene, with large wood carvings and quiet fountains. Try the panang chicken, green curry and pad eggplant, which comes in a spicy black bean sauce. For dessert, the mango sticky rice is unbeatable.

Adams Morgan

American

The Diner

2453 18th Street, NW, between Kalorama & Columbia Roads (1-202 232 8800). Dupont Circle Metro then 42 bus or Woodley Park-Zoo/Adams Morgan Metro. **Open** 24hrs daily. **Main courses** $4-$18. **Credit** MC, V. **Map** p250 G3 ㊴

Tryst. *See p123.*

Tabaq Bistro. *See p127.*

One of DC's few 24-hour joints, the Diner is brought to you by the same folks who own coffee lounge Tryst (*see below*) just two doors away. The Diner is constantly packed with neighbourhood hipsters and night owls. True to its name, there's home-style chow (and more), but we don't think it's the food that keeps people going back for more. It's those long counters, great for flirting, sipping coffee and playing with your food behind the Sunday paper.

LeftBank

2424 18th Street, NW, between Belmont & Columbia Roads (1-202 464 2100/www.leftbankdc.com). Dupont Circle Metro then 42 bus or Woodley Park-Zoo/Adams Morgan Metro. **Open** 7am-2am Mon-Thur, Sun; 7am-3am Fri, Sat. **Main courses** $6-$18. **Credit** AmEx, Disc, MC, V. **Map** p250 G3 ⓴

A trendy interior – concrete floor, mod furniture, giant U-shaped bar – and young clientele conspire to make LeftBank feel like the place to be in Adams Morgan, whether late on a Saturday night or in the middle of a working day. The place is huge, and so is the menu – there are plates small and large for dinner, omelettes and pancakes for weekend brunch, even sushi in the evenings. And if you happen to wander inside in the middle of an afternoon's sightseeing, you won't be denied a chance to order from the lunch menu. Happy hour is, of course, prime time, especially on spring nights, when the storefront opens up to the lively street scene. **Photo** *p120.*

Cafés & coffeehouses

Tryst

2459 18th Street, NW, between Belmont & Columbia Roads (1-202 232 5500/www.trystdc.com). Dupont Circle Metro then 42 bus, or Woodley Park-Zoo/Adams Morgan Metro. **Open** 6.30am-2am Mon-Thur; 6.30am-3am Fri, Sat; 7am-2am Sun. **Credit** AmEx, Disc, MC, V. **Map** p250 G2/3 ㉛

Not quite a club, a bar, or even a coffeehouse for that matter, Tryst makes a great community living room. Overstuffed chairs, comfy sofas and country-style kitchen tables – not to mention the free wireless Internet access – create a hip, relaxed vibe without feeling collegiate. If you want to drink alcohol, fine. If not, the coffee, served in enormous mugs, is very good. There are also a dozen sandwiches (half of which are vegetarian; we recommend the Alisha, a houmous-and-veggie combo on thick farm bread) and several small plates for nibbling. **Photo** *p121.*

Cajun/Creole

Bardia's

2412 18th Street, NW, at Belmont Road (1-202 234 0420). Dupont Circle Metro then 42 bus or Woodley Park-Zoo/Adams Morgan Metro. **Open** 11am-10pm Mon-Fri; 10am-10pm Sat, Sun. **Main courses** $7-$14. **Credit** AmEx, MC, V. **Map** p250 G3 ㊷

Perry's. *See p125.*

Eat, Drink, Shop

There really is a Bardia – he's here, most days, making sure the shrimp étouffée at his tiny restaurant has that pleasantly burnt flavour that serves to distinguish it from the lesser versions. Bardia's New Orleans specialities – gumbo, jambalaya, po'boys, and the like – along with the egg dishes that are served all day long account for most, but not all, of the charm at his New Orleans Café. The rest of the pleasure is supplied by sitting at the window table, whiling away the afternoon and taking in the street scene. If you play your cards right, Bardia may even bring you some beignets.

Contemporary

Cashion's Eat Place

1819 Columbia Road, NW, between Biltmore Street & Mintwood Place, Adams Morgan (1-202 797 1819/www.cashionseatplace.com). Dupont Circle Metro then 42 bus or Woodley Park-Zoo/Adams Morgan Metro then 90, 92, 93, L2 bus. **Open** 5.30-10pm Tue; 5.30-11pm Wed-Sat; 11.30am-2.30pm, 5.30-10pm Sun. **Main courses** $19-$30. **Credit** MC, V. **Map** p250 G3 ❹❸

Often recognised as one of the very best chefs in the region, Ann Cashion puts on a good show, with classic food to match her classic yet informal dining room. With John Fulchino in charge of front of house and the master of the wine list they make for an exciting team of restaurateurs. The menu itself is seasonal – in fact, it's decided daily, based on what Cashion's local purveyors have to hand and what she fancies cooking. This does mean, unfortunately, that the food can be somewhat hit-or-miss, but it's range is from (at worst) the above average to the truly outstanding. There's room at the bar for eating, but if you want a table, be sure to book. In warm months, the outdoor seating area is festive.

Upscale but not uptight

It can hardly be said that Washington is a city lacking in formality. If you want to dress up for a big, splashy fine-dining experience, there are plenty of restaurants that can cater to you. (Most of the downtown name restaurants adhere to a 'business casual' dress code – and that means serious business.) But if you've arrived in town without your best duds – or want to show that you're a slick urbanite, not a preening peacock – there are still plenty of excellent choices. There's no reason you can't be treated like a prince, and eat some of the best food in town, in surroundings and clothes that are comfortable and fun.

One of the city's best-orchestrated dinner experiences is at **Obelisk** (*see p120*), an unassuming walkup a stone's throw from Dupont Circle. The uncostumed servers seat you promptly and immediately begin plying you with treats; a steady march of antipasti is followed by a stately procession of courses until you look at your watch and realise you've made an evening of it. **Komi** (*see p119*), a similarly understated space with equally lofty culinary ambitions, is patrolled by fresh-faced staff whose enthusiasm for the food is infectious. It's all very up to the minute, and you get a homemade lollipop at the end.

The Adams Morgan neighbourhood is home to heaps of fun restaurants, but only **Cashion's Eat Place** (*see above, pictured right*) is both ambitious enough that it consistently makes top-10 lists and unpretentious enough that you can read a newspaper at the bar. Unless you have to, though, skip the reading material

– Cashion's bartenders are among the friendliest to be found anywhere in town.

Cleveland Park's **Palena** (*see p130*) manages a clever trick: the chef has turned his bar area into the 'Palena Café', serving hauted-up versions of American fast food. It's ostentatiously casual – though the decor is easily the equal of the main dining room's. And so is the cooking: you can have any of the chef's first-rate Italian offerings at the bar, without making a reservation. In fact, reservations aren't accepted in the café – you may need to go early to beat the crowd.

Fusion

Perry's

1811 Columbia Road, NW, at Biltmore Street (1-202 234 6218/www.perrysadamsmorgan.com). Dupont Circle Metro then 42 bus or Woodley Park-Zoo/ Adams Morgan Metro then 90, 92, 93, L2 bus. **Open** 5.30-10.15pm Mon-Thur; 5.30-11.30pm Fri, Sat; 10.30am-2.30pm, 5.30-10.15pm Sun. **Main courses** $17-$22. *Set brunch* $22.95. **Credit** AmEx, Disc, MC, V. **Map** p250 G2/3 **44**

Stand smack in the middle of Adams Morgan Party Central, the intersection of 18th Street and Columbia Road, NW (and the traffic is so gridlocked on weekend nights that you can often do so without any significant risk to either life or limb), and you'll see the illuminated rooftop of Perry's, hangout of beautiful people and their attendant wannabes. The largely twentysomething crowd is attracted not just to the lights – and the lively scene under them – but to the array of well-executed sushi prepared downstairs, where a classic wood-panelled dining room offers a more sedate setting for unwinding. Along with sushi, the menu features a short list of New American starters and entrées, with such favorites as heirloom tomatoes in season, lamb chops with mint jelly, and duck breast with polenta. **Photo** *p123.*

Middle Eastern

Amsterdam Falafelshop

2425 18th Street, NW, at Belmont Road (1-202 234 1969/falafelshop.com). Dupont Circle Metro then 42 bus or Woodley Park-Zoo/Adams Morgan Metro. **Open** 11am-midnight Mon, Sun; 11am-2.30am Tue, Wed; 11am-3am Thur; 11am-4am Fri, Sat. **Main courses** $3.50-$7. **No credit cards**. **Map** p250 G3 **45**

This is the perfect place for a quick bite, whether it's two in the afternoon or two in the morning (although beware the long, hungry lines that form in the early hours). The choices at the counter are simplicity itself: small or large? Wholewheat pitta or white? Fries with that? (Say yes – they're the best in town.) You'll face tougher decisions at the extensive toppings bar, which includes houmous, grilled eggplant (aubergine), marinated cucumber, and more – much more, sadly, than can fit in one pitta. This might be the best deal in town.

Logan Circle

Asian

Rice

1608 14th Street, NW, between Q & Corcoran Streets (1-202 234 2400/www.ricerestaurant.com). Dupont Circle or U Street/African-American Civil War Memorial/Cardozo Metro. **Open** 11am-2.30pm, 5-10.30pm Mon-Thur; 11am-11pm Fri, Sat; 11am-10.30pm Sun. **Main courses** $12-$16. **Credit** Disc, MC, V. **Map** p250 H4 **46**

The chicest of urban-chic Thai places, Rice takes minimalism to the max. The expanse of its celadon-green and exposed-brick walls is interrupted only by a small fountain; its coconut-milk-scented rice arrives artistically mounded in the centre of the plate. Appetisers and entrées are divided into categories of authentic Thai food, healthy options and house specialties; stick with the latter two for originality and assurance of execution. There's no reason not to order a saké Martini or other fancy drink from your young, black-clad server.

Vegetarian

Vegetate

1414 Ninth Street, NW, between O & P Streets (1-202 232 4585/www.vegetatedc.com). Shaw-Howard University or Mount Vernon Square-Convention Center Metro. **Open** 6-9.30pm Thur; 6-11pm Fri, Sat; 11am-2.30pm, 6-9.30pm Sun. **Main courses** $12-$16. **No credit cards.** **Map** p251 J4 **47**

Housed in a subtly marked townhouse on a largely ungentrified block near the Washington Convention Center, Vegetate has the aura of an insider's secret. Hipsters populate both the clientele and the staff, which serves all-vegetarian, largely vegan fare in sleekly stylish surroundings. One season's menu might include cauliflower lasagna and slivered and sautéed turnips; another's might feature chilled carrot soup. The prices are low, but the portions are also on the small side, so you'll want to order multiple entrées for sharing. For drinks, you can pick from a variety of fruit and vegetable juices.

U Street/14th Street Corridor

American

Ben's Chili Bowl

1213 U Street, NW, between 12th & 13th Streets (1-202 667 0909/www.benschilibowl.com). U Street/ African-American Civil War Memorial/Cardozo Metro. **Open** 6am-2am Mon-Thur; 7am-4am Fri, Sat; noon-8pm Sun. **Main courses** $3-$6. **No credit cards.** **Map** p250 H3 **48**

Looking like a museum piece on the yuppified, bup-pified stretch of U Street once known as Black Broadway, Ben's Chili Bowl, opened in 1958, is in no danger of moldering away, thankfully. This family-owned institution's appeal rests on three legs: nostalgia (past customers include Duke Ellington, Miles Davis and Bill Cosby), the insatiable late-night hunger of young partiers, and of course the great bang for the buck afforded by burgers, fries and chilli. In-the-know customers order chilli on a dog or half-smoke (arguably Washington's signature speciality) and cheese fries, but you can also get a turkey sub or a veggie burger. These days, in fact, you can even order Ben's over the internet.

Eat, Drink, Shop

If you think the food looks good, wait until you see the view at **Tabaq Bistro**. *See p127.*

Busboys and Poets

2021 14th Street, NW, between U and V Streets (1-202 387 7638/www.busboysandpoets.com). U Street/African-American Civil War Memorial/ Cardozo Metro. **Open** 10am-midnight Mon-Thur, Sun; 10am-2am Fri, Sat. **Main courses** $8-$18. **Credit** MC, V. **Map** p250 H3 ㊾

It may not have the most exciting food (burgers, salads, sandwiches, pizza), but no matter. Busboys and Poets is an exciting space in and of itself. Located at the corner of 14th and U Streets, NW, and a mecca of civil rights activism in the 1960s, this restaurant-coffee house-bookstore-café-meeting space is a breath of fresh air in a neighbourhood that has long needed new life. With its communal tables, sofas and cushy chairs, Busboys is the ultimate urban living room, where people meet for coffee or drinks or a snack in between meals. Laptops are welcome to take advantage of the free wireless internet access. Open-mike poetry readings, live music and book discussions are also on the menu.

Cafés & coffeehouses

Love Cafe

1501 U Street, NW, at 15th Street (1-202 265 9800/ www.cakelove.com). U Street/African-American Civil War Memorial/Cardozo Metro. **Open** 8am-11pm Mon-Fri; 9am-11pm Sat; 10am-10pm Sun. **Credit** AmEx, MC, Visa. **Map** p250 H3 ㊿

Run by the folks behind Cake Love, a high-end bakery just across the street, this cosy spot offers a place to sample the bakery's wares – including a wide array of cupcakes and, weight watchers beware, what have to be the largest slices of cake in town. Not in the mood for sweets? Sip a latte while browsing the internet (there's free wifi), or snack on a sandwich. It really would be a shame to leave without a at least one little treat, though – so why not try the 'buzz balls' (cream-filled pastries) or the 'crunchy feet' (miniature pound cakes)?

Contemporary American

Crème Café

1322 U Street, NW, at 13th Street (1-202 234 1884). U Street/Cardozo Metro. **Open** 6-10.30pm Mon-Thur; 6pm-midnight Fri, Sat; 11am-3pm, 6-9pm Sun. **Main courses** $11-$20. **Credit** AmEx, Disc, MC, V. **Map** p250 H3 (51)

One gets the sense while dining at Crème, U Street's new culinary star, that chef Terrell Danley has a sense of humour. On the short menu are such seemingly low-brow options as chicken soup, pork and beans, and shrimp with grits – each dressed up and reinterpreted to be subtle and modern enough to suit the trendy clientele, while remaining down-home satisfying. Vegetarians beware – you won't find many options at this meat-heavy joint.

Fusion

Simply Home

1410 U Street, NW, between 14th and 15th Streets (1-202 232 8424/www.simplyhomedc.com). U Street/African-American Civil War Memorial/ Cardozo Metro. **Open** 11am-2.30pm Mon-Sat. **Main courses** $14-$22. **Credit** Disc, MC, V. **Map** p250 H3 (52)

Part restaurant, part clothing-jewellery-housewares boutique, Simply Home is simply beautiful. We'd go so far as to say it's sexy, with its white leather banquette and lounge-area stools and shiny bamboo tables. That's the work of Washington artist Mike Weber, who teamed up with restaurateur Sak Pollert (owner of Rice, *see p125*), to offer 'world cuisine with

Thai flavour'. If you're suspicious of the fusion, don't be. Pallert does an extraordinarily good job of melding flavours, infusing the same old Caesar salad with lemongrass and Kaffir lime, for instance. Wontons are stuffed with Greek feta, crab cakes get paired with avocado, kiwi and mango salsa. Even dessert has a twisty turn – cheesecake flavoured with green tea powder (which works, by the way).

Mediterranean

Tabaq Bistro

1336 U Street, NW, at 13th Street (1-202 265 0965/ www.tabaqdc.com). U Street/Cardozo Metro. **Open** 5-11pm Mon-Thur; 3pm-midnight Fri; 11am-4pm, 5pm-midnight Sat; 11am-4pm, 5-11pm Sun. **Main courses** $14-$21. **Credit** AmEx, Disc, MC, V. **Map** p250 H3 ❸

Unlike nearby Crème Café (*see p126*), the attraction here lies more in the setting than in the menu. Diners enjoy a dramatic rooftop view year-round in the glass-enclosed terrace, which opens up in summer for fresh air. (Be prepared to climb several flights of stairs to reach it, though.) Not that the food – kebabs, roast chicken and lamb, plus small plates from Turkey, Morocco and elsewhere – is particularly bad. Far from it. But sadly it doesn't quite meet the mark. It may simply be a case of the kitchen staff trying a little too hard to live up to the spectacular location. But what a view to aspire to. **Photo** *p126*.

Pizza/Italian

Coppi's Organic

1414 U Street, NW, between 14th & 15th Streets (1-202 319 7773/www.coppisorganic.com). U Street/ African-American Civil War Memorial/Cardozo Metro. **Open** 6-11pm Mon-Thur; 5pm-midnight Fri, Sat; 5-10pm Sun. **Main courses** $11-$23. **Credit** AmEx, Disc, MC, V. **Map** p250 H3 ❸

Crispy-crusted pizzas and chewy calzones come dressed in the finest mozzarella and fresh basil, with gourmet toppings like pancetta and portobellos – and it's all organic. For pudding, treat yourself to a Nutella dessert calzone. It's pure heaven. The space is dimly lit and cosy.

Georgetown

Cafés & coffeehouses

Pâtisserie Poupon

1645 Wisconsin Avenue, NW, between Q Street & Reservoir Road (1-202 342 3248). Foggy Bottom-GWU Metro then 30, 32, 34, 35, 36, Georgetown Metro Connection bus. **Open** 8am-6.30pm Tue-Sat; 8am-4pm Sun. **Credit** AmEx, MC, V. **Map** p249 E4 ❸

Light and airy in a modern European sort of way, Pâtisserie Poupon gets points for presentation and attitude. The tarts and cakes are just like you'd find in Paris, and the menu is short but oh-so-French:

salade niçoise, crudités, quiches and baguettes. All coffee drinks are made in the back at the espresso bar and delivered by the barista himself.

Contemporary American

Clyde's of Georgetown

3236 M Street, NW, between Wisconsin Avenue & Potomac Street (1-202 333 9180/www.clydes.com). Foggy Bottom-GWU Metro then 30, 32, 34, 35, 36, 38B, Georgetown Metro Connection bus. **Open** 11.30am-midnight Mon-Thur; 11.30am-1am Fri; 10am-1am Sat; 9am-midnight Sun. **Main courses** $11-$16 lunch; $13-$23 dinner. **Credit** AmEx, DC, Disc, MC, V. **Map** p249 E5 ❸

No visit to Georgetown's see-and-be-scene M Street promenade is complete without a stop at one of the neighbourhood's many watering holes, and Clyde's of Georgetown is first among the local equals. High-volume in both senses of the word, the place easily absorbs busfuls of tourists yet somehow still manages to attract regulars to its brass-railed bar. Perhaps it's the food. In addition to serving tavern staples – the turkey burger is a standout, moist and flavourful – Clyde's showcases seasonal, local ingredients in such dishes as a bright-tasting Bowl of Spring, featuring fiddlehead ferns, asparagus and wild mushrooms. Well-chosen wines and craft-brewed beers complete your meal, served by efficient, preternaturally cheery youngsters.

1789

1226 36th Street, NW, at Prospect Street (1-202 965 1789/www.1789restaurant.com). Foggy Bottom-GWU Metro then 30, 32, 34, 35, 36, 38B, Georgetown Metro Connection bus. **Open** 6-10pm Mon-Thur, Sun; 6-11pm Fri; 5.30-11pm Sat; 5.30-10pm Sun. **Main courses** $21-$34. **Credit** AmEx, DC, Disc, MC, V. **Map** p249 E5 ❺

Georgetown's 1789, site of countless graduation fêtes and anniversary dinners, is evocative of a Washington of old, when men unfailingly wore ties and women smiled and nodded. These things still happen, of course, and the main dining room, with its antique-style china and gold-framed historical prints, is an appropriate setting for them. It's also the setting for the cooking of chef Nathan Beauchamp, who respects tradition but favours such menu items as kurobuta pork and beef tartare topped with quail egg. The food is exceptional; the service, as might be expected, impeccable.

French

Café La Ruche

1039 31st Street, NW, between K & M Streets (1-202 965 2684/www.cafelaruche.com). Foggy Bottom-GWU Metro then 30, 32, 34, 35, 36, 38B, Georgetown Metro Connection bus. **Open** 11.30am-11.30pm Mon-Thur; 11.30am-1am Fri, Sat; 10am-11.30pm Sun. **Main courses** $9-$14. *Set brunch* $10.95. **Credit** AmEx, MC, V. **Map** p249 E5 ❸

Power playgrounds

You don't get to be a member of Congress – or even a lowly legislative correspondent – without a serious commitment to your career. These people never stop thinking – and talking – about their jobs. And you can easily eavesdrop on them, in venues great and small, high-dollar and divey, if you can withstand the onslaught of acronyms.

The obvious place to hear money talk is along and around the lobbyists' lanes of K Street and Pennsylvania Avenue, NW; the obvious place to see democracy in action is in the clusters of eateries near the Capitol and the legislative-branch offices. Along the 300 block of Massachusetts Avenue, NE, just east of Union Station, is a strip that includes the old-fashioned **Café Berlin** (No.322, 1-202 543 7656), its outdoor tables the closest thing Washington has to a beer garden; the shabby-chic (and inarguably romantic) **2Quail** (No.320, 1-202 543 8030); and the **White Tiger** (No.301, 1-202 546 5900), serving well-priced Indian food. **La Loma** (No.316,

1-202 548 2550), better liked for its drinks than its less-than-authentic Mexican fare, is a likely redoubt for young Senate staffers.

On the other side of Union Station is a trio of taverns where Hill rats of all persuasions can frequently be seen, if not always heard over the din. The most striking location of the local **Capital City Brewing Company** (2 Massachusetts Avenue, NE, 1-202 842 2337) chain is housed in the same building as the National Postal Museum; its cavernous interior and ever-changing selection of beers are its main selling points. Across the way, on F Street at the corner of North Capitol, are **Kelly's Irish Times** (1-202 543 5433) and the slightly swankier **Dubliner** (1-202 737 3773), where senators and staffers alike go to quaff the occasional Guinness.

The venerable **La Colline**, home of congressional receptions for 20-some years, has closed, its spot at 400 North Capitol Street to be filled by the popular **Johnny's Half Shell** (*see p118*), its spot in the establishment pecking order still up for grabs. The equally stalwart **Monocle** (107 D Street, NE, 1-202 546 4488), meanwhile, soldiers on, attracting senators with its steaks, seafood and convenient location. Closer still to the Capitol is **Charlie Palmer Steak** (101 Constitution Avenue, NW, 1-202-547 8100), with wine from every state in the union; it's a privilege to eat here, one for which numerous legislators seem quite willing to pay. Also serving steaks – and many House members –

Quaint from the outside, a little more hip on the inside, La Ruche (which means 'beehive') is a comfort zone for Francophiles who don't want to drop a big wad of cash on their cuisine of choice. They gather here in swarms, making a buzz of conversation while waiting for chef Jean-Claude Cauderlier's cooking. The food comes café-style, with a wide range of choices in the quiche/sandwich/salad range, plus a smattering of daily entrée specials such as mussels and duck à l'orange. Desserts, which include a range of traditional tarts, are made in-house. Brunch (10am-3pm weekends) is popular, especially in the garden when the weather's good.

Michel Richard Citronelle

Latham Hotel, 3000 M Street, NW, at 30th Street (1-202 625 2150/www.citronelledc.com). Foggy Bottom-GWU Metro then 30, 32, 34, 35, 36, 38B, Georgetown Metro Connection bus. **Open** 6.30-10.30am, 6-10pm Mon-Thur; 6.30-10.30am, 6-10.30pm Fri, Sat; 6.30-10.30am, 6-9.30pm Sun. **Dining room** *Set menus* $85-$155. **Lounge** *Main courses* $14-$38. **Credit** AmEx, DC, Disc, MC, V. **Map** p249 F5 ⑤⑨
This is the sort of place where diners have an 'experience' rather than just a meal. Hailed as one of the country's best chefs, Michel Richard has built a reputation for innovative combinations, with a presen-

is the **Capital Grille** (610 Pennsylvania Avenue, NW, 1-202 737 6200).

Watering holes on the House of Representatives side (south and east of the Capitol) include the lovable **Tune Inn** (*see p135*), a hangout for Democratic staffers and the drinkers among their bosses; the **Pour House** (319 Pennsylvania Avenue, 1-202 546 1001); the **Hawk & Dove** (*see p134*); and, resurrected after a devastating fire, the **Capitol Lounge** (229 Pennsylvania Avenue, NW, 1-202 547 2098). At the corner of First and D Streets SE are **Bullfeathers** (*see p134*), beloved of GOP staff, and **Tortilla Coast** (400 First Street, SE, 1-202 546 6768), favourite of Dems.

Any big-ticket restaurant within striking distance of the White House is a good bet for a little executive action, but you'll be hard pressed to listen in on other tables at such discreet venues as **Equinox** (*see p113*) and the **Oval Room** (800 Connecticut Avenue, NW, 1-202 463 8700). The **Bombay Club** (*see p115*) has been a first-family favourite since before the current administration; you're more likely to spot Laura than George, though, and you won't get within spitting distance. For true insider feel, if not access, head to the very posh **Caucus Room** (401 Ninth Street, NW, 1-202 393 1300), founded by members of both parties ostensibly to create a place of bipartisan camaraderie? Bipartisanship is a dubious prospect these days, but with its hobnail-and-leather chairs, wood-panelled walls, and patterned carpets – not to mention the well-connected clientele – the restaurant feels like not just an imitation but an extension of the corridors of power.

tation that introduces a touch of whimsy. While Richard's creations might encompass the likes of foie gras and venison, dishes are light and imaginative, never heavy. The 8,000 or so bottles of wine, sitting comfortably in their state-of-the-art cellar, get equal billing. Be prepared to shell out in a big way.

Fusion

Mendocino Grill & Wine Bar

2917 M Street, NW, between 29th & 30th Streets (1-202 333 2912/www.mendocinodc.com). Foggy Bottom-GWU Metro then 30, 32, 34, 35, 36, 38B, Georgetown Metro Connection bus. **Open** 11.30am-3pm, 5.30-10pm Mon-Thur; 11.30am-3pm, 5.30-11pm Fri, Sat; 5.30-10pm Sun. **Main courses** 18-$31. **Credit** AmEx, MC, V. **Map** p249 F5 ⑩

The cuisine is West Coast, the ingredients East Coast – Mendocino has a commitment to local producers. In the wine bar, and in the intimate, mirror-decked dining room, patrons are treated to simple, well-executed plates along with interesting wines, mostly from California, of course. The young servers are well informed about not only the wine but the excellent variety of artisanal cheeses.

Italian

Café Milano

3251 Prospect Street, NW, at Wisconsin Avenue (1-202 333 6183/www.cafemilanodc.com). Foggy Bottom-GWU Metro then 30, 32, 34, 35, 36, 38B, Georgetown Metro Connection bus. **Open** 11.30am-1am Mon-Tue; 11.30am-2am Wed-Sat; 11.30am-11pm Sun. **Main courses** $17-$45. **Credit** AmEx, MC, V. **Map** p249 E5 ⑪

The crowd here is as much of an attraction as the food; you might spot Michael Jordan or a visiting movie star in this multi-room complex. Even the non-famous clientele are for the most part young, rich and glamorous. The menu – and the atmosphere – ranges from casual to chic; you can choose from a selection of pizzas and pastas, or opt for roasted veal with mushroom risotto or grilled liver.

Mediterranean

Moby Dick House of Kabob

1070 31st Street, NW, at M Street (1-202 333 4400/www.mobysonline.com). Foggy Bottom-GWU Metro then 30, 32, 34, 35, 36, 38B, Georgetown Metro Connection bus. **Open** 11am-10pm Mon-Thur; 11am-4pm Fri, Sat; noon-10pm Sun. **Main courses** $6-$11. **No credit cards. Map** p249 E5 ⑫

This tiny establishment, like its cousins throughout the metro area, serves simple, traditional Middle Eastern dishes – felafel, houmous, kebabs of chicken or lamb – with little fanfare and to many fans. You order at the counter, get a number, and then take your place at one of only two small communal tables – sit even if you're getting takeout, because this fast food isn't necessarily fast. The houmous is exceptionally creamy; the pita bread, made fresh throughout the day, manages to be simultaneously lighter and more substantial than the ordinary.

Thai

Bangkok Joe's

3000 K Street, NW, at 29th Street (1-202 333 4422/www.bangkokjoes.com). Foggy Bottom-GWU Metro then 30, 32, 34, 35, 36, 38B, Georgetown Metro Connection bus. **Open** 11am-10.30pm Mon-Thur; 11am-11.30pm Fri; noon-11.30pm Sat; noon-10.30pm Sun. **Main courses** $10-$16. **Credit** AmEx, Disc, MC, Visa. **Map** p249 F5 ⑬

Vibrant colours and sleek design set the tone at this stylish Thai establishment, definitely the best bet for food among the restaurants in Washington Harbour, on the Georgetown waterfront. While the cooking lacks some of the complex flavours you'll find at the Regent (*see p121*), Bangkok Joe's features a dumpling bar (try the mushroom and ginger dumplings), plus lots of delicious noodle dishes.

Upper Northwest

Asian

Sushi-Ko

2309 Wisconsin Avenue, NW, between Calvert Street & Observatory Lane, Glover Park (1-202 333 4187/ www.sushiko.us). Foggy Bottom-GWU Metro then 30, 32, 34, 35, 36 bus. **Open** 6-10.30pm Mon; noon-2.30pm, 6-10.30pm Tue-Thur; noon-2.30pm, 6-11pm Fri; 5.30-11pm Sat; 5.30-10pm Sun. **Main courses** $14-$25. **Credit** AmEx, MC, V. **Map** p249 D3 ❻❹

Behind a mock-industrial façade is a sleek little dining room containing one of the city's best sushi bars. The decor is simple – design within reach, as the furniture store name would have it – the menu compact, venturing beyond sushi and sashimi but not detracting from their star power. Tuna Six Ways, a frequent special, accentuates variations of texture and flavour; simple preparations showcase unusual fish nightly. The vibe is casual: neighbours stop by for carryout, club kids come in to start their nights, and solo diners make friends at the sushi bar.

Italian/pizza

Palena

3529 Connecticut Avenue, NW, between Ordway & Porter Streets (1-202 537 9250/www.palena restaurant.com). Cleveland Park Metro. **Open** 5.30-10pm Tue-Sat. **Set menus** $50-$68. **Credit** AmEx, Disc, MC, V. **Map** p249 F1 ❻❺

A terracotta Minerva presides over the elegant formal dining room at the back, where chef Frank Ruta's tasting menu offers seasonal and fashionable Italian delicacies; a bar menu of American favourites is served in the casual and equally elegant café at the front. The former might feature gnocchi with nettles in spring or Roman-style braised oxtail in winter; the latter, an impossibly upscale hamburger, hotdog and fries (including not only potatoes but also onions and, yes, those are lemon slices). You can order from the tasting menu in the café; whatever your choice, consider leaving room for Ann Amernick's much-loved caramels, cookies or pastries.

Mediterranean

Lebanese Taverna

2641 Connecticut Avenue, NW, at Woodley Road, Woodley Park (1-202 265 8681/www.lebanese taverna.com). Woodley Park-Zoo/Adams Morgan Metro. **Open** 11.30am-3pm, 5.30-10.30pm Mon-Thur; 11.30am-3pm, 5.30-11.30pm Fri; 11.30am-3.30pm, 5.30-11.30pm Sat; 5-10pm Sun. **Main courses** $13-$20. **Credit** AmEx, DC, Disc, MC, V. **Map** p249 F2 ❻❻

This popular family-owned operation, part of a local mini chain, starts filling up early for dinner. The friendly crowd is a mix of families, couples and more formal business groups. Make a meal of appetisers, which are quite substantial, fun to share and a bit more of a bargain. There's the familiar tabouleh and falafel as well as more interesting variations, such as houmous bel shawarma (houmous with pieces of lamb), shankleesh (herbed and spiced feta with a tomato salad) and manakish b'sabanigh, a special bread topped with a spinach, pine nut and cheese mixture. Save room for baklava, and round things off with an Arabic coffee scented with cardamom. **Other locations**: 5900 Washington Boulevard, between McKinley Road & Nicholas Street, Arlington, VA (1-703 241 8681); Pentagon Row, 1101 S Joyce Street, VA (1-703 415 8681).

Mount Pleasant & north

American

Tonic Restaurant

3155 Mt Pleasant Street, NW, between 16th & 17th Streets (1-202 986 7661/www.tonicrestaurant.com). Columbia Heights Metro. **Open** 5-11pm Mon-Thur; 5pm-midnight Fri; 10am-3pm, 5pm-midnight Sat; 10am-3pm Sun. **Main courses** $8-$16. **Credit** AmEx, DC, Disc, MC, V. **Map** p250 H2 ❻❼

The funky, still-in-transition neighbourhood of Mount Pleasant has been graced with a few tasty new arrivals, including Tonic, a homey two-storey bar/restaurant on the main drag. Depending on your mood, you've got a choice of dining experiences: upstairs is for a quieter, sit-down, tablecloth vibe; downstairs is a cavernous bar, with dark wood, television and plenty of beer on tap. No matter where you choose, the menu is the same, a shout-out to comfort food with regional American touches. Think macaroni and cheese, meatloaf sandwiches, pulled pork, home-made baked beans and a killer side of garlicky sautéed spinach.

Capitol Hill

American

Market Lunch

Eastern Market, 225 Seventh Street, SE, between Pennsylvania & North Carolina Avenues (1-202 547 8444/www.easternmarket.net). Eastern Market Metro. **Open** 7.30am-3pm Tue-Sat; 11am-3pm Sun. **Main courses** $2-$5. **No credit cards**. **Map** p253 L7 ❻❽

On weekends, the barbecue and crab-cake sandwiches at this counter-service-only restaurant vie with outdoor craft vendors as Eastern Market's main draw. But Market Lunch is perhaps best

Montmartre: a little bit of the city of light in the city on the hill.

visited on weekdays – the line is shorter then, and you're more likely to get a seat at the communal table in the center aisle of the historic food hall. Breakfast is a favourite meal for locals, who order such Southern staples as grits, scrapple (yes, that's made of pig scraps), and the fried fish breakfast – huge crusty fillets accompanied by sweetish, dark potato slices, cooked to a dense softness and dusted with Old Bay seasoning.

Ugly Mug

723 8th Street, SE, at G Street, Capitol Hill and Around (1-202 547 8459/www.uglymugdc.com). Eastern Market Metro. **Open** 11.30am-1.30am Mon-Thur; 11.30am-2.30am Fri; 11am-2.30am Sat; 11am-1.30am Sun. **Main courses** $9-$14. **No credit cards**. **Map** p253 M8

At first glance, the Ugly Mug is a neighbourhood pub with plenty of beer (20-plus on tap) and sports TV (five flat screens). Attracting both old timers and new college grads, the Mug is undoubtedly a popular local watering hole, but it's not the beer alone that's roping them in – it's the food. Departing from standard old bar grub, the Mug offers a twist on some of the old classics: instead of a burger, consider the trio of mini-burgers on brioche buns, served with a mound of Parmigiano-accented shoestring onion rings. The fish that goes with the chips gets a dip in a local beer batter. Among the many toppings for its Housemaid pizza is Maryland crab.

French

Montmartre

327 Seventh Street, SE, between C Street & Pennsylvania Avenue (1-202 544 1244). Eastern Market Metro. **Open** 11.30am-2.30pm, 5.30-10pm Tue-Thur; 11.30am-2.30pm, 5.30-10.30pm Fri, Sat; 11.30am-2.30pm, 5.30-9pm Sun. **Main courses** $12-$22. **Credit** AmEx, Disc, MC, V. **Map** p253 L7 ⑦

Its dining room bustling even when it's not full, its patio seats constantly occupied, Montmartre is much-beloved of Capitol Hill residents, who stop by for weekend brunch and people-watching (Eastern Market is just steps away) as well as reliable daily dinners. The walls bear the inevitable Moulin Rouge poster, but the vibe is sophisticated, and the elegantly presented food is more than just café fare: in addition to hanger steak and duck confit, the menu includes such dishes as braised rabbit leg and an appetiser of *brandade de morue*, its salt cod and potato combination homey, warm and comforting.

Alexandria

Middle Eastern

100 King

100 King Street, at South Union Street, Alexandria, VA. (1-703 299 0076/www.100king.com). Ballston Metro then 10B bus. **Open** 11.30am-3pm, 5-10pm Mon-Thur; 11.30am-3pm, 5-11pm Fri; 11.30am-11pm Sat; 11am-10pm Sun. **Main courses** $8-14. **Credit** AmEx, DC, Disc, MC, V.

The Abi-Najms have done it again. Locally known for its popular empire of Lebanese restaurants (Lebanese Taverna, *see p130*), the family has expanded its consistently good Middle East repertoire (albeit slightly) to include the Mediterranean coast – Turkey, France, Spain, even Morocco – at 100 King, located in the heart of Old Town Alexandria. Small plates dominate the menu, which in addition to Middle Eastern standards such as kefta kebab, grilled halloumi cheese and baba ghanouj, opens up to possibilities such as lamb shank tagine, duck leg confit and Turkish zucchini cake. The restaurant is a two-storey affair: upstairs is more formal; downstairs is more suitable for grazing, with a wine bar showcasing 40 by the glass.

Southern

Majestic Café

911 King Street, between North Patrick & Alfred Streets, Alexandria, VA (1-703 837 9117/ www.majesticcafe.com). King Street Metro, then Dash Bus 2 or 7. **Open** 11.30am-2.30pm, 5.30-10pm Mon-Thur; 11.30am-2.30pm, 5.30-11pm Fri, Sat; 11am-2.30pm, 5.30-10pm Sun. **Main courses** $7-$14 lunch; $11-$16 dinner. **Credit** AmEx, Disc, MC, V.

The menu at the Majestic Café is Southern, the mood sweetly nostalgic. Framed black-and-white photos from the '30s and '40s line the walls, heels click on the terrazzo floor, and art deco touches abound. There's nothing old-fashioned about the food presentation, though. Fried green tomatoes arrive in a 'napoleon'; an appetiser invokes a fried-chicken picnic. There is always a vegetarian option too. The dining room is frequently full, particularly during Sunday brunch, but there are often seats at the bar. Dessert is worth saving room for.

Arlington, VA

Asian

Little Viet Garden/Clarendon Crab House

3012 Wilson Boulevard, between Highland & Garfield Streets (1-703 522 9686). Clarendon Metro. **Open** 11am-10pm Mon-Fri; noon-11pm Sat; noon-10pm Sun. **Main courses** $5-$12. **Credit** AmEx, DC, Disc, MC, V.

A Clarendon stalwart with excellent curb appeal, thanks to its expansive patio and twinkling tropical lights, Little Viet Garden has hedged its bets by

Majestic Café.

adding crab to its menu and sign (call ahead for the availability of crustaceans). That perhaps wasn't necessary; in an increasingly restaurant-clotted and gentrified neighbourhood, the place would stand out anyway for its honest Vietnamese food at reasonable prices. The menu goes beyond basic, with a whole page of chef's specialities as well as the expected summer rolls and noodle dishes. Crispy squid, available as appetiser or entrée, is outstanding: the spicy rings are surprisingly tender inside, their accompanying bed of lettuce and onions made delicious by their sweet-hot, salty sauce.

Pho 75

1721 Wilson Boulevard, between Rhodes & Quinn Streets, Rosslyn (1-703 525 7355). Rosslyn Metro. **Open** 9am-8pm daily. **Main courses** $5-$7. **No credit cards.**

'Pho' signifies an experience as much as it does Vietnamese soup. Diners sit at a long communal table in a bare-bones dining room and slurp, unmindful of the inevitable splashes as noodles slip off chopsticks and back into the bowl. The only real choices are which cuts of beef (brisket, tendon and tripe are among the options) to order for your broth – this arrives redolent of star anise and Thai basil – and which condiments (hot sauce, sprouts and jalapeños are all winners) to top it with. People eat pho for breakfast, lunch and dinner, and often finish with Pho 75's sweet, strong iced coffee.

Cafés & coffeehouses

Misha's

102 S Patrick Street, at King Street, Alexandria. (1-703 548 4089/http://pages.alexandriacity.com/ dining/mishas.htm). King Street Metro, then Dash bus 2, 5, or 7. **Open** 6.30am-8pm daily. **Main courses** $3-$7. **Credit** MC, V.

There are two independent coffee shops in this town of sip-worthy attention. Misha's is one of them (Murky's, is the other). Located in Old Town Alexandria, Misha's is one of the few remaining places in the entire Washington area where you can light up with your java. (Smokers bond around a communal table in a separate room.) Beans are roasted on the premises; customer favourites include Caravan Blend and the famous Route 66, which is always available brewed by the cup. Food is limited to a tantalising array of carbs, all the more reason for an intra-meal pit stop. Straight-ahead jazz is always blaring from the speakers, and we like that just fine.

Murky Coffee

3211 Wilson Boulevard, at intersection of North Fairfax Drive and Clarendon Boulevard, Arlington (1-703 312 7001/www.murkycoffee.com). Clarendon Metro. **Open** 7am-9pm Mon-Thur; 7am-10pm Fri; 8am-10pm Sat; 8am-9pm Sun. **Main courses** $2-$8. **Credit** MC, V.

The brainchild of local entrepreneur Nick Cho, Murky has two locations – a small shop in Eastern Market and a larger, living-room-style branch in the

The Ethiopian connection

Both healthy (lots of vegetables) and heavy (lots of grease), Ethiopian food is a mainstay in the diet of many young Washingtonians. You sit around a communal platter of *injera* – a spongy, pleasantly sour giant pancake of bread. Stews are served on the top – and diners scoop up bites of food with more *injera*, torn into bite-sized pieces. Meat tends to come in conveniently sized chunks; vegetables, in properly textured piles. It's great fun, it's economical, and it's a good base for a night on the town.

For many years, Adams Morgan was the epicentre of Ethiopian cuisine, with senior statesman **Meskerem** (2434 18th Street, NW, between Columbia & Belmont Roads, 1-202-462-4100) holding its own over competitors with its decor: a radiant sunbeam painted on the ceiling, and mushroom-shaped straw tables to cradle the *injera* platter perfectly. The vegetarian sampler here is a great way to go; the spicy red-lentil purée is particularly winning. A block south is **Awash** (No. 2218, 1-202 588 8181), less of a looker but easily Meskerem's match for cuisine.

Recently, the locus of Ethiopian activity has shifted down on to U Street, NW, and Ninth Street, a strip now informally dubbed Little Ethiopia. Some are large venues with bars and established nightlife, others mere townhouses with tables. **Dukem**, an old-timer at the corner of 11th and U (1114-1116 U Street, 1-202 667 8735), is one of the former, beloved for its outdoor seating and its multiple versions of *kitfo*, spiced raw minced beef. At **Axum** (1934 Ninth Street, 1-202 387 0765), a pleasant, sociable dining room serves not only such dishes as crispy, pleasantly chewy *derek tibs* – lamb cubes cooked with onions and jalapeños, accompanied by a pool of fiery sauce – but also Italian-style *cotoletta* sandwiches. **Etete** (1942 Ninth Street, 1-202 232 7600), another small wonder, is a critics' darling – especially for its spicy beef and lamb dishes. **Roha** (1212 U Street, 1-202 462 1212), named for an ancient holy city, tries to do it all, with a sleek bar, a dining room that showcases the work of Ethiopian artists, and, at weekends, live music until late into the night.

Arlington neighbourhood of Clarendon. For the best people watching, we recommend the latter, which is always packed with nearby George Mason University students and plenty of coffee shop characters to keep you entertained. The food, limited to baked goods (mostly French and consistently good), pairs beautifully with the coffee, which is handled to championship barista standards. Cho works with a roaster in North Carolina and is partial to beans from smaller coffee co-operatives and farms. Although the coverage is spotty, free wireless internet access is available.
Other locations: 660 Pennsylvania Ave, SE, at Seventh Street (1-202 546 5228).

Contemporary American

Restaurant Eve

110 S Pitt Street, at King Street Alexandria, VA (1-703 706 0450/www.restauranteve.com). King Street Metro, then Dash bus 2 or 5. **Open** 11.30am-2.30pm, 5.30-10pm Mon-Fri; 5.30-10pm Sat. **Bistro** *main courses* $13-$34. **Tasting Room** *prix fixe* $95. **Credit** AmEx, DC, Disc, MC, V.
There are two ways to eat at Restaurant Eve: in the Bistro, a bar/lounge area, and in the Tasting Room, where only a five- or nine-course prix-fixe menu is offered. Either way is pretty special, as you'll get to taste the culinary work of Dublin native Cathal Armstrong, whose creative menu is chock-full of

local and seasonal ingredients. Named a Best New Chef of 2006 by *Food and Wine* magazine, Armstrong is whipping up stuff like confit of house-cured pork belly, housemade garlic veal sausage and lobster crème brulée. The Bistro is decidedly more casual and you'll notice neighbours drop in for a quick bite and one of the bartender's signature cocktails (we've heard that he makes his own tonic water!).

Steakhouses

Ray's the Steaks

1725 Wilson Boulevard, at North Quinn Street (1-703 841 7297). Court House or Rosslyn Metro. **Open** 6-10pm. **Main courses** $18-$47. **Credit** AmEx, MC, V.
Ray's positions itself as the anti-steakhouse steakhouse, substituting bare walls for clubby panelling, happy clamour for cigar-bar murmur, hipsters and young parents for besuited fat cats. Some of the frills you'll miss – the tiny storefront restaurant does not take reservations, and it can be thronged on weekend nights (the practised staff are excellent at estimating the wait). Some you won't – the prices are notably lower than at downtown steakhouses, without a commensurate drop in quality. There are seafood options, even a mushroom entrée, but big, hand-cut, well-cooked meat is the order of the day.
Other locations: 8606 Colesville Road, Silver Spring, MD (1-301 588 7297).

Eat, Drink, Shop

Bars

Work hard, drink harder.

All right, nothing will ever displace politics from its central position in Washington's life, not even drinking. And the stereotype of Washingtonians as workaholics is not without foundation. However, it is not the whole story either. The fact is that lots of people like to have a good time, and right now new bars are as common as lobbyists.

The legal drinking age in the US is 21 and, for the most part, it's strictly enforced, especially in the Adams Morgan and Georgetown districts, which get a lot of college-age traffic and, thus, under-age chancers. In those areas, if you don't have a passport or driver's licence, you probably won't even make it in through the door. So bring photo ID with you even if you're just going to have a glass of wine with your food and look to be over 30. But don't bother putting that packet of cigarettes in your pocket. DC has approved a broad ban on smoking in bars and restaurants, which becomes effective from January 2007.

The Metro runs until 3am on Friday and Saturday nights, although the last train from your station is often earlier. If you're partying late, it's often easier to get a cab home. For gay-oriented bars and clubs, see p178.

The White House & around

Old Ebbitt Grill

675 15th Street, NW, between F & G Streets (1-202 347 4800/www.ebbitt.com). Metro Center Metro. **Open** 7.30am-2am Mon-Thur; 7.30am-3am Fri; 8.30am-3am Sat; 8.30am-2am Sun. **Credit** AmEx, DC, Disc, MC, V. **Map** p252 H6 ❶
The Old Ebbitt first opened in 1856 as a boarding house, and over the years its more illustrious guests have included presidents Grant, Johnson, Cleveland and Teddy Roosevelt. Just a block from the White House, it's a popular place for the power lunch (in the main dining room, that is, not in the atrium). The two bars – one at the back, one at the front – are always packed, usually with men who ensure that no nubile young thing has to pay for her own drinks.

Capitol Hill & around

Bullfeathers

410 First Street, SE, between D & E Streets (1-202 543 5005/www.bullfeatherscapitolhill.com). Capitol South Metro. **Open** 11.15am-2am Mon-Sat. **Credit** AmEx, DC, Disc, MC, V. **Map** p253 L7 ❷

Got you! **Bar Pilar**. *See p139.*

'Bullfeathers,' President Teddy Roosevelt used to snort every time he wanted people to know that they were full of it, but didn't want to use the other, scatological, bovine expletive. It's an all-too-appropriate name for this place, which is full of trash-talking Hill aides, interns and politicos drinking up a storm. Thursday nights are particularly popular.

Hawk & Dove

329 Pennsylvania Avenue, SE, between Third & Fourth Streets (1-202 543 3300/www.hawk anddoveonline.com). Capitol South or Eastern Market Metro. **Open** 10am-2am Mon-Thur, Sun; 10am-3am Fri, Sat. **Credit** AmEx, DC, Disc, MC, V. **Map** p253 L7 ❸
The Hawk & Dove is the classic Capitol Hill bar, attracting partisan staffers who enjoy the political atmosphere as much as the pool games. It's a hunting lodge-esque relic from the Vietnam War era (hence the name, which recalls the heated debates from those days). To go with the hunting lodge theme, the political memorabilia has to compete for attention with game trophies (aka dead animals).

Today, it attracts a slightly older and wealthier Hill crowd than the Tune Inn (*see below*) next door – in other words, plenty of thirtysomething types in suits – though the free food at happy hour is a big draw for the young and the hungry.

Tune Inn
331½ Pennsylvania Avenue, SE, at Fourth Street (1-202 543 2725). Capitol South Metro. **Open** 8am-2am Mon-Thur, Sun; 8am-3am Fri, Sat. **Credit** AmEx, MC, V. **Map** p253 L7 ❹
The Tune Inn is one of the few places in DC that starts serving beer at 8am – and you'll probably need a pint to deal with the rowdy blue-collar crowd and the sometimes surly staff. There are no fancy artisan brewed beers on offer here – this place regularly wins awards for being Washington's best dive dar, with prices to match.

The Federal Triangle

Round Robin Bar
Willard Inter-Continental Hotel, 1401 Pennsylvania Avenue, NW, at 14th Street, Federal Triangle (1-202 637 7348/www.washington.intercontinental.com/ washa). Metro Center Metro. **Open** 11am-1am Mon-Sat; 11am-midnight Sun. **Credit** AmEx, DC, Disc, MC, V. **Map** p252 H6 ❺
See p138 **Hotel havens**.

Union Station & around

Flying Scotsman
233 Second Street, NW, between C Street & Louisiana Avenue (1-202 783 3848/www.flying scotsman-dc.com). Judiciary Square Metro. **Open** 11am-2am Mon-Thur, Sun; 11am-3am Fri, Sat. **Credit** AmEx, MC, V. **Map** p253 K6 ❻
This Scottish-themed restaurant and bar has a loyal clientele of lobbyists, Federal workers and Hill staffers who come for the fun ambience, great food and a selection of drinks that includes, as you'd expect, an extensive list of quality Scotches and some hard-to-find beers. The popular kitchen dishes out everything from fish and chips to leg of lamb, and there's a pool table and dartboard.

Union Pub
201 Massachusetts Avenue, NE, at Second Street (1-202 546 7200/www.unionpubdc.com). Union Station Metro. **Open** 11.30am-2am Mon-Thur; 11.30am-3am Fri; noon-3am Sat; noon-2am Sun. **Credit** AmEx, MC, V. **Map** p253 L6 ❼
Not all outdoor patios are created equal. At Union Pub a giant awning covering the 80 or so seats elevates the al fresco concept to greatness. Happy hour is also bumped up a few notches, with an extraordinary array of cut-price drinks available seven nights a week. Wednesday happy hour boasts $1.50 bottled beers until 10pm, while on Tuesday night women can drink for free (domestic beer and rail drinks, ie the cheaper brands of spirits) from 5pm to 7pm, with no strings attached.

Downtown

Gordon Biersch
900 F Street, NW, at 9th Street (1-202 783 5454/ www.gordonbiersch.com). Gallery Place-Chinatown Metro. **Open** 11.30am-midnight Mon-Thur; 11.30am-1am Fri, Sat; 11.30am-11pm Sun. **Credit** AmEx, Disc, MC, V. **Map** p253 J6 ❽
The California microbrew chain's first appearance in the region is an impressive one. Inside a beautifully restored 1890s bank, four traditional German lagers are brewed on site – no stouts or ales, though.

Poste
Hotel Monaco, 555 Eighth Street, NW, between E & F Streets, Downtown (1-202 783 6060/www.poste brasserie.com). Gallery Place/Chinatown Metro. **Open** 11.30am-1am daily. **Credit** AmEx, DC, Disc, MC, V. **Map** p253 6J ❾
See p138 **Hotel havens**. **Photo** p138.

The best Bars

For al fresco drinks
Poste (*see above*); **Sequoia** (*see p140*); **Trio's Fox & Hounds** (*see p137*); **Union Pub** (*see left*).

For beer
Birreria Paradiso (*see p139*); **Brickskeller** (*see p136*); **Gordon Biersch** (*see above*).

For cocktails
Degrees Bar & Lounge (*see p139*); **Firefly** (*see p137*); **Fly Lounge** (*see p137*); **Poste** (*see above*).

For drinking with a theme
Fly Lounge (*see p137*); **Palace of Wonders** (*see p140*); **Science Club** (*see p136*).

For listening in to political arguments
Bullfeathers (*see p134*); **Hawk & Dove** (*see p134*); **Tune Inn** (*see above*).

For memorable decor
Aroma (*see p140*); **Bar Rouge** (*see p136*); **Firefly** (*see p137*); **Leftbank** (*see p137*); **Rosa Mexicano** (*see p136*); **Temperance Hall** (*see p140*).

For vodkas
Russia House Restaurant & Lounge (*see p137*).

For whiskies
Flying Scotsman (*see left*); **J Paul's** (*see p139*); **Temperance Hall** (*see p140*).

Eat, Drink, Shop

Russia House Restaurant & Lounge.

Rosa Mexicano

575 7th Street, NW, at F Street (1-202 783 5522/ www.rosamexicano.com). Gallery Place-Chinatown Metro. **Open** 11.30am-3pm, 5-10.30pm Mon-Thur; 11.30am-3pm, 5-11.30pm Fri; noon-3pm, 5-11.30pm Sat; noon-3pm Sun. **Credit** AmEx, DC, MC, V. **Map** p253 6J ⑩

Sit back, sip a pomegranate Margarita and watch the beautiful people – made even more gorgeous by a backdrop of glittering blue tiles and rose petals embedded in clear Lucite (a glossy clear plastic) – eye each other's press credentials under the pink-hued lights. Then order up some guacamole, which comes in strengths from mild to medium to wowee. All the varieties taste delicious and are whipped up tableside in a volcanic stone mortar and pestle. And remember, things really do look better when seen through rose-coloured sangria glasses.

Science Club

1136 19th Street, NW, between L & M Streets (1-202 775 0747/www.scienceclubdc.com). Farragut North Metro. **Open** 5pm-2am Mon-Thur; 5pm-3am Fri, Sat. **Credit** MC, V. **Map** p252 G5 ⑪

Rest assured, you don't need to know the difference between the second law of thermodynamics and the third law of motion to get in here. In fact, the name comes from the decor: bar-goers in this four-level space sit on round metal stools salvaged from a high-school chemistry lab. Apart from that, Science Club sticks with tried and trusted new bar practice. The $3 bottles of Yuengling are mixed with DJs who

spin dub and funk, plus there's a basement bar that looks like a Prohibition speakeasy. It all makes for one positively charged evening.

Dupont Circle

Bar Rouge

Rouge Hotel, 1315 16th Street, NW, at Scott Circle, Dupont Circle (1-202 232 8000/www.roughotel.com). Dupont Circle Metro. **Open** 11.30am-midnight Mon-Wed, Sun; 11.30am-2am Thu-Sat. **Credit** AmEx, DC, Disc, MC, V. **Map** p250 H4 ⑫

See p138 **Hotel havens**.

Brickskeller

1523 22nd Street, NW, between P & Q Streets (1-202 293 1885/www.thebrickskeller.com). Dupont Circle Metro. **Open** 11.30am-2am Mon-Thur; 11.30am-3am Fri; 6pm-3am Sat; 6pm-2am Sun. **Credit** AmEx, DC, Disc, MC, V. **Map** p250 G4 ⑬

The labyrinthine saloon that is Brickskeller claims to have the world's largest selection of beers: more than 1,000 brands from all over the world, from America to Africa. Not, of course, that all 1,000 of these often-expensive bottles are available at the same time – seasonal varieties, availability and shipping play havoc with the list. Still, the Brickskeller is a popular place for friends to meet and sample the diverse menu of brews – ordering a Bud light may draw stares. The food is typical bar fare, featuring buffalo burgers, and fish and chips. **Photo** *p140*.

Russia House Restaurant & Lounge

1800 Connecticut Avenue, NW, at Florida Avenue (1-202 234 9433/www.russiahouselounge.com). Dupont Circle Metro. **Open** 5pm-midnight Mon-Thur; 5pm-2am Fri; 6pm-2am Sat. **Credit** AmEx, MC, V. **Map** p250 G3

Once a private restaurant and lounge, Russia House retains something of the mystery of the Kremlin, despite the fact that any Tom, Dick or Vladimir can now down vodka here. The walls are covered in bordello-red silk and serious Russian oils, with cushy sofas and low coffee tables adding to the room's intimacy. A selection of more than 50 vodkas – a mix of Russian favourites, Eastern European brands and American blends – further aids foreign affairs. There's also a downstairs restaurant, serving the likes of chicken kiev and beef stroganoff.

Tabard Inn

1739 N Street, NW, between 17th & 18th Streets, Dupont Circle (1-202 785 1277/www.tabardinn.com). Dupont Circle Metro. **Open** 11.30am-2.30pm, 6-10pm Mon-Thur; 11.30am-2.30pm, 6-10.30pm Fri; 8-10am, 11am-2.30pm, 6-10.30pm Sat; 10.30am-2.30pm, 6-10pm Sun. **Credit** AmEx, DC, MC, V. **Map** p250 G4

See p138 **Hotel havens.**

Trio's Fox & Hounds

1533 17th Street, NW, between Church & Q Streets (1-202 232 6307). Dupont Circle Metro. **Open** 11am-2am Mon-Thur, Sun; 11am-3am Fri; 10am-3am Sat. **Credit** AmEx, Disc, MC, V. **Map** p250 G4

A local pub that's dim and cave-like, with hardcore drinkers hunched over the bar. It becomes a real biergarten in warm weather, when crowds pack the patio and swarm the jukebox. This is a place for lingering, a reputation that the sometimes painfully slow staff takes a little too seriously.

Firefly

Hotel Madera, 1310 New Hampshire Avenue, NW, between N Street & Sunderland Place, Dupont Circle (1-202 861 1310/www.firefly-dc.com). Dupont Circle Metro. **Open** 5.30pm-10pm Mon-Thur; 5.30-10.30pm Fri; 5-10.30pm Sat, Sun. **Credit** AmEx, DC, Disc, MC, V. **Map** p250 G4

See p138 **Hotel havens.**

Fly Lounge

1802 Jefferson Place, NW, intersection of 18th Street, Connecticut Avenue & Jefferson Place (1-202 828 4433/www.flyloungedc.com). Dupont Circle Metro. **Open** 9pm-2am Tue-Thur; 9pm-3am Fri, Sat; 9pm-1am Sun. **Credit** AmEx, MC, V. **Map** p250 G5

If your idea of bacchanalian bliss is downing your Snow Queen vodka on the inside of a 747, then Fly Lounge's friendly sky (in this case, a dropped ceiling that resembles a fuselage) is just what you've been looking for. Join the hipper-than-thou mile-high club and order a bottle of something bubbly. Your flight attendant/cocktail server (in a low-cut stewardess dress – complete with neckerchief) will land it gently in the built-in ice bucket in the middle of your table which, in keeping with the aeronautical theme, is modelled on the afterburner of an F-15 fighter plane. At the centre of Fly is the DJ booth, with one of the best sound systems in the city. With the seatbelt sign permanently off, late-night revellers dance, often on top of the padded banquettes, to everything from Madonna to deep house.

Adams Morgan

Bedrock Billiards

1841 Columbia Road, NW, between 18th Street & Belmont Road (1-202 667 7665/www.bedrock billiards.com). Dupont Circle Metro, then 42 bus or Woodley Park-Zoo Metro. **Open** 4pm-2am Mon-Thur; 4pm-3am Fri; 1pm-3am Sat; 1pm-2am Sun. **Credit** AmEx, MC, V. **Map** p250 G3

An unpretentious pool hall/games room (with 30 pool tables, plus Scrabble, Connect Four and other childhood favourites) that aims for a prehistoric look, with caveman drawings on the green walls (although these often get covered with photos, murals and paintings from local artists). The place is popular with a young, beer-drinking crowd that doesn't take itself too seriously.

Leftbank

2424 18th Street, NW, at Columbia Road (1-202 464 2100). Dupont Circle Metro, then L2 bus or Woodley Park-Zoo/Adams Morgan Metro, then 98 bus. **Open** 7am-2am Mon-Thur, Sun; 7am-3am Fri, Sat. **Credit** MC, V. **Map** p250 G3

Eat, Drink, Shop

Hotel havens

Poste.

Come on, you're in Washington, spook central, surely you want to have a secret assignation in a hotel bar? The trouble is, it's much harder these days to find somewhere quiet where you and your personal Deep Throat can plot the downfall of governments and decide what to do after dinner: those pesky locals have commandeered all the best bars. Still, on the basis that if you can't beat them you might as well drink with them, we offer here some hotel bars suitable for meeting a generous lobbyist.

And where better to start than the bar where, it's said, the term lobbying was first invented. Those wanting a quiet word in President Grant's ear used to hang around in the lobby of the Willard Inter-Continental Hotel hoping perhaps to stand the president or one of his advisors a drink in the **Round Robin Bar** (listings p135). The lobbyists may have moved on but you'll find that the bar is still reminiscent of an old-fashioned gentlemen's club. Take a seat in the dark green bar and see how many of the portraits of previous

guests you can recognise: Walt Whitman, Mark Twain, Nathaniel Hawthorne and President Abraham Lincoln, who lived at the hotel for two weeks before his inauguration, are among the distinguished subjects.

A generous lobbyist would be an ideal drinking companion at **Degrees Bar & Lounge** (listings p139) in the Ritz-Carlton Georgetown: if you have to buy your own classic-with-a-twist cocktails be prepared to hand over $10-$15 a go. Degrees aims to capture the clubby feel of a 1940s supper club, and patrons can pose to their heart's content at the sleek 25-seat bar.

A different kind of chic dominates **Bar Rouge** (listings p136) at the Hotel Rouge. The bedrooms here have a singular sense of style, with red vinyl headboards and pop-culture design. The bar is more understated and comfortable, with throne-like armchairs, long couches and white leather seats. Cocktails are pricey ($8-$14) and a little too syrupy, but strangely addictive nonetheless, especially in combination with the hypnotic acid jazz oozing out of the sound system.

Another Kimpton Group hotel, the Hotel Madera, goes for a 'contemporary rustic' aesthetic with its **Firefly** bar (listings p137), which features a huge tree trunk, with miniscule copper lanterns hanging from the branches. Seating is comfy, with intimate nooks and low, expansive tables for cocktails and small plates of food. Set among office buildings, it's popular for after-work drinking.

Heading downtown, **Poste** (listings p135), part of the Monaco Hotel, is set in the restored sorting office of the 1841 General Post Office, which explains the high ceilings and skylights: they made it easier for the letter sorters to read addresses. The courtyard – reached through a long arcade that was designed for horse-drawn mail wagons – is one of the most beautiful outdoor spots in Washington. Cocktails are full of fresh herbs and vegetables – like the Basil Lemontini, courtesy of the hotel's herb garden.

Finally, the **Tabard Inn** (listings p137) makes for a most relaxing place to start, end or break a day of sightseeing. The bar is set in a shabby-chic, living-room-like front room, where patrons can relax on Victorian sofas in front of a log fireplace that might have come straight from the pages of *Wuthering Heights*, while sipping a fortifying glass of wine or brandy.

Eat, Drink, Shop

With its flat white and glass walls, low furniture aesthetic and piles of orange cushions, you may think you're in the waiting lounge of a Pan Am terminal, circa 1971. But pull up your pseudo-Knoll stool, take a listen to Leftbank's state-of-the-art sound system, and catch a peep at the $300-dollar-jeaned patrons. Leftbank's style, like its crowd, is cool and fun – and miles from the nearest airport.

Reef

2446 18th Street NW, between Belmont & Columbia Roads (1-202 518 3800/www.thereefdc.com). Woodley Park-Zoo/Adams Morgan Metro, then 98 bus or Dupont Circle Metro then 42 bus. **Open** 5pm-2am Mon-Thur; 5pm-3am Fri, Sat; 11am-2am Sun. **Credit** AmEx, MC, V. **Map** p250 G3 ㉑

Fish tanks as decorations, trippy fluorescent lighting, long lines to get in: all are hallmarks of the Reef. The second-storey floor-to-ceiling windows offer a good vantage point for watching the foot traffic on 18th Street. The bar showcases a wide selection of beers – nothing in bottles – and is spacious enough to facilitate the requisite hook-up mingling.

U Street/ 14th Street Corridor

Bar Pilar

1833 14th Street, NW, between S & T Streets (1-202 265 1751/www.barpilar.com). U Street/ African-American Civil War Memorial/Cardozo Metro. **Open** 5pm-2am Mon-Thur, Sun; 5pm-3am Sat, Sun. **Credit** AmEx, MC, V. **Map** p250 H3 ㉒

The younger and less popular sister of Café Saint-Ex, Bar Pilar is affectionately referred to as a dive bar, dressed up. The vibe is intimate, with just 38 seats, and the low-key attractions include bacon bloody marys at brunch (sort of a liquefied BLT, hold the lettuce) and a kitschy photo booth. **Photo** *p134.*

Bohemian Caverns

2001 11th Street, NW, at U Street (1-202 299 0801/www.bohemiancaverns.com). U Street/ African-American Civil War Memorial/Cardozo Metro. **Open** 6pm-1am Tue; 8pm-2am Wed; 9pm-2am Thur; 9.30pm-3am Fri, Sat. **Credit** AmEx, MC, V. **Map** p250 J3 ㉓

Dance, dine, drink, it's all available at this throwback of a bar. The chandelier-hung main floor restaurant is complete 1920s glamour. The lower-level Caverns Jazz Lounge is a nightclub; upstairs, you'll find a bar and a dance floor. *See also p187.*

Café Saint-Ex

1847 14th Street, NW, at T Street (1-202 265 7839/ www.saint-ex.com). U Street/African-American Civil War Memorial/Cardozo Metro. **Open** 5pm-1.30am Mon; 11am-1.30am Tue-Thur; 11am-2.30am Fri, Sat; 11am-1.30am Sun. **Credit** AmEx, MC, V. **Map** p250 H3 ㉔

Named for Antoine de Saint-Exupery, the French aviator and author of *The Little Prince*, this brasserie aims to evoke the watering holes of Paris's Latin

Quarter and, in the basement-level lounge, the heroic days of aviation. And if pressed-tin ceilings, tobacco-stained walls and borderline service are your thing, then *voilà*! DJs spin ironically hip new wave nightly for the usual crush.

Velvet Lounge

915 U Street, NW, between Vermont Avenue & Ninth Street (1-202 462 3213/www.velvetlounge dc.com). U Street/African-American Civil War Memorial/Cardozo Metro. **Open** 8pm-2am Mon-Thur, Sun; 8pm-3am Fri, Sat. **Credit** MC, V. **Map** p251 J3 ㉕

Comfy, funky and groovy, the Velvet Lounge is a popular place to stop off for a drink when on the way out for the night, or on the way back after a concert at the nearby 9:30 Club. It's like a neighbourhood bar that just happens to have live music: many come to enjoy Martinis and beers with friends, others are here for the music. *See also p186.*

Georgetown

Birreria Paradiso

3282 M Street, NW, between Potomac Street & Georgetown Park (1-202 337 1245/www.eatyour pizza.com). Farragut West Metro, then 35 bus or Foggy Bottom-GWU Metro, then 32 bus. **Open** 11.30am-11pm Mon-Thur; 11.30am-midnight Fri, Sat; noon-10pm Sun. **Credit** AmEx, MC, V. **Map** p249 E5 ㉖

Pizza paradise above, beer heaven below, what more could you want? Birreria Paradiso, one of Georgetown's newest destinations, is in the basement of the hugely popular Pizzeria Paradiso (*see p121*) and the English-style hand pumps behind the bar serve up cask-conditioned ales that will soon produce heavenly visions in imbibers. The brews on offer include Britain's Old Speckled Hen, Belgium's Chimay Cinq Cents and a blood-coloured Flemish beer named the Duchesse de Bourgogne. Manager Thor Cheston has created some three-taste flights (with three little glasses of beer to try), so sensation seekers can sample a cross-section of Birreria's extensive offerings – culled from a six-page menu.

Degrees Bar & Lounge

Ritz-Carlton Georgetown, 3100 South Street, NW, at 31st Street, Georgetown (1-202 912 4100/www.ritzcarlton.com/hotels/georgetown). Foggy Bottom/George Washington University Metro, then 34 bus. **Open** 2.30pm-midnight Mon-Thur, Sun; 2.30pm-2am Fri, Sat. **Credit** AmEx, DC, MC, V. **Map** p249 E5 ㉗

See p138 **Hotel havens**.

J Paul's

3218 M Street, NW, at Wisconsin Avenue (1-202 333 3450/www.j-pauls.com). Foggy Bottom-GWU Metro, then 30, 32, 34, 35, 36, Georgetown Metro Connection bus. **Open** 11.30am-2am Mon-Thur; 11.30am-3am Fri, Sat; 10.30am-2am Sun. **Credit** AmEx, DC, Disc, MC, V. **Map** p249 E5 ㉘

Building a hangover one **Brickskeller** at a time. *See p136.*

In good weather, young DC professionals fight for the seats of choice along the open windows facing M Street. They're also drawn to the good raw shellfish and the 55 varieties of Scotch. Like almost every other drinking hole in Georgetown, this bar gets its fair share of student drinkers.

Sequoia

3000 K Street, NW, at Wisconsin Avenue, Washington Harbour (1-202 944 4200/www.arkrestaurants.com). Foggy Bottom-GWU Metro, then 30, 32, 34, 35, 36, Georgetown Metro Connection bus. **Open** 11.30am-11.30pm Mon-Sat; 10.30am-10.30pm Sun. **Credit** AmEx, Disc, MC, V. **Map** p249 E5 ㉙

This enormous bar and restaurant is people-watching central. The interiors are spacious, with high ceilings and tall windows. The outside bar, which looks out over the Potomac River and has views of Georgetown University and the Kennedy Center, is a popular nightspot-cum-pickup joint in the summer, crowded with singles, university students and tourists.

Cleveland Park

Aroma

3417 Connecticut Avenue, NW, between Newark & Ordway Streets (1-202 244 7995). Cleveland Park Metro. **Open** 6pm-2am Mon-Thur, Sun; 6pm-3am Fri, Sat. **Credit** AmEx, DC, MC, V. **Map** p249 F1 ㉚

After making its name as a cigar bar, Aroma has become a modernist local hangout. The amoeba-shaped tables and leopard skin-clad couches are packed at weekends, as crowds turn out for a mix of live jazz, DJs spinning loungey tunes, excellent mixed drinks, and some of the city's best bartenders.

Nanny O'Brien's

3319 Connecticut Avenue, NW, between Macomb & Newark Streets (1-202 686 9189www.nannyobriens. com). Cleveland Park Metro. **Open** 4pm-1.30am Mon-Thur; 4pm-2.30am Fri; noon-2.30am Sat; noon-1.30am Sun. **Credit** AmEx, DC, Disc, MC, V. **Map** p249 F1 ㉛

Much smaller (and more crowded) than the Four Provinces across the street, Nanny's is closer to an 'authentic' Irish pub than most DC bars. The traditional music sessions, held every Monday night, are legendary. Three dartboards in the back attract many locals and some of the city's sharpest shooters.

Petworth

Temperance Hall

3634 Georgia Avenue, NW, between Otis & Princeton Places, Mount Pleasant & North (1-202 722 7669/ www.temperancehalldc.com). Georgia Avenue-Petworth Metro. **Open** 5pm-1.30am Mon-Thur, Sun; 5pm-2.30am Fri, Sat. **No credit cards. Map** p251 J1 ㉜

Should Josephine Baker rise and take the stage again, she would feel right at home among the Jazz Age fittings – dramatic torchières, flock wallpaper and gilt-edged mirrors – of Temperance Hall. And so will you. The Hall's simple neighbourhood vibe tempers the decor's opulence and the impressive rye whiskey selection will have you feeling even more at ease. Don't miss the great jukebox, which is tucked away down a flight of stairs and past the kitchen in the speakeasy-like Whiskey Room.

Capitol Hill

Palace of Wonders

1210 H Street, NE, at 12th Street (1-202 398 7469/ www.palaceofwonders.com). Union Station Metro. **Open** 7pm-2am Mon-Thur, Sun; 7pm-3am Fri, Sat. **Credit** DC, MC, V.

It may have the vibe of a travelling freak show, but it's actually a brand new bar up and running in DC's latest up and coming district – the area of H Street running east from Union Station. Hot dogs are a whole foot long, there are arm-wrestling competitions every Tuesday and punters are promised all sorts of extraordinary events: trapeze, vaudeville and comedy to name but a few.

Shops & Services

Spend, spend, spend.

Heated political debate at **Uncle Brutha's Hot Sauce Emporium**. *See p154.*

It's just as well that most of DC's museums and tourist attractions are free, given the city's burgeoning number of shops ready to relieve you of your cash. As neighbourhoods across town have redeveloped, the retail scene has followed. Of course, Washington has all the international brands, and if your stay in the capital would be incomplete without a Banana Republic shirt take a look at the one-stop shopping section beginning on page 142. However, what any real shopper wants is the inside information on the stores and services only a resident would know, and we aim to provide that here.

SHOPPING DISTRICTS

We begin in the district of **Georgetown**. It's a great place to shop and, assuming you're the owner of a well-endowed bank balance, to live. You'll find a positive portmanteau of fine antique stores on upper Wisconsin Avenue, NW, and a veritable outdoor mall of global retail chains – from Armani Exchange to Zara – around lower Wisconsin Avenue and along M Street, NW. At the western end of M Street,

nearing Key Bridge, is Cady's Alley, a new hub of high-end home-furnishings stores.

You can walk from Georgetown to **Dupont Circle**, home to several of DC's favourite local merchants selling books, records, clothes, jewellery and household wares. From there, you'll find that Dupont's retail energy is spreading eastward, expanding with the march of new apartment blocks along the **14th Street, NW** corridor, **U Street, NW**, and **Logan Circle**. To the continuing amazement of local folks, the once left-for-dead 14th Street has reawakened as a bona fide retail row. At the northern end of this precinct, along U Street, a new-ish Metro station has encouraged the arrival of stylish new shops as well.

Just north of Dupont Circle, the 18th Street strip in **Adams Morgan** has more food and beverage (especially beverage) purveyors than anything, but if you go there to eat, you'll come across plenty of good finds in its clothing, music and home stores. South of Dupont, lower **Connecticut Avenue, NW**, on the way to the White House, has an array of excellent if businesslike clothiers (Brooks Brothers,

Eat, Drink, Shop

Find a funky collection of shoes at **Carbon**. *See p149.*

Burberry, et al). And across Downtown, in **Chinatown**, the city and its developer handmaidens have more or less ensured the disappearance of anything authentically Chinese and redeveloped the area around the MCI Center with popular brand stores such as Benetton, Urban Outfitters and a gigantic underground site known as Bed Bath & Beyond.

Away from everything else is Capitol Hill – perhaps you've heard of it – a hotbed of lobbying and, occasionally, legislation. But influence is not all that the place sells. There are fresh foods galore and, at weekends, arts and crafts at **Eastern Market**, a creditable remnant of a more agrarian age, and an expanding row of shops along **Eighth Street, SE**.

For the fancy stuff, follow the money to **Friendship Heights** along upper Wisconsin Avenue, NW at DC's border with Maryland, where you can stare into a firmament that includes Neiman Marcus, Saks Fifth Avenue, Chanel, Louis Vuitton and Jimmy Choo.

Note: in DC, the sales tax is 5.75 per cent added to the ticket price. In Maryland it's five per cent, and in Virginia 5.5 per cent.

One-stop shopping

Malls

Chevy Chase Pavilion
5335 Wisconsin Avenue, NW, at Western Avenue, Friendship Heights, Upper Northwest (1-202 686 5335/www.ccpavilion.com). Friendship Heights Metro. **Open** 9am-9pm Mon-Sat; 11am-6pm Sun. **Credit** varies.

Feeding mainly off the better stores across the street at Mazza Gallerie (*see below*) this minor mall offers clothing and home stuff, plus a food court. Highlights include Pottery Barn and Linens-N-Things.

The Collection at Chevy Chase
5471 Wisconsin Avenue, Chevy Chase, MD (www.thecollectionatchevychase.com). Friendship Heights Metro. **Open** 10am-9pm Mon-Sat; 11am-6pm Sun. **Credit** varies.

Quite near Mazza Gallerie, this long-awaited shopping centre – still to open at the time of writing – is set to combine a lineup of magnetic retail names under one roof, including Ralph Lauren, Lacoste, CO-OP Barney's New York, Max Mara, Tiffany & Co, Christian Dior, Cartier and Gucci.

Fashion Centre at Pentagon City
1100 South Hayes Street, between Army Navy Drive & 15th Street, Arlington, VA (1-703 415 2400/ www.simon.com). Pentagon City Metro. **Open** 10am-9.30pm Mon-Sat; 11am-6pm Sun. **Credit** varies.

Not bad for an old-school mall, with copious daylight and royal palms in its deep, plunging atria. Anchored by department stores Macy's and Nordstrom, this mall offers better (but not the best) apparel, gifts and speciality goods from 160-odd national franchises such as Gap, Limited and Kenneth Cole, and is surrounded by big-box discount stores (Marshalls, Best Buy, Costco) to its east and a flank of decent shops (Bombay, Sur La Table) in a too-cute outdoor mall to its west.

Mazza Gallerie
5300 Wisconsin Avenue, NW, between Western Avenue & Jenifer Street, Friendship Heights, Upper Northwest (1-202 966 6114/www.mazzagallerie.net). Friendship Heights Metro. **Open** 10am-8pm Mon-Fri; 10am-7pm Sat; noon-6pm Sun. **Credit** varies.

Stores here run from snooty (Neiman Marcus) to congenially high-end (Saks Fifth Avenue's Men's Store) to over-a-barrel discount (Filene's Basement). Also houses a Williams-Sonoma ($30 cookie-decorating kits!), Foot Locker, fine china at Villeroy & Boch, and a multi-screen cinema.

Shops at Georgetown Park

3222 M Street, NW, at Wisconsin Avenue, Georgetown (1-202 298 5577/www.shopsatgeorge townpark.com). Foggy Bottom-GWU Metro then 30, 32, 34, 35, 36 bus. **Open** 10am-9pm Mon-Sat; noon-6pm Sun. **Credit** varies. **Map** p249 E5.

Tucked between M Street and the C&O Canal, this skylit, air-conditioned escape from Georgetown's hectic streets has major clothing chains such as Bebe, Polo Ralph Lauren and J Crew, fancy sundries at Crabtree & Evelyn, and frivolous gadgets at Sharper Image. But if you get peckish, skip the meagre food court and pay a visit to Dean & Deluca (*see p154*) next door on M Street, NW.

Shops at Union Station

50 Massachusetts Avenue, NE, at North Capitol Street, Union Station & Around (1-202 371 9441/ 1-202 289 1908/www.unionstationdc.com). Union Station Metro. **Open** 10am-9pm Mon-Sat; noon-6pm Sun. **Credit** varies. **Map** p253 L6.

In the 1980s, before all the airports became malls, the refurbished Union Station assembled a lively range of boutiques and cafés beneath its soaring, coffered vaults. Thus the future of this magnificent building, under threat of demolition due to the long-term decline in the numbers of rail passengers, was ensured. Before travelling you can shop at B Dalton Booksellers, visit Appalachian Spring for handmade crafts and ceramics or try the jeweller at Taxco Sterling. There's also a luggage shop, a liquor store, a tie store and several newsstands.

Tysons Corner Center

1961 Chain Bridge Road, McLean, VA (1-888 289 7667/1-703 893 9400/www.shoptysons.com). West Falls Church-VT/UVA Metro then 28A, 28B or 3T bus. By car: Route 66 west to Route 7 west to Tysons Corner. **Open** 10am-9.30pm Mon-Sat; 11am-7pm Sun. **Credit** varies.

You could spend an entire weekend inside TCC, grounded at one end by Bloomingdale's and at the other by Nordstrom, with shops such as Benetton, Lane Bryant and West Elm elsewhere on two levels. For the better-off consumer, the Galleria also holds higher-end retailers like Bose and Cartier.

Watergate Shops

2650 Virginia Avenue, NW, at 26th Street, Foggy Bottom (1-202 944 3920). Foggy Bottom-GWU Metro. **Open** 10am-6pm daily. **Credit** varies. **Map** p252 F5.

Upper-bracket consumers come here to find Valentino, Saks Jandel or Yves St Laurent. Brides-to-be return for a zillion-dollar wedding gown at the Vera Wang Bridal Boutique or a wedding shower at the swank Watergate Hotel.

Department stores

Don't forget **Nordstrom** and **Bloomingdales** at Tysons Corner Center (*see above*) and **Macy's** at the Fashion Centre at Pentagon City (*see p142*).

Lord & Taylor

5255 Western Avenue, NW, at Wisconsin Avenue, Chevy Chase, Upper Northwest (1-202 362 9600/ www.lordandtaylor.com). Friendship Heights Metro. **Open** 10am-9.30pm Mon-Thur, Sat; 10am-10pm Fri; 11am-7pm Sun. **Credit** AmEx, Disc, MC, V.

Grown-ups' and children's dress and sportswear with broad, basic appeal by the likes of Calvin Klein and Perry Ellis, with the requisite cosmetics and jewellery departments. Plus sizes for women, too.

Macy's

1201 G Street, NW, at 12th Street, Downtown (1-202 628 6661/www.macys.com). Metro Center Metro. **Open** 10am-8pm Mon-Sat; noon-6pm Sun. **Credit** AmEx, Disc, MC, V. **Map** p252 H6.

What was Hecht's now belongs to Macy, so you know what to expect: reasonably priced, mid-range fashions by famous makers, and an outstanding source of undies, socks, ties, shades and cologne. If you see a cool cake mixer at Williams-Sonoma, you can probably buy it slightly cheaper here.

Other locations: 5400 Wisconsin Avenue, at Western Avenue, Chevy Chase (1-301 654 7600).

Neiman Marcus

5300 Wisconsin Avenue, NW, at Western Avenue, Upper Northwest (1-202 966 9700/www.neiman marcus.com). Friendship Heights Metro. **Open** 10am-8pm Mon-Fri; 10am-7pm Sat; noon-6pm Sun. **Credit** AmEx, DC, Disc, MC, V.

With Corneliani men's suits, Ugg handbags, flirty Anna Sui dresses, Prada shoes, Wedgwood dinner services and Acqua di Parma cosmetics you can smell the money when you walk in.

Saks Fifth Avenue

5555 Wisconsin Avenue, NW, at South Park Avenue, Chevy Chase, MD (1-301 657 9000). Friendship Heights Metro. **Open** 10am-7pm Mon-Wed, Fri; 10am-8pm Thur; 10am-6pm Sat; noon-6pm Sun. **Credit** AmEx, DC, Disc, MC, V.

Luxury a go-go from casual to couture, with designers such as Marc Jacobs, Michael Kors and John Varvatos, and cosmetics by La Prairie, Chanel, and Kiehl's. Guys would rue missing the Saks men's shop at 5300 Wisconsin Avenue.

Other locations: Tysons Corner Center, 2051 International Drive, McClean VA (1-703 761 0700).

Discount & factory outlets

Filene's Basement

1133 Connecticut Avenue, NW, Downtown (1-202 872 8430/www.filenesbasement.com). Farragut North Metro. **Open** 9.30am-8pm Mon-Sat; noon-5pm Sun. **Credit** AmEx, Disc, MC, V. **Map** p250 G5.

Massive markdowns on every category of clothing and accessories by familiar names.
Other locations: National Press Building, 529 14th Street, NW, Downtown (1-202 638 4110); Mazza Gallerie, 5300 Wisconsin Avenue, NW, Chevy Chase (1-202 966 0208).

H&M

1025 F Street, NW, Downtown (1-202 347 3306/ www.hm.com). Metro Center Metro. **Open** 10am-8pm Mon-Sat; noon-6pm Sun. **Credit** AmEx, DC, Disc, MC, V. **Map** p252 J6.
The Swedish retailer has taken DC by storm, selling sportswear and dresswear (including plus sizes) for men, women and children under its own label.
Other locations: shops at Georgetown Park, 3222 M Street, NW (1-202 298 6792).

Antiques

Most of the fancier antiques stores are in Georgetown, but they're ideal for browsing (although beware Sunday closing) and they do provide free guides to Washington's other antiques shops.

Dragonfly Design Décor

1457 Church Street, NW, Shaw: Logan Circle (1-202 265 3359). Dupont Circle or U Street/African-Amer Civil War Memorial/Cardozo Metro. **Open** *Winter*
11am-6pm Wed-Sat; noon-5pm Sun. *Summer* 11am-6pm Wed, Sat; 11am-8pm Thur, Fri; noon-5pm Sun. **Credit** AmEx, MC, V. **Map** p250 H4.
Inside this tranquil storefront you'll find exquisite Asian antiques handpicked by the roving owner. Among them are handcrafted tables, cabinets and seating, as well as ceramic vessels, statuary, screens, wall art and a selection of silk pieces.

Goodwood

1428 U Street, NW, U Street Corridor (1-202 986 3640). U Street or U St/African-Amer Civil War Memorial/Cardozo Metro. **Open** 5pm-9pm Thur; 11am-7pm Fri, Sat; 11am-5pm Sun. **Credit** AmEx, MC, V. **Map** p250 H3.
Scouting the best auctions in the mid-Atlantic, Goodwood brings in amazing wood tables, armoires, bookcases and mirrors, plus ornamental follies you won't find elsewhere for the prices. Go Thursday evening for the picks of the week.

Miss Pixie's

2473 18th Street, NW, between Belmont & Columbia Roads, Adams Morgan (1-202 232 8171). Woodley Park-Zoo/Adams Morgan Metro, then 90, 92, 93 bus. **Open** noon-9pm Thur; noon-7pm Fri-Sun. **Credit** AmEx, Disc, MC, V. **Map** p250 G3.
Miss Pixie's brings in country and vintage furnishings at very reasonable prices. Take home a porch rocker, a 1950s sofa or cool garden ornaments.

Museum pieces

DC is museum central for the US. People travel hundreds, if not thousands of miles to visit the capital's collections and many of the visitors want to take something home with them. That's where the museum shops come in. We list those most worth visiting.

Arthur M Sackler Gallery & Freer Gallery of Art

1050 Independence Avenue, SW, between 11th & 12th Streets, The Mall & Tidal Basin (1-202 633 4880/www.asia.si.edu). Smithsonian Metro. **Open** 10am-5.30pm daily. **Credit** AmEx, Disc, MC, V. **Map** p252 J7.
Books, music and video relevant to the museum's Asian focus, plus teapots, crystal objects, kimono gift sets, Chinese and Japanese prints, and arty umbrellas.

National Building Museum

401 F Street, NW, between Fourth & Fifth Streets, Judiciary Square area (1-202 272 7706/www.nbm.org). Judiciary Square Metro. **Open** 10am-5pm Mon-Sat; 11am-5pm Sun. **Credit** AmEx, MC, V. **Map** p253 J6.

Often rated the best museum store in DC, and with good reason. Opening on to the museum's loggia, the store sells a lot of one-off, beautiful items such as toys and gizmos, bowls, pillows, vases, mobiles, neckties, architect-designed watches and a library's worth of design books.

National Gallery of Art

West Building: Constitution Avenue, between Fourth & Seventh Streets, NW; East Building: Constitution Avenue & Fourth Street, NW, The Mall & Tidal Basin (1-202 737 4215/www. nga.gov). Archives-Navy Memorial/Judiciary Square or Smithsonian Metro. **Open** 10am-5pm Mon-Sat; 11am-6pm Sun. **Credit** AmEx, Disc, MC, V. **Map** p253 J6.
In the cool lower floors of both National Gallery Buildings are huge shops with fine collections of books, prints, posters, cards and calendars.

National Museum of the American Indian

Fourth Street & Independence Avenue, SW, The Mall & Tidal Basin (1-202 633

Books

All the big national chain bookstores have stores in Washington. There are two branches of **Borders** downtown (1801 K Street, NW, 1-202 466 4909; and 600 14th Street, NW, at F Street, 1-202 737 1385) plus a **Barnes & Noble** in Georgetown (3040 M Street, NW, 1-202 965 9880). The notable local chain, **Olsson's Books & Records** (418 Seventh Street, NW, 1-202 638 7610) packs nearly as many books into stores that are on a slightly more intimate scale. Listed below are DC's independent and speciality booksellers.

ADC Map & Travel Center

1636 I Street, NW, between Connecticut Avenue & 17th Street, Downtown (1-800 544 2659/www.adcmaps.com). Farragut West Metro. **Open** 8am-6.30pm Mon-Thur; 8am-5.30pm Fri; 11am-5pm Sat. **Credit** AmEx, Disc, MC, V. **Map** p252 G5.
Paradise for wanderers, squeezed into a tiny space. The store, as you would expect, sells maps covering pretty nearly every region of the world.

Big Planet Comics

3145 Dumbarton Street, NW, between 31st & 32nd Streets, Georgetown (1-202 342 1961). Foggy Bottom-GWU Metro, then 30, 32, 34, 35, 36 bus. **Open** 11am-7pm Mon, Tue, Thur, Fri; 11am-8pm Wed; 11am-6pm Sat; noon-5pm Sun. **Credit** AmEx, MC, V. **Map** p249 E4.
Underground comics and graphic novels.

Candida's World of Books

1541 14th Street, at Q Street, NW, between P & Q Streets, 14th Street Corridor (1-202 667 4811). Dupont Circle Metro. **Open** 10am-10pm Tue-Sat; noon-8pm Sun. **Credit** MC, V. **Map** p250 H4.
A smart shop offering travel guides and atlases, plus language aids, dictionaries and phrasebooks for the linguistically or cartographically curious.

Capitol Hill Books

657 C Street, SE, at Seventh Street, Capitol Hill (1-202 544 1621/www.capitolhillbooks-dc.com). Eastern Market Metro. **Open** 11.30am-6pm Mon-Fri; 9am-6pm Sat, Sun. **Credit** AmEx, MC, V. **Map** p253 L7.
Two floors of secondhand books – fiction, mysteries, politics, cooking and more – plus rare and first editions. An excellent place for browsing.

Chapters, a Literary Bookstore

445 11th Street, at E Street, NW, between Pennsylvania Avenue & E Street, Downtown (1-202 737 5553). Metro Center Metro. **Open** 10am-7pm Mon-Fri; noon-7pm Sat; 2-7pm Sun. **Credit** AmEx, Disc, MC, V. **Map** p252 J6.

1000/www.nmai.si.edu). Smithsonian or Archives-Navy Memorial Metro. **Open** 10am-5.30pm daily. **Credit** AmEx, Disc, MC, V. **Map** p253 K7.
In the newest museum on the Mall, you'll find books and CDs, calendars, cards and blankets resonant of the many Indian tribes that once populated North America.

Renwick Gallery of the Smithsonian American Art Museum

17th Street & Pennsylvania Avenue, NW, The White House & Around (1-202 633 8998/ 377 2700/http://americanart.si.edu). Farragut North or Farragut West Metro. **Open** 10am-5.30pm daily. **Credit** AmEx, Disc, V. **Map** p252 G5.
Pieces in ceramic, wood and glass, plus jewellery nearly as good as the stuff on display. There is also a wide selection of books on American crafts.

Textile Museum

2320 S Street, NW, between 23rd & 24th Streets, Dupont Circle (1-202 667 0441/ www.textilemuseum.org). Dupont Circle Metro. **Open** 10am-5pm Mon-Sat; 1-5pm Sun. **Credit** AmEx, MC, V. **Map** p250 F4.
A comprehensive selection of books on weaving and fabrics, plus, naturally, the final product: ties, scarves, shawls and other fabric goods.

Washington National Cathedral

Massachusetts & Wisconsin Avenues, NW, Upper Northwest (1-202 537 6200/www.cathedral.org). 30, 32, 34, 35, 36 bus. **Open** *Sept-May* 10am-5.30pm Mon-Fri; 10am-4.30pm Sat; 8am-6.30pm Sun. *June-Aug* 10am-8pm Mon-Fri; 10am-4.30pm Sat; 8am-6.30pm Sun. **Credit** AmEx, Disc, MC, V. **Map** p249 E2.
For $565 you can pick up an actual oil lamp from the Bronze Age, but for somewhat less you can take home stained-glass reproductions, liturgical material, rosaries, books, cards and the like. Also visit the Greenhouse (for plants) and Herb Cottage (for herbs and other food products) in the grounds. Opening times for the cathedral can vary, so it's best to check first.

Eat, Drink, Shop

De Vinos. *See p157.*

The independent literary bookstore of Washington. New book releases are highlighted at the front of the store, and the staff's own reading picks are prominently displayed within.

Kramerbooks

1517 Connecticut Avenue, NW, at Q Street, Dupont Circle (1-202 387 1400). Dupont Circle Metro. **Open** 7.30am-1am Mon-Thur, Sun; 24hrs Fri, Sat. **Credit** AmEx, Disc, MC, V. **Map** p250 G4.

Not just a bookshop, but an episode of *Blind Date*, Kramerbooks is an oft-used venue for a first assignation. First, meet in the bookshop, then repair to the café (Afterwords, *see p119*). Romance aside, the book selection is good, the staff indifferent.

Lambda Rising

1625 Connecticut Avenue, NW, between Q & R Streets, Dupont Circle (1-202 462 6969). Dupont Circle Metro. **Open** 10am-midnight Fri, Sat. **Credit** AmEx, Disc, MC, V. **Map** p250 G4.

Pioneers in the book business and in DC's gay community, Lambda has serious (and frivolous) gay fiction, history (and 'herstory'), self-help and health-care titles, periodicals, and note cards and trinkets.

Politics & Prose

5015 Connecticut Avenue, NW, between Fessenden Streets & Nebraska Avenue, Upper Northwest (1-800 722 0790/1-202 364 1919/www.politics-prose.com). Van Ness-UDC Metro, then northbound L1, L2, L4 bus. **Open** 9am-10pm Mon-Thur; 9am-11pm Fri, Sat; 10am-8pm Sun. **Credit** AmEx, Disc, MC, V.

As you might guess, Politics & Prose carries a lot of both, plus a large section that is set aside for children and teenagers, and a coffee shop downstairs. The store is a must-stop for prominent authors who are on the reading-tour circuit.

Second Story Books

2000 P Street, NW, at 20th Street, Dupont Circle (1-202 659 8884/www.secondstorybooks.com). Dupont Circle Metro. **Open** 10am-10pm daily. **Credit** AmEx, Disc, MC, V. **Map** p250 G4.

A venerated, musty space, chock-a-block with all kinds of curious used titles, plus second-hand music and prints. Check the sidewalk bins for bargains.

Cameras & film processing

CVS (*see p158*) offers a one-hour photo developing service.

Penn Camera

840 E Street, NW, between Eighth & Ninth Streets, Penn Quarter (1-202 347 5777/www.penncamera.com). Gallery Place-Chinatown Metro. **Open** 8.30am-6pm Mon-Fri; 10am-5pm Sat. **Credit** AmEx, Disc, MC, V. **Map** p253 J6.

All the equipment a pro could need, but the smart staff will help novices too.
Other locations: throughout town. Check phone book for details.

Electronics

Radio Shack has stores throughout the area. Check the phone book for your nearest.

Best Buy

4500 Wisconsin Avenue, NW, at Albemarle Street, Tenleytown, Upper Northwest (1-202 895 1580/ www.bestbuy.com). Tenleytown-AU Metro. **Open** 10am-9pm Mon-Sat; 11am-7pm Sun. **Credit** AmEx, Disc, MC, V.

A carnival of mass-media gizmos that offers just about anything you want – if it's in stock.

Graffiti

1219 Connecticut Avenue, NW, between M & N Streets, Dupont Circle (1-202 296 8412/www.graffiti audio.com). Dupont Circle or Farragut North Metro. **Open** 10am-7pm Mon-Sat; noon-6pm Sun. **Credit** AmEx, Disc, MC, V. **Map** p250 G4.

TV and audio equipment of the better kind.
Other locations: 4914 Wisconsin Avenue, NW, Upper Northwest (1-202 244 9643); 7810 Old Georgetown Road, Bethesda, MD (1-301 907 3660).

Fashion

Most of the mainstream clothiers make appearances in the District – **American Apparel**, **Banana Republic**, **J Crew**, **Gap**. Georgetown has one of nearly all of them, plus choicer chains like **Club Monaco**, **French Connection**, **Diesel** and **Armani Exchange**.

Boutiques

Betsy Fisher

1224 Connecticut Avenue, NW, between N Street & Jefferson Place, Dupont Circle (1-202 785 1975/ www.betsyfisher.com). Dupont Circle Metro. **Open** 10am-7pm Mon-Wed; 10am-9pm Thur, Fri; 10am-6pm Sat; noon-4pm Sun. **Credit** AmEx, DC, Disc, MC, V. **Map** p250 G4.

Approachable chic, from the tailored to the saucy. Ensembles, dresses, and the rest by the likes of Caractere, Gazebo and Three Dots.

Junction

1510 U Street, NW, between 15th & 16th Streets, U Street/14th Street Corridor (1-202 483 0260). Dupont Circle or U St/African-Amer Civil War Memorial/Cardozo Metro. **Open** 3-7pm Tue, Wed; noon-7pm Thur-Sat; noon-5pm Sun. **Credit** AmEx, MC, V. **Map** p250 H3.

A collectively run boutique selling original designs for men and women, plus vintage pieces, accessories, photography and handmade gifts.

Nana

1528 U Street, NW, between 15th & 16th Streets, U Street/14th Street Corridor (1-202 667 6955/ www.nanadc.com). Dupont Circle Metro. **Open** *Winter* noon-7pm daily. *Summer* noon-7pm Tue-Sun. **Credit** MC, V. **Map** p250 H3.

Green your **Garden District**. See p152.

Wearing escapism on its sleeveless little dress, Nana sells fun, funky dresses, blouses, skirts and more by Classic Girl, Elaine Perlov and Uppsee Daisees. Then she tosses some wonderful accessories from the likes of Angela Adams (handbags) and Lilian Hartman (jewellery) into the mix. Fresh!

Pop

1803A 14th Street, NW, at S Street, U Street/14th Street Corridor (1-202 332 3312/www.shoppop.com). U Street/African-American Civil War Memorial/ Cardozo Metro. **Open** noon-8pm Mon-Fri; 11am-7pm Sat; noon-5pm Sun. **Credit** AmEx, MC, V. **Map** p250 H4.
Set in a bright little loft, this groovy store sells scenester favourites like Ben Sherman, Penguin, Le Tigre and Members Only.

Relish

3312 Cady's Alley, NW, M Street between 33rd & 34th Streets, Georgetown (1-202 333 5343/www. cadysalley.com). Foggy Bottom Metro, then 38B bus. **Open** 10am-6pm Mon-Wed, Fri-Sat; 10am-7pm Thur. **Credit** AmEx, MC, V. **Map** p249 E5.
Relish is in an airy loft on Georgetown's design oriented Cady's Alley, and its designer lines are similarly rarefied: dresses by Marni, DVN or Missotten for women and shirts by Comme des Garcons, Dries van Noten and Junya Wantanabe for men. Plus shoes by Collection Privee and Punkt.

Children

Don't leave the children out of the style equation. You can find clothes and shoes for youngsters at **H&M** (*see p144*), **Macy's** (*see p143*), and **Lord & Taylor** (*see p143*). There's a **Gap Kids** in Georgetown (1267 Wisconsin Avenue, NW, 1-202 333 2411) and in Chevy Chase. Any **CVS** drug store (*see p158*) has baby and child sundries galore. And check the museum shops (*see p144* **Museum pieces**) for one-of-a-kind toys.

K Baby

3112 M Street, NW, between 31st Street & Wisconsin Avenue, Georgetown (1-202 333 3939/ www.k-baby.com). Foggy Bottom/GWU Metro, then 30, 32, 34, 35, 36 bus. **Open** 11am-7pm Mon-Sat; noon-5pm Sun. **Credit** AmEx, MC, V. **Map** p249 E5.
This pastel microcosm sells baby fashions from premature to toddler sizes for girls (couture by Jean Bourget) and boys (Charlie Rocket).

Kid's Closet

1226 Connecticut Avenue, NW, at N Street, Dupont Circle (1-202 429 9247). Dupont Circle Metro. **Open** 10am-6pm Mon-Fri; 11am-5pm Sat. **Credit** AmEx, Disc, MC, V. **Map** p250 G4.
Lines by Little Me, Carter's, Absorba, plus higher-end miniature fashions by Baby Trousseau.

Designer

The greatest concentration of designer clothing is to be found in Washington's better department stores, such as **Neiman Marcus** (*see p143*) and **Saks Fifth Avenue** (*see p143*). **Betsey Johnson** keeps her wacky slip dresses at 1319 Wisconsin Avenue, NW (1-202 338 4090). If you're feeling especially thin, you can visit **Chanel**'s boutique in the Willard Hotel (1455 Pennsylvania Avenue, NW, 1-202 638 5055). Women of a certain quiet sophistication have shopped at **Claire Dratch** for 59 years (7615 Wisconsin Avenue, Bethesda, MD, 1-301 656 8000). Or they visit **Rizik**'s downtown (1100 Connecticut Avenue, NW, Downtown, 1-202 223 4050), across the street from which is a convenient **Burberry** store (1155 Connecticut Avenue, NW, 1-202 463 3000).

Dry cleaning & laundry

Imperial Valet

1331 Connecticut Avenue, NW, between Dupont Circle & N Street, Dupont Circle (1-202 785 1444). Dupont Circle Metro. **Open** 7.30am-6.30pm Mon-Fri; 9am-3pm Sat. **Credit** AmEx, MC, V. **Map** p250 G4.
In an hour, you can have a hat dry cleaned. In a day, laundry done. Imperial Valet also undertakes reasonably fast alterations and repairs.

Hats

Proper Topper

1350 Connecticut Avenue, NW, between Dupont Circle & N Street, Dupont Circle (1-202 842 3055/ www.proppertopper.com). Dupont Circle Metro. **Open** 10am-8pm Mon-Fri; 10am-7pm Sat; noon-6pm Sun. **Credit** AmEx, Disc, MC, V. **Map** p250 G4.
The chic hat selection covers both women and men, but the combs and jewellery are for the ladies.

Jewellery & accessories

Jewelerswerk Galerie

2000 Pennsylvania Avenue, NW, between 20th & 21st Streets, Foggy Bottom (1-202 293 0249). Farragut West or Foggy Bottom-GWU Metro. **Open** 10am-7pm Mon-Fri; 11am-6pm Sat. **Credit** AmEx, Disc, MC, V. **Map** p252 G5.
This cool little gallery, nestled inside a small arcade, sells jewellery made by international artists in a variety of media.

Tiny Jewel Box

1147 Connecticut Avenue, NW, between L & M Streets, Downtown (1-202 393 2747/www.tiny jewelbox.com). Farragut North or Farragut West Metro. **Open** 10am-5.30pm Mon-Sat. **Credit** AmEx, MC, V. **Map** p252 G5.
A vast range of pieces, from classic to contemporary, lines the three floors of this old-line downtown favourite. Other products for sale include scarves, bags, gloves and gifts.

Menswear

BOSS Hugo Boss

1517 Wisconsin Avenue, NW, between P & Q Streets, Georgetown (1-202 625 2677/www. hugoboss.com). Foggy Bottom-GWU Metro, then 30, 32, 34, 35, 36 bus. **Open** 11am-8pm Mon-Sat; noon-6pm Sun. **Credit** AmEx, Disc, MC, V. **Map** p249 E4.
Less drapey than they used to be, the designer's suits, shirts and trousers combine an excellent choice of materials with reasonable prices.

Brooks Brothers

1201 Connecticut Avenue, NW, at M Street, Dupont Circle (1-202 659 4650). Farragut North or Dupont Circle Metro. **Open** 9.30am-7pm Mon-Fri; 9.30am-6pm Sat; noon-5pm Sun. **Credit** AmEx, Disc, MC, V. **Map** p250 G5.
Ever the classicists, Brooks Brothers has elegant men's and women's clothes and furnishings. **Other locations**: 5504 Wisconsin Avenue, Chevy Chase, MD (1-301 654 8202).

District Line

2118 18th Street, NW, between California Street & Wyoming Avenue, Adams Morgan (1-202 558 5508). Woodley Park-Zoo/Adams Morgan Metro, then 90, 92, 93 bus. **Open** noon-8pm Mon-Sat; noon-5pm Sun. **Credit** AmEx, Disc, MC, V. **Map** p250 G3.

Take a ride on the District Line for the sort of English style that normally terminates before it reaches the capital: preppy shirts by Fred Perry and English Laundry, jackets by Lonsdale, and some perfectly soigné accessories and watches.

Everard's Clothing

1802 Wisconsin Avenue, NW, at S Street, Georgetown (1-202 298 7464/www.everards clothing.com). Foggy Bottom-GWU Metro then 30, 32, 34, 35, 36 bus. **Open** 10am-6pm Mon-Sat. **Credit** AmEx, DC, Disc, MC, V. **Map** p249 E3.
The well-dressed Washington man knows Louis Everard, and Mr Everard knows the well-dressed Washington man, or at least his measurements. This is the place to come for suits beautifully made to customer specifications. You never know which of the rich and powerful you might see within, or upstairs browsing through the fine women's collections.
Other locations: Omni Shoreham Hotel, 2500 Calvert Street, NW (1-202 234 5040).

Outdoor

City Bikes

2501 Champlain Street, NW, at Euclid Street, Adams Morgan (1-202 265 1564/www.citybikes. com). Woodley Park-Zoo/Adams Morgan Metro, then 90, 92, 93 bus. **Open** 10am-7pm Mon-Wed, Fri, Sat; 10am-9pm Thur; 10am-5pm Sun. **Credit** MC, V. **Map** p250 G2.
Hardcore cyclists frequent City Bikes for its excellent bikes, parts and mechanics. More casual cyclists show up to rent bicycles for a short ride.

Hudson Trail Outfitter

4530 Wisconsin Avenue, NW, at Brandywine Street, Tenleytown (1-202 363 9810/www.hudsontrail.com). Tenleytown-AU Metro. **Open** 10am-9pm Mon-Sat; 11am-6pm Sun. **Credit** AmEx, Disc, MC, V.
Hudson Trail offers an extensive array of hiking clothes, shoes and gear, plus bicycles and stuff for climbing, kayaking, snow sports and fly fishing.

Shoes

Georgetown has several good shoe stores, including **Kenneth Cole** (1259 Wisconsin Avenue, NW, 1-202 298 0007), **Steve Madden** (3109 M Street, NW, 1-202 342 6194) and the **Walking Company** (3101 M Street, NW, 1-202 625 9255).

Carbon

1203 U Street, NW, between 12th & 13th Streets, U Street/14th Street Corridor (1-202 986 2679/ www.carbondc.com). U Street/African-American Civil War Memorial/Cardozo Metro. **Open** 11.30am-7.30pm Tue-Sat; 11.30am-5pm Sun. **Credit** MC, V. **Map** p250 H3.
Hard-to-find brands for men include Mark Nason, Blackstone and Pikolinos; women may choose among Biviel, Matiko and Shoola. Plus gorgeous handcrafted belts and jewellery. **Photos** *142*.

Eat, Drink, Shop

Church's English Shoes

1820 L Street, NW, between 18th & 19th Streets, Downtown (1-202 296 3366). Farragut North Metro. **Open** 10am-6pm Mon-Sat. **Credit** AmEx, Disc, MC, V. **Map** p252 G5.

This long-standing English company produces handcrafted men's leather shoes in subdued styles.

Shake Your Booty

2439 18th Street, NW, between Belmont & Columbia Roads, Adams Morgan (1-202 518 8205). Woodley Park-Zoo/Adams Morgan Metro, then 90, 92, 93 bus. **Open** noon-8pm Mon-Fri; noon-9pm Sat; noon-6pm Sun. **Credit** AmEx, Disc, MC, V. **Map** p250 G3.

Sassy shoes and a fun attitude mark this home-grown favourite. The highest of heels and the flattest of flats, plus things for the upper body as well.

Specialist

Backstage

545 Eighth Street, SE, at G Street, Capitol Hill (1-202 544 5744). Eastern Market Metro. **Open** 11am-7pm Mon-Sat. **Credit** AmEx, MC, V. **Map** p253 M8.

While the masses might pile in here for Hallowe'en, it's the troupers in Washington's enormous theatre community who constantly bang on the doors for costumes, masks, hair and nails.

Georgetown Formal Wear & Custom Tailor

1083 Wisconsin Avenue, NW, at M Street, Georgetown (1-202 625 2247). Foggy Bottom-GWU Metro, then 30, 32, 34, 35, 36 bus. **Open** 10am-7pm Mon-Sat. **Credit** AmEx, Disc, MC, V. **Map** p249 E5.

Sudden invitation to a formal state dinner. Forgot to pack the black tie and tails in your luggage? Head here for a tux and all the trimmings.

Sporting goods & sportswear

Fleet Feet

1841 Columbia Road, NW, between Biltmore Street & Mintwood Place, Adams Morgan (1-202 387 3888/www.dcnet.com/fleetfeet). Woodley Park/ Adams Morgan Metro, then 90, 92, 93 bus. **Open** 10am-8pm Mon-Fri; 10am-7pm Sat; noon-4pm Sun. **Credit** AmEx, DC, Disc, MC, V. **Map** p250 G3.

Judging by the number of runners that hang around here at weekends, it would seem that athletes can't tear themselves away from the first-rate selection of well-priced shoes to actually go running.

Sports Zone

3140 M Street, NW, at Wisconsin Avenue, Georgetown (1-202 337 9773). Foggy Bottom-GWU Metro, then 30, 32, 34, 35, 36 bus. **Open** 10am-10pm Mon-Sat; 10am-8pm Sun. **Credit** AmEx, MC, V. **Map** p249 E5.

Suits and shoes to get you out running on track or field or road by Ecko, Adidas and Avirex.

Streetwear

Commander Salamander

1420 Wisconsin Avenue, NW, between O & P Streets, Georgetown (1-202 337 2265). Foggy Bottom-GWU Metro, then 30, 32, 34, 35, 36 bus. **Open** 10am-9pm Mon-Wed; 10am-10pm Thur-Sat; 11am-7pm Sun. **Credit** AmEx, Disc, MC, V. **Map** p249 E4.

Goth and punk clothing, and accessories by von Dutch, Gucci and more are available at this underground headquarters for those who want to advertise their non-conformity in expensive clothes.

Urban Outfitters

3111 M Street, NW, between 31st & 32nd Streets, Georgetown (1-202 342 1012). Foggy Bottom-GWU Metro then 30, 32, 34, 35, 36 bus. **Open** 10am-10pm Mon-Sat; 11am-8pm Sun. **Credit** AmEx, Disc, MC, V. **Map** p249 E5.

Young neo-bohemians troll the creaky floors of this bazaar for geek fashions and groovy housewares. **Other locations**: 737 7th Street, NW, between G & H Streets, Chinatown (1-202 737 0259).

Vintage & second-hand

Annie Creamcheese

3279 M Street, NW, between 32nd & 33rd Streets, Georgetown (1-202 298 5555/www.anniecream cheese.com). Foggy Bottom Metro then 38B bus. **Open** 11am-8pm Mon-Wed; 11am-9pm Thur-Sat; noon-6pm Sun. **Credit** AmEx, Disc, MC, V. **Map** p249 E5.

Vintage designer clothes from Pucci, Missoni, Lanvin, and the like. Also imports new items from minor designers in Miami and Los Angeles.

Meep's & Aunt Neensie's

2104 18th Street, NW, between California Street & Wyoming Avenue, Adams Morgan (1-202 265 6546/ www.meepsdc.com). Woodley Park-Zoo/Adams Morgan Metro, then 90, 92, 93 bus. **Open** noon-7pm Tue-Sat; noon-5pm Sun. **Credit** MC, V. **Map** p250 G3.

Remember that shirt you had when you were 16? The one that, when you put it on, you knew made you look the absolute business. Would you like to find it again? It's at Meep's, where DC's slackers and band kids flock to get that *Quadrophenia* look. They don't sell mopeds, but have all the other retro-chic essentials for both sexes.

Florists & garden suppliers

Allan Woods Florist

2645 Connecticut Avenue, NW, at 26th Street, Woodley Park (1-202 332 3334). Woodley Park-Zoo/Adams Morgan Metro. **Open** 9am-7pm Mon-Fri; 9am-6pm Sat. **Credit** AmEx, Disc, MC, V.

Fresh, seasonal favourites abound at this shop – hydrangeas, peonies, lilies and lilacs in spring and summer and a parade of poinsettias at Christmas – alongside a deluge of cut flowers.

The best of Brazilian design at **Artefacto**. *See p152.*

Future Green.

Garden District

1801 14th Street, NW, at S Street, U Street/
14th Street Corridor (1-202 797 9005). Dupont
Circle or U St/African-Amer Civil War Memorial/
Cardozo Metro. **Open** *9am-7pm Mon-Sat; 10am-5pm*
Sun. Closed Jan. **Credit** *AmEx, Disc, MC, V.*
Map *p250 H4.*

A compact resource for urban gardeners, with plants in all sizes, from bonsais to bedding plants to larger trees, plus all the supplies you'll need. **Photo** *p148.*

A Little Shop of Flowers

2421 18th Street, NW, between Belmont & Columbia
Roads, Adams Morgan (1-202 387 7255). Woodley
Park-Zoo/Adams Morgan Metro, then 90, 92, 93
bus. **Open** *9am-7pm Mon-Sat; noon-5pm Sun. Closed*
Aug. **Credit** *AmEx, Disc, MC, V.* **Map** *p250 G3.*

Stop in for sunflowers or alstromeria to freshen your room, or order a bouquet of any size for a friend.

Furniture & home accessories

A Mano

1677 Wisconsin Avenue, NW, at Reservoir Road,
Georgetown (1-202 298 7200/www.amano.bz). Foggy
Bottom-GWU Metro, then 30, 32, 34, 35, 36 bus.
Open *10am-6pm Mon-Sat; noon-5pm Sun.* **Credit**
AmEx, MC, V. **Map** *p249 E4.*

Welcome to a world of handmade (hence the name) earthen vessels, glass and linen.

Apartment Zero

406 Seventh Street, NW, between D & E Streets,
Penn Quarter (1-202 628 4067/www.apartment
zero.com). Archives-Navy Memorial or Gallery
Place-Chinatown Metro. **Open** *11am-6pm Wed-*
Sat; noon-5pm Sun. **Credit** *AmEx, Disc, MC, V.*
Map *253 J6*

Cool-hunters shop at Apartment Zero for furniture by Konstantin Grcic, Ron Arad and Moooi.

Artefacto

3333 M Street, NW, between 33rd & 34th Streets,
Georgetown (1-202 338 3337/www.artefacto.com).
Foggy Bottom Metro, then 38B bus. **Open** *10am-*
7pm Mon-Sat; noon-6pm Sun. **Credit** *AmEx, MC, V.*
Map *p249 E5.*

Brazil's design secrets are becoming known to the world through Artefacto, with its minimalist hardwood and steel pieces covered in leathers, silks, taffeta, crocodile or cane. **Photos** *p151.*

Contemporaria

3303 Cady's Alley, NW, M Street between 33rd &
34th Streets, Georgetown (1-202 338 0193/www.
contemporaria.com). Foggy Bottom Metro, then 38B
bus. **Open** *10am-6pm Mon-Fri; 11am-6pm Sat; noon-*
5pm Sun. **Credit** *AmEx, MC, V.* **Map** *p249 E5.*

Cruise down the curved concrete ramp to a minimalist world of Kartell chairs, Cappellini wall systems and Minotti sofas. Less is more, particularly when you come to paying the bill.

Future Green

1469 Church Street, NW, between 14th & 15th
Streets, Logan Circle (1-202 234 7110/www.
futuregreen.net). Dupont Circle Metro. **Open**
11am-7pm Mon-Sat; 11am-5pm Sun. **Credit**
AmEx, Disc, MC, V. **Map** *p250 H4.*

Shop with a clean conscience for eco-friendly home supplies, clay-dyed clothing, linens and bedding, 'fair trade' foods, and Peace Fleece knitting yarns.

Good Eye

4918 Wisconsin Avenue, NW, between Ellicott & Fessenden Streets, Upper Northwest (1-202 244 8516/www.goodeyeonline.com). Tenleytown-AU or Friendship Heights Metro. **Open** noon-6pm Thur-Sun. **Credit** Disc, MC, V.

Appealing to lovers of mid 20th-century throwbacks, Good Eye sells mint-condition upholstered and wooden furniture, and a fine array of lighting.

Home Rule

1807 14th Street, NW, at S Street, Shaw: U Street/ 14th Street Corridor (1-202 797 5544/www.home rule.com). U Street/African-Amer Civil War Memorial/ Cardozo Metro. **Open** 11am-7pm Mon-Sat; noon-6pm Sun. **Credit** AmEx, Disc, MC, V. **Map** p250 H4.

In this arresting little shop, the walls are lined with the latest kitchen utensils, desk supplies, incredible soaps and lotions, and tons of stocking fillers.

Illuminations

415 Eighth Street, NW, between D & E Streets, Penn Quarter (1-202 783 4888/www.illuminc.com) Archives-Navy Memorial Metro. **Open** noon-6pm Mon-Fri; 11am-5pm Sat. **Credit** AmEx, MC, V. **Map** p253 J6.

Two showrooms display lighting from Artemide, Ingo Maurer, Flos and Neidhardt, among others. **Other locations**: 3323 Cady's Alley, NW, Georgetown (1-202 965 4888).

Millennium Decorative Arts

1528 U Street, NW, between 15th & 16th Streets, U Street/14th Street Corridor (1-202 483 1218). U Street/African-American Civil War Memorial/ Cardozo Metro. **Open** noon-7pm Fri, Sat; noon-6 pm Sun. **Credit** AmEx, MC, V. **Map** p250 H3.

Stylish 1940s to 1960s-vintage European furniture is stocked at this two-level store, but you'll find graphic glassware, vases and coaster sets too.

100% Mexico Hecho a Mano

1612 14th Street, between Q & R Streets, Shaw: U Street/14th Street Corridor (1-202 332 2888/www. 100mexico.net). U Street/African-Amer Civil War Memorial/Cardozo or Dupont Circle Metro. **Open** noon-7pm Tue-Fri; 11am-7pm Sat; noon-6pm Sun. **Credit** AmEx, MC, V. **Map** p250 H4.

Goods from Mexico's remoter areas: Servin ceramics, Oaxacan wood carvings, masks, Zapotec rugs and embroidered *guayaberas*.

Reincarnations

1401 14th Street, NW, at Rhode Island Avenue, U Street/14th Street Corridor (1-202 319 1606). Dupont Circle Metro. **Open** 11am-8pm Tue-Sun. **Credit** AmEx, MC, V. **Map** p250 H4.

Furniture and accessories with great wit, with styles from the baroque to the contemporary. You'll find something to suit any setting.

Simply Home

1412 U Street, NW, between 14th & 15th Streets, U Street/14th Street Corridor (1-202 986 8607/ www.simplyhomedc.com). U Street/African-Amer

Civil War Memorial/Cardozo Metro. **Open** 11am-9pm daily. **Credit** AmEx, Disc, MC, V. **Map** p250 H3.

The Thai proprietor brings in garments, linens, bedding and pillows in modish fabrics from weavers in his homeland, and also runs an adjoining café that serves some sublime Thai food. **Photos** *p155*.

Sur La Table

5211 Wisconsin Avenue, NW, between Ingomar & Harrison Streets, Chevy Chase, Upper Northwest (1-202 237 0375/www.surlatable.com). Friendship Heights Metro. **Open** 10am-6pm Mon-Wed, Sat; 10am-8pm Thur, Fri; noon-6pm Sun. **Credit** AmEx, Disc, MC, V.

All the kitchen gadgets you could possibly want and some you had never dreamed of. The staff members are knowledgeable and happy to help those uncertain of the utility of a rechargeable milk frother.

Tabletop

1608 20th Street, NW, between Q & R Streets, Dupont Circle (1-202 387 7117/www.tabletop dc.com). Dupont Circle Metro. **Open** noon-8pm Mon-Sat; noon-6pm Sun. **Credit** AmEx, Disc, MC, V. **Map** p250 G4.

The owners favour lesser-known makers of playful, clean accessories, such as Klein Reid for vases and Panek Tobin for ceramics. These are sold alongside contemporary lighting and modern jewellery.

Vastu

1829 14th Street, NW, between S & T Streets, U Street/14th Street Corridor (1-202 234 8344/ www.vastudc.com). U Street/African-American Civil War Memorial/Cardozo Metro. **Open** 11am-7pm Tue-Sat; noon-5pm Sun. **Credit** AmEx, DC, Disc, MC, V. **Map** p250 H3.

Unifying this store is the warm modernism of Steven Anthony upholstered furniture, tables and cabinets by escribaStudio of Brazil, and Babette Holland spun-metal lamps. Vastu also sells Knoll furniture.

Food & drink

See also p156 **Unpack your palate**. *For cafés, see pp134-40.*

Bakeries

La Madeleine

3000 M Street, NW, at 30th Street, Georgetown (1-202 337 6975). Foggy Bottom-GWU Metro, then 30, 32, 34, 35, 36 bus. **Open** 7am-10pm daily. **Credit** AmEx, Disc, MC, V. **Map** p249 F5.

A decent chain French bakery, with all the classics and yummy coffee, too.

Marvelous Market

3217 P Street, NW, at Wisconsin Avenue, Georgetown (1-202 333 2591/www.marvelous market.com). Foggy Bottom-GWU Metro, then 30, 32, 34, 35, 36 bus. **Open** 8am-9pm Mon-Sat; 8am-8pm Sun. **Credit** AmEx, MC, V. **Map** p249 E4.

Eat, Drink, Shop

Delicious breads, rolls, scones and pastries (alas, no biscuits) along with a smattering of packaged goods. **Other locations**: throughout town. Check phone book for details.

Patisserie Poupon

1645 Wisconsin Avenue, NW, between Q & R Streets, Georgetown (1-202 342 3248). Foggy Bottom-GWU Metro, then 30, 32, 34, 35, 36 bus. **Open** 8am-6.30pm Tue-Fri; 8am-5pm Sat; 8am-4pm Sun. **Credit** AmEx, DC, Disc, MC, V. **Map** p249 E4.
All the calorific French classics are here. Arrive early at weekends if you want to grab a table.

Ethnic

DC's suburbs have long since globalised, and as they have, much of the good ethnic shopping lies in places like Wheaton, Rockville, Arlington and Falls Church.

Addisu Gebeya

2202 18th Street, NW, between Wyoming Avenue & Kalorama Road, Adams Morgan (1-202 986 6013). Woodley Park-Zoo/Adams Morgan Metro, then 90, 92, 93 bus. **Open** 9am-9pm daily. **Credit** AmEx, MC, V. **Map** p250 G3.
Everything Ethiopian is stocked here, from spices and lentils to spongy injera bread and the teff flour that is used to make it.

Casa Peña

1636 17th Street, NW, between Corcoran & R Streets, Dupont Circle (1-202 462 2222). Dupont Circle Metro. **Open** 8am-11pm daily. **Credit** AmEx, DC, Disc, MC, V. **Map** p250 G4.
Beans, rice, chillies, and just about everything else you'd need for a hot meal, plus tropical herbs and produce, and meats from the adjacent butcher.

Vace

3315 Connecticut Avenue, NW, at Macomb Street, Cleveland Park (1-202 363 1999). Cleveland Park Metro. **Open** 9am-9pm Mon-Fri; 9am-8pm Sat; 10am-5pm Sun. **Credit** AmEx, Disc, MC, V.
Take out a crisp, aromatic slice of pizza – or order a whole pie – and get fresh pasta, condiments, meats and wines at great prices at this premier Italian deli.

Farmers' markets

The growing season in the DC region is quite long, hence the ever-flowing bounty of fruits and vegetables, not to mention artisanal cheeses, baked goods, and cut flowers. **Eastern Market**, open year-round, is the gold standard, open every day but Monday from 8am-6pm (closes at 4pm Sunday; 225 Seventh Street, SE, between C Street & North Carolina Avenue, Capitol Hill; 1-202 544 0083). At the year-round **Freshfarm Market**, open 9am-1pm Sun (Riggs Bank parking lot, 20th & Q Streets, NW, Dupont Circle, 1-202 362 8889; seasonal locations in Georgetown and Penn Quarter),

food vendors all sell food that has been grown, raised or made on their own premises. The same applies to the surfeit of foods at the **Takoma Park Farmers' Market** (Laurel Avenue, between Eastern & Carroll Avenues, Takoma Park, 1-301 422 0097; Takoma Park Metro). Leave your plastic behind when browsing, all the markets accept cash only.

Fish

Wharf at Maine Avenue, SW

L'Enfant Plaza or Waterfront-SEU Metro. **Map** p252 J8.
Fish, crabs, spices, sauces, you name it, they're at Captain White Seafood (1-202 484 2722), the big tuna of this market. Subtropical fruits and vegetables sit alongside the goodies del mar at Jessie Taylor Seafood (1-202 554 4173). You'll find that Pruitt Seafood (1-202 554 2669) is slightly cheaper.

Gourmet

Dean & Deluca

3276 M Street, NW, at Potomac Street, Georgetown (1-202 342 2500/www.deandeluca.com). Foggy Bottom-GWU Metro, then 30, 32, 34, 35, 36 bus. **Open** *Shop* 10am-8pm Mon-Thur, Sun; 10am-9pm Fri, Sat. *Café* 8am-8pm Mon-Thur, Sun; 8am-9pm Fri, Sat. **Credit** AmEx, MC, V. **Map** p249 E5.
Fresh produce, salads, pastries, meats and more, all of exceptional quality and for prices higher than you ever thought you'd pay.

Uncle Brutha's Hot Sauce Emporium

323 7th Street, SE, between C Street & Pennsylvania Avenue, Capitol Hill (1-202 546 3473). Eastern Market Metro. **Open** 10am-7pm Tue-Thur; 10am-8pm Fri; 9am-7pm Sat; 10am-5pm Sun. **Credit** AmEx, Disc, MC, V. **Map** p253 L7.
Choose from some 300 types of hot sauces – 'from mild to wild' – including a proprietary line, plus Cajun seasonings and dry rubs. Water, please. **Photo** *p141*.

Health & beauty

Beauty products, body care & spas

Aveda

1325 Wisconsin Avenue, NW, between N & Dumbarton Streets, Georgetown (1-202 965 1325/www.aveda.com). Foggy Bottom-GWU Metro, then 30, 32, 34, 35, 36 bus. **Open** 10am-7pm Mon, Sun; 10am-8pm Tue; 10am-9pm Wed, Thur; 8.30am-8pm Fri, Sat. **Credit** AmEx, MC, V. **Map** p249 E4.
Disappear into this well-regarded salon and spa to treat your scalp, wax your brows, have a massage (hot stones optional), or reward your tired feet. **Other locations**: throughout the city. Check phone book for details.

Blue Mercury

*3059 M Street, NW, between 30th & 31st Streets,
Georgetown (1-202 965 1300/www.bluemercury.
com). Foggy Bottom-GWU Metro then 30, 32, 34,
35, 36 bus.* **Open** 10am-8pm Mon-Sat; noon-6pm
Sun. **Credit** AmEx, Disc, MC, V. **Map** p249 E5.
Try the wide range of body treatments, then browse
through the fine selection of cosmetics, fragrances
and moisturisers, including Acqua di Parma and
Bumble & Bumble, and take some nirvana home.
Other locations: (store only): 1619 Connecticut
Avenue, NW (1-202 462 1300).

Celadon

*1180 F Street, NW, between 11th & 12th Streets,
Downtown (1-202 347 3333). Metro Center Metro.*
Open 8.30am-6pm Mon-Wed, Fri; 8.30am-7pm
Thur; 8.30am-4pm Sat. **Credit** AmEx, Disc, MC,
V. **Map** p252 J6.

Downtown's workaholics defuse their tensions at
this subdued salon and spa, and often leave with a
bag of skin and beauty products for carrying on the
good work at home.

Grooming Lounge

*1745 L Street, NW, between Connecticut Avenue &
18th Street, Downtown (1-202 466 8900). Farragut
North Metro.* **Open** 9am-7pm Mon-Fri; 9am-6pm Sat;
11am-4pm Sun. **Credit** AmEx, MC, V. **Map** p252 G5.
Men finally have a place to call their own in DC. This
modern retreat with an old barber shop mood offers
haircuts, hot shaves, facials and nail care, plus product lines by Anthony, Dermalogica and Jack Black.

Ilo

*1637 Wisconsin Avenue, NW, between Q Street
& Reservoir Road, Georgetown (1-202 342 0350).
Foggy Bottom-GWU Metro then 30, 32, 34, 35,*

Simply Home. *See p153.*

Unpack your palate

You may be planning a picnic, or have just been invited to a backyard gathering and don't want to show up empty-handed. Or you want to assemble your own little charcuterie tray and you need something nice to wash it down with. In any case, who needs an excuse to enjoy excellent cheeses, meats and a good bottle of wine?

Best Cellars

1643 Connecticut Avenue, NW, between Q & R Streets, Dupont Circle (1-202 387 3146). Dupont Circle Metro. **Open** *10am-9pm Mon-Thur; 10am-10pm Fri, Sat.* **Credit** *AmEx, MC, V.* **Map** *p250 G4.*
With stores in several US cities, these wine realists take you beyond the freemasonry of

wine snobs and their secret codes and boil it down to a simple glossary of 'luscious' (an Alsatian Pinot Gris, for example), 'big' (Californian Zinfandel or Syrah from France), 'smooth' (Chilean Merlot), and so on. For less than $15 a bottle, you can find about 100 different choices. Also 'handcrafted' beers (makes for wet hands) and some small-batch spirits.

Calvert Woodley

4339 Connecticut Avenue, NW, at Windom Place, Upper Northwest (1-202 966 4400/www.calvertwoodley.com). Van Ness-UDC Metro. **Open** *10am-8.30pm Mon-Sat.* **Credit** *Disc, MC, V.*
The old hands here have mounted a large yet well-focused selection of voluptuary treats. The extensive wine shop is especially strong in Burgundy and Bordeaux and always has affordable specials – say, a 2004 Wishing Tree Shiraz from Australia for $9.99. At the deli, the prodigious selection includes prosciutto, Serrano and pâtés, and a world of cheeses from Cotswold to Mimolette.

Cowgirl Creamery

919 F Street, NW, between 9th & 10th Streets, Downtown (1-202 393 6880/ www.cowgirlcreamery.com). Gallery Place-

36 bus. **Open** 10am-7pm Tue, Wed, Fri; 10am-8pm Thur; 9am-6pm Sat. **Credit** AmEx, MC, V. **Map** p249 E4.
In town to accept an award and – gasp! – not looking your best after the red-eye flight? This spa offers traditional services, plus laser hair removal, microdermabrasion and botox to prepare you for your close-up. And it works just as well if you need to make a presentation in front of important new clients.

Sephora

3065 M Street, NW, between 30th & 31st Streets, Georgetown (1-202 338 5644). Foggy Bottom-GWU Metro, then 30, 32, 34, 35, 36 bus. **Open** 10am-9pm Mon-Sat; noon-6pm Sun. **Credit** AmEx, Disc, MC, V. **Map** p249 E5.
The celebrated French chain is a beauty junkie's paradise, with skincare, cosmetics and designer scents for both men and women.

Splash at the Sports Club/LA

Ritz Carlton Hotel, 1170 22nd Street, NW, at M Street, Foggy Bottom (1-202 974 6601). Foggy Bottom-GWU or Dupont Circle Metro. **Open** 8am-9pm Mon-Fri; 9am-6pm Sat, Sun. **Credit** AmEx, Disc, MC, V. **Map** p250 G5.
Athletes and actors have been spotted at this plush spa, checking in for facials, massages, body treatments, waxing and the like. No doubt their wallets are lighter upon leaving.

Hairdressers & barbers

Axis

1509 Connecticut Avenue, NW, between Dupont Circle & Q Street, Dupont Circle (1-202 234 1166). Dupont Circle Metro. **Open** 10am-7.30pm Tue-Fri; 9am-5pm Sat. **Credit** AmEx, MC, V. **Map** p250 G4.

Chinatown or Metro Center Metro. **Open** 10am-8pm Tue-Fri; 9am-6pm Sat. **Credit** MC, V. **Map** p253 J6.

From their original creamery in Point Reyes, California, the owners, daughters of the DC area, have flown back to offer their celebrated cheeses here. Among the choices are the triple-cream Mt Tam, earthy Alpine Shepherd, buttery Constant Bliss, as well as cottage cheese and crème fraiche.

Rodman's

5100 Wisconsin Avenue, NW, at Garrison Street, Friendship Heights, Upper Northwest (1-202 363 3466). Friendship Heights Metro. **Open** 9am-9.30pm Mon-Sat; 10am-7pm Sun. **Credit** AmEx, Disc, MC, V.

Open since 1955, this family-owned discount drugstore has expanded greatly and now offers one of the best selections of wine in Washington. Possibilities range from a Turning Leaf Cabernet marked down to $3.99 to a rare Dominus Cabernet Sauvignon for $115. Plus gourmet cheeses, exotic snacks, coffees and teas to round out the repast.

Vace

3315 Connecticut Avenue, NW, at Macomb Street, Cleveland Park (1-202 363 1999). Cleveland Park Metro. **Open** 9am-9pm Mon-Fri; 9am-8pm Sat; 10am-5pm Sun. **Credit** MC, V. **Map** p249 F1.

There's not that much fresh Italian produce in DC, but most of what there is can be found at Vace. The aroma of freshly rolled and baked pizzas (slices or pies) will draw you inside, where you'll find freezers of ready-to-heat pastas, and coolers of soft, delicious linguines plus awesome imported Parmesan and other cheeses, all across from a deli case of carpaccio, salamis, hams and, last but certainly not least, olives. And don't overlook the wine selection.

De Vinos

2001 18th Street, NW, at Florida Avenue, Adams Morgan (1-202 986 5002). Dupont Circle Metro. **Open** noon-10pm daily. **Credit** Amex, Disc, MC, V. **Map** p250 G3.

The wines at this relatively new but friendly shop are arranged by country and region – including those from Armenia and, as if to please neighborhood expats, Ethiopia. The store also stocks a selection of tasty beers, plus soft and hard cheeses and the gourmet crackers necessary to carry them. The wine selection is adventurous – bottles range in price from $6 to $500, and you'll find appellations you've never heard of. But then, you only learn by learning, right?

Whole Foods

1440 P Street, NW, between 14th & 15th Streets, Logan Circle (1-202 332 4300). Dupont Circle Metro. **Open** 8am-10pm daily. **Credit** AmEx, DC, Disc, MC, V. **Map** p250 H4.

Besides its piles of organic produce, mountains of granola and organically raised meats, this wonderful store has an excellent stock of wines, cheeses, antipasti and other grown-up finger foods. Though the store as a whole can be expensive, the wines are available in all price ranges. And if you buy a case there's ten per cent off.

The prices may rise, but those in need of a cut or a trim keep coming, attracted in part by the cheeky window displays and funky storefront.

Christophe

1125 18th Street, NW, between L & M Streets, Foggy Bottom (1-202 785 2222/www.christophe.com). Farragut North Metro. **Open** 9am-7pm Tue, Wed; 9am-8pm Thur, Fri; 9am-5pm Sat. **Credit** AmEx, MC, V. **Map** p252 G5.

The Washington branch of the Beverly Hills salon. You know what to expect: good haircuts, at a price.

Evolve

2905 M Street, NW, between 29th & 30th Streets, Georgetown (1-202 333 9872). Foggy Bottom-GWU Metro, then 30, 32, 34, 35, 36 bus. **Open** 10am-2pm, 3-6pm Tue-Sat. **Credit** AmEx, Disc, MC, V. **Map** p249 F5.

Two decades of keeping DC's ladies beautiful attests to the excellent standards of this salon, which also offers hair treatments and facials.

Ipsa

1629 Wisconsin Avenue, NW, between Q & R Streets, Georgetown (1-202 338 4100). Foggy Bottom-GWU Metro, then 30, 32, 34, 35, 36 bus. **Open** 8am-4pm Mon; 10am-6pm Tue, Thur, Fri; 10am-7pm Wed; 9am-5pm Sat. **Credit** Disc, MC, V. **Map** p249 E4.

A chilled atmosphere makes for a pleasant visit and a satisfying hair-do.

Roche

3050 K Street, NW, at Thomas Jefferson Street, Georgetown (1-202 775 0775/www.rochesalon.com). Foggy Bottom-GWU Metro, then 30, 32, 34, 35, 36 bus. **Open** 10am-7pm Tue-Fri; 8.30am-5pm Sat. **Credit** AmEx, MC, V. **Map** p249 F5.

Eat, Drink, Shop

Fashionistas know Roche because they see it written up in the glossies. With its poppy interior and cool attitude, it will send you out a changed person – and for the better, at least in externals.

Pharmacies

CVS
6 Dupont Circle, NW, between Massachusetts & New Hampshire Avenues, Dupont Circle (1-202 833 5704). Dupont Circle Metro. **Open** 24hrs daily. **Credit** AmEx, DC, Disc, MC, V. **Map** p250 G4.
Locals have a love-hate affair with this chain drugstore. It carries just about anything you'd need at 2am, but some of the staff can be a bit clueless. **Other locations**: throughout the city. Check phone book for details.

Music & DVDs

CD Warehouse
3001 M Street, NW, at 30th Street, Georgetown (1-202 625 7101). Foggy Bottom-GWU Metro, then 30, 32, 34, 35, 36 bus. **Open** 11am-9pm Mon-Thur; 11am-10pm Fri, Sat; noon-7pm Sun. **Credit** AmEx, Disc, MC, V. **Map** p249 F5.
Stacks and stacks of new and not-so-new compact discs and DVDs, including new releases and imports, most of which you can audit before buying. CD Warehouse also buys and trades CDs. Check out the work on the walls by local artists.

DJ Hut
2010 P Street, NW, at 20th Street, Dupont Circle (1-202 659 2010/www.djhut.com). Dupont Circle Metro. **Open** noon-9pm Mon-Thur, Sat; noon-10pm Fri; 1-6pm Sun. **Credit** AmEx, Disc, MC, V. **Map** p250 G4.
Dance, dance, dance. This DJ destination sells all manner of hip hop, house, jungle, trance and beats, plus paraphernalia for working turntablists.

Melody Records
1623 Connecticut Avenue, NW, between Q & R Streets, Dupont Circle (1-202 232 4002). Dupont Circle Metro. **Open** 10am-10pm Mon-Thur, Sun; 10am-11pm Fri, Sat. **Credit** AmEx, MC, V. **Map** p250 G4.
Tunes in every imaginable genre are stuffed into this small, owner-operated landmark, which has the city's biggest collection of world music. Knowledgeable staff make you wish digital music had never dawned, because there's no place like a great record store.

Revolution Records
4215 Connecticut Avenue, NW, at Van Ness Street, Upper Northwest (202 237 2480). Van Ness-UDC Metro. **Open** 10am-9pm Mon-Fri; 11am-7pm Sat; noon-6pm Sun. **Credit** AmEx, Disc, MC, V.
Run by members of the local indie-rock band Gist, this small but friendly and discerningly stocked shop is particularly strong in hip hop and alt-rock CDs, both new and used. There's also a small vinyl selection. Live music sets most afternoons.

Sankofa Video
2714 Georgia Avenue, NW, between Girard & Fairmont Streets, Shaw (1-202 234 4755/www. sankofa.com). Shaw-Howard U Metro. **Open** 10am-7.30pm daily. **Credit** AmEx DC, Disc, MC, V. **Map** p251 J2.
The Ethiopian-born filmmaker Haile Gerima owns this store and stocks it with a spectrum of titles from around the world, especially Africa.

Musical instruments

Guitar Shop
1216 Connecticut Avenue, NW, between M & N Streets, Dupont Circle (1-202 331 7333). Dupont Circle or Farragut North Metro. **Open** noon-7pm Mon-Fri; 11am-6pm Sat. **Credit** Disc, MC, V. **Map** p250 G4.
Guitar heads in and around DC – and they are legion – consider this store their own, not least for the rare and exotic items alongside the standard inventory.

Speciality & gift shops

Appalachian Spring
1415 Wisconsin Avenue, NW, at P Street, Georgetown (1-202 337 5780). Foggy Bottom-GWU Metro then 30, 32, 34, 35, 36 bus. **Open** 10am-8pm Mon-Fri; 10am-9pm Sat; noon-6pm Sun. **Credit** AmEx, MC, V. **Map** p249 E4.
Why buy household gifts at the national chains when you can find wonderful handmade ceramics, blown glass, carved-wood items, blankets and jewellery at this regional crafts boutique?

Georgetown Tobacco
3144 M Street, NW, at Wisconsin Avenue, Georgetown (1-202 338 5100/www.gttobacco.com). Foggy Bottom-GWU Metro, then 30, 32, 34, 35, 36 bus. **Open** 10am-9pm Mon-Thur; 10am-10pm Fri, Sat; noon-8pm Sun. **Credit** AmEx, MC, V. **Map** p249 E5.
Tobacco in every form, along with everything you'd ever need for smoking it.

Ginza
1721 Connecticut Avenue, NW, between R & S Streets, Dupont Circle (1-202 331 7991/www. ginzaonline.com). Dupont Circle Metro. **Open** 11am-7pm Mon-Sat; noon-6pm Sun. **Credit** AmEx, Disc, MC, V. **Map** p250 G4.
Did you leave your heart in Tokyo? This intimate but comprehensive shop sells Japanese household items (dinnerware, and so on), plus specialities such as origami paper and garden ornaments.

Sullivan's Toy Store
3412 Wisconsin Avenue, NW, between Norton Avenue & Newark Street, Cleveland Park (1-202 362 1343). Tenleytown-AU Metro, then 30, 32, 34, 35, 36 bus. **Open** 10am-6pm Mon, Tue, Sat; 10am-7pm Wed-Fri; noon-5pm Sun. **Credit** AmEx, Disc, MC, V.
Before the onslaught of Toys 'R' Us, the world was full of toy stores like this one, which stocks craft kits, kites and puzzles, dolls and action figures.

Arts & Entertainment

Features

National Zoo. See p166.

Festivals & Events

Hanging out at the Mall.

Washington offers all the state ceremonies you would expect of a capital. Happily, it also has a calendar bursting with less formal occasions, from events associated with the big cultural institutions to lively weekends of streetside fun celebrating the diverse neighbourhoods where the District's real people live – Anacostia, Adams Morgan, Chinatown, Dupont Circle, Mount Pleasant, and many more. Keep track of events with the *Washington Post*'s Friday 'Weekend' section (www.washingtonpost.com/weekend), the *Washington City Paper* (www.washingtoncitypaper.com), or the events database at the Washington.org tourist site. Note that most events are free unless otherwise stated; phone near the time to check. For information on Washington's various film festivals, *see p170*. For a list of national holidays, *see p235*.

Spring

St Patrick's Day Celebrations

Constitution Avenue, NW, from Seventh to 17th Streets, The Mall & Tidal Basin (1-202 637 2474/ www.dcstpatsparade.com). Smithsonian, Federal Triangle, L'Enfant Plaza or Archives-Navy Memorial Metro. **Date** 17 Mar. **Map** p253 J6.
DC's St Patrick's Day revelries draw the crowds with a parade of dancers, bands, bagpipes and floats. In true Irish style, the partying continues in pubs around the city. If 17 March doesn't fall on a Sunday, the festivities take place the previous Sunday. Celebrations are also held in Alexandria in Virginia, where they're organised by a charity called Ballyshaners (1-703 237 2199/www.ballyshaners.org).

Annual White House Easter Egg Roll

White House South Lawn, 1600 Pennsylvania Avenue, NW, between 15th & 17th Streets (information 1-456 2200/2322/www.whitehouse. gov/easter). McPherson Square Metro. **Date** 1st Mon after Easter. **Map** p252 H6.
Since 1878, when Congress kicked them off the Capitol lawn, kids aged three to six have been invited to hunt Easter eggs – the egg count is up to 24,000-plus these days – hidden on the south lawn of the Executive Mansion. A festival on the Ellipse features storytelling, children's authors, even astronauts sometimes – and, crucially for cranky parents, food. In this most political city, even the Easter Bunny can become a focus for politicking: in 2006, a group of gay families attended en masse, quietly

making the point that they exist, even if United States law barely acknowledges it. The event kicks off at the Southeast Gate at the corner of East Executive Avenue and E Street; it gets very crowded, so arrive early. Make sure the kids are with you around 7-7.30am, when the tickets are handed out (though the actual festivities run from 10am to 2pm).

Easter celebrations

Mount Pleasant & Adams Morgan. **Date** Good Friday.
The procession of the Stations of the Cross on Good Friday through Mount Pleasant and Adams Morgan is dramatically Latin. At the time of writing it was not certain if the procession would take place in 2007 – check the local press for details nearer the time. On Easter Monday there is traditionally a big African-American gathering at the National Zoo, in memory of the time when African Americans were not welcomed at the Easter Egg Roll.

Smithsonian Annual Kite Festival

Washington Monument Grounds, The Mall & Tidal Basin (information 1-202 357 2700/ www.kitefestival.org). Smithsonian Metro. **Date** Sun late Mar. **Map** p252 H7.
Kite lovers of all ages proudly show off their handmade contraptions (and the serious ones even take part in competitions). There are also demonstrations with novelty and sport kites by 'kite-making masters'. Usually held on first day of National Cherry Blossom Festival (*see below*).

Cherry Blossom Festival

Information 1-202 547 1500/www.nationalcherry blossomfestival.org. **Date** late Mar-mid Apr.
Cherry blossom time is a big deal in Washington. In 1912, 3,000 cherry trees were donated to the city by Mayor Yukio Ozaki of Tokyo as a symbol of friendship between Japan and the United States. These original trees were planted along the Tidal Basin; today, the path that rings the basin becomes clogged during bloom time with ogling tourists – and even normally blasé Washingtonians. Ironically enough, given the World War II fate of the 'friendship' between Japan and the US, the city has become famous for the immigrant blossoms, and celebrates them with near-pagan worship and a weekend (31 March-15 April 2007) of special events, including a National Cherry Blossom Festival Parade and the Sakuri Matsuri Street Festival, a celebration of Japanese art, food and culture held on 12th Street between Pennsylvania and Constitution Avenues. To witness this explosion of colour, try to visit between late March and mid April; the atmosphere is congenial and the blossoms are truly glorious.

Arts & Entertainment

Eastern Market Day

Seventh Street, SE, at Pennsylvania Avenue, Southeast (information 1-202 675 9050/www. friendshiphouse.net). Eastern Market Metro. **Date** 1st Sun in May. **Map** p253 L7.

A neighbourhood festival, held from 11am to 6pm, featuring arts and crafts, games, rides, entertainment and food. All the funds raised go to Friendship House, a local social services agency.

Memorial Day celebrations

Date Memorial Day weekend (last Mon in May).

On the Sunday evening, the National Symphony Orchestra performs a free concert on the West Lawn of the US Capitol (there's another one on Labor Day in September; details on 1-800 444 1324 or www.kennedy-center.org/nso). On Monday, the presidential wreath-laying and memorial services are held at Arlington National Cemetery (1-703 607 8000/www.arlingtoncemetery.org), the Vietnam Veterans Memorial (1-202 426 6841) and the US Navy Memorial (1-202 737 2300 ext 768). Rolling Thunder's Ride for Freedom, a massive motorcycle parade on Sunday morning, remembers POWs/MIAs and honours those who died in wars while serving the United States.

Memorial Day Jazz Festival

Alexandria, VA (1-703 838 4844). King Street Metro. **Date** around Memorial Day (last Mon in May).

Quaint Old Town Alexandria is the location for this day-long affair, which features half a dozen or so jazz artists, plus food stalls.

Black Pride

Multiple venues (1-202 737 5767/www.dcblack pride.org). **Date** Memorial Day weekend (last Mon in May).

Exhibitions, workshops and concerts over four days, when around 10,000 African-American gays and lesbians hit the city for Black Pride.

Capital Pride

Multiple venues (1-202 797 3510/ www.capitalpride.org). **Date** early June.

Washington's GLBT community marks Capital Pride Week with parties, pageants, political forums, a Pennsylvania Avenue street festival, the inevitable parade – and even a mini film festival.

Summer

Also check out the two-week Shakespeare Free For All festival held at the Carter Barron Amphitheatre in Rock Creek Park (*see p100*).

Fort Reno Summer Concert Series

Fort Reno Park, NW, between Wisconsin & Nebraska Avenues, Upper Northwest (www.fortreno.com). Tenleytown-AU Metro. **Date** June-Aug.

Both up-and-coming and well-known bands take to the outdoor stage at Fort Reno Park, on a hill overlooking Washington. Concerts are free and bands

play for nothing; not surprisingly, long-term funding is a concern. Bring a picnic and soak up the music. No booze or glass bottles allowed.

Marine Band's Summer Concert Series and Evening Parades

West Terrace of the US Capitol *Capitol Hill, The Capitol & around. Capitol South or Smithsonian Metro.* **Date** Wed, June-Aug. **Map** p253 K7.

US Marine Corps War Memorial *Arlington, VA Rosslyn Metro.* **Date** Tue, June-Aug. **Both** *1-202 433 4011/433 6060/www.marine band.usmc.mil.*

'The President's Own' – once led by John Phillip Sousa – performs free, twice-weekly outdoor concerts at the Capitol and/or on the Mall; the repertoire ranges from classical music to brass-band favourites, and the action starts at 8pm. (See website for days and locations.) On summer Fridays, the band is also a featured element of the showy Evening Parade, which includes impressive precision formation drills; it begins at 8.45pm on the manicured grounds of the Marine Barracks (Eighth & I Streets, SE), the corps' oldest post. Reservations are required, though unclaimed seats are sometimes available at the time: see www.mbw.usmc.mil/ parades for details. The affiliated Commandant's Own drum and bugle corps performs a weekly Sunset Parade at the Iwo Jima memorial statue, adjacent to Arlington Cemetery; start time is 7pm and reservations are not required.

Capital Jazz Fest

Merriweather Post Pavilion, Columbia, MD (1-301 218 0404/www.capitaljazz.com). **Date** June.

Billed as 'the Woodstock of jazz festivals', this outdoor extravaganza serves up food, crafts, and of course some of the best jazz musicians around. Dave Koz, Eric Benét, Walter Beasley, David Benoit, Incognito, and India Arie are among past headliners. A recent addition: a *Pop Idol*-style talent challenge with a $5,000 prize.

National Race for the Cure

Starts at Constitution Avenue, NW, at Ninth Street for runners and 12th Street for walkers, The Mall & Tidal Basin (1-703-848 8884/www.nat-race-for-the-cure.org). Federal Triangle Metro. **Date** early June. **Map** p252 H6.

It's said to be the biggest five-kilometre run/walk in the world and the National Race for the Cure draws tens of thousands of participants to raise money for and awareness of breast cancer.

Dupont-Kalorama Museum Walk Weekend

Information 1-202 387 4062 ext 12/www.dk museums.com. **Date** early June.

Hidden-treasure museums and historically important houses in Dupont Circle and the neighbouring Kalorama neighbourhood take part in an 'off the Mall' museum day for the public. Free food, music, tours and crafts are added bonuses.

Arts & Entertainment

National Capital Barbecue Battle

Pennsylvania Avenue, NW, between Ninth &
14th Streets, Federal Triangle (1-301 860 0630/
www.barbecuebattle.com). Metro Archives-Navy
Memorial. **Date** late June. **Map** p252/p253 J6.

For more than a decade, barbecue wizards have
gathered to compete for titles that now, astonish-
ingly, carry more than $25,000 in prize money. Tens
of thousands throng the nation's Main Street to sample glorious ribs, chicken and every other form of
barbecue imaginable. Celebs, music, children's activities and much more to go with the food.

DanceAfrica DC: The
Annual Festival

Dance Place, 3225 Eighth Street, NE, at Monroe
Street, Northeast (1-202 269 1600/www.dance
place.org). Brookland-CUA Metro. **Date** mid June.
Map p251 M2.

A week of masterclasses culminates in a weekend
festival celebrating African and African-American
dance, with free outdoor performances, crafts and
food, plus ticketed mainstage events indoors. Note
that an admission price is charged for some events.

Caribbean Festival

Georgia Avenue, NW, between Missouri Avenue
& Banneker Park, Mount Pleasant & North
(1-202 726 2204/www.dccaribbeancarnival.com).
Date last weekend in June.

Hundreds of thousands of islanders and others line
Georgia Avenue for the DC Caribbean Carnival's big
parade, the climax of a week of festivities featuring
soca, calypso, steel band music, African drumming,
stilt dancers and a few thousand people dancing
through the streets while wearing some spectacular
carnival costumes. A Sunday festival caps off the
madness at Banneker Park.

Smithsonian Folklife Festival

National Mall, between Tenth & 15th Streets, The
Mall & Tidal Basin (1-202 357 2700/recorded info
1-202 633 9884/www.folklife.si.edu). Smithsonian
Metro. **Date** last weekend in June and 1st weekend
in July. **Map** p252 H7.

This monster festival celebrates the arts, crafts and
food of selected US states and other countries (2007's
focus: contemporary Northern Ireland, the roots of
Virginia culture, and the interconnected populations
influenced by Southeast Asia's Mekong River). Food
and demonstration booths stretch down the National
Mall, and there are evening celebrations and music
performances. The atmosphere is cheerful, the
weather usually hot and sticky, and parking very
limited, so use the Metro.

Independence Day

Various venues (information 1-202 789 7000).
Date 4 July.

Steer clear of this one if you hate crowds (nearly
700,000 people generally turn up), or if the now
rather pervasive security makes you think of Mr
Orwell (the legacy of 9/11 means that Fourth of July
revellers now encounter a fenced-off National Mall,
with checkpoints through which to enter). Official
events begin at 10am at the National Archives, with

Smithsonian Folklife Festival.

The Open House – centrepiece of the sprawling autumn Prelude Festival – is a day-long weekend extravaganza celebrating the Center's birthday and showcasing the diversity of the arts it plays host to. Local and national artists strut their stuff on the plazas, on the river terrace overlooking the Potomac, and on the Kennedy Center stages. The 2006 open house, held just after the one-year anniversary of Hurricane Katrina, celebrated Gulf Coast arts and artists, with folkabilly queen Nanci Griffith, zydeco legends Beausoleil avec Michael Doucet, and swamp pop dynamo Marcia Ball, among many others. Children are kept entertained, too, with a National Symphony Orchestra 'petting zoo' where they get to bow, blow, drum or strum their favourite instruments. The weeks-long Prelude Fest is the unofficial kick-off of the city's autumn performing arts season, including symphony performances, a jazz series, and the Page to Stage theatre event over Labor Day weekend; the latter is a new-works mini festival, with readings and performances involving no fewer than 35 local troupes.

Adams Morgan Day
18th Street, NW, between Columbia Road & Florida Avenue, Adams Morgan (1-202 328 9451/www. adamsmorgandayfestival.com). Dupont Circle or Woodley Park Metro. **Date** second Sunday in Sept. **Map** p250 G2.
For over a quarter of a century, thousands of DC residents have come out to celebrate this community, home to large Latino, white, African and African-American populations. Musicians, crafts and ethnic foods are in ample supply.

Black Family Reunion
National Mall/Washington Monument (1-202 383 9130/www.ncnw.org/events/reunion.htm). Smithsonian Metro. **Date** early to mid Sept. **Map** p252 H7.
Tens, if not hundreds, of thousands descend on the National Mall each year to celebrate 'the enduring strengths and traditional values of the African-American family'. Among the offerings: R&B and gospel concerts, a prayer breakfast, and a festival with a food fair and myriad themed pavilions.

Washington National Cathedral Open House
Massachusetts & Wisconsin Avenues, NW, Upper Northwest (1-202 537 3129/www.cathedral.org/ cathedral). Tenleytown/AU Metro then 30, 32, 35 or 36 bus. **Date** 10am-4pm Sat late Sept/early Oct. **Map** p249 E2.
This event, which in 2007 celebrates the anniversary of the laying of the cathedral's foundation stone, is great for children. As well as demonstrations of stone carving, there are performances by dancers, choirs, strolling musicians, jugglers and puppeteers. Hardier visitors can climb to the top of the central tower for a look at the bells (only one of two times a year that visitors are allowed to do this) and take in the amazing views from there.

a dramatic reading of the Declaration of Independence, demonstrations of colonial military manoeuvres, and more. Just before noon, the Independence Day parade starts to wind its way down Constitution Avenue (from the National Archives to 17th Street), and later (5-9.15pm) the grounds of the Washington Monument hosts entertainment – folk music, jazz, marching bands, military singers – and hordes of revellers. The National Symphony Orchestra performs a concert on the West Lawn of the US Capitol building at 8pm, traditionally concluding with a battery of cannons assisting in the finale of Tchaikovsky's *1812 Overture*; then, at roughly 9pm, a stupendous array of fireworks are set off over the Washington Monument. Logistical hassles or no, it's a grand sight: the monuments are lovely in the summer dusk, and the barrages involve literally thousands of rounds of explosives. Walk to the festivities if you can: Fourth of July crowds eat up parking spots and test the limits of the public transport system. Check local listings for smaller celebrations.

Autumn

Kennedy Center Open House Arts Festival/Prelude Festival
2700 F Street, NW, at New Hampshire Avenue & Rock Creek Parkway, Foggy Bottom (1-202 416 8000/www.kennedy-center.org). Foggy Bottom-GWU Metro. **Date** early-mid Sept. **Map** p252 F6.

Arts & Entertainment

National Book Fair

National Mall, NW, between Seventh & 14th streets (1-202 888 714 4696/www.loc.gov/ bookfest). Archives-Naval Memorial or Federal Triangle Metro. **Date** late Sept or early Oct. **Map** p252 H7.

Sponsored by the Library of Congress, the Book Fair features dozens of authors, illustrators, poets and storytellers, all reading, performing and signing in block after block of pavilions themed around 'Fiction and Imagination', 'History and Biography', 'Mysteries and Thrillers' and so on. Admission is free.

Annual High Heel Race

17th Street, NW, between S & P Streets, Dupont Circle (information from JR's bar 1-202 328 0090). Dupont Circle Metro. **Date** on or around 31 Oct. **Map** p250 H4.

Dupont Circle residents and gawkers from across the city swarm to 17th Street to catch this ultimate drag race, which features outrageously costumed contestants promenading up and down – then sprinting down a two-block stretch in the heart of the capital's gay ghetto. The event itself lasts only minutes, but the street-party atmosphere is festive and the scenery fabulous.

Marine Corps Marathon

1-800 786 8762/www.marinemarathon. com. **Date** late Oct (race starts 8.30am).

The 'Marathon of Monuments' draws runners from around the world, and no wonder: the course winds along the banks of the Potomac, through Georgetown and Rock Creek Park, past the city's most famous sites and monuments, finishing up at the Marine Corps War Memorial. Spectators and supporters turn the route into a 26-mile street party.

Veterans' Day ceremonies

Arlington National Cemetery, Memorial Drive, Arlington Drive, VA (1-703 607 8000/www. arlingtoncemetery.org). Arlington Cemetery Metro. **Date** 11am Veterans' Day (11 Nov).

A solemn ceremony with military bands, in honour of the country's war dead. Ceremonies are also held at the Vietnam Veterans' Memorial (details on 1-202 426 6841), Mount Vernon (1-703 780 2000) and the US Navy Memorial (1-202 737 2300).

Winter

National Christmas Tree Lighting

The Ellipse, The Mall & Tidal Basin (1-202 426 6841). Federal Triangle Metro. **Date** early Dec. **Map** p252 H6.

The president kicks off the holiday season by switching on the lights on the giant National Christmas Tree. (There's a National Menorah, too, which gets lit on the appropriate night.) For a seat in the enclosure, you'll need a ticket: apply at least six weeks in advance as they run out fast. The ticketless, though, can usually get a glimpse from the other side of the fence. The ceremony begins at 5pm;

arrive early. From now until New Year's Day, the Ellipse hosts Christmas performances as part of the annual Pageant of Peace.

New Year's Eve celebrations

Events around town range from relatively inexpensive celebrations at the Kennedy Center (music and dancing in the Grand Foyer) to dinners at some of the area's more upscale dining establishments costing hundreds of dollars. Restaurants and clubs often offer jazz, dinner and a champagne toast for a fixed but generally substantial price (most start taking reservations early); check ads in the *Washington City Paper* and the *Washington Post*.

Martin Luther King Jr's Birthday Celebrations

1-202 727 1186/WPAS concert information 1-202 833 9800/www.wpas.org. **Date** 3rd week Jan.

A birthday celebration is held on the steps of the Lincoln Memorial, where Dr King gave his famous 'I have a dream' speech in 1963. That's just one of many, many commemorations in DC. Among others: The Washington Performing Arts Society (WPAS) hosts an annual children's concert with Sweet Honey in the Rock, who combine gospel, African rhythms and rap into a cappella combinations. A tremendous show.

Chinese New Year

Chinatown, H Street, NW, between Sixth & Ninth Streets, Downtown. Gallery Place-Chinatown Metro. **Date** 18 Feb 2007, 7 Feb 2008 (determined by the lunar calendar). **Map** p253 J5.

Celebrations kick off with a bang – dancers, dragons, firecrackers and parades – and continue, a bit more muted, for ten days. Look out for details near the time or contact the Chinese Consolidated Benevolent Association at 1-703 851 5685.

Black History Month

Date Feb.

The Smithsonian Institution holds special events, exhibitions and cultural programmes throughout the month. For more information on the activities on offer, check newspaper listings or contact the Martin Luther King Library (*see p87*).

Famous birthdays

Information Lincoln 1-202 426 6841/Washington 1-703 780 2000/Douglass 1-202 426 5960. **Date** Feb.

A trio of famous men's birthdays. A celebration of Abe Lincoln's birthday (12 February) is held at the Lincoln Memorial; Lincoln's Gettysburg address is read and a wreath is laid. For hard-core history buffs only. George Washington's birthday celebration, with a patriotic military programme and a George Washington impersonator, is held (on the third Monday in February) at Mount Vernon, Virginia (*see p212* **Presidential seats**). The Frederick Douglass birthday tribute is held on or near 14 February at the Frederick Douglass National Historic Site, 1411 W Street, SE, at 14th Street, Anacostia.

Children

Capital!

National Zoo. See p102.

Walk along the National Mall, especially on a summer day or weekend, and you'll find children everywhere. It's the museums and monuments that are the attraction. They're some of the world's finest, and most – including the Smithsonian museums, the Supreme Court and the Capitol – are free. This helps make the city a relatively low-budget destination.

The scale of Washington DC – low-rise buildings, tourist attractions centred in a compact area and plenty of open space – is inviting, and children are welcome nearly everywhere. To get a taste of the major sights – and to avoid the ever-present transport hassles – consider taking one of the tours offered by a company like the National Park Service-approved Tourmobile (1-202 554 5100/www.tourmobile.com). The city is also pedestrian-friendly, so a family walking tour like those offered by Washington Walks (1-202 484 1565, www.washingtonwalks.com) can be delightful, especially in the spring or autumn, to escape summer's heat and humidity.

Babysitting

If you plan on leaving the children behind, be advised that childcare in Washington is not cheap, but most large hotels and those with concierge services can provide it, using in-house services or local companies. Last-minute requests can usually be accommodated (with extra fees), but it's best to book ahead. The leading childcare agencies include **White House Nannies** (1-800 266 9024, www.whitehousenannies.com), a well-respected service that uses thoroughly screened, independent carers at a flat fee. **Mothers' Aides Inc** (1-800 526 2669, www.mothersaides.com) charges a $55 agency fee a day plus the caregiver's hourly wage (normally $15-$20 per hour).

Entertainment

The listings below focus on attractions in or near central DC. For places further afield and in the suburbs, including parks and outdoor recreational facilities, buy a copy of *Going Places With Children in Washington, DC* ($14.95) or *Around Washington, DC With Kids* ($9.95), both excellent specialist guides available from most decent bookshops.

Eating out

Children are welcome at all but the fanciest restaurants – where you're unlikely to want to take them anyway. For quick budget meals, fast-food restaurants are plentiful and easy to find, but if your offspring aren't fussy eaters, you might want to try one of the many moderately priced ethnic restaurants like the Ethiopian choices found along Adams Morgan's 18th Street. A surefire winner for sports-crazy youngsters is the **ESPN Zone** (555 12th Street, NW, corner of 11th and E Streets, 1-202 783 3776), with its huge game room worthy of an amusement park. The food court in the **Pavilion at the Old Post Office** (1100 Pennsylvania Avenue, NW, between 11th and 12th Streets) is near the museums of Natural History and American History, while the **National Gallery of Art** (Constitution Avenue and Fourth Street, NW, 1-202 737 4215, www.nga.gov) has a nice self-service café with plentiful seating. Famished families on Capitol Hill can find sustenace at **Marty's** (527 Eighth Street, SE, 1-202 546 4952), whose menu has something for even the pickiest eaters, or the food court at Union Station (50 Massachusetts Avenue, NE, 1-202 289 1908), where '50's-style burger joint **Johnny Rockets** is a favourite.

Museums

All Smithsonian museums offer at least a few exhibits geared towards children, though three are consistently highly rated: the **National Air & Space Museum** (*see p66*), the **National Museum of American History** (*see p62*) and the **National Museum of Natural History** (*see p69*). Close behind are the **National Building Museum** (*see p93*), the **International Spy Museum** (*see p91*) and the relatively new **Museum of the American Indian** (*see p68*). And though it's not a museum per se, don't miss the **Bureau of Engraving & Printing** (*see p82*). Children are fascinated by its 35-minute tour, where they can look at currency being printed and even buy a souvenir bag of shredded cash.

Two more child-friendly museums:

National Postal Museum

2 Massachusetts Avenue, NE, Capitol Hill (1-202 633 5533/www.postalmuseum.si.edu). Union Station Metro. **Open** 10am-5.30pm daily. **Admission** free. **Credit** AmEx, MC, V. **Map** p253 K6.
More than 35 interactive games and screens make the mail fascinating for even the most technology-addled youngsters. Myriad stamp collections and a 'personal postcard' machine complete the experience.

National Geographic Museum at Explorers Hall

17th & M Streets, NW, Downtown (1-202 857 7588/www.nationalgeographic.com/museum). Farragut North Metro. **Open** 9am-5pm Mon-Sat; 10am-5pm Sun. **Admission** free. **Credit** AmEx, Disc, MC, V. **Map** p252 H5.
Filled with hands-on, science-oriented exhibits for the younger visitor, this museum-from-the-magazine offers free family programmes each Friday morning.

Animals & the outdoors

Within the District, the best outdoor activity for children, bar none, is a trip to the **National Zoo** (*see p102*). Particularly popular are the zoo's two giant pandas and their superstar cub, Tai Shan ('peaceful mountain'), the prairie dog community and the 11.30am daily sea lion feeding and training. Survival tip: the zoo slopes steeply downhill to Rock Creek from the entrance on Connecticut Avenue, so to avoid a long, hot climb at the end of your visit, plan a circular route that gets you back to the entrance before you run out of energy.

Rock Creek Nature Center & Planetarium

5200 Glover Road, NW, at Military Road, Upper Northwest (1-202 895 6070/www.nps.gov/rocr/naturecenter). Friendship Heights Metro then E2, E3 bus. **Open** 9am-5pm Wed-Sun. **Admission** free.

Rock Creek is a great place for cycling, skating, horse riding and exploring the old mill and the site of the Civil War battle at Fort Stevens. As well as the Nature Center's guided hikes, there's the highly entertaining Creature Feature programme (4pm on Fridays), which takes a close look at the park's wildlife. The planetarium (located on the park's western edge) hosts several free shows: 4pm Wednesday, Saturday and Sunday for ages seven-plus and 1pm Sunday for ages 4 and up.

Shopping

For clothes shops, *see p148*. For a good classic toy shop, try **Sullivan's Toy Store**, *see p158*.

Sport & fitness

Washington is a fantastic city for bike riding, with miles of family-friendly trails. Try the picturesque C&O Canal Towpath (www.nps.gov/choh, *see p196*) – where mule-drawn barge rides are also available – or the beautiful Mount Vernon Trail river ride (www.nps.gov/gwmp/mvt.html, *see p196*). The latter ends at George Washington's estate, where a tour is offered that younger children enjoy hugely (*see p213*). Also great are the 11 miles of the Capital Crescent Trail (*see p196*) and the loop through East Potomac Park. For maps and details, contact the Washington Area Bicyclist Association (*see p195*). For bike shops, *see p149*. For bike rental, *see p197*.

Less physically demanding is a summertime trip to see the Washington Nationals (*see p195*), whose arrival once again restored the 'national pastime' (professional baseball) to the capital.

Theatre & the arts

The 'Saturday's Child' column of the 'Weekend' section of Friday's *Washington Post* (www.washingtonpost.com) covers the current week's performances and other activities for children in and around DC. Other institutions that occasionally offer art and theatre programmes include the **National Gallery of Art** (*see p67*), the **Corcoran Museum of Art** (*see p73*), the **Hirshhorn Museum & Sculpture Garden** (*see p65*) and the **National Building Museum** (*see p92*).

Arthur M Sackler Gallery & Freer Gallery of Art

1050 Independence Avenue, SW, between 11th & 12th Streets, The Mall & Tidal Basin (1-202 633 4880/www.asia.si.edu). Smithsonian Metro. **Open** 10am-5.30pm daily. ImaginAsia times vary. **Admission** free. **Map** p252 J7.
The Sackler and Freer galleries offer ImaginAsia several days a week (call 1-202 357 2700 for schedules). Children aged six to 14, who must be accom-

panied by an adult, are given an activity book before entering the exhibition, and take part in an art workshop at the end. For reservations call 1-202 633 0461.

Glen Echo Park

7300 MacArthur Boulevard, at Goldsboro Road, Glen Echo, MD (1-301 492 6229/www.glenechopark. org). Friendship Heights Metro then Ride-On Bus 29.
Until 1968 Glen Echo was a popular amusement park just a trolley ride from Downtown. Today it is preserved by the National Park Service (2pm weekend tours) and run by a non-profit group as a site for theatre, art and dance. It also has a playground, picnic tables, a lovely 1921 carousel (open May-Aug, 10am-2pm Wed, Thur; noon-6pm Sat, Sun. Sept noon-6pm Sat, Sun) and plenty of places to explore. The following are highlights of the activities on offer:
Adventure Theatre *(1-301 320 5331, www. adventuretheatre.org; 1.30pm, 3.30pm Sat, Sun; admission $7).*
The DC area's longest-running children's theatre presents one-hour plays for fours and overs based on fables, fairy tales, musicals and children's classics, using puppets and actors.
Discovery Creek Children's Museum *(1-202 337 5111, www.discoverycreek.org; 10am-3pm Sat, Sun; admission $5, free under-2s).*
This small nature centre offers interactive events designed to teach children about nature and geography, as well as wildlife treks through the park.

Puppet Company Playhouse *(1-301 320 6668, www.thepuppetco.org; 10am, 11.30am Wed-Fri; 11.30am, 1pm Sat, Sun; admission $6).*
Plays are presented for all ages, most of them adaptations of classic stories for children like *Cinderella* and *The Jungle Book.* Reservations recommended.

Kennedy Center

2700 F Street, NW, at New Hampshire Avenue & Rock Creek Parkway, Foggy Bottom (1-800 444 1324/1-202 467 4600/www.kennedy-center.org). Foggy Bottom-GWU Metro. **Admission** varies. **Credit** AmEx, DC, Disc, MC, V. **Map** p252 F6.
The Kennedy Center offers an amazing variety of dance, music and theatre for youngsters. With subjects as diverse as West African dance and the history of Mexico in song, there is truly something for every taste (although most events are best for fives and over). The National Symphony also presents occasional family concerts here.

Saturday Morning at the National

National Theatre, 1321 Pennsylvania Avenue, NW, between 13th & 14th Streets, The Federal Triangle (1-202 783 3372/www.nationaltheatre.org). Metro Center Metro. **Admission** free. **Map** p252 H6.
On Saturdays at 9.30am and 11am, from September to April, the National Theatre offers free entertainment for both children and adults. The one-hour events include theatre, music, dance and magic.

Mighty ducks

How best to see the city? How about by duck? DUKW, to be exact: an acronym for amphibious personnel carriers that were devised in the wake of Pearl Harbor as a way to transport supplies from ships to areas that did not have port facilities. Meaning, essentially, that military minds took two-and-a-half-ton trucks, made them watertight and added propellers, allowing them to cruise like their web-footed namesakes. Little ones thrill at actual 1942 DUKWs (fully updated, natch) that now haul visitors on all-encompassing 90-minute tours that begin at Union Station. Narrated – though the 'wise-quacking' may get on grown-ups nerves after a bit – jaunts take in the major monuments, National Mall and adjunct sites, then splash in to the Potomac. A half-hour river cruise floats appropriately by the Pentagon and other war-related buildings, then tacks toward Gravely Point, where planes headed into Reagan National Airport buzz the craft. Tykes are occasionally offered a chance to steer the craft, adding a thrill – for both driver and passengers – before it drips its way back to Union Station. As an all-round travel-oddity, child-pleaser and good starting point for a first-time visit to the city, the duck turns out to be a pretty cool bird.

DC Ducks

Union Station, 50 Massachusetts Avenue, NE, Capitol Hill (1-202 832 9800/www. dcducks.com). Union Station Metro. **Open** mid-Apr-Nov 10am-4pm daily. Closed Memorial Day, 4 July. Check in at Union Station Ticket desk. **Tours** hourly Mon-Fri; every 30 mins Sat, Sun. Phone for firm schedule. **Rates** $32 adult; $16 4-12s; free under-3s. **Credit** AmEx, Disc, MC, V.

Arts & Entertainment

Film

The usual multiplexes – and a whole lot more.

The current fashion in American cinemas is for megaplexes containing up to 25 screens, which show essentially all the new mainstream releases. These behemoths slot more easily into brand new suburban developments than cities, but local developers have found room for two 14-screen complexes, both opened since the millennium. There are also a range of older moviehouses, one of which dates from the 1920s (the **Avalon**). Most of these cinemas show the same formulaic product that's seen from coast to coast (and around the world), but declining returns for Hollywood-made films have encouraged the major exhibitors to book more documentaries and independent films. Washington also has several theatres that specialise in non-Hollywood fare. These are complemented by an extensive array of non-commercial repertory film programmes.

Local filmmakers often claim that DC has the country's third-largest film industry, after LA and New York, but few features are produced locally. Instead, the emphasis is on documentaries, many of them made for the DC-based Discovery and National Geographic cable channels. There are many local showcases for non-fiction films, including the **Silverdocs** festival every June at the AFI Silver.

Washington has long been a useful location for Hollywood movies, but the crews often spend just a few days in town, filming at conspicuous landmarks before heading back to LA or continuing the shoot in cheaper locales. The Metro doesn't allow violent acts to be staged on its property, so subway scenes in Washington-based action movies are often shot in Baltimore. Still, Hollywood filmmakers keep coming. Washington is most often used as a setting for spy thrillers, such as *Mission Impossible 3*, but occasionally appears in comedies such *Wedding Crashers*.

THE CINEMAS

A series of recent mergers that combined four leading chains put most DC cinemas in the hands of a single company, AMC Loews. Landmark, the leading US arthouse chain, opened the eight-screen **E Street Cinema** in early 2004, followed later that year by Regal's 14-screen **Gallery Place** megaplex. The city currently has only one independently owned cinema, the **Avalon**. The E Street and Gallery Place cinemas returned cinema to Downtown, which was once full of opulent movie palaces. But most of the city's cinemas are found along Connecticut or Wisconsin Avenues, the major commercial arteries of the city's affluent west side.

TICKETS AND INFORMATION

Most cinemas have two or three screenings a night (usually between 7pm and 7.45pm, and 9pm and 9.45pm) and often a late show at the weekend. All DC theatres feature weekday and weekend matinées. Landmark E Street and Bethesda Row sometimes do weekend cult-film midnight shows. Washington filmgoers usually don't book in advance, although it's advisable to do so for the opening of heavily promoted new movies. Advance tickets for AMC Loews theatres are available at www.moviewatcher. com. Purchase tickets for Landmark theatres at www.movietickets.com, Regal Gallery Place at www.fandango.com and for Phoenix Union Station at www.phoenixtheatres.com.

Mainstream films

AMC Loews Georgetown
3111 K Street, NW, between 31st Street & Wisconsin Avenue, Georgetown (1-202 342 6033). 30, 32, 34, 35, 36, 38, D2, D4, D6, G2, DC Circulator or Georgetown Connection bus. **Tickets** $6.50-$9.50. **Credit** AmEx, Disc, MC, V. **Map** p249 E5.
This 14-screen cinema, part of a complex that incorporates the old Georgetown Incinerator, has a large, dramatic lobby. The theatres themselves, the biggest of which have 300 seats, are standard stadium-seating houses, with large screens and clear views.

AMC Loews Mazza Gallerie
5300 Wisconsin Avenue, NW, at Jenifer Street, Upper Northwest (1-202 537 9553). Friendship Heights Metro. **Tickets** $6.50-$12.50. **Credit** AmEx, Disc, MC, V.
When Massa Gallerie opened in 1999 the seven-screen cinema was the city's first with stadium seating, boasting large screens and excellent sight lines. Alcoholic beverages and an expanded snack menu are available in the two 'club cinemas'. The latter auditoriums are restricted to viewers over 21, although that doesn't guarantee that the movie shown will be suitable for adults.

AMC Loews Uptown
3426 Connecticut Avenue, NW, between Porter & Ordway Streets, Cleveland Park (1-202 966 5400). Cleveland Park Metro. **Tickets** $6.50-$9.50. **Credit** AmEx, Disc, MC, V. **Map** p249 F1.

With the destruction of the last of the Downtown movie palaces in the 1980s, what was once just an average neighbourhood theatre became the city's premier cinema. The 1936 art deco movie palace – with 1,500 seats it's the city's largest – now shows blockbusters and would-be blockbusters. Not everyone applauds the curved screen, originally installed in the 1960s for Cinerama movies.

AMC Loews Wisconsin Avenue

4000 Wisconsin Avenue, NW, at Upton Street, Upper Northwest (1-202 244 0880). Tenleytown-AU Metro. **Tickets** $6.50-$9.50. **Credit** AmEx, Disc, MC, V.

Now 15 years old, the six-screen Wisconsin lacks some of the more modern amenities such as stadium seating. But the sightlines are generally good, and the two largest auditoriums have bigger screens than any in the new 14-plexes.

Phoenix Theatres Union Station

Union Station, 50 Massachusetts Avenue, NE, at N Capitol Street, Union Station & Around (1-703 998 4262/www.phoenixtheatres.com). Union Station Metro. **Tickets** $6.50-$9.50. **Credit** AmEx, Disc, MC, V. **Map** p253 K6.

Located in an intriguing, cavern-like space under Union Station's waiting room, the Phoenix contains nine auditoriums, each named for a vanished Washington moviehouse. The largest theater has good sightlines and one of the city's biggest screens; the others are acceptable.

Regal Gallery Place

701 Seventh Street, NW, at G Street, Downtown (1-202 393 2121). Gallery Place-Chinatown Metro. **Tickets** $6.50-$9.50. **Credit** AmEx, Disc, MC, V. **Map** p253 J5.

Across the plaza north of Verizon Center and up two flights of escalators awaits a sparkling new but otherwise standard contemporary megaplex, with 14 auditoriums. The screens are big for the size of the houses, which range from 100 seats to about 300.

Foreign & independent films

AMC Loews Dupont Circle

1350 19th Street, NW, near N Street, Dupont Circle (1-202 333 3456). Dupont Circle Metro. **Tickets** $6.50-$9.50. **Credit** AmEx, Disc, MC, V. **Map** p250 G4.

AMC Loews' principal DC venue for foreign and independent films, the five-screen Dupont Circle is a bit cramped, but its bookings are usually exclusive, so for most films that play here it's the only option.

Avalon

5612 Connecticut Avenue, NW, at McKinley Street, Chevy Chase (1-202 966 6000/www.theavalon.org). Friendship Heights Metro/E2, E3, E4, E6, L1, L2, L4 bus. **Tickets** $6.50-$9.50. **Credit** MC, V.

Abandoned by its corporate operator, the city's oldest surviving moviehouse was rescued and restored by a neighbourhood group. Both inside and out, the 1923 structure has more charm than any number of

In search of **Avalon**.

the cookie-cutter megaplexes that have sprouted like mushrooms in the suburbs. It now shows a mix of foreign, independent, documentary and Hollywood fare, as well as classic and children's films. The small second screen upstairs is nothing special.

Landmark E Street Cinema

555 11th Street, NW (entrance on E Street), Downtown (1-202 452 7672/www.landmark theatres.com). Metro Center or Gallery Place Metro. **Tickets** $6.75-$9.50. **Credit** AmEx, Disc, MC, V. **Map** p252 J6.

The eight-screen Landmark is the city's leading arthouse. The screens are big, even in the smallest of the auditoriums, and all but one of the theatres have stadium seating. This is one of only two DC cinemas with a liquor licence. Landmark also operates the roomier Bethesda Row in suburban Maryland, but the downtown theatre's bookings tend to be more adventurous.

Other locations: Bethesda Row 7235 Woodmont Avenue, Bethesda, MD (1-301 652 7273).

Repertory

Washington no longer has any commercial repertory cinemas. It does, however, boast one of the country's most extensive non-commercial rep film scenes. Keeping abreast of the programmes at these venues is a major undertaking, but not an expensive one: most of the screenings are free.

Arts & Entertainment

Among the many other local institutions that frequently screen films are the **National Archives** (documentaries from its collection or that used its footage; 1-202 501 5000); the **Goethe Institut** (films about Germany, 1-202 289 1200); the **DC Jewish Community Center** (Jewish-related films, tickets 1-800 494 8497/information 1-202 518 9400 ext 229); the **National Museum of Women in the Arts** (films by women or linked to current exhibits, 1-202 783 7370); and several foreign embassies. See *Washington City Paper* for listings.

AFI Silver Theatre & Cultural Center

8633 Colesville Road, at Georgia Avenue, Silver Spring (1-301 495 6720/www.afi.com/silver). Silver Spring Metro. **Tickets** $9.25. **Credit** AmEx, Disc, MC, V.

As part of a suburban redevelopment project, the American Film Institute opened this handsome, state-of-the-art complex in 2003. The largest of the three houses is a restored (and reduced) version of the Silver, a 1938 art deco cinema. After drawing few patrons in its first two years, it began to emphasise first-run foreign, indie and documentary films. But it still hosts retrospectives of directors and stars, overviews of national cinemas, and series devoted to African and Latin-American cinema.

Films on the Hill

Capitol Hill Arts Workshop, 545 Seventh Street, SE, Capitol Hill (1-202 547 6839/www.filmsonthe hill.com). Eastern Market Metro. **Tickets** $5. **Screenings** usually 7pm several weeknights. **No credit cards. Map** p253 L8.

Early films, many of them silent, with an emphasis on vintage Hollywood movies.

Freer Gallery of Art

Meyer Auditorium, Jefferson Drive, SW, at 12th Street, Mall & Tidal Basin (1-202 357 2700/www. asia.si.edu). Smithsonian Metro. **Tickets** free. **Screenings** usually 7pm Fri; 2pm Sun. **Map** p252 J7.

The films shown here come from the countries represented in the gallery's collection, predominantly Asia and the Middle East. It is one of the best places in town to see movies from India and Iran, but arrive early – the theatre soon fills up with emigrés from those countries. Recently, the Freer split a Mikio Naruse retrospective with the National Gallery of Art and AFI. Annual events include anime movies to mark the Cherry Blossom Festival and a mid-summer survey of Hong Kong films.

Hirshhorn Museum & Sculpture Garden

Seventh Street & Independence Avenue, SW, Mall & Tidal Basin (1-202 357 2700/www.hirshhorn.si.edu). L'Enfant Plaza Metro. **Tickets** free. **Screenings** usually 8pm Thur, Fri. **Map** p253 J7.

The Hirshhorn showcases work by upcoming and experimental directors, often fresh from their suc-

cesses on the international film festival circuit. Highlights from several alternative festivals are shown annually and filmmakers sometimes show works in progress. Programmer Kelly Gordon was one of the first Americans to champion such directors as Peter Greenaway and Tsai Ming-Liang, leading to some exclusive US premieres of their films.

Library of Congress

Mary Pickford Theater, Madison Building, First Street & Pennsylvania Avenue, SE, Capitol & Around (1-202 707 5677/www.loc.gov/rr/mopic/ pickford). Capitol South Metro. **Tickets** free; reservations recommended. **Screenings** usually 7pm several weeknights. **Map** p253 L7.

The Library of Congress draws on its own extensive holdings to programme its small cinema, named after the iconic silent movie star. It may have the only copies of some of the early films it shows, although it screens better-known titles in its ongoing series of movies that have been appointed to the National Film Registry. It usually operates two to three nights a week; recent series include 'Bob Hope and the American Comedy Tradition' and 'Don't Touch that Vase! The True Desperate Housewives'.

National Gallery of Art

East Building Auditorium, Fourth Street & Constitution Avenue, NW, Mall & Tidal Basin (1-202 842 6799/www.nga.gov). Judiciary Square or Archives-Navy Memorial Metro. **Tickets** free. **Screenings** afternoon Sat, Sun, some weekdays. **Map** p253 J6.

This auditorium has one of the biggest screens and some of the most interesting programming in the city, as well as the most leg room. Film series are sometimes linked to major exhibitions, but the museum also hosts major retrospectives; recent ones include the work of Luchino Visconti and Benoit Jacquot. Documentaries about art and related topics are shown on weekdays.

Film festivals

The largest local annual festival is **Filmfest DC** (www.filmfestdc.org), which shows about 75 films, most of them international, during a two-week period beginning in late April. Its organisers also sponsor an overview of Arab films in January. In October and November, the American Film Institute (www.afi.com) presents the **European Film Showcase**, introducing new European films that recently premiered at the continent's leading festivals.

Other festivals of note are the **Environmental Film Festival** (www.dc environmentalfilmfest.org) in March; **Reel Affirmations** (www.reelaffirmations.org), the gay and lesbian film fest, in October; and the **Jewish Film Festival** (www.wjff.org) in December. Check the *Washington City Paper* listings for details.

Arts & Entertainment

Galleries

The best young shoots of DC's art scene are bursting out of their traditional spaces.

Washington's efforts to transform its gallery network into a version of New York's Chelsea South invite comparisons to *The Little Engine that Could*, but in this case the train is still chugging uphill. The problem is provincialism: the city has two parallel artistic universes, one inhabited by local artists who cater to home-grown tastes, the other populated by artists and gallery owners working to boost the city's national and international reputation.

In recent years, the savviest District gallery owners and real estate developers – the latter population mushroomed early in the decade when a condominium boom gripped the city – have concluded that space matters. Breaking out of the city's traditional domestic-scaled gallery spaces – Dupont Circle's elegant but cramped brownstones – into more open, New York-style art venues, is the new norm (*see p173* **Art on 14th Street**). The trend has invigorated the city's scene.

DC still retains its less-polished venues and art events; the city's DIY spirit, so often manifest in local music, bleeds into visual arts too, as younger artists crowd into alternative spaces and create one-off art shows. Local artists are known for co-opting fallow spaces in downtown office buildings. Legislation mandating an arts district in the area around Penn Quarter ensured that new commercial developments were required to incorporate arts components. This stipulation resulted in some lacklustre lobby galleries but, as in the case of Gallery at Flashpoint, has also managed to cultivate interesting gallery spaces. Elsewhere, furniture and design stores stage mini exhibitions on their walls – so you may run into a show when you least expect it.

Washington collectors are becoming younger and savvier. While the commercial gallery scene is less avant-garde or large-scale than New York's, Washington patrons can still find ambitious work made by local artists as well as national and international ones. In general, the gallery-going community here is casual and supportive (some might argue insular). **Logan Circle**, the new heart of the scene, shows the most refreshing art the city has to offer and should be the first stop on any aficionado's tour. **Dupont Circle** once boasted a dense gallery concentration – the townhouses lining R Street between Connecticut and Florida Avenues still house well-loved galleries – but the work here tends toward local artists of middling repute. Like Dupont, the downtown Seventh Street corridor in **Penn Quarter** was once home to both galleries and artists, but while the area's soaring property prices gained the galleries wider audiences, the area became prohibitively expensive for most resident artists. **Georgetown**, meanwhile, serves up a hotchpotch of art: galleries varying from avant-garde to conservative cater to both the blue-haired and the blue bloods. *Washington City Paper* is the best publication for gallery listings, including one-off events. Admission for all galleries is free. Note that many galleries are closed on Sunday and Monday.

The best Galleries

For art per square foot
Curator's Office (*see p172*).

For beautiful painting
Addison/Ripley Fine Art (*see p175*).

For checking your email after checking out the show
Provisions Library (*see p175*).

For contemporary work
Numark Gallery (*see p172*).

For local artists and craftspeople
Torpedo Factory Arts Center (*see p176*).

Downtown/Penn Quarter

Galleries in this arts and entertainment district cluster near the corner of Seventh and E Streets, NW. Monthly third Thursday joint openings (6-8pm) feature volunteer-led gallery walks and drinks specials at local bars and restaurants.

Gallery at Flashpoint
916 G Street, NW, between Ninth & Tenth Streets (1-202 315 1305/www.flashpointdc.org). Gallery Place-Chinatown Metro. **Open** noon-6pm Tue-Sat; also by appointment. **Credit** MC, V. **Map** p253 J6.

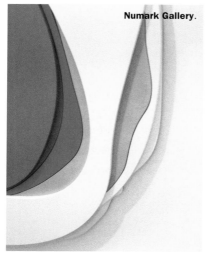

Numark Gallery.

For upwards of a century, the Rupperts clan has owned this and several other storefronts on the block. In the mid '90s, Molly Ruppert and son Paul started throwing art parties in the former hardware store. Soon they got serious about the art space and renovated it, which meant leaving the walls unfinished and the floors worn. But there's a generous skylight now, and some proper walls, along with a full-time café that displays works of art.

Logan Circle

Curator's Office
1515 14th Street, NW, Suite 201, at Church Street (1-202 387 1008/www.curatorsoffice.com). Dupont Circle or Shaw-Howard University Metro. **Open** noon-6pm Wed-Sat; also by appointment. **No credit cards. Map** p250 H4.
This tiny gallery might only be the size of most people's closets but it has an impact many times its dimensions. The curator is Andrea Pollan and this is indeed her office. It's also where extraordinary Washington artist Jiha Moon exhibits, as does rising international artist Virgil Marti.

David Adamson Gallery
1515 14th Street, NW, Suite 202 at P Street (1-202 232 0707/www.adamsoneditions.com). Dupont Circle or Shaw-Howard University Metro. **Open** 11.30am-5pm Tue-Fri; noon-5pm Sat. **Credit** MC, V. **Map** p250 H4.
A long-time downtown favourite, David Adamson decamped to Logan during the great gallery exodus of 2004 (*see p173* **Art on 14th Street**). Now a stand-alone exhibition space that's separate from its internationally recognised printmaking studio, the gallery continues to exhibit the fruits of its printmaking collaborations with contemporary art heavyweights such as Jim Dine and Chuck Close. One of Washington's most innovative spaces.

G Fine Art
1515 14th Street, Suite 200, NW, at Church Street (1-202 462 1601/www.gfineartdc.com). Dupont Circle or Shaw-Howard University Metro. **Open** 11am-6pm Tue-Sat. **Credit** AmEx, MC, V. **Map** p250 H4.
Annie Gawlak's gallery began life on M Street, but she's since left for hipper pastures. Her Logan Circle space is impressive in scale and ambition, with a programme rivalling power dealer Cheryl Numark and sometimes even exceeding it; G recently mounted a compelling group show organised by one of the Hirshhorn museum's curators. Artists, from French legend Daniel Buren to performance artist Vanessa Beecroft to Washington-based star Iona Rozael Brown show here.

Hemphill Fine Arts
1515 14th Street, NW, Suite 300, at Church Street (1-202 234 5601/www.hemphillfinearts.com). Dupont Circle or Shaw-Howard University Metro. **Open** 10am-5pm Tue-Sat; also by appointment. **Credit** MC, V. **Map** p250 H4.

Gallery at Flashpoint occupies a multi-arts complex sponsored by the city's Cultural Development Corporation. Though the exhibitions vary widely, programming is getting better with age. The complex also houses a blackbox theatre and dance studio.

Numark Gallery
625-627 E Street, NW, between Sixth & Seventh Streets (1-202 628 3810/www.numarkgallery.com). Archives-Navy Memorial or Gallery Place-Chinatown Metro. **Open** 11am-6pm Tue-Sat. **Credit** MC, V. **Map** p253 J6.
Cheryl Numark is Washington's power dealer: her openings draw legions of artists and discerning patrons to see works by recognised New Yorkers and promising Washingtonians. Her move, in 2003, to a spacious, Chelsea-inspired white cube space only enhanced her reputation. Nikki Lee shows here, as do local favourites like Dan Steinhilber. Numark's group shows are some of the sharpest in town.

Touchstone Gallery
406 Seventh Street, NW, between D & E Streets (1-202 347 2787/http://gallery.infosrc.com). Archives-Navy Memorial or Gallery Place-Chinatown Metro. **Open** 11am-5pm Wed-Fri; noon-5pm Sat, Sun. **Credit** AmEx, MC, V. **Map** p253 J6.
Touchstone, an artist-owned cooperative gallery, shows works by area artists and lesser-known internationals. Although quality can be hit or miss, the gallery's size increases the chances of finding a gem.

Warehouse Gallery
1021 Seventh Street, NW, between L Street & New York Avenue (1-202 257 5989/www.warehousetheater.com). Mt Vernon Square/7th Street-Convention Center Metro. **Open** 10am-7.30pm Mon-Sat; also by appointment. **No credit cards. Map** p253 J5.

George Hemphill's contemporary art gallery plays host to many of Washington's strongest, and safest, artists. Occasional group shows, such as a gripping exhibition of Vietnam War-era photojournalism, add depth to the regular parade of solo exhibitions. The art tends mainly towards the decorative, but important works do still come through. **Photo** *p175*.

Irvine

1412 14th Street, NW, at Rhode Island Avenue (1-202 332 8767/www.irvinecontemporaryart.com). McPherson Square Metro. **Open** 11am-6pm Tue-Sat; also by appointment. **Credit** AmEx, MC, V. **Map** p250 H4.

Martin Irvine focuses on painting and drawing, with favourites including the Brooklynites Teo Gonzalez and Andrew Lyght. He is beginning to investigate more innovative fare, but sometimes veers towards the painfully superficial. In 2006, the gallery moved into a fine space formerly occupied by that legend of the DC artworld, Fusebox. At the moment, it struggles to live up to its predecessor. **Photo** *p174*.

Plan b

1530 14th Street, NW, between Church & Q Streets (1-202 234 2711/www.galleryplanb.com). Dupont Circle Metro. **Open** noon-7pm Wed-Sat; 1-5pm Sun. **Credit** MC, V. **Map** p250 H4.

Not the most riveting art space in town, but worth stopping by if you're in the area. You might find something interesting among the paintings and prints, most by local artists.

Transformer

1404 P Street, NW, between 14th & 15th Streets (1-202 483 1102/www.transformergallery.org). Dupont Circle Metro. **Open** *during exhibitions* 1-7pm Wed-Sat; also by appointment. **No credit cards. Map** p250 H4.

Despite its size, this tiny, one-room non-profit space hosts the city's most daring shows. Some are duds, some gems, but each one makes a mark. And don't be alarmed by the gallery's downmarket digs; they're actually an asset: since no wall or window is sacred, artists can transform the place as they like.

Art on 14th Street

The success of New York's Chelsea neighbourhood, with its nearly unfathomable concentration of galleries, has rippled southward. Though Manhattan's massive art mall has its proponents and detractors, money talks, and developers – in this case Giorgio Furioso – listen. Furioso, landlord to defunct alternative space Signal 66, solidified the Logan Circle gallery scene with the September 2004 opening of **1515 14th Street**. The building he chose – a three-storey former car dealership built in the 1920s – collects some of the city's strongest dealers under a single roof.

Furioso and his gallery tenants were doing what gentrifiers usually do: they followed the pioneers. Erstwhile gallery Fusebox opened in late 2001 and launched the neighbourhood as an art destination; alternative space Transformer (*see p173*) followed soon afterwards. As chain stores and high-end furniture outlets moved in and condominiums mushroomed, Furioso and the galleries recognised an opportunity. Indeed, to some observers, the institutionalisation of the Logan Circle neighbourhood was more death knell than jubilee.

Still, the gallery spaces number among the city's best. As a purpose-built seat of government, the city lacks the industrial core that provides other cities – New York, Philadelphia – with ideal real estate for studio and gallery conversions. But in the 14th Street building, Furioso found the elegant proportions, generous spaces and period details he was looking for; his team then refurbished the interior plasterwork and preserved exterior details, including the original rosettes and Greek motifs occupying the structure's cornice and lintels.

The gallery tenants of 1515 14th Street are: **David Adamson Gallery, Curator's Office, G Fine Art** and **Hemphill Fine Arts** (for all, *see p172*).

Hmm. What is that? **Irvine**. *See p173.*

U Street

Nevin Kelly Gallery

1517 U Street, NW, between 15th Street & New Hampshire Avenue (1-202 232 3464/www.nevin kellygallery.com). Dupont Circle Metro. **Open** noon-6pm Wed, Sun; noon-8pm Thur-Sat. **Credit** AmEx, MC, V. **Map** p250 H3.

Former lawyer Nevin Kelly concentrates on art from Eastern Europe, especially Poland.

Project 4

903 U Street, NW, at Ninth Street (1-202 232 4340/ www.project4gallery.com). U-Street/African Amer Civil War Memorial/Cardoza Metro. **Open** 2-6pm Wed-Fri; noon-6pm Sat; also by appointment. **No credit cards. Map** p251 J3.

Four friends, two of them architects, founded Project 4 on the fringes of the U street restaurant and shopping scene. The 900sq ft space is gorgeous, the selections as varied as the guest curators who run the shows. A gallery worth watching.

Dupont Circle

Most galleries line R Street between Connecticut and Florida Avenues; a handful are tucked in Hillyer Court, an alley south of R Street between Florida Avenue and 21st Street, and a few others stand on Connecticut Avenue. Many of the following are involved in joint gallery openings on the first Friday of the month (6-8pm).

Conner Contemporary Art

1730 Connecticut Avenue, NW, 2nd Floor, between R Street & Florida Avenue (1-202 588 8750/www. connercontemporary.com). Dupont Circle Metro. **Open** 10am-5pm Tue-Sat. **Credit** MC, V. **Map** p250 G4.

Since Leigh Conner opened her gallery in 1999, she has been showing prints, photographs, paintings and sculptures by the kind of cutting-edge artists Washingtonians usually travel to New York to see. Recent shows have spotlit Leo Villareal and photographer David Levinthal; strong shows by DC's younger artists have been well received.

Fondo Del Sol

2112 R Street, NW, between 21st Street & Florida Avenue (1-202 483 2777/1-202 265 9235). Dupont Circle Metro. **Open** 12.30-5.30pm Tue-Sat. **No credit cards. Map** p250 G4.

Around the corner from the Phillips Collection, this non-profit gallery dedicates exhibitions and symposia to arts of the Americas; call for the performance and poetry reading schedule.

Gallery 10 Ltd

1519 Connecticut Avenue, NW, at Q Street (1-202 232 3326/www.gallery10dc.com). Dupont Circle Metro. **Open** 11am-5pm Wed-Sat. **Credit** MC, V. **Map** p250 G4.

Many of the District's most respected artists jumpstarted careers with shows at Gallery 10. Now the place shows an older generation of District artists whose exhibitions vary from undisciplined to cohesive – you never know what you'll get.

International Art & Artists

9 Hillyer Court, NW, 2nd Floor, off 21st Street, between Q & R Streets (1-202 338 0680/www. artsandartists.org). Dupont Circle Metro. **Open** by appointment. **No credit cards. Map** p250 G4.

A handsome gallery space inside the headquarters of a company that organises travelling art exhibitions. The programme of exhibits juxtaposes Washington- based and international artists.

Jane Haslem

2025 Hillyer Place, NW, between 21st Street & Connecticut Avenue (1-202-232-4644/www.jane haslemgallery.com). Dupont Circle Metro. **Open** by appointment. **Credit** AmEx, MC, V. **Map** p250 G4.

A long-time DC gallery owner, Haslem has only recently returned to public viewing in this charming Dupont home. Prints by artists such as Alex Katz are usually on view.

Kathleen Ewing Gallery

1609 Connecticut Avenue, NW, between Q & R Streets (1-202 328 0955/www.kathleenewing gallery.com). Dupont Circle Metro. **Open** noon-6pm Tue-Sat; also by appointment. **Credit** MC, V. **Map** p250 G4.

Director Kathleen Ewing's unpretentious approach to art dealing, coupled with her eagle eye for talent, have earned her a reputation as the city's finest photography dealer. Her laid-back gallery has evolved

Arts & Entertainment

into a focal point for local photographers, who regularly drop in to chat and network. Since the space opened in 1976, Ewing's stable of 19th- and 20th-century photographers has grown to include the likes of Berenice Abbott, Arnold Newman and DC photographer Frank DiPerna.

Marsha Mateyka Gallery

2012 R Street, NW, between Connecticut Avenue & 21st Street (1-202 328 0088/www.marshamateyka gallery.com). Dupont Circle Metro. **Open** 11am-5pm Wed-Sat; also by appointment. Closed Aug. **Credit** MC, V. **Map** p250 G4.

Marsha Mateyka exhibits painting, sculpture and works on paper by established contemporary American and European artists. Past highlights have included museum-quality paintings by Sam Gilliam and L C Armstrong. The gallery is worth a peek for its architecture too: the late 19th-century brownstone's interior features spectacular cherrywood fireplaces, wainscoting and carved wood transoms.

Provisions Library

1611 Connecticut Avenue, NW, off Q Street (1-202 299 0460/www.provisionslibrary.org). Dupont Circle Metro. **Open** noon-7pm Tue-Fri; noon-5pm Sat. **No credit cards. Map** p250 G4.

Though Provisions Library calls itself a 'resource center for activism and arts', you don't have to be a Green/communist/World Bank protester to enjoy the nearly-always-empty visual arts library-cum-lefty recreation centre. The exhibitions programme has, as you'd expect, a strongly political bent.

St Luke's Gallery

1715 Q Street, NW, between 17th & 18th Streets (1-202 328 2424). Dupont Circle Metro. **Open** 10am-6pm Sat; also by appointment. **Credit** AmEx, MC, V. **Map** p250 G4.

Dupont's only Old Master gallery, St Luke's brims with oils, watercolours and etchings by the likes of Domenichino, Whistler and Piranesi. The airy townhouse is a favourite with local curators, who cite the gallery's print collection as the best in the city.

Georgetown

There's no real gallery epicentre in Georgetown. Showrooms are located on or near M Street, the area's main east–west artery. Several galleries of middling quality occupy the Canal Square complex (1054 31st Street, NW), which hosts joint openings every third Friday of the month; in warmer weather, bands play music.

Addison/Ripley Fine Art

1670 Wisconsin Avenue, NW, at Reservoir Road (1-202 338 5180/www.addisonripleyfineart.com). Foggy Bottom-GWU Metro then 30, 32, 34, 35, 36 bus. **Open** 11am-6pm Tue-Sat; also by appointment. **Credit** MC, V. **Map** p249 E4.

Addison/Ripley shows and sells high-calibre painting, photography and prints by contemporary American and European artists to an upscale and well-moneyed clientele. Gallerists Christopher Addison and Sylvia Ripley make an effort to look

Hemphill Fine Arts. *See p172.*

for nationally recognised names who might not otherwise be seen in Washington. Their selections, while always lovely, do tend towards the excruciatingly safe. Wolf Kahn shows regularly.

Govinda Gallery
1227 34th Street, NW, at Prospect Street (1-202 333 1180/www.govindagallery.com). Rosslyn Metro. **Open** 11am-6pm Tue-Sat. **Credit** MC, V. **Map** p249 E5.
Although the Govinda Gallery is set some distance away from Georgetown's commercial fray, it's worth a trip out to see its rock 'n' roll-themed photography and painting shows. The gallery represents the estate of artist and former Beatle Stuart Sutcliffe as well as rock photographers Bob Gruen and Gered Mankowitz, and often shows classic images of the Rolling Stones and the Beatles.

Mu Project
1521 Wisconsin Avenue, NW, No. 2, between P Street & Volta Place (1-202 333 4119/www.mu project.com). Farragut West Metro, then 34, 36 bus. **Open** 11am-5pm Wed-Sat; also by appointment. **No credit cards.** **Map** p249 E4.
Proprietor Shigeko Bork has a line on some of the hottest and most important young artists out of Asia, but her schedule is irregular so call ahead before making a trip to her gallery.

Maurine Littleton Gallery
1667 Wisconsin Avenue, NW, at Reservoir Road (1-202 333 9307/www.littletongallery.com). Foggy Bottom-GWU Metro then 30, 32, 34, 35, 36 bus. **Open** 11am-6pm Tue-Sat. **Credit** AmEx, MC, V. **Map** p249 E4.
The daughter of studio glass art pioneer Harvey Littleton founded her eponymous gallery to show glasswork that transcends the obvious goblet or bowl (although these are available as well) by incorporating photo images and collage.

Parish Gallery
1054 31st Street, NW, at M Street (1-202 944 2310/www.parishgallery.com). Foggy Bottom-GWU Metro then 30, 32, 34, 35, 36 bus. **Open** noon-6pm Tue-Sat; also by appointment. **Credit** AmEx, DC, MC, V. **Map** p249 E5.
Specialising in the art of the African diaspora, the Parish Gallery shows a mixed bag of abstraction and realism. The quality varies too.

Strand on Volta
1513 33rd Street, NW, at Volta Place (1-202 333 4663/www.strandonvolta.com). Foggy Bottom-GWU Metro then 30, 32, 34, 35, 36 bus. **Open** 11am-4pm Thur, Fri; 11am-6pm Sat; also by appointment. **No credit cards.** **Map** p249 E4.
James Strand Alefantis's airy, one-room gallery exudes typical Georgetown elegance. But his artists certainly aren't stuffy. One month you might see playful aeroplane drawings by Los Angeles up-and-comer Jay Stuckey; and then the next these will be replaced by paintings on paper from District abstract expressionist Mindy Weisel.

Arlington Arts Center
3550 Wilson Boulevard, at Monroe Street, Arlington, VA (1-703 797 4574/www.arlingtonartscenter.org). Virginia Square-GMU Metro. **Open** 11am-5pm Tue-Sat.
After a lengthy renovation and expansion, this non-profit, non-collecting contemporary visual arts centre now shows a regular roster of local names.

District of Columbia Arts Center (DCAC)
2438 18th Street, NW, between Belmont & Columbia Roads, Adams Morgan (1-202 462 7833/ www.dcartscenter.org). Woodley Park-Zoo/Adams Morgan Metro. **Open** 2-7pm Wed-Sun. **Credit** MC, V. **Map** p250 G3.
This independent company programmes its small gallery and 50-seat theatre in Adams Morgan with a selection of innovative avant-garde exhibitions.

Ellipse Art Center
4350 North Fairfax Drive, Arlington, VA (1-703 228 7710/www.arlingtonarts.org/ellipseartscenter. htm). Ballston Metro. **Open** 11am-7pm Wed-Fri; 11am-2pm Sat.
An Arlington County-sponsored space, its interest level varies according to who occupies the helm.

Fraser Gallery Bethesda
Suite E, 7700 Wisconsin Avenue, at Middleton Lane, Bethesda, MD (1-301 718 9651/www.thefraser gallery.com). Bethesda Metro. **Open** 11.30am-6pm Tue-Sat; also by appointment. **Credit** AmEx, MC, V.
A bright, glass-walled gallery that exhibits realist painting and photography.

McLean Project for the Arts
1234 Ingleside Avenue, McLean, VA, at McLean Community Center (1-703 790 1953/www.mclean art.org). Ballston Metro then 23A, 23C bus. **Open** 10am-4pm Tue-Fri; 1-5pm Sat; also by appointment. **Credit** MC, V.
Posh, suburban location; urban attitude.

Osuna Art
7200 Wisconsin Avenue, in the Artery Plaza Lobby, between Bethesda Avenue & Elm Street, Bethesda (1-301 654 4500/www.osunaart.com). Bethesda Metro. **Open** 11.30am-5.30pm Tue-Sat. **Credit** MC, V.
So it seems you *can* please all of the people all of the time: dealer Ramon Osuna sells hits from DC's Color School days – Tom Downing and Ken Noland – as well as Regency candelabras and 18th-century sculpture.

Torpedo Factory Arts Center
105 N Union Street, at King Street, Alexandria, VA (1-703 838 4565 ext 4/www.torpedofactory.org). King Street Metro then 28A, 28B bus or Dash bus AT2, AT3, AT5, AT7. **Open** noon-5pm Wed-Sun; also by appointment. **Credit** AmEx, MC, V.
Alexandria's Torpedo Factory Arts Center woos tourists with three floors of studios and galleries. More homespun than sophisticated, the centre's principal appeal is its warm atmosphere.

Gay & Lesbian

Even partying can be political.

Halo. *See p179.*

Washington's gay and lesbian scene has been inching further east ever since it first staked its claim in Dupont Circle. These days it has reached 14th Street, Logan Circle and Shaw, and is still heading eastwards, making its presence felt all the way to North Capitol Street. The gay community's activists – who once received a great deal of attention by staging a 'nude-in' on the Mall – have found that they get even more respect with their clothes on. The AIDS crisis and its need for loud voices and charismatic leaders took the perennial outsiders off the city's streets and planted them inside the Capitol. Gays transformed themselves from a marginalised minority into a force to be reckoned with, complete with a smart downtown HQ for lobbying organisation the Human Rights Campaign.

After a hard day's lobbying, the District's gays and (to a lesser extent) lesbians have taken advantage of a steady stream of bars, clubs and discos that keep them occupied after dark, and often right up until dawn. But it was only a matter of time before the issue of partying would itself become political. The second half of the millennium's first decade has changed the rhythm of the night for Washington's gay crowd, as institutions

have gone dark and some of the scene's biggest parties have danced their last.

The building of a new stadium for the District's baseball team, the Washington Nationals, brought about the closing of Ziegfeld's – a strip bar and DC institution – as well as Nation, the home of the city's mega-party, Velvet. Lizard Lounge, a successful Sunday night event that attracted one of the District's more diverse crowds, pulled its own plug when promoter Mark Lee decided the new smoking ban would clear the dance floor of more than just smoke. And Be Bar, a venture set to open in the Shaw neighbourhood, was met with resistance from a local religious group who claimed a gay bar in its midst would run contrary to that community's moral code.

None of this has come even close to derailing DC's queer community, though. The music plays on. Saturday nights will soon belong to **Blowoff**, the late-night party at the 9:30 Club, hosted by tag-team DJs Bob Mould, founder of punk band Husker Du, and Rich Morel. Even before Velvet's demise, some party boys had already started splitting their weekend nights between the Mould & Morel Show and **Apex** (the latter winning the *Washington Blade*'s readers' pick for Best Dance Club in 2005).

The **Blowoff** duo.

Those looking for better lighting have been hitting newcomer **Halo** on P Street, while Thursday nights belong to the **Duplex Diner** (aka 18th & U Street Diner), the part-bar/part-restaurant hangout on (you guessed it) 18th Street, and the **Green Lantern**, where the shirtless drink free for an hour.

As one would expect in a town that has become increasingly partisan over the last decade, divisions abound in Washington's gay community as well. Bears and bikers and those who love them frequent Blowoff and the **DC Eagle**, while DC's D&G crowd are more likely to be found in the other dance venues.

Finding places that separate the men from the boys might be easy enough but sadly the same can't be said for the District's lesbian bars; one would find it much easier to point to where the girls aren't, rather than are, in this town. **Phase One** remains the only nightly option for women, and it has done much to move beyond its image of a place where gals shoot pool and watch the Redskins. Live performances dot its calendar and even if it's not the glitziest place in town, it is the city's longest running gay bar, making it worthy of a visit. **Club Chaos** still turns Wednesday night over to the girls, and **Liquid Ladies** spills on to the dance floor of Apex on Saturday. One of Washington's more ambitious undertakings in finding a solution for the lack of lesbian spots

has been the roving party known as **A Different Kind of Ladies' Night**. Keeping women in the loop via a website of the same name, sans apostrophe, the ADKLN teams up with the local Kimpton Hotel bars and throws sophisticated mixers.

Washington's gay and lesbian scene is as diverse as one would expect in a capital city. To capitalise on all that the scene has to offer, *Metro Weekly* and the *Washington Blade* remain the go-to guides. Or check for flyers announcing up-and-coming events like alt-favourite *Taint*, which dots the first Sunday night of the month spot at club DC9. You'll find towering stacks of these cards at Lambda Rising (*see p147*) or **Caribou Coffee**. And with the amount of cruising that goes on you might just find something else as well.

Clubs & bars

Apex

1415 22nd Street, NW, between O & P Streets, Dupont Circle (1-202 296 0505). Dupont Circle Metro. **Open** 5pm-2am Mon-Wed, Sun; 9pm-2am Thur; 9pm-3am Fri, Sat. **Admission** $1-$6. **Credit** MC, V. **Map** p250 G4.
This dance club recently snatched the crown from the now defunct Velvet Nation as the favourite in the *Washington Blade*'s annual readers' poll for the best venue. While it doesn't have the vastness of its cavernous rival, Apex goes in the opposite direction by keeping things tight and intimate. There's lots of action both on and off the dancefloor, but if you're still bored then the video bar in the back of the club will help to keep you entertained.

Blowoff

930 Club, 815 V Street, NW, at Ninth Street, Shaw U Street/14th Street Corridor (1-202 393 0930/www.930.com/www.blowoff.us). U Street/African-American Civil War Memorial/Cardozo Metro. **Open** varies. **Admission** varies. **Credit** AmEx, DC, MC, V. **Map** p251 J3.
Ever since this monthly party had its humble beginnings playing to a handful of partygoers in the cramped quarters of Velvet Lounge, before moving on and into the 9:30 Club's basement, there was never any doubt that it would one day aspire to and achieve bigger and better things. Now housed in the main room of the 9:30 Club, Bob Mould and Rich Morel's 'diva-free' dance party is pumping some real muscle into the District's nightlife. Expect anything from Black Legend to Madonna to Secret Machines to Mould and Morel's own remixes and compositions. Check the website for dates and times of events.

Club Chaos

1603 17th Street, NW, at Q Street, Dupont Circle (1-202 232 4141/www.chaosdc.com). Dupont Circle Metro. **Open** 6pm-2am Tue-Thur; Sun; 6pm-3am Fri, Sat. **Admission** free. **Credit** AmEx, DC, MC, V. **Map** p250 G4.

Mustachioed drag kings, Latin drag queens, shirtless dancing hotties and audience-participation party games. No, it's not one of Pedro Almodóvar's earlier films but Club Chaos. Even on theme nights, the club is very inclusive. Check the *Metro Weekly* or the *Washington Blade* for what's going on.

Cobalt/30 Degrees

1639 R Street, NW, between 16th & 17th Streets, Dupont Circle (1-202 462 6569/www.cobaltdc.com). Dupont Circle Metro. **Open** 5pm-2am Mon-Thur, Sun; 5pm-3am Fri, Sat. **Admission** $1-$5. **Credit** AmEx, MC, V. **Map** p250 G4.

Twentysomethings and those who won't admit they're fortysomething gather upstairs around the small dancefloor in Cobalt. Downstairs at 30 Degrees it's quieter and the attitude is less ageist. Dress among the good-looking crowd throughout leans towards club-fashionable, not club-fabulous. Cobalt/ 30 Degrees is primarily a good place to begin your evening. By 1am most of the boys have moved on.

DC Eagle

639 New York Avenue, NW, between Sixth & Seventh Streets, Downtown (1-202 347 6025/ www.dceagle.com). Mount Vernon Square/7th Street-Convention Center Metro. **Open** 4pm-2am Mon-Thur, Sun; 4pm-3am Fri, Sat. **Admission** free. **Credit** MC, V. **Map** p253 J5.

Those familiar with the Eagle standard, set in clubs across the country, will know what to expect. For the uninitiated, DC's version of the popular club offers the usual trappings – pool, pinball and a rock/industrial dance mix. However, what the unfamiliar might find most surprising is the lack of pretence and attitude among the bar's patrons. A great, but dimly lit, club for those who love men in leather (or just the smell of them).

Green Lantern

1335 Green Court, NW, behind lot at 1335 L Street, between 13th & 14th Streets, Downtown (1-202 347 4533/www.greenlanterndc.com). McPherson Square Metro. **Open** 4pm-2am Mon-Thur; 4pm-3am Fri, Sat; 1pm-3am Sun. **Admission** free. **Credit** MC, V. **Map** p252 H5.

After a recent makeover, the Green Lantern still draws the same burly types that it always has, especially on Thursday nights when 'shirtless men drink free'. Pool tables, karaoke, a dancefloor and video screens provide plenty of entertainment, but the real action here is the cruising.

Halo

1435 P Street, NW, between 14th & 15th Streets, Logan Circle (1-202 797 9730). Dupont Circle Metro. **Open** 5pm-2am Mon-Thur; Sun; 5pm-3am Fri, Sat. **Credit** AmEx, Disc, MC, V. **Map** p250 H4.

This stylish hang raised the bar for DC's night-time landscape. Sure, other bars in other cities had this sort of sleekness years earlier, but for the once style-deficient capital, Halo's appearance has been a pleasant departure from the pool 'n' pub trappings of other gay haunts in the neighbourhood. The clientele tends to be well dressed if not well heeled (or at least well versed in the affectation). That the club was smoke-free from night one has made it heaven-sent for many. The newly opened first floor allows the festive air to flow from the club into the street, and vice versa. A must for happy hour. **Photo** *p177.*

JR's

1519 17th Street, NW, at P Street, Dupont Circle (1-202 328 0090/www.jrswdc.com). Dupont Circle Metro. **Open** 2pm-2am Mon-Thur, Sun; 2pm-3am Fri, Sat. **Admission** free. **Map** p250 G4.

Bar staff move at lightning speed to serve customers in this tight space. Nightly happy-hour specials and occasional seasonal events (such as the annual Easter bonnet contest) keep the crowd entertained. Videos and pool tables are the main entertainment – aside from cruising, that is – as there's no dancefloor.

Phase One

525 Eighth Street, SE (1-202 544 6831). Eastern Market Metro. **Open** 7pm-2am Thur, Sun; 7pm-3am Fri, Sat. **Admission** free. **Credit** AmEx, DC, MC, V.

It's lamentable that an international capital like DC doesn't have more options for its lesbian denizens and visitors. But if girls just want to have fun, club nights aside, this is it. Phase One has done its best to overcome its image of a rough-gurl hangout where fist-flying bar brawls were the norm. The oldest gay and lesbian operation in the District now has open mic events, regular entertainment and even dance nights, though you're most likely to find the place packed out when the Redskins game is projected on to a gigantic screen.

Remington's

639 Pennsylvania Avenue, SE, between Sixth & Seventh Streets, Capitol Hill (1-202 543 3113/ www.remingtonswdc.com). Eastern Market Metro. **Open** 4pm-2am Mon-Thur, Sun; 4pm-3am Fri, Sat. **Admission** $2-$5. **No credit cards. Map** p253 L7.

The waning popularity of the 'new Nashville' and two-stepping craze has made this Capitol Hill bar a little bit easier to walk through. As the District's only gay country music venue, Remington's is still a draw for those who like to Roll the Rug and do the Tush Push. The club itself is one of the cleanest and friendliest environments in the city, and the recently expanded dancefloor does its best to accommodate all comers. Dance lessons are available at the beginning of most nights.

Gyms

Bodysmith

1622 14th Street, NW, at Corcoran Street, Logan Circle (1-202 939 0800/www.bodysmithdc.com). Shaw-Howard University Metro. **Open** varies. **Credit** AmEx, MC, V. **Map** p250 H4.

Bodysmith's personal trainers are well qualified and, judging by the look of the patrons, they do their job well. Best to book ahead, however, as appointments go fast at this small personal training facility.

Arts & Entertainment

Crew Club

1321 14th Street, NW, between N Street & Rhode Island Avenue, Logan Circle (1-202 319 1333/ www.crewclub.net). McPherson Square Metro. **Open** 24hrs daily. **Rates** day membership $9; 30-day $14. **Credit** AmEx, MC, V. **Map** p250 H4.

A licensed nudist facility, Crew Club caters to those looking for a workout that's uninhibited – or at least undressed. Showers, lockers and towels are all available, as are condoms. There's a TV room too.

Results, The Gym

1612 U Street, NW, between 16th & 17th Streets, U Street/14th Street Corridor (1-202 518 0001/ www.resultsthegym.com). U Street/African-Amer Civil War Memorial/Cardozo Metro. **Open** 5am-11pm Mon-Fri; 7am-9pm Sat; 8am-9pm Sun. **Rates** day membership $20. **Credit** MC, V. **Map** p250 H3.

Results used to be *the* gym of choice for the gay community. The facility is still better than most, but the posing and chatting boys can bring your workout to a standstill during peak hours (6pm onwards). If it's a social scene you want, with patrons as steely and polished as the equipment, you'll be ecstatic. If it's a serious workout you're looking for, hit Results. **Other locations**: 315 G Street, SE, Capitol Hill (1-202 234 5678).

Restaurants & cafés

There really aren't any restaurants that are exclusively gay in the District. But there are joints where the community tends to congregate as much for the scene as for the sustenance.

Annie's Paramount Steak House

1609 17th Street, NW, between Q & Corcoran Streets, Dupont Circle (1-202 232 0395). Dupont Circle Metro. **Open** 11.30am-11.30pm Mon-Wed; 11.30am-1.30am Thur; 11.30am Fri-11pm Sun. **Main courses** $10-$22. **Credit** AmEx, DC, Disc, MC, V. **Map** p250 G4.

A DC institution: having served DC's gay community for more than 50 years, it's worth grabbing a burger at Annie's just to say 'I was there'. There's nothing remarkable about the decor or the service – or the food, for that matter. Many of the patrons seem to come to reminisce about the glory of their youth, giving the restaurant even more of a neighbourhood feel. Midnight brunch is served at weekends and holidays, and the kitchen remains open round the clock from Friday night until Sunday night.

Caribou Coffee

1400 14th Street NW, at Rhode Island Avenue, Logan Circle (1-202 232 4552/www.caribou coffee.com). Dupont Circle Metro. **Open** 5.30am-10pm Mon-Fri; 6.30am-10pm Sat; 7am-9pm Sun. **Credit** AmEx, Disc, MC, V. **Map** p250 H4.

Yes, it's part of a chain and no, that chain is not a gay-oriented business. Nevertheless, this Caribou has become a favourite among gay and lesbian locals. It's the kind of spot where heads spin towards the door each time it opens, as everyone looks for a friend or a face they'd like to know better. Weekends are particularly active and it can be hard to get a table. The patio gets equally crowded in summer as it provides a good vantage point for people watching.

Dakota Cowgirl/Titan Bar

1337 14th Street, NW, between N Street & Rhode Island Avenue, Logan Circle (1-202 232 7010/ www.dakotacowgirldc.com). McPherson Square Metro. **Open** 11am-10.30pm Mon-Thur; Sun; 10.30am-11pm Fri, Sat. **Credit** MC, V. **Map** p250 H4.

Dakota Cowgirl serves up burgers and fries and offers another option for Sunday brunch. Its second floor plays host to the Titan Bar where anything from bingo to a gay trivia game can take place. Friday happy hour is popular with those who prefer not to need to look so polished as the working week ends.

Duplex Diner

2004 18th Street, NW, at Vernon Street, Adams Morgan (1-202 265 7828/www.duplexdiner.com). Dupont Circle Metro then 42 bus. **Open** 6-11pm Mon, Sun; 6pm-12.30am Tue, Wed; 6pm-1am Thur; 6pm-1.30am Fri, Sat. **Main courses** $6-$12. **Credit** AmEx, Disc, MC, V. **Map** p250 H3.

The Duplex Diner, or the 18th & U as it's also known, has the casual feel of the 1950s eateries it emulates and a reputation for *au courant* cocktails. Some nights attract more patrons than others; for instance, the Thursday night bar and club crowd often relies on the Duplex as its opening act. The menu lists diner favourites – burgers and fries, natch – but the real draw is the neighbourhood feel.

Dupont Italian Kitchen (DIK)

1637 17th Street, NW, at R Street, Dupont Circle (1-202 328 3222/www.dupontitaliankitchen.com). Dupont Circle Metro. **Open** noon-11.30pm Mon-Fri; 10.30am-11.30pm Sat; 10.30am-10.30pm Sun. **Main courses** $6-$13. **Credit** AmEx, Disc, MC, V. **Map** p250 H4.

It's not the food that keeps this place in business, but rather the prime vantage point it offers for viewing the 17th Street fauna and flora. The meals are modestly priced and the mood is casual (and service, unfortunately, can be sketchy). It's a great place to spend a lazy afternoon outside, or to socialise on a warm summer night. But note that when patrons get a seat here, they're not likely to give it up in a hurry, and table turnovers can be few and far between. Upstairs is a favourite hang of those of a certain age who don't fancy the loud, late club scene.

L'Enfant Café

2000 18th Street, NW at corner of U Street & Florida Avenue, Adams Morgan (1-202 319 1800/ www.lenfantcafe.com). Dupont Circle Metro then 42 bus. **Open** 6pm-midnight Mon-Fri; 10am-midnight, Sat, Sun. **Main courses** $7.95-$12.95. **Credit** AmEx, Disc, MC, V. **Map** p250 H3.

L'Enfant does its best to deliver decent French stalwarts, like boeuf bourguignon, at a reasonable price with reasonable speed. Dimly lit but welcoming and warm, it's an ideal spot to spend a winter afternoon.

Meet Joe Solmonese

In a town where access is power and power is everything, few people in the GLBT community wield the kind of influence that Joe Solmonese does. As president of the Human Rights Campaign, the nation's largest lobbying group for gay, lesbian bisexual and transgender people, Solmonese fights the good fight in the nation's capital on a daily basis for people whose interests some might not want to consider, let alone represent. And he's just as likely to be found fielding questions in the produce aisle of Whole Foods Market as he is fighting for non-discrimination legislation in the workplace. This approachable approach may seem unlikely for one of DC's more powerful players. 'I live where a lot of people in the GLBT community live,' Solmonese explains. 'I shop and go to the gym and go out and do things with lots of members of the community and I think that kind of life experience really shapes how I go about the work.'

For Solmonese, that work hasn't been easy. Since taking over Human Rights Campaign, he's had to face the Republican-controlled federal government's efforts to roll back any advances made by gays and lesbians during the friendlier times of the Clinton-Gore era. HRC and Solmonese have been on the front lines, fighting issues like the Federal Marriage Amendment while working towards federal hate crimes legislation.

It's a battle that he and the organisation have had to wage, one opinion at a time. 'The fights now are more locally fought,' Solmonese says. 'If you're going to change things nationally now you've got to change things locally.'

It's the same grassroots mentality that he carries with him at all times, whether lending a hand in a political race in western Pennsylvania, walking on the streets of his neighbourhood or while resting in between sets at the gym. 'I find that when people come up and talk to me at the gym, or in the checkout line at Whole Foods, or even at Halo, that is where I get my best feedback,' Solmonese says. And in keeping with his accessible nature, this not-so-average Joe encourages more of the same. 'I need people to take the initiative. I want them to come up and talk to me about issues and concerns, or even just make an observation. And when they do, I just love it!'

Food Bar DC

1639 R Street, NW, between 16th & 17th Streets, Dupont Circle (1-202 462 6200/www.foodbardc.com). Dupont Circle Metro. **Open** 5-10pm Mon-Thur; 5-11pm Fri; 11am-11pm Sat; 11am-9pm Sun. **Main courses** $3-$23. **Credit** AmEx, MC, V. **Map** p250 H4. Food Bar DC is an all-in-one address for the city's gay scene. Its location on the street level in the same building as Cobalt means you can eat, drink and dance under one roof. Anyone looking for an ultra-chic hang with a super-modish menu will be disappointed, but if you want a good meal in a convenient spot, your needs should be met. Even if you don't eye something on the menu to suit your tastes you'll find plenty of eye candy at the surrounding tables.

Health Bar

1612 U Street, NW, between 16th & 17th Streets, U Street/14th Street Corridor (1-202 588 9255). U Street/African-Amer Civil War Memorial/Cardozo Metro. **Open** 7am-2am Mon-Fri; 8am-2am Sat, Sun. **Main courses** $10-$14. **Credit** MC, V. **Map** p250 H3. Health Bar, in the same building as Results, The Gym, has become a de facto community centre, a one-stop spot for fuelling up, working out and unwinding. The interior is sleek without being icy; both the long community table and the winding banquette encourage conversation. There are booths, too, for those who prefer a little privacy. The menu does its best to accommodate diets of various kinds. Weekend brunches and Monday nights attract the biggest crowds.

Music

This city has its own sounds.

Birchmere. *See p183.*

Washington is a southern city with an East Coast attitude and an international population, and its music scene reflects that diversity. A rockabilly, bluegrass and country centre in the 1950s, 1960s and 1970s, Washington would, in the mid '70s, give birth to go-go – DC's distinctive black music – and, around the turn of the 1980s, to the brand of hardcore punk of which locals were so possessive that they styled it 'harDCore'. Large Latin American, Caribbean and African communities contribute alternative beats, and there is also an active classical music scene whose wingspan extends from embassies and churches to museums and concert halls.

VENUES

Washington has venues for practically every musical taste. The **Kennedy Center**, DC's landmark arts centre, still plays host to those artists who require a more refined setting, though its Millennium Stage series is casual (and free). Mammoth acts – Mariah Carey, Dixie Chicks, Shakira – head straight for the **Verizon Center** (*see p198*), whereas all-day festivals like Warped Tour, Ozzfest and the HFStival

set up shop at Columbia, Maryland's **Merriweather Post Pavilion** (www.merri weathermusic.com); Bristow, Virginia's **Nissan Pavilion** (www.nissanpavilion.com) and DC's own **RFK Stadium** (*see p198*).

Yet there is no shortage of smaller stages around the District and acts like the Streets, Gerald Albright, Buckwheat Zydeco and Snow Patrol can all be heard – and seen – in relatively intimate settings, rather than in cavernous arenas. Many of these venues are in the U Street Corridor, known as Black Broadway in its 1930s heyday and revitalised in the 1990s.

LISTINGS AND INFORMATION

The free weekly *Washington City Paper* has good music listings. The *Washington Post* has an extensive 'Weekend' section on Fridays. *Express*, a free commuter paper owned by the *Washington Post* and available at most Metro and bus stops, offers entertainment previews on Thursdays. (It's also at readexpress.com.)

Websites can lead your ears to music, too. For a little bit of everything (including tons of non-music options and news), try www.dcist.com, www.cityguide.aol.com/washington or the City

Guide at www.washingtonpost.com. For indie and punk, www.heresahint.org and www.bigyawn.net will help. For dancehall and reggae, check www.bashmentlinkup.com. For go-go, try www.tmottgogo.com.

Tickets for most performances can be obtained direct from the venue. Ticket agencies such as Ticketmaster (1-800 551 7328/432 7328) and ProTix (1-703 218 6500) allow you to order by phone but add high surcharges.

Rock, roots & R&B

From small rooms to large arenas, DC's stages host every type of rock and pop performance imaginable, including the pretty bog standard. Be warned: there are numerous 'bar band' type spots in the environs of Adams Morgan and Georgetown, where cover bands might punctuate their repertoire of audience-winning cover versions with one or two original cuts.

Folk, country and bluegrass music acts are now generally booked into rock clubs as well, although the **Birchmere**, **Iota Club & Café** and **Jammin' Java** have more than their share of unplugged acts.

Whatever you're going to see, get tickets well in advance, as many shows sell out quickly. Younger punters should check venues' admissions policies: many require patrons to be 21 or over, though **9:30 Club**, **Black Cat** and **Warehouse Next Door** admit any age group (no alcoholic drinks served to under-21s). Always carry ID. Most places will card you no matter how old you may look.

9:30 Club

815 V Street, NW, at Ninth Street, Shaw: U Street/ 14th Street Corridor (1-202 265 0930/393 0930/ www.930.com). U Street/African-Amer Civil War Memorial/Cardozo Metro or 66, 68, 70, 71, 90, 92, 93, 96, 98 bus. **Open** varies. **Admission** varies. **Credit** AmEx, DC, MC, V. **Map** p251 J3.
This mid-sized concert hall has come a long way since its legendary beginnings. Once a cramped dive on F Street, renowned for its heat (and smell), the 9:30 has, since relocating a decade ago, boasted state-of-the-art sound and ventilation, as well as a healthy slate of microbrews. A few long-lived (or reunited) punk and post-punk bands have played both incarnations, among them the Flaming Lips, Wire and Mission of Burma, but these days you're as likely to see the Black Crowes, Damian Marley and Death Cab for Cutie (not on the same bill, of course) as the Decemberists, MF Doom and Sean Paul. The open floor and balcony layout is supposed to guarantee unrestricted viewing of the stage from anywhere in the club, and for the most part it succeeds. However, arriving early, scoping out the best vantage point and then standing your ground for the rest of the night is the best way to ensure a good view.

Birchmere

3701 Mount Vernon Avenue, between W Reed Avenue & Russell Road, Alexandria, VA (1-703 549 7500/www.birchmere.com). Pentagon Metro then 10A or 10E bus, or Crystal City Metro then 10P bus. **Open** from 6pm on gig nights. **Admission** $15-$45. **Credit** AmEx, MC, V.
Originally a bluegrass, folk, and country institution, the Birchmere is one of those venues artists can't bear to outgrow. Patty Loveless might play a couple of nights here in the fall before heading to Wolf Trap in the spring, and Merle Haggard's annual gigs always sell out. Now the Birchmere also serves up the kind of pop, smooth jazz, world music and rock that appeals to a over-30s. The Band Stand area has a dance floor, but most of the shows are in the larger Music Hall. This is a listeners' club, not some chicken-wire honky-tonk, and a few house rules apply in the table-service Music Hall: no standing, no smoking, no recording, no talking. It is, however, acceptable to whisper to the waitress a request for bourbon-sauced bread pudding. Rowdier patrons can head for the bar and the pool tables. **Photo** *p182.*

Black Cat

1811 14th Street, NW, between S & T Streets, Shaw: U Street/14th Street Corridor (1-202 667 7960/www.blackcatdc.com). U Street/African-Amer Civil War Memorial/Cardozo Metro. **Open** 8pm-2am Mon-Thur, Sun; 8pm-3am Fri, Sat. *Red Room Bar* 8pm-2am Mon-Thur, Sun; 7pm-3am Fri, Sat. **Admission** $8-$20. **No credit cards** (ATM in club). **Map** p250 H3.

Black Cat.

DC sounds: indie

Beginning with Minor Threat's first tour in 1981, Washington indie-rock's reputation centred on Dischord Records and its bands – especially the ones featuring charismatic frontman (and Dischord co-owner) Ian MacKaye. The label and his best-known band, Fugazi, established an ethos of fierce independence, social activism and anti-commercialism that continues to influence local musicians, as well as such current punk-rooted indies as Lovitt, Exotic Fever, District and Red Stapler.

Even at the peak of Dischord's influence, however, its brand of lean, vehement post-punk was not the whole story. The city has also spawned such diverse musical phenomena as the jazzy 'downtempo' music of Thievery Corporation and its label, ESL; the non-disco electronica of Chessie, 302 Acid and Manhunter; art-metal instrumental groups that verge on classical (Tone) or jazz (Orthrelm); and such post-punk singer-songwriters as Brandon Butler (late of Canyon), Benjy Ferree (recently signed to Britain's Domino) and Jenny Toomey (co-founder of the now-defunct Simple Machines label).

Fugazi has been on hiatus since late 2002, but MacKaye performs regularly with the Evens, a folk-punk duo. Of the band's other members, bassist Joe Lally is playing solo with electronic accompaniment, and drummer Brendan Canty has toured with Hüsker Dü veteran Bob Mould, who moved to DC in 2002. Other veterans who are currently active include Weird War's Ian Svenonius (once of Nation of Ulysses), Travis Morrison (Dismemberment Plan), Channels' J Robbins (Jawbox) and Ris Paul Ric's Chris Richards (Q and Not U). Younger bands of note include the prog-hardcore Mass Movement of the Moth, the pop-punk Washington Social Club, the heavy-organ Apes and the rustic-rock Nethers.

Likely venues for such bands include the **Black Cat**, **Warehouse Next Door**, **DC9**, the **Red and the Black** and the **Velvet Lounge**. Check fliers and websites for shows at occasional and non-commercial venues; in the summer, local bands play for free outdoors at Fort Reno Park (fortreno.com).

Fugazi.

As famous for having Foo Fighter Dave Grohl as a backer as it is for the bands it books – which says something for Grohl, considering the subsequent status of some of those acts – the Black Cat has picked up where the old 9:30 left off when it comes to hosting smaller, less mainstream acts, such as Rainer Maria or Camera Obscura'. Opened in 1993, the Black Cat began with the Fall, Stereolab and Slant 6 and has been continuing pretty much along those lines ever since. The vibe is dark and homey. A downstairs area – Backstage – hosts spoken-word performances, retro dance parties, independent films, and greener local and out-of-town bands. The indie regulars here can make for a rather focused, undemonstrative crowd; if your idea of fun is toe-tapping, head-nodding and staring at the stage, the upstairs Mainstage is your kind of place. **Photo** *p183*.

Crossroads

4103 Baltimore Avenue (Alternate Route One), north of Annapolis Road (Route 202), Bladensburg, MD (1-301 927 1056/www.crossroadsclub.com). Cheverly Metro then F1, F8 bus. **Open** Wed-Sun; door times vary. **Admission** varies. **Credit** AmEx, MC, V.

The area's premier club for Caribbean music, from roots reggae and dancehall to soca and steel bands, Crossroads is a mixture of concert venue, restaurant and social club for the area's West Indian diaspora. The music is loud and the vibe is usually casual. Most evenings feature DJs, but the club averages about four to six concerts every month, featuring the likes of Stephen Marley, Lee 'Scratch' Perry, Bunji Garlin and Baby Cham. Bear in mind that buses will have stopped running by the end of the show.

DC9

1940 Ninth Street, NW, at U Street, Shaw: U Street/14th Street Corridor (1-202 483 5000/ www.dcnine.com). U Street/African-Amer Civil War Memorial/Cardozo Metro. **Open** 8pm-2am Mon-Thur, Sun; 7pm-3am Fri, Sat. **Admission** $5-$15. No advance tickets. **Credit** MC, V. **Map** p251 J3.

This club's long, thin, vintage-looking first-floor bar leads to an oddly shaped upstairs performance space. It showcases the same sort of local and touring indie bands that play Galaxy Hut, Velvet Lounge and the Red & The Black, but has a larger capacity.

Galaxy Hut

2711 Wilson Boulevard, between Danville & Edgewood Streets, Arlington, VA (1-703 525 8646/ www.galaxyhut.com). Clarendon Metro. **Open** 5pm-2am Mon-Fri; 7pm-2am Sat, Sun. **Admission** $5.

This petite bar offers up-and-coming acts (mostly indie-rock) for a small cover charge. With a capacity of only 48, the place fills up easily, but in good weather you can watch the bands from outside, through the club's picture window.

IOTA Club & Cafe

2832 Wilson Boulevard, between Edgewood & Fillmore Streets, Arlington, VA (1-703 522 8340/ www.iotaclubandcafe.com). Clarendon Metro. **Open** 5pm-2am daily. **Admission** $10-$15. **Credit** AmEx, MC, V.

A good reason to pop across the River Potomac to nearby Virginia, IOTA boasts an intimate atmosphere that makes it an excellent place in which to hear singer-songwriters such as the child-friendly Dan Zanes or the all-grown-up Ron Sexsmith. Unfortunately, the surroundings can be a little too intimate and it's not unknown for patrons to be asked to shut up or leave the premises – sometimes by the performers themselves – as even the slightest bit of talking can interfere with the music. The artist-comes-first policy has its benefits: Norah Jones and John Mayer played their first DC shows here. The layout of the tiny club doesn't provide many optimum vantage points, so early arrival is advised.

Jammin' Java

228 Maple Avenue, East Vienna, VA (1-703 255 1566/www.jamminjava.com). **Open** 7am-11pm Mon-Thur; 7am-midnight Fri; 8am-midnight Sat; noon-10pm Sun. **Admission** $10-$22. **Credit** AmEx, MC, V.

A Christian coffeehouse bought out and turned secular, Jammin' Java has earned a place on the folk, blues and roots circuits, with fare ranging from John Renbourn and Jacqui McShee to Roy Book Binder to a regular Monday-night open mic. Owners Luke and Daniel Brindley also occasionally take the stage as pop-rock duo the Brindley Brothers.

Jaxx

6355 Rolling Road, at Old Keene Mill Road, Springfield, VA (1-703 569 5940/www.jaxx roxx.com). **Open** times vary. **Admission** $6-$30. **Credit** AmEx, MC, V.

A hard-rock has-been haven par excellence, Jaxx is the room of choice for diehards who would see a Sebastian Bach-less Skid Row and a Glenn Danzig-less Misfits on back-to-back nights. Year after year, bands you didn't think still existed (WASP, Dokken, Warrant) crank it up to 11 and dust off the Gibsons for the long-haired faithful. Jaxx also books a regular schedule of internationally renowned death-metal acts like Cryptopsy and Napalm Death. The club has great sound and lights, which gives the up-and-coming local groups that fill out the schedule a chance to jam in a professional environment. All this in a suburban shopping plaza.

Love

1350 Okie Street, NE, at New York Avenue, Northeast (1-202 636 9030/www.welcometo dream.com). Union Station Metro then D4 bus. **Open** 9pm-3am Thur; 6pm-4am Fri; 9pm-4am Sat. **Admission** $10-$40. **Credit** AmEx, MC, V.

Formerly Dream, this is primarily a huge, plush, upscale urban dance club (*see p192*), but Love also occasionally hosts live R&B and hip hop (Fat Joe, T.I., Busta Rhymes). Note that the dress code prohibits athletic wear, no matter how much you paid for it. Many patrons report trouble with condescending staff and long lines, and Dream was reportedly called 'Club Nightmare' by the police for a variety of crimes that happened in and around the venue. It's probably best to drive or take a cab to Love as there's no Metro nearby and the neighbourhood can be dangerous.

The Red & the Black

1212 H Street, NE, at 12th Street (1-202 399 3201/ www.redandblackbar.com). McPherson Square or Gallery Place/Chinatown Metro then X2 bus. **Open** 6pm-2am Mon-Thur; 6pm-3am Fri, Sat. **No credit cards.**

Opened in 2006, the Red & the Black is run by the same folks who own DC9. There's a bar on the main floor and the performance space is on another, making this smaller club feel a lot like its big brother. The New Orleans-themed decor and menu complements a full music schedule featuring singer-songwriters, alt-country and indie-rockers from DC, as well as touring bands.

State Theatre

220 N. Washington Street (Lee Highway/Route 29), Falls Church, VA (1-703 237 0300/www.thestate theatre.com). East Falls Church Metro then 2A, 3A bus. **Open** 7pm on show nights; closing time varies. **Credit** AmEx, Disc, MC, V.

Another converted movie theatre, the State is a favourite haunt of jam bands, blues, folk and reggae artists from near and far. Recent acts include Dirty Dozen Brass Band, Kaki King, James Cotton and the Easy Star All-Stars. The club has ample seating in the back and upstairs, plus a raked floor for good sight lines throughout the room. It may feel like a hike to get out there, but it's actually a 15-minute walk or a speedy bus journey from the East Falls Church Metro station on the Orange line.

Arts & Entertainment

DC sounds: go-go

Ask a black Washingtonian (of just about any age) what the sound of the city is and the response will be 'go-go'. This has nothing to do with bikini-clad women doing the frug in cages circa 1967. The term refers rather to a kind of beat-driven big-band R&B that was pioneered by Chuck Brown and the Soul Searchers and has thrived inside the Beltway for three decades while remaining virtually unheard around the rest of the country. Incorporating elements of funk and hip hop, it features call-and-response shout-outs to the audience and is built on a syncopated rhythm bed that is unmistakeable once you've heard it. Go-go is so unshakeable a sound that many of the old-school acts are still performing several nights a week, every week – not just Brown but also EU, Rare Essence, Backyard Band, Junk Yard Band and more. Plus, it seems like new bands are popping up all the time.

The bad news is that the go-go scene has a not-unearned reputation for violence, making it hard for outsiders to keep up with the go-go clubs that come and go. The best way to find out where the bands are playing is to check the listings in *Washington City Paper* or to click through the ad fliers at TMOTTGoGo.com; there's another go-go clearing house online at funkmasterj.tripod.com/gogo.htm. As for your own safety, there are no guarantees, but if you don't go looking for trouble, the chances are that it won't come looking for you.

Velvet Lounge

915 U Street, NW, between Vermont Avenue & Ninth Street, Shaw: U Street/14th Street Corridor (1-202 462 3213/www.velvetloungedc.com). U-Street/African-Amer Civil War Memorial/Cardozo Metro. **Open** 8pm-2am Mon-Thur, Sun; 8pm-3am Fri, Sat. **Admission** $3-$12 **Credit** MC, V. **Map** p250 J3.
Often the province of local bands and their friends whooping them on from the audience, the Velvet Lounge also books cult acts and indie-rockers from outside the Beltway. The place still has the feel of a neighbourhood bar that just happens to have a small stage upstairs. A good place to drop in after attending a show at the nearby 9:30 Club.

Warehouse Next Door

1017 Seventh Street, NW, at K Street, Downtown. (1-202 783 3933/www.warehousenextdoor.com). Gallery Place/Chinatown or Mount Vernon Square/7th Street Convention Center Metro. **Open** show nights 8pm-2am. **Admission** $5-$15. **Map** p251 J5.
Part of a complex that includes a café, a gallery and two live theatres, this small performance space specialises in the more experimental varieties of indie-rock, post-punk and metal. It's a good place to catch the side projects of local luminaries, and it books hipster out-of-town acts like Shearwater and Oneida as well as putting on plenty of multi-band metal and hardcore punk bills. When full up, the venue can get a little on the claustrophobic side, but at least Warehouse strives to makes up for that with incredibly cheap drinks and a no-smoking policy.

Zanzibar on the Waterfront

700 Water Street, SW, at Seventh Street, Southwest Waterfront (1-202 554-9100/www.zanzibar-otw.com). Waterfront-SEU Metro. **Open** Wed-Sun, times vary. **Admission** varies. **Credit** AmEx, MC, V. **Map** p253 J8.

An upscale gathering place for the Washington's African and Caribbean communities, Zanzibar is a beautifully designed, multilevel club and restaurant that offers a spectacular view out over the Potomac River. The majority of the nights feature DJs spinning everything from hip hop, R&B and reggae to salsa, Senegalese mbalax and Malian pop. But there is also a handful of live performances every month, featuring Caribbean greats like Super Cat and the Mighty Sparrow and African stars like Hugh Masekela and Alpha Blondy.

Jazz

Washington has a rich jazz history, claiming the legendary likes of Duke Ellington and Shirley Horn as its own, though you wouldn't know it from the relatively few clubs hosting the music. But with jazz enshrined as 'American classical music', the **Kennedy Center** (*see p188*), particularly its KC Jazz Club, and the **Smithsonian** (*see p189*) help pick up the slack.

Blues Alley

1073 Wisconsin Avenue, NW, at M Street, Georgetown (1-202 337 4141/www.bluesalley.com). Foggy Bottom-GWU Metro then 30, 32, 34, 35, 36, 38B, Georgetown Metro Connection bus. **Open** 6.30pm-12.30am daily. **Admission** $16-$50. **Credit** AmEx, DC, MC, V. **Map** p249 E5.
Some patrons consider the cover charges here outrageously high, especially as there is also a two-drink minimum per person for each set, which usually lasts just under an hour. Others are just so thankful that they have a small space where first-rate acts such as Mose Allison or Pieces of a Dream will perform that money is not an object. Table service can be on the inconsistent side, but if you're

Arts & Entertainment

coming for the music you'll find the acoustics to be as top-notch as the talent on the stage. Don't be surprised to see a surcharge on your bill that goes to the Blues Alley Jazz Society, which supports jazz activities for young people.

Bohemian Caverns

2003 11th Street, NW, Shaw: U Street/14th Street Corridor (1-202 299 0800/www.bohemiancaverns. com). U Street/African-Amer Civil War Memorial/ Cardozo Metro. **Open** 6pm-1am Tue; 8pm-2amWed; 9pm-2am Thur; 9.30pm-3am Fri, Sat. **Credit** AmEx, MC, V. **Map** p250 J3.

After being shuttered for 30 years, the legendary Bohemian Caverns reopened in 2000. While it has not quite brought back the jazz glory days of U Street – it's not even the best jazz club in the immediate area – it has found a place among the revitalised nightlife in the historic African-American corridor. A management change in 2006 may help spur better word of mouth about this expensive venue, which has suffered from iffy service and uninspired bookings. Most of the acts are local, but occasionally an out-of-towner will stage a concert in the club's cave-like setting.

HR-57

1610 14th Street, NW, between Corcoran & R Streets, Shaw: Logan Circle (1-202 667 3700/ www.hr57.org). U Street/African-Amer Civil War Memorial/Cardozo or Dupont Circle Metro. **Open** phone for details. **Admission** varies. **No credit cards. Map** p250 H4.

From the outside, this store-front club looks like the type of place where a secret handshake is required to gain admittance. But you just need a few dollars to enter, which by the end of the night you'll feel was a bargain. Named after the US House of Representatives' resolution recognising jazz as a national treasure, this unassuming club is about music. You won't find big names here, unless they

stop in to jam after Kennedy Center gigs, but you will find huge talent. There's no bar, but a plate of greens and beans can be had for the same price as the cover charge. Hit it on a good night, and you've got the best dinner-and-a-show value in town.

Twins Jazz/Twins Lounge

Twins Jazz *1344 U Street, NW, between 13th & 14th Streets, Shaw: U Street/14th Street Corridor (1-202 234 0072/www.twinsjazz.com). U Street/ African-Amer Civil War Memorial/Cardozo Metro.* **Open** 6pm-midnight Tue-Thur, Sun; 6pm-1am Fri, Sat. **Credit** AmEx, MC, V. **Admission** $5-$20. **Map** p250 H3.

Twins Lounge *5516 Colorado Avenue, NW, at Longfellow Street (1-202 882 2523/www.twins jazz.com). McPherson Square Metro then S2, S4 bus.* **Open** 6pm-2am Wed, Fri, Sat. **Admission** $10-$30. **Credit** AmEx, DC, Disc, MC. V.

The twins here are owners Kelly and Maze Tesfaye, though their jazz/supper club also has dual locations. Both rooms regularly feature local (Lenny Robinson, Michael Thomas) and national (David 'Fathead' Newman, Eddie Henderson) players, though the bigger names usually appear downtown; the lounge is almost literally a hole in the wall. The headlining cuisine is that of the twins' native Ethiopia, with Caribbean and American dishes rounding out the menu. Like with most jazz clubs, there's a cover charge ($10-$30) and a two-drink minimum at the downtown location.

Utopia

1418 U Street, between 14th & 15th Streets, Shaw: U Street/14th Street Corridor (1-202 483 7669/ www.utopiaindc.com). U Street/African-Amer Civil War Memorial/Cardozo Metro. **Open** 5pm-2am Mon-Thur; 5pm-3am Fri, Sat. **Tickets** $7-$10. **Credit** AmEx, DC, Disc, MC, V. **Map** p250 H3.

One of the first places to open as part of the regeneration of the Shaw neighbourhood, this small space

Blues Alley. *See p186.*

has settled into a regular schedule of local jazz and blues. Exhibits by local artists and a nice international cuisine all go towards making Utopia a sophisticated but relaxed local joint.

Classical & Opera

Washington, DC's classical music and opera scene can reflect the 'by the book' mentality of the city when it comes to the arts. Everything is professional and top notch, of course, but there's not a lot that could be considered as daring. Still, there are numerous embassies here with active cultural departments, offering an incredible number of opportunities to hear musicians from around the world. Many embassy-related events – held in the embassies themselves or in venues around town – can be found at www.embassyseries.com, www. embassyevents.com and www.cultural tourismdc.org. If you're around in June, be sure to catch a few of the concerts put on by the spunky, volunteer-run Washington Early Music Festival (www.earlymusicdc.org).

Companies

Choral Arts Society
1-202 244 3669/www.choralarts.org. **Tickets** $17-$50. **Credit** AmEx, Disc, MC, V.
Under the direction of Norman Scribner, this 190-member chorus has a very popular subscription series for its performances at the Kennedy Center. Occasional international appearances are also part of its itinerary, and it routinely performs locally with the National Symphony Orchestra. Not bad for a bunch of volunteers.

National Symphony Orchestra
1-202 416 8100/www.kennedy-center.org/nso. **Tickets** $40-$75. **Credit** AmEx, DC, MC, V.
The National Symphony, which performs mainly in the Kennedy Center Concert Hall, tries to live up to its name by offering something for everyone, and that's not always easy. Leonard Slatkin is the director of the orchestra and he has focused on making the music more accessible. Sometimes, as with the learning programmes and concerts geared towards children, he hits his mark. Other decisions, like that of naming Marvin Hamlisch as Principal Pops Conductor, are applauded by many but questioned by others. Overall, though, the NSO delivers a variety of engaging performances throughout the year, including composer-themed festivals.

Washington National Opera
1-202 295 2400/www.dc-opera.org. **Tickets** $45-$290. **Credit** AmEx, MC, V.
Started in 1956, and under the direction of Placido Domingo since 1996, the Washington Opera, resident at the Kennedy Center Opera House, is one of the city's best national performing arts groups. Recent productions include *Madame Butterfly* and *The Valkyrie*. The season usually sells out to subscribers but there is the chance that a call to the KenCen's box office will result in a lucky score of tickets. All productions have English subtitles.

Main venues

Kennedy Center
2700 F Street, NW, at New Hampshire Avenue & Rock Creek Parkway, Foggy Bottom (tickets & information 1-800 444 1324/1-202 467 4600/office 1-202 416 8000/www.kennedy-center.org). Foggy Bottom-GWU Metro (free shuttle 9.45am-midnight Mon-Fri; 10am-midnight Sat; noon-midnight Sun). **Box office** 10am-9pm Mon-Sat; noon-9pm Sun. **Peformances** times vary. **Tickets** vary. **Credit** AmEx, DC, MC, V. **Map** p252 F6.
The John F Kennedy Center for the Performing Arts – the national cultural centre of the United States – hosts a great variety of music, particularly on its free Millennium Stage. However, its primary focuses are classical and jazz. A welcome addition is the slate of intimate KC Jazz Club shows scheduled in the Terrace Gallery. The Center has five auditoriums. The Concert Hall is where the National Symphony Orchestra and Washington Chamber Symphony (among others) perform; its acoustics are first class. The Opera House hosts dance and ballet troupes, Broadway-style musical performances, and is the home of the Washington Opera. Productions in the Eisenhower Theater tend to have more of an edge, while the Theater Lab and Terrace Theater are the Center's most intimate spaces. **Photo** *p189.*

Folger Shakespeare Library
201 East Capitol Street, SE, Capitol Hill (1-202 544 7077/www.folger.edu). Capitol South or Union Station Metro. **Open** *Library* 10am-4pm Mon-Sat. **Performances** times vary. **Tickets** vary. **Credit** AmEx, MC, V. **Map** p253 L7.
The Globe isn't, though the convincing back-lit canopy does manage to convey the appearance of an outdoor theatre from Shakespeare's time. The Folger Consort ensemble presents period recitals of medieval, Renaissance and baroque chamber music. Interesting for the casual fan and a must for anyone with a passion for lyres and lutes.

National Academy of Sciences
2100 C Street, NW, at 21st Street, The Northwest Rectangle (1-202 334 2436/www7.national academies.org/arts/). Foggy Bottom-GWU Metro. **Performances** times vary. **Tickets** free. **Map** p252 G6.
A favourite of chamber ensembles, this space hosts groups such as the Jupiter Symphony Chamber Players and the Mendelssohn String Quartet. The performances are free but the seating is on a first-come, first-served basis. Navigating the one-way streets around the Academy can be tricky so either take a cab or study your map before you set out.

Kennedy Center. *See p188.*

Other venues

Museums & galleries

Venturing out to the city's numerous museums and galleries can often provide an unexpected bonus to visitors – choral and musical performances to accompany the visual arts on display.

Corcoran Gallery of Art

500 17th Street, NW, at New York Avenue, The White House & around (1-202 639 1700/www. corcoran.org). Farragut West Metro. **Performances** times vary. **Tickets** vary. **Credit** AmEx, MC, V. **Map** p252 G6.

Music at the Corcoran Gallery is best enjoyed in the setting of the modest Hammer Auditorium, where cabaret singers and jazz groups have taken over from chamber ensembles. The Sunday Gospel Brunch, which is held in the main lobby, is very popular, but if you're expecting an environment where the music is in the background, be warned: it can be extremely loud, irritatingly so depending on your taste and the performers concerned, and the musicians are often placed opposite the ticket/information desk, making for awkward transactions.

Phillips Collection

1600 21st Street, NW, at Q Street, Dupont Circle (1-202 387 2151/www.phillipscollection.org). Dupont Circle Metro. **Performances** *Oct-May* 5pm. **Tickets** concert included with museum admission. **Credit** AmEx, Disc, MC, V. **Map** p250 G4.

The Phillips, as it's known locally, carries with it a certain status that seems to lift it above the other, smaller venues in Washington. Its Sunday afternoon concerts are thus fittingly first-rate as well. If it's name-recognition you're looking for, however, you won't always find it on the bill. But if it's an excellent performance of chamber music in an environment where such things are truly appreciated that you're seeking, then you won't be disappointed.

Smithsonian Institution

Various buildings of the Smithsonian Institution (1-202 357 2700/www.si.edu). For listings, see p70.

As part of its varied programme, the Smithsonian regularly sponsors music events that can range from jazz performances and chamber music recitals to the two-week Folklife Festival that takes place in late June and early July. Call ahead for the locations as they can change depending upon the seating required. Also of interest to music lovers are the performances on the early instruments that are part of the permanent collection in the Museum of American History and the Friday evening IMAX Jazz Café at the Museum of Natural History.

Churches

Several of the city's churches, cathedrals and synagogues open their doors for special performances. Others are known for the calibre of the choirs at their weekend services. In addition to those listed below, the Church of the Epiphany (1317 G Street, between 13th & 14th Streets, NW, Downtown, 1-202 347 2635) has an outstanding musical programme.

Basilica of the National Shrine of the Immaculate Conception

400 Michigan Avenue, NE, at Fourth Street, Northeast (1-202 526 8300/www.national shrine.com). Brookland-CUA Metro. **Performances** times vary. **Tickets** free. **Map** p251 L1.

Occasional choral performances, or carillon and organ recitals, which are healthily attended.

St Augustine Roman Catholic Church

1419 V Street, NW, at 15th Street, Shaw: U Street/ 14th Street Corridor (1-202 265 1470/www.saint augustine-dc.org/music.html). U Street/African-Amer Civil War Memorial/Cardozo Metro. **Performances** times vary. **Tickets** free. **Map** p250 H3.

As the Mother Church of the local African-American Roman Catholic community, St Augustine's is best known for its wonderful Easter vigil service. The Sunday 12.30pm mass is also popular. Led by the more sedate choir and choral group, the latter complete with ensemble accompaniment of bass, guitar and drums, the service becomes a mix of Gospel, old-time revival and traditional mass.

Multi-use venues

Clarice Smith Performing Arts Center

University of Maryland, College Park, MD (1-301 405 2787). College Park/U of Md Metro. **Tickets** vary. **Credit** AmEx, DC, MC, V.

The Center major in 'the unfamiliar, the unpredictable and the developing'. There are all kinds of theatre, dance and music performances. Eclectic music programming can feature anything from Maryland high school choirs to jazz from the McCoy Tyner Septet to fado singer Dulce Pontes.

Coolidge Auditorium, Library of Congress

Independence Avenue, between First & Second Streets, SE, The Capitol & around (1-202 707 5502/ www.loc.gov). Capitol South Metro. **Performances** times vary; most begin 8pm. **Tickets** free. **Map** p253 L7.

The problem with a number of Washington venues is that the standard of architecture and the acoustics doesn't always match – with monumental buildings matched to muffled sound. The Coolidge Auditorium in the Jefferson Building, however, rises to the occasion on both counts. Programming is intriguing and intimate: genres performed here run the gamut from classical to country to world music, with acts ranging from the Daedalus Quartet and Chick Corea to Laura Cantrell and the River Boys Polka Band.

George Mason University Center for the Arts

Roanoke Lane & Mason Drive, Fairfax, VA (1-703 993 8888/www.gmu.edu/cfa). Vienna/Fairfax Metro then Cue Gold or Cue Green bus. **Tickets** $17.50-$84. **Credit** AmEx, Disc, MC, V.

It's a shame that one of the area's best concert facilities is located so far out of the District. Until the issue is addressed, however, folks will have to travel to the George Mason campus for some of the best in music, experimental drama and modern dance. The main hall seats nearly 2,000 and has hosted artists from the Canadian Brass to Dr John to the Dresden Philharmonic. The university's 10,000-seat stadium, the Patriot Center, hosts big-name musical acts as well as sports matches.

Lincoln Theatre

1215 U Street, NW, between 12th & 13th Streets, Shaw: U Street/14th Street Corridor (1-202 328 6000/www.thelincolntheatre.org). U Street/African-Amer Civil War Memorial/Cardozo Metro. **Tickets** $10-$50. **Credit** AmEx, MC, V. **Map** p250 H3.

DC's one-time answer to Harlem's Apollo Theater, this magnificent structure has received a new lease of life thanks to the continuing renewal of U Street. The site of jazz and pop performances and neo-'Chitlin Circuit' theatre, the Lincoln also plays host to annual events like Reel Affirmations (Gay and Lesbian Film Festival, *see p170*) and various pageants, concerts and lectures.

Lisner Auditorium

730 21st Street, NW, at H Street, Foggy Bottom (1-202 994 6800/www.lisner.org). Foggy Bottom-GWU Metro. **Tickets** vary. **No credit cards**. **Map** p252 G5.

Located in George Washington University, Lisner hosts a variety of performers and performances. Dance troupes and opera companies have taken the stage, as has Senegalese singer Youssou N'Dour. Author readings and rock shows are scheduled as well, sometimes on the same night, as when Dave Eggers split the bill with They Might Be Giants.

Strathmore

5301 Tuckerman Lane, North Bethesda, Maryland (1-301 581 5100/www.strathmore.org). Grosvenor-Strathmore Metro. **Tickets** vary. **Credit** AmEx, Disc, MC, V.

The DC-area home of the Baltimore Symphony Orchestra is beautiful and acoustically gorgeous. Opened in 2005, the concert hall's walls are blond wood, lending a light and airy feel. The Strathmore is part of a larger arts complex, and the bookings here reflect that, running from South African a capella group Ladysmith Black Mambazo to goth-rock legends Bauhaus. But the room is ideal for acoustic music, best heard in performances by luminous visiting classical artists and the Baltimore Symphony, which has added some much-needed competition to the sometimes staid National Symphony.

Warner Theatre

13th & E Streets, NW, The Federal Triangle (1-202 783 4000/www.warnertheatre.com). Metro Center Metro. **Tickets** vary. **Credit** AmEx, Disc, MC, V. **Map** p252 H6.

Built in 1924, the Warner Theatre has seen a variety of acts on its stage. The early deco design of the auditorium gives it either a decadent gaudiness or a stately individuality, depending on the performance. Comedians, dance troupes and Broadway plays dominate, but music acts still surface now and then.

Wolf Trap

1645 Trap Road, Vienna, VA (1-703 255 1900/ www.wolf-trap.org). West Falls Church Metro then Wolf Trap shuttle bus. **Tickets** $10-$70. **Credit** AmEx, Disc, MC, V.

Calling itself 'America's National Park for the Performing Arts', Wolf Trap consists of two essentially separate performance spaces – the Barns and the Filene Center. Don't let the name, the Barns, fool you. Yes, the space is rustic, but that doesn't mean you'll be sitting on a milking stool. The acoustics here are top notch, as are the seating and facilities. The Filene Center is the sprawling outdoor concert facility with lawn and pavilion seating. The scope of the performances at both spaces is broader than that at many venues in the District that also use the name 'national'. Depending on the night you visit, you might catch the resident opera company tackling Salieri's *Falstaff*, or Del McCoury laying down some plaintive, high-lonesome bluegrass.

Nightlife

Work hard. Play harder.

Get one of your **Five** a day. *See p192.*

We've said it before and we'll say it again: yes, there's more to Washington than politics; and no, its nightlife isn't boring. Neither is this city a wannabe New York. In its nightlife, as well as everything else, it has its own very distinct flavour, with a wide range of venues for all breeds of clubbers. Here we pick some of the best: just a soupçon of what the District has to offer. For bars with music, see **Bars**, *pp134-40*.

DC's nightlife hub of Adams Morgan, beloved of the college-aged and notable for its Saturday-night crowds packing the streets, ubiquitous pizza slices and grime, has lost more sophisticated nightlifers to areas like the revitalised U Street, 18th Street and Connecticut Avenue (which is mobbed at weekends), and Georgetown (for the swanky and pricey).

Information on club nights and parties can be found in the *Washington City Paper* and the *Washington Post*'s 'Night Watch' column in Friday's 'Weekend' section. Natural-born scruffs should note that some of the DC scene operates a dress code: think slightly smart. Access to upscale joints will be denied those wearing jeans, sneakers and hats. The legal drinking age in the US is 21 and it is strictly enforced in DC. Though many clubs will let under-21s in, they can't buy booze.

Clubs & lounges

Another lounge of the moment – also a restaurant – is **Indebleu** (*see p115*), with top DJs from Wednesday to Saturday night.

Bar Nun

1326 U Street, NW, between 13th & 14th Streets, Shaw: U Street/14th Street Corridor (1-202 667 6680/ www.dcbarnun.com). U Street/African-Amer Civil War Memorial/Cardozo Metro. **Open** 8pm-2am Mon; 6pm-2am Tue-Fri; 9pm-3am Sat, Sun. **Admission** $5-$10. **Credit** AmEx, DC, MC, V. **Map** p250 H3.

The vibe at Bar Nun is eclectic, with open mic poetry sessions, live jazz and Saturday nights devoted to 'couples and women'. Early in the evening the candlelit club's atmosphere is loungey and relaxed, but by 10.30pm hard-core dance machines can pump away amid the pulsating beats of house and hip hop on the two packed dancefloors. The crowd is serious about its music, but not so serious about itself – a refreshing attitude for a club of this calibre.

Impress your date with classical learning. **MCCXXIII** means **1223**. *See p194.*

Bravo! Bravo!

1001 Connecticut Avenue, NW, between K & L Streets,
Downtown (1-202 223 5330/www.bravobravodc.com).
Farragut North Metro. **Open** 11am-9pm Mon, Tue,
Thur; 11am-3am Wed, Fri, Sat. **Admission** $10-$15.
Credit AmEx, DC, Disc, MC, V. **Map** p252 G5.

For almost ten years this unassuming nightclub three
blocks from the White House has been attracting
upwards of 400 polished dancers on Wednesday and
Saturday and Friday (world music) nights.
The mood is flirty; the music is a combination of
Spanish-language club hits and up-tempo remixes.
This is one of the few 18-and-over dance nights in the
city. Lighting is harsh and security tight.

Bukom Café

2442 18th Street, NW, between Belmont & Columbia
Roads, Adams Morgan (1-202 265 4600/www.
bukom.com). Dupont Circle then 42 bus. **Open** 4pm-
2am Mon-Thur; 4pm-3am Fri, Sat. **Admission** free.
Credit AmEx, Disc, MC, V. **Map** p250 G3.

The crowd is West African and African American
but everyone's welcome to get lost in the sway. The
Ghanaian menu is reason alone to visit (try the beef
wrapped in cassava leaves) but arrive after 10pm
and it's standing room only: be prepared to dance
with whoever's next to you. Nightly bands play reggae, soca and funk.

Chi-Cha Lounge

1624 U Street, NW, between 16th & 17th Streets
(1-202 234 8400). Dupont Circle or U Street/African-
Amer Civil War Memorial/Cardoza Metro. **Open**
5.30pm-1.30am Mon-Thur, Sun; 5.30pm-2.30am Fri,
Sat. **Admission** usually free. **Map** p250 H3.

Ecuadorean entrepreneur Mauricio Fraga-Rosenfeld
has taught DC to relax to a Latin beat. Since opening Chi-Cha, he's expanded to Dupont Circle
(Gazuza), Georgetown (Mate), Silver Spring
(Ceviche) and Arlington (Gua-Rapo). All follow the
same formula: deep velvet couches, candlelight,
Andean tapas, sangria, Latin jazz and hookah pipes
filled with honey-cured tobacco. Chi-Cha hosts live
bands from Sunday to Thursday; on these nights
there's a $15 minimum consumption fee. No hats,
ties or sportswear. That's right, no ties.

Eighteenth Street Lounge

1212 18th Street, NW, between M Street & Jefferson
Place, Dupont Circle (1-202 466 3922). Farragut
North or Dupont Circle Metro. **Open** 5.30pm-2am
Tue-Thur; 5.30pm-2.30am Thur, Fri; 9.30pm-2.30am
Sat. **Admission** $5-$10. **Credit** AmEx, MC, V.
Map p250 G5.

Love it or hate it, ESL remains the city's trendiest
and most exclusive lounge, widely renowned (or
notorious) for its strict door policy. Should your
attire (or your connections) please the notoriously
fickle doormen and you're granted entrance through
the unmarked wooden door, you'll find hipsters mingling and dancing to live jazz or downtempo electronic music spun by the city's best DJs.

Five

1214B 18th Street, NW, between M Street &
Jefferson Place, Dupont Circle (1-202 331 7123).
Dupont Circle or Farragut North Metro. **Open** 9pm-
3am Wed; 10pm-2am Thur; 9pm-5am Fri; 10pm-5am
Sat; 6am-noon alternate Sun. **Admission** $5-$10.
Credit AmEx, MC, V. **Map** p250 G5.

Randomness reigns supreme at Five, with music as varied as the crowd it attracts. With three large dancefloors, Five is ideal for those whose main interest is dancing to anything and everything, from hip hop to trance to break beats and reggae. **Photo** *p191*.

Fur

33 Patterson Street, NE, at North Capitol Street, Northeast (1-202 542 3401/www.furnightclub.com). New York-Florida Avenue/Gallaudet U Metro. **Open** 8pm-2am Thur; 9pm-3am Fri, Sat. **Admission** $10-$25. **Credit** AmEx, Disc, MC, V.

Dress up and wait in line at the city's latest upscale super-club. What makes Fur different from DC's other multi-level entertainment venues? All boast chic interiors, VIP rooms, music's biggest names and vast dance spaces. But what sets Fur apart is its intimate lounges, which provide a haven from the audio-visual show pulsating from the club's dancefloors. They have louche names like the Mafia Room and the Mink Room, and they feel like your living room – provided your living room looks like an interiors magazine. Theme nights are frequent so check the website in advance.

Habana Village

1834 Columbia Road, NW, between Biltmore Street & Mintwood Place, Adams Morgan (1-202 462 6310/ www.habanavillage.com). Dupont Circle Metro then 42 bus. **Open** 6.30pm-3am Wed-Sat. **Admission** $5. **Credit** AmEx, DC, MC, V. **Map** p250 G2.

This multi-level salsa palace caters to most whims, with a couple of lounges, multiple dance floors and live sounds. The music, clientele and decor will appeal to Latin lovers but also those who've grown tired of the largely Anglo-focused clubs in Adams Morgan.

Heaven & Hell

2327 18th Street, NW, at Kalorama Road, Adams Morgan (1-202 667 4355). Dupont Circle Metro then 42 bus. **Open** 7.30pm-2am Mon-Thur, Sun; 7pm-3am Fri, Sat. **Admission** $5 (includes 1 drink). **Credit** AmEx, DC, Disc, MC, V. **Map** p250 G3.

If the '80s were your idea of heaven, then head here on Thursday nights for the best party in town. After getting your glow-in-the-dark halo at the door, head up to Heaven and immerse yourself in retro land. If you're looking for a young singles meat market and a trite but fun theme night, this is the place to be. Whatever you do, avoid Hell (downstairs) – it's a small bar where nothing interesting ever happens.

H2O

800 Water Street, SW, between Seventh & L Streets, Southwest Waterfront (1-202 484 6300). Waterfront-SEU Metro. **Open** 5-11pm Thur; 5pm-3am Fri; 9pm-3am Sat. **Admission** varies. **Credit** AmEx, Disc, MC, V. **Map** p253 J8.

A glistening waterfront club with nightly specials and a parade of superstar DJs. The 42,000sq ft club is a warren of private nooks and expansive dance floors. And it's big: more than 1,500 people come through on a regular night. 'International Fridays' feature a complimentary buffet for early arrivals, and salsa bands long into the night. 'Soul Food Saturdays' are designed to feed the body and spirit – pick up a bag of hot rum buns as you leave. It's also *the* club for celeb sightings. Natalie Portman, P Diddy, and Bill Clinton are just a few of the famous faces to have made an appearance.

Love

1350 Okie Street, NE, at New York Avenue, Northeast (1-202 636 9030/www.welcometodream.com). **Open** 9pm-3am Thur-Sat. **Admission** $10-$40. **Credit** AmEx, MC, V.

Love, formerly called Dream, is still one of the hottest dance clubs in town. While the recent name change hasn't altered the club's popularity, Love is still a nightmare to reach (best to drive or take a cab, as there's no Metro nearby and the area can be dangerous). A refurbished four-storey warehouse in an industrial neighbourhood off New York Avenue, the club is an evening's commitment. But dress to impress and it's worth it. Inside are myriad bars, rooms pumping hip hop, world music, salsa, house and trance. Catch live shows Friday nights from the likes of DMX and Busta Rhymes.

Mantis

1847 Columbia Road, NW, at Mintwood Place, Adams Morgan (1-202 667 2400). Dupont Circle Metro then 42 bus. **Open** 5.30pm-1.30am Mon-Thur, Sun; 5.30pm-2.30am Fri, Sat. **Credit** AmEx, MC, V. **Map** p250 G3.

IndeBleu, fusing east and yeast. *See p191.*

A large gold Buddha presides like a harvest moon over this apple-green lounge in Adams Morgan. Philippe Starck chairs and modular leather furniture provide a playful space to sip Cosmos and nibble on bar food. In the basement a small DJ space gets things moving at around 10pm.

MCCXXIII (1223)

1223 Connecticut Avenue, NW, at 18th Street, Dupont Circle (1-202 822 1800/www.club1223.com). Dupont Circle or Farragut North Metro. **Open** 9pm-2am Tue; 6pm-2am Wed, Thur; 5pm-3am Fri; 9pm-3am Sat; 8pm-2am Sun. **Admission** varies. **Credit** AmEx, Disc, MC, V. **Map** p250 G5.

The Roman numerals reveal the address of this chic nightspot. Past the velvet rope, interior columns support high ceilings above couches and a dancefloor the size of a postage stamp. The crowd is international and celebrities such as Michael Jordan and George Clooney have been spotted. It's also the domain of professional athletes and the women who date them. On Fridays, dress to impress and arrive by 6pm for the $20 happy hour. **Photo** *p192.*

Mie N Yu

3125 M Street, NW, between 31st Street & Wisconsin Avenue, Georgetown (1-202 333 6122). Foggy Bottom-GWU Metro then 30, 32, 34, 36, Georgetown Metro Connection bus. **Open** 5pm-1.30am Mon, Tue; 11.30am-1.30am Wed, Thur, Sun; 11.30am-2.30am Fri, Sat. **Admission** free. **Credit** AmEx, DC, Disc, MC, V. **Map** p249 E5.

If you have the patience and the cash, a trip down the Silk Road can be a kick. Launched as a restaurant, the bar culture all but takes over after 11pm. Skip the fussy food and camp out in any of the overdressed oriental theme areas (the Turkish tent is fab). The house cocktail menu is a good read but unnecessary. The fun here is the people-watching: richie-rich undergraduates and ex-wives.

Modern

3287 M Street, NW, between 33rd & Potomac Streets, Georgetown (1-202 338 7027). Foggy Bottom-GWU Metro then 30, 32, 34, 36, Georgetown Metro Connection bus. **Open** 9pm-2am Thur; 9pm-3am Fri, Sat. **Admission** varies; up to $10. **Credit** AmEx, MC, V. **Map** p249 E5.

Another of John Boyle's successes (Five, Mie N Yu), this swanky lounge is popular with young Georgetown. Of the places to chill out, the favourite-has to be the ring of leather cubes around the sunken bar. Order into the well and the bartenders hand up your bevs. The hanging bubble chair off the dance floor is the best seat in the house.

Platinum

915 F Street, NW, between Ninth & Tenth Streets, Downtown (1-202 393 3555/www.platinum clubdc.com). Gallery Place-Chinatown or Metro Center Metro. **Open** 10pm-3am Thur-Sat; 10pm-2.30am Sun. **Admission** $10-$15; free for women before 11pm Fri; or sign up for free admission via the website. **Credit** AmEx, MC, V. **Map** p253 J6.

Without question, Platinum is one of the city's most beautiful clubs. Built as a bank at the turn of the last century, the space has endured several incarnations, but once the lights, smoke and dance music start, the effect is entrancing. Don't sit down unless you want bottle service ($50-$500).

Republic Gardens

1355 U Street, NW, between 13th & 14th Streets, Shaw: U Street/14th Street Corridor (1-202 232 2710). U Street/African-Amer Civil War Memorial/ Cardozo Metro. **Open** 5.30pm-1.30am Wed, Thur; 6.30pm-2.30am Fri, Sat. **Admission** free Wed, Thur; $10 Fri; $20 Sat. **Credit** AmEx, MC, V. **Map** p250 H3.

Republic Gardens remains Washington's upscale lounge for African Americans. Born in U Street's heyday, the 1920s, the club saw performances by Charlie Parker, Pearl Bailey and native son Duke Ellington. It closed in the 1960s, reopened in the '90s and, after extensive renovations and new management, was reborn in 2003. Dine in the Mahogany Room, rest up or play pool in the Library, or dance on whatever patch of floor you can claim.

Zanzibar on the Waterfront

700 Water Street, SW, between Sixth & Seventh Streets, Southwest Waterfront (1-202 554 9100). Waterfront-SEU Metro. **Open** 5pm-2am Wed, Thur; 5pm-3am Fri; 9pm-4am Sat; 9pm-2am Sun (Sky Lounge only). **Admission** varies; up to $15. **Credit** AmEx, MC, V. **Map** p253 J8.

Zanzibar has reclaimed the waterfront. Sit near the wide windows at lunchtime and watch the boats chug by while noshing on Afro-Caribbean food. Return for Wednesday night's salsa party, which welcomes wonks in suits and hotties in little dresses. Take the free dance lesson at seven o'clock, and you can be using your new moves by eight. To enjoy the view from the top-floor Sky Club, however, you'll need to, well, join the club.

Zengo

781 Seventh Street, NW, at H Street, Downtown (1-202 393 2929). Chinatown/Gallery Place Metro. **Open** 5-10pm Mon-Thur, Sun; 5pm-12.30am Fri, Sat. **Admission** free. **Credit** AmEx, MC, V. **Map** p253 J5.

One of the few DC hot spots where the pricey cocktails are actually worth the money (try the Mojito De Mango), Zengo's drinks, vibrant atmosphere and food from renowned chef Richard Sandoval make it a favourite among the trendy crowd. The one drawback to this sleek Latin-Asian lounge is that it closes early – 12.30am – even at weekends.

Comedy & cabaret

Improv

1140 Connecticut Avenue, NW, between L & M Streets, Downtown (1-202 296 7008/www.dcimprov.com). Farragut North Metro. **Open** *Shows* 8.30pm Tue-Thur; 8pm, 10.30pm Fri, Sat; 8pm Sun. **Admission** $15-$35. **Credit** AmEx, MC, V. **Map** p252 G5.

The most common assessment of Improv is that the service is disappointing but the material hysterical.

Sport & Fitness

Get out from behind the desk.

Washington may be more associated with politics and monuments than sport, but the superb natural resources surrounding the city provide a great environment for outdoor activities. For more on the Washington area's great outdoors, *see p214-18*. Some of the Washington area's most famous city sights and beautiful rural spots can best be seen while rollerblading, biking, boating – or even on a Segway (a scooter-like device, *see p197*). And for spectators, DC has a new baseball team, the Washington Nationals (*see p196* **Go Nationals**), as well as established basketball (Wizards), football (Redskins) and soccer (DC United) sides.

But sport does not have to come prearranged or ready packaged: check out the National Mall or Rock Creek Park in the spring and summer for pick-up games. So grab a baseball glove, kayak or football, go out and play.

Participation Sports

Boating & fishing

In March and April, when the cherry blossoms are in peak bloom, a popular way to see the sights is on a peddleboat on the calm Tidal Basin. **Tidal Basin Peddle Boats** (1501 Maine Avenue, SW, 1-202 479 2426, www.tidal basinpeddleboats.com) rents out peddleboats from mid March to mid October. It's $8 an hour for a two-seater and $16 for a four-seater.

Annapolis (*see p217*), about a 45-minute drive from DC, is on the Chesapeake Bay, the largest estuary in the US. **South River Boat Rentals** (Sunset Drive, Edgewater, MD, 1-410 956 9729, www.annapolisboatrental.com) rents out sailing boats and power boats for a day on the bay. **J World Annapolis** (213 Eastern Avenue, Annapolis, MD, 1-800 966 2083, www.sailjworld.com) and the **Annapolis Sailing School** (601 Sixth Street, Annapolis, MD, 1-800 638 9192, www.annapolis sailing.com) offer sailing classes. Annapolis is also a great place to go sea-fishing. **Rod & Reel Charters** (Route 261 & Mears Avenue, Chesapeake Beach, MD, 1-301 855 8450, www.rodnreelinc.com) is among several companies that offer fishing excursions for groups in the spring, summer and autumn.

It's best to call several days in advance in order to be sure of reserving yourself a spot.

Below are companies hiring boats in DC and the immediate area.

Fletcher's Boat House
4940 Canal Road, NW, at Reservoir Road, Upper Northwest (1-202 244 0461/www.fletchersboat house.com). **Open** *Early Mar-Oct* 7.30am-6pm daily. **No credit cards. Map** p248 B3.
Fletcher's rents out boats, canoes, bicycles and fishing equipment, and is convenient for the Potomac River and the C&O Canal.

Jack's Boathouse
3500 K Street, NW, under the Key Bridge, Georgetown (1-202 337 9642/www.jacksboat house.com). *Rosslyn Metro*. **Open** 10am-sunset Mon-Fri; 8am-sunset Sat, Sun. **Credit** MC, V. **Map** p249 E5.
Canoes, kayaks and tandem kayaks are hired for $15 an hour or $35 for a whole day on the Potomac. The company also offers lessons throughout the year.

Thompson Boat Center
2900 Virginia Ave, NW, at Rock Creek Parkway, Foggy Bottom (1-202 333 9453/www.thompson boatcenter.com). *Foggy Bottom-GWU Metro*. **Open** *Mar-Oct* 6am-8pm Mon-Sat; 7am-7pm Sun. **Credit** MC, V. **Map** p252 H7.
Canoes and kayaks for rent from spring to autumn. Rowing lessons and bike hire are available too.

Washington Sailing Marina
1 Marina Drive, off George Washington Memorial Parkway, Alexandria, VA (1-703 548 9027/www. washingtonsailingmarina.com). **Open** *Summer* 9am-6pm daily. *Winter* 10am-5pm daily.
This outfit rents out three types of sailboats, from a 14ft Sunfish to a 19ft Flying Scot, and rental costs range from $10 to $19 an hour. You must be certified or pass a written test to rent.

Cycling

Paved bicycle trails abound in Washington. They're easy to spot, being marked clearly with a green sign that has a picture of a bike on it. But for rougher terrain, you'll have to leave the city environs. Check out Scott Adams' *Washington Mountain Bike Book* – available at local bicycle shops.

Trail maps and on-street bike routes can be found at bike shops and the ADC Map & Travel Store (*see p145*). Also, the Washington Area Bicyclist Association (1803 Connecticut

Arts & Entertainment

Go Nationals

For the first time since 1972, Washington is home to Major League Baseball. Until recently, the nearest team was the Baltimore Orioles. But in 2005, the Montreal Expos moved to DC, renamed themselves the Washington Nationals and posted a very creditable 81 win, 81 loss record in their first season.

The honeymoon ended in 2006, not with a bang but a whimper. The Nats were among the worst teams in a hopelessly weak National League, limping along at the bottom of the NL East for much of the season despite some excellent trades pulled off by Jim Bowden, the team's oft-maligned general manager. However, some good did come out of the season when, after four years in limbo, the team finally found a new owner in May: real

estate millionaire Ted Lerner, who brought in son Mark (part-owner of the Capitals hockey team) and Stan Kasten (erstwhile president of the Atlanta Braves) to run the operation. It remains to be seen how much money the new owners will allocate for player contracts

Though a new ballpark is being built along the Southwest waterfront, hopefully in time for the 2008 season, the team currently plays at the RFK Stadium (*see p198*). The season runs from April to early October; see http://washington.nationals.mlb.com for a schedule. Tickets ($7-$115) are available in advance from the website or on 1-888 632 6287; however, although a few games each year do sell out, you should be able to get tickets for most games on the day.

Avenue, NW, 1-202 518 0524, www.waba.org) has an informative website with maps and other resources for cycling enthusiasts.

Metro riders note that you can take your bicycle on the trains only during off-peak hours – between 10am and 2pm and after 7pm during the week, and all day at weekends and holidays.

Below are a list of popular cycling trails.

C&O Canal Towpath

An 184-mile gravel path that starts at the corner of the Pennsylvania Avenue, NW, ramp of the Rock Creek Parkway (which is near the Foggy Bottom Metro stop) and finally ends up in Cumberland, Maryland. For a popular biking trip, take the trail 19.9 miles to Great Falls Park in Virginia.

Capital Crescent Trail

This trail makes its way from the Thompson Boat Center on the Potomac river in Georgetown all the way to Silver Spring, Maryland. The 11-mile trail also links with the Mount Vernon Trail. The paved part of the trail terminates in Bethesda, Maryland, but more advanced cyclists can take the crushed stone Georgetown Branch Trail to Silver Spring.

Mount Vernon Trail

An asphalt trail that takes riders along the Potomac river. It starts out on Theodore Roosevelt Island in Rosslyn, Virginia (near the Rosslyn Metro stop) and travels 18.5 miles through Old Town Alexandria, ultimately terminating, as the name suggests, at George Washington's historic home.

Rentals & tours

Big Wheel Bikes

1034 33rd Street, NW, at Cady's Alley, Georgetown (1-202 337 0254/www.bigwheelbikes.com). Bus 38B.
Open 11am-7pm Mon-Thur; 10am-6pm Sat, Sun.
Credit AmEx, MC, V. **Map** p249 E5.
A basic bicycle is $5 an hour or $25 a day.
Other locations: 3119 Lee Highway, Arlington, Virginia (1-703 522 1110); 6917 Arlington Road, Bethesda, Maryland (1-301 652 0192); 2 Prince Street, Alexandria, Virginia (1-703 739 2300).

Bike the Sites

Tour starts at the Old Post Office Pavillion, 1100 Pennsylvania Avenue, NW, (1-202 842 2453/www.bikethesites.com). Federal Triangle Metro.
Open 9am-6pm Mon-Sat; 9.30am-6pm Sun. **Rates** phone for details. **Credit** AmEx, MC. V. **Map** p252 H7.
See Washington on two wheels. Tours are typically three or four hours and from four to eight miles, usually costing $40 for adults and $30 for children, including bike and helmet hire.

Gyms

Many hotels have fitness centres; *see p40-55.*

Gold's Gym

409 Third Street, SW, between D & E Streets, Southwest (1-202 554 4653/www.goldsgym.com). Federal Center SW Metro. **Open** 5am-10pm Mon-Fri; 8am-8pm Sat; 9am-6pm Sun. **Rates** $15 per day; $50 per wk. **Credit** AmEx, Disc, MC, V. **Map** p253 J7.
Gold's has branches throughout DC and its suburbs; this location offers classes. Call ahead to register.

National Capital YMCA

1711 Rhode Island Avenue, NW, at 17th Street, Dupont Circle (1-202 862 9622/www.ymcanational capital.org). Farragut North Metro. **Open** 6am-11pm Mon-Fri; 8am-7pm Sat; 9am-6pm Sun. **Rates** *YMCA members* $7 per day. *Non-members* $15 per day.
Credit MC, V. **Map** p250 G5.
Good equipment, a pool and fitness classes.

Washington Sports Clubs

1990 M Street, NW, at 20th Street, Foggy Bottom (1-202 785 4900/www.mysportsclubs.com). Dupont Circle Metro. **Open** 6am-10pm Mon-Fri. **Rates** phone for details. **Credit** AmEx, MC, V. **Map** p252 G5.
Popular with locals, this sports club offers classes, machines, weights and squash courts.

Hiking

Virginia and Maryland's sumptuous scenery makes for popular hiking territory, and the District has its own wide expanse of green in Rock Creek Park (which stretches into Maryland). A few well-known trails are listed below, but see www.trails.com or *60 Hikes Within 60 Miles: Washington, DC* by Paul Elliott for more.

Appalachian Trail

www.patc.net.
The AT, as it is known, stretches 2,168 miles from Georgia to Maine, making it a little long for a day trip. However, there are lots of shorter walks that take you along parts of the trail in Virginia and Maryland.

Catoctin Mountain Park

www.nps.gov/cato.
Tucked away in Thurmont, Maryland, the park has 25 miles of trails with scenic mountain views. Check out the 78-foot plummet at Cunningham Falls.

Rock Creek Park

www.nps.gov/rocr/.
A good starting point for the park's 25 miles of trails is the seven-mile hike from the Meadowside Nature Center (5100 Meadowside Lane, Rockville, MD, 1-301 924 4141). You can also pick up trails at Lake Needwood (15700 Needwood Lake Circle, Rockville, MD, 1-301 924 4141) or on Beach Drive.

Ice & in-line skating

For ice skaters, parks and area town centres often set up ice rinks in the winter months, usually from late October through to March. In DC, Pershing Park (1-202 737 6938) is on Pennsylvania Avenue, NW, between 14th and 15th Street near the White House. There is also a popular rink in the sculpture garden at the National Gallery of Art (*see p66*).

While many of the bike paths listed above are fair game also for in-line skaters, they're often too narrow and crowded. As an alternative, try Beach Drive, north of Blagden Road in Rock Creek Park, on weekends when it's closed to traffic. Visit www.skatedc.org for more information on where to skate.

Pick-up games

At evenings and weekends Washingtonians of all ages enjoy playing in amateur sports teams and in pick-up games (where anyone's welcome). The Mall is the most popular location but the Ellipse, just south of the White House, and the fields around the Lincoln Memorial are also hot spots. For listings of local clubs and events get a copy of *MetroSports Magazine* (free in street boxes) or check its website at www.metrosportsdc.com.

Segway tours

Segway Human Transporters are like self-balancing scooters that automatically respond to your body's movements. Try out one of these unique modes of transport on a Segway tour of DC. City Segway Tours offers four-hour, day and night tours for $70 per person. Reserve in

Arts & Entertainment

advance at www.citysegwaytours.com or call 1-877 734 8687. All tours meet at the Willard Hotel (1445 Pennsylvania Avenue, NW).

Swimming

Cooling off on a hot day in DC is easy – there are nearly three dozen indoor public swimming pools in the area, as well as public outdoor pools. Outdoor pools are usually open from Memorial Day (late May) to Labor Day (early September). The best are the Capitol East Natatorium (635 North Carolina Avenue, SE, 1-202 724 4495) and Francis Pool (25th & N Streets, NW, 1-202 727 3285). For more options, check out the government listings (blue-edged) in the *Yellow Pages* under 'District of Columbia, Parks and Recreation', or phone Aquatic Services at 1-202 576 8884. Some local gyms have pools that are open to the public for a fee.

Tennis

Aside from these public facilities, check out parks and schools for outdoor-only courts. It's first come, first serve, so be prepared to wait for a spot and cut your playing time to 30 minutes to an hour if others are in line.

East Potomac Tennis Center

1090 Ohio Drive, SW, at Buckeye Drive, Southwest (1-202 554 5962/www.eastpotomactennis.com). Smithsonian Metro then 20min walk. **Open** 7am-10pm daily. **Rates** $8-$17 per hr. Credit MC, V. **Map** p284 H8.

A public facility at Hains Point that has 24 courts, including 10 clay and 14 hard. There's also a pro shop and you can call in advance to set up a lesson.

Rock Creek Tennis Center

16th & Kennedy Streets, NW, Upper Northwest (1-202 722 5949/www.rockcreektennis.com). Bus S1, S2, S3, S4, S5. **Open** 7am-11pm Mon-Thur; 7am-8pm Fri-Sun. **Rates** $8-$29.75 per hr. **Credit** MC, V.

25 outdoor courts, five of which can be covered in the winter. Racquets and a ball machine for hire.

Spectator Sports

Tickets for nearly all professional sporting events in Washington are distributed by **Ticketmaster** (1-301 808 4300, www.ticket master.com). There is a service charge for all ticket purchases.

American football

Three-time Super Bowl winners the **Washington Redskins** play in Landover, Maryland at FedEx Field. All the tickets at FedEx Field are season tickets, so you can't

just walk up, buy tickets and watch a game – there's a decades-long waiting list. If you're desperate to see a match, try Craigslist.org, the *Washington Post*'s classified ads section, or try your luck with the touts (scalpers) at FedEx's front gate. If you travel to Baltimore, you have a better chance of seeing some American football action. The **Baltimore Ravens**' season tickets go on sale in August. Phone 1-410 261 7283 or check www.baltimoreravens.com for the latest information. The football season runs from August to January.

Basketball

Both men's and women's basketball are popular in DC. The **Washington Wizards** of the NBA made it to the playoffs in 2005 and 2006, and the women's **Washington Mystics** have stars like Alana Beard in their lineup.

Tickets are usually relatively easy to get and cost $10-$775 for the Wizards, or as low as $4 for the Mystics. The men play from November to May, the women from May to September.

Verizon Center

601 F Street, NW, at Seventh Street, Downtown (1-202 628 3200/www.mcicenter.com). Gallery Place-Chinatown Metro. **Map** p253 J6.

Recently renamed (it was previously called the MCI Center), the arena cost $200 million to build and seats nearly 20,000 fans.

Hockey

After the National Hockey League strike that cancelled the 2004-5 season, the **Washington Capitals**, along with the rest of American hockey, are back up and running. The Caps don't usually sell out and tickets cost $20-$140. Phone the Verizon Center (*see above*) for match information. Tickets are available from Ticketmaster (*see above*).

Soccer

Since baseball returned to DC at the RFK Stadium, the Nationals have somewhat overshadowed Washington's soccer team, **DC United**. But United has proved itself as a talented squad, with talented teen phenomenon Freddy Adu playing midfield.

RFK Stadium

22nd & East Capitol Street, NE, Northeast (office 1-202 547 9077/DC United office 1-202 587 5000/www.dcsec.com). Stadium-Armory Metro. **Open** 8.30am-5.30pm Mon-Fri. **Tickets** vary. **Credit** MC, V.

Tickets are available from DC United (1-202 587 5000, www.dcunited.com) or through the ubiqitous services of Ticketmaster (*see above*).

Arts & Entertainment

Theatre & Dance

DC's theatre and dance scenes are in a state of rude health.

Like any theatre town worth its greasepaint, Washington can point to posh troupes with a roster of distinguished directors as well as scrappy little outfits that get by on foundation grants and volunteer sweat. And Washington's theatre world is growing – never mind that the post-9/11 economy shook out a few of the smaller companies, including one of the two local French-language troupes. And never mind that Chocolate City – so called for its majority African-American population and thriving black middle class – still boasts just one professional theatre ensemble (the African Continuum Theatre Company) devoted to exploring the African-American experience.

On the whole, though, the stage scene here remains one of the healthiest in the United States – the second healthiest after New York, if you believe the Helen Hayes Awards Society, which hands out the local equivalent of the UK's Oliviers or New York's Tonys. And while the museums and monuments still draw the biggest swarms of out-of-town visitors, locals are spotting a new species of seasonal migrant: the theatrical tourist. The **Kennedy Center**'s smash-hit Sondheim Festival attracted musical-theatre junkies in the summer of 2002, a similar endeavour in 2004 brought fans and critics from afar to get reacquainted with the smothering mothers and deranged belles of Tennessee Williams, and it will host performances in a city-wide Shakespeare festival scheduled for the first six months of 2007 (*see p200* **Doing it the Bard way**).

The bigfoot on the Potomac isn't the only ambitious outfit, though: in January 2004, the **Signature Theatre** drew Rodgers & Hammerstein devotees for the world premiere of a heavily revised *Allegro*, the 1950s concept musical that was the duo's first major flop, and its 2006 premiere of *Nevermore* likewise proved a magnet for Edgar Allan Poe junkies. On Capitol Hill, the **Folger Theatre** has played host to star performers (including Michael Learned) and celebrity audience members (including Kenneth Branagh) with such high-profile productions as *Elizabeth the Queen* and *Melissa Arctic*, the latter a world-premiere reworking of *The Winter's Tale* from white-hot dramatist Craig Wright. And in the summer of 2006, a mad young bunch of Irish specialists called Solas Nua staged *La Corbière*, a play

about French prostitutes drowned off Jersey's La Corbière lighthouse, by Jersey-born writer Anne le Marquand Hartigan, in a municipal swimming pool. (That's right, *in* it.)

When it comes to festivals, Shakespeare is not the only theme in town. Two transplanted veterans of the Philadelphia Fringe recently asked why there was no DC equivalent. And hey, presto: the inaugural **Capital Fringe** Festival sold 17,000 tickets to 400-plus performances by 96 acts – from a 'ukulele operetta' to the abovementioned *La Corbière* – in more than 20 venues over 10 days in July 2006. For a first-year effort it represents a pretty big success, and Washington's audiences and art-makers responded voraciously. The consensus: Shakespeare in Washington may be one whopper of a one-off, but the annual Capital Fringe (www.capfringe.org) looks to be the latest landmark on DC's performing-arts landscape.

H Street Playhouse: home to Theater Alliance. *See p205.*

LISTINGS AND INFORMATION

For comprehensive information on dates, times and venues, check the *Washington City Paper* (www.washingtoncitypaper.com), the *Washington Post* (www.washingtonpost.com), or the Helen Hayes Awards site (www.helen hayes.org). Look for flyers in coffeehouses, theatres and bookshops. Try Ticketplace (1-202 638 2406, www.ticketplace.org), at 407 Seventh Street, NW, for last-minute half-price tickets, and eavesdrop on DC theatre news and gossip at Theaterboy (www.theaterboy.net).

Theatre

Major venues

Arena Stage

1101 Sixth Street, SW, at Maine Avenue, Southwest (1-202 488 3300/www.arenastage.com). Waterfront-SEU Metro. **Box office** 10am-8pm Mon-Sat; noon-8pm Sun. **Tickets** $40-$45. **Credit** AmEx, Disc, MC, V.
The city's theatrical grande dame and a pioneer in the American resident theatre movement may be emerging from nearly a decade of torpor. Blessed (and cursed) with an affluent establishment audience, artistic director Molly Smith has disappointed some critics by programming unchallenging audience-pleasers. But there have been a few bold ventures nonetheless: an epic trilogy of one-acts (Sarah Ruhl's vividly imagined Passion Play) and the archival excavation of a protofeminist rarity (Intimations for Saxophone, from Machinal author Sophie Treadwell) are just two. A long-gestating musical from Pulitzer Prize winner Paula Vogel – A Civil War Christmas – was announced for 2006-7, then postponed, but fundraising continues for a $100-million expansion plan that will upgrade facilities, create a 200-seat new-play incubator, and wrap the existing Fichandler and Kreeger theatres in a glittering glass box.

Kennedy Center

2700 F Street, NW, at New Hampshire Avenue & Rock Creek Parkway, Foggy Bottom (1-800 444 1324/ 1-202 467 4600/www.kennedy-center.org). Foggy Bottom-GWU Metro then free shuttle 9.45am-midnight Mon-Fri; 10am-midnight Sat; noon-midnight Sun. **Box office** 10am-9pm Mon-Sat; noon-9pm Sun. **Tickets** $5-$105. **Credit** AmEx, DC, MC, V. **Map** p252 F6.

Doing it the Bard way

Shakespeare? In Washington? Believe it or not. Though it's not quite Stratford, the national capital handily trounces the nation's theatrical capital, New York, when it comes to its range of classical theatre programming – and even the British Library must feel an occasional twinge of envy over the 79 *First Folios* crowning the vast Shakespearean hoard at the Folger Shakespeare Library. So when ex-Covent Garden chief Michael Kaiser dreamed up a six-month city-wide Shakespeare in Washington festival, DC responded with a collective 'Why didn't we think of that?'

From January to June 2007, decreed Kaiser (now poobah at the John F Kennedy Center for the Performing Arts, *see p200*), tiny local theatres and world-famous troupes alike would produce the bard both straight up (the RSC promised to ship in Gregory Doran's *Coriolanus* for a spring run) and with a twist (Washington Shakespeare Company, *see p205*, scheduled a largely silent *King Lear*.)

Opera companies programmed the Verdi adaptations, while Dame Cleo Laine signed on for a concert based on her 1960s-vintage *Shakespeare and All That Jazz* album. And the Smithsonian Jazz Masterworks Orchestra scheduled a night of Shakespeare-inspired music from Duke Ellington and Billy Strayhorn, spiced with soliloquies and scenes read by African-American stage and screen stars.

World-class ballets were booked – the American Ballet Theatre with Lar Lubovitch's controversial modernist *Othello*, the Kirov with Leonid Lavrovsky's 1940 *Romeo & Juliet*, and more – while theatrical futurists at Montreal's 4D Art and DC's)musica(aperta, respectively, offered up a one-act multimedia *La Tempête* and a genre-defying *Six Degrees of Hamlet*.

Festival curator Michael Kahn (artistic director at the Shakespeare Theatre Company, *see right*) signed on to direct a *Richard III* starring Geraint Wyn-Davies (TV's *Slings and Arrows* and *Forever Knight*), plus a *Hamlet* with hot young actor Jeffrey Carlson (Broadway's *Taboo*) – and booked in Australian director Gale Edwards (*Whistle Down the Wind*) to stage *Titus Andronicus*. And at least three variations on the Scottish play – including a naked *Macbeth* and a Native American *Macbeth* – were proposed by this group or that, as if to deny custom the chance to make Shakespeare feel stale.

All told, upward of 45 organisations jumped at the chance to celebrate the Bard. A complete schedule is at www.kennedy-center.org/shakespeare.

As part of its broad-spectrum programming, the national cultural centre puts on a full theatre season each year. It's mostly imports and tours – not since the 1980s has the house had a resident company – but now and again the imports are remarkable. (The Royal Shakespeare Company has visited regularly in recent years, and the revamped Kennedy Center Fund for New American Plays brings in one major regional company each season.) Home-grown productions are picking up too: a splashy *Mame* revival, starring Tony Award winner Christine Baranski, sold out to the rafters in the summer of 2006, and the handsome new Kennedy Center Family Theater space hosts originals and adaptations by the likes of movie star Whoopi Goldberg and Japanese-American dramatist Naomi Iizuka. And with ex-Covent Garden guru Michael Kaiser at the helm, the centre has sponsored a series of ambitious festivals (*see p200* **Doing it the Bard way**).

National Theatre

1321 Pennsylvania Avenue, NW, between 13th & 14th Streets, The Federal Triangle (1-202 628 6161/ www.nationaltheatre.org). Metro Center of Federal Triangle Metro. **Box office** *Performance days* until performance begins. *Non-performance days* 10am-6pm Mon-Sat; noon-6pm Sun. **Tickets** $15-$75. **Credit** AmEx, DC, Disc, MC, V. **Map** p252 H6.

One of the city's oldest theatres (it dates from 1835), the National has a history as a Broadway tryout house – productions have included the flamingly awful jukebox musical *Hot Feet*, which went on to an ignoble 97 New York performances in 2006. But in recent decades it has been home mostly to touring fluff – when it doesn't sit empty, that is. Another recent tenant: a revival of *Legends!* starring… wait for it… Linda Evans and Joan Collins.

Shakespeare Theatre Company

450 Seventh Street, NW, between D & E Streets, Penn Quarter (1-202 547 1122/www.shakespeare theatre.org). Gallery Place-Chinatown Metro. **Box office** *Performance days* 10am-6pm Mon; 10am-6.30pm Tue-Sat; noon-6.30pm Sun. *Non-performance days* 10am-6pm Mon-Sat; noon-6pm Sun. **Tickets** $17-$66. **Credit** AmEx, Disc, MC, V. **Map** p253 J6.

Led for two decades by noted director Michael Kahn and hailed by the *Economist* as 'one of the world's three great Shakespearean theatres', the Shakespeare Theatre is probably the top classical company in the US – and now it's adding an $85-million second house to its portfolio, the better to produce plays in rep and host visiting troupes. It currently stages five major works each season, serving up not just intelligent, inventive Bardolatry (its go-go-booted 1960s update of *Love's Labour's Lost* was a guest at the RSC's complete-works marathon in August 2006), but classics from the likes of Ben Jonson (an uproarious *Silent Woman*), Eugene O'Neill (a titanic *Mourning Becomes Electra*), and Aeschylus (a shattering new translation of *The Persians*). The company also makes a speciality of Tennessee Williams and Oscar Wilde, while experimenting with rarities by the likes of Alfred de Musset (a lusty 2005 *Lorenzaccio*) – which is why it regularly attracts big-name directors (Chicago's Mary Zimmerman, Australian Gale Edwards, rising American light Ethan McSweeny, who launched his career here) and actors (Keith Baxter, Kelly McGillis, Dixie Carter, Hal Holbrook). The season expands to eight plays when the company's new Harmon Hall, nearly twice as large, opens in autumn 2007 around the corner at 650 F Street, NW.

Studio Theatre

1333 P Street, NW, at 14th Street, Shaw: Logan Circle (332 3300/www.studiotheatre.org). Dupont Circle or U Street/African-American Civil War Memorial/Cardozo Metro. **Box office** *Performance days* 10am-6pm Mon, Tue; 10am-9pm Wed-Sat; noon-8pm Sun. *Non-performance days* 10am-6pm Mon-Fri.* **Tickets** $20-$40. **Credit** AmEx, Disc, MC, V. **Map** p250 H4.

Slick productions, smart directors and substantial plays (occasional cerebral musicals too) make the Studio Theatre a serious player on the capital city's dramatic scene. It was home to the first DC production of the docudrama *Guantanamo* (Donald Rumsfeld didn't attend); a chamber-sized *Caroline, or Change* (the brooding, bittersweet Tony Kushner/ Jeanine Tesori musical) and a wrenching take on Bryony Lavery's *Frozen* were concurrent triumphs in 2006. And the brutalist playwright Neil LaBute apparently liked a month-long festival of his work enough to offer the company a world premiere for the 2006-7 season. Co-founder and artistic director Joy Zinoman has built an almost absurdly healthy organisation: not long after a $12-million expansion that added a third 200-seat theatre plus a black-box space, Studio started shopping for $4.5 million worth of artists' housing in its Logan Circle neighbourhood.

Other theatres & companies

Folger Theatre

201 East Capitol Street, SE, between Second & Third Streets, The Capitol & Around (1-202 544-7077/ www.folger.edu). Capitol South Metro. **Box office** noon-4pm Mon-Sat. **Tickets** $15-$45. **Credit** AmEx, MC, V. **Map** p253 L7.

When the Shakespeare Theatre decamped for downtown in the early 1990s, the Folger lay fallow for a year or two. But it has since revived, and its stable of regular directors (including British actor Richard Clifford) produces solid, intelligent fare. It was here that Lynn Redgrave developed what became the Broadway hit *Shakespeare For My Father*, and here that mischievous DC Shakespearean Joe Banno dramatised Hamlet's internal debates by splitting the title role into four parts – and casting women in three of them.

Ford's Theatre

511 Tenth Street, NW, between E & F Streets, Downtown (1-202 347 4833/www.fordstheatre.org). Metro Center or Gallery Place-Chinatown Metro.

The best guides to enjoying London life

(but don't just take our word for it)

'More than 700 places where you can eat out for less than £20 a head... a mass of useful information in a genuinely pocket–sized guide'

Mail on Sunday

'Armed with a tube map and this guide there is no excuse to find yourself in a duff bar again'

Evening Standard

'I'm always asked how I keep up to date with shopping and services in a city as big as London. This guide is the answer'

Red Magazine

'Get the inside track on the capital's neighbourhoods'

Independent on Sunday

'A treasure trove of treats that lists the best the capital has to offer'

The People

Rated 'Best Restaurant Guide'

Sunday Times

Available at all good bookshops and
timeout.com/shop from £6.99

100% Independent

Box office 10am-6pm Mon-Fri. **Tickets** $29-$45. **Credit** AmEx, Disc, MC, V. **Map** p252 J6.
President Abraham Lincoln's assassination – in 1865, during a performance of *Our American Cousin* – shuttered this house for a century, but crusading producer Frankie Hewitt helped bring its stage back to life in the late 1960s. Much of what Ford has offered since has been easy-to-swallow fare, but now and again producers surprise theatregoers with an edgy imported offering (Anna Deavere Smith's *Twilight: Los Angeles, 1992* had its DC run here). Since Hewitt's death in 2003, Alley Theatre veteran Paul Tetreault has steered the house gingerly in the direction of more substantial fare – including, in January 2007, a production of August Wilson's devastating *Jitney*.

Olney Theatre Center

2001 Olney-Sandy Spring Road (Route 108), Olney, MD (Box office 1-301 924 3400/information 1-301 924 4456/www.olneytheatre.org). Glenmont Metro then Y5, Y7, Y8, Y9 bus. **Box office** 10am-6pm Mon-Sat; noon-5pm Sun. **Tickets** $10-$31. **Credit** MC, V.
It's a hike, but the hour-long drive to this suburban Maryland house can be worth the trouble. Founded as a summer theatre in the 1930s, it has seen performances by a startlingly starry roster: Helen Hayes, Tallulah Bankhead, Olivia de Havilland, Hume Cronyn, Jessica Tandy, Uta Hagen and Ian McKellen are just a few of the names. These days, Olney's season is largely subscriber-friendly fluff, but now and again artistic director Jim Petosa will programme something gratifying: a gorgeous *Camille*, David Hare's agonised *Racing Demon*, the hypnotic Calderón adaptation *Sueño*, a bracingly blunt staging of that reliably irascible Ibsen fellow. (*An Enemy of the People*, coming just after government leakers exposed domestic spying programmes in 2006, seemed especially apt.) A new 440-seat mainstage completes a campus with no fewer than four performance spaces.

Round House Theatre

Bethesda *7501 Wisconsin Avenue, at Waverly Street, Bethesda, MD (Box office 1-240 644 1100/information 1-240 644 1099/www.round-housetheatre.org). Bethesda Metro.* **Box office** noon-5pm Mon-Fri.
Silver Spring *8641 Colesville Road, between Georgia Avenue & Fenton Street, Silver Spring, MD (1-240 644 1099). Silver Spring Metro.* **Box office** noon-5pm Mon-Fri.
Both Tickets $10-$38. **Credit** AmEx, MC, V.
An established company bold and successful enough to have opened not one but two new houses in recent years, Round House was home in 2005 to Alain Timar's adaptation of *The Chairs* (imported after its success at 2003's Avignon Festival) and to the world premiere of *Columbinus*, a thoughtfully disturbing response to the Colorado school massacre. (It went on to a well-received run off-Broadway.) Round House's main home is in the close-in suburb of Bethesda, but it also offers a

regular slate of performances (including a cabaret series) near the other end of the Metro's Red Line, in a black-box space at the AFI Silver complex in Silver Spring. On the 2006-7 roster: *Orson's Shadow*, a backstage drama whose characters include Orson Welles, not to mention Laurence Olivier, Joan Plowright and Viven Leigh.

Signature Theatre

3806 South Four Mile Run Drive, at Oakland Drive, Arlington, VA (1-703 218 6500/www.sig-online.org). Pentagon Metro, then 7A (daily), 7F, 7H, 17F, 17G, 22A, 22B, FC306 bus (weekdays only). **Box office** 10am-6pm Mon-Fri. **Tickets** $28-$30. **Credit** AmEx, Disc, MC, V.
Signature's signature is first-rate Sondheim, and if its instincts for straight plays aren't as keen, it's still an ambitious outfit: Sarah Kane's *Crave* and a Hebrew version of *Hamlet* were both on the house's 2007 calendar, as if a move into a $7-million, two-theatre complex weren't enough of a challenge. Also in 2007: the US premiere of *The Witches of Eastwick* – yes, the same musical staged in London by Signature artistic director Eric Schaeffer back in 2000, to decidedly mixed reviews. Landmark productions in past seasons include the first *Assassins* outside New York, a *Passion* that put the house on the map with New York critics, and a world-premiere Van Gogh musical (*The Highest Yellow*) from Tony-nominated composer Michael John LaChiusa.

Woolly Mammoth Theatre Company

649 D Street, NW, at Seventh Street, Penn Quarter (1-202 393 3939/www.woollymammoth.net). Archives/Navy Memorial of Gallery Place/Chinatown Metro. **Box office** 10am-6pm Mon-Fri. **Tickets** $24-$29. **Credit** AmEx, MC, V. **Map** p253 J6.
This brash and often brilliant company has been pushing boundaries (both theatrical and personal) for a quarter-century, most recently in a superb new $7-million, 265-seat downtown home. Notable playwrights who've called Woolly home include *Six Feet Under* scribe Craig Wright, Pulitzer Prize finalist Sarah Ruhl (*The Clean House*) and that poet of neurosis, Nicky Silver. **Photo** *p204*.

Small companies

Washington is a terrific theatre town: there are far too many fringe-y, flaky, fearless small companies to list here. But look for anything involving the **Actors Theatre of Washington** (queer-themed stuff, www.atwdc. org), **American Century Theater** (neglected 20th-century American greats, www.american century.org), **Forum Theatre + Dance** (smart, politically aware stuff from contemporary writers and 20th-century giants, www.forum theatredance.org), **Longacre Lea** (fearsomely intelligent, and fun to watch, www.longacrelea. org), **Synetic Theater** (gorgeous movement-based theatre, www.synetictheater.org), and

Arts & Entertainment

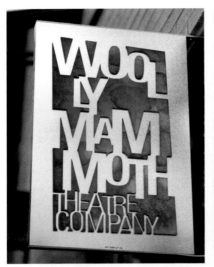

Woolly Mammoth Theatre Company.
See p203.

Solas Nua (the swimming-pool nutters mentioned atop this section).

For the following companies, fixed addresses are given where possible; for information about performances by roving companies, call the number listed. Note that box office hours have not been given; it's generally a case of leaving a message on the answerphone for the company to call you back.

African Continuum Theatre Company

Information: 3523 12th Street NE, Second Floor (1-202 529 5763/www.africancontinuumtheatre.com).
Tickets $15-$28. **Credit** AmEx, MC, V.

A solo hip hop odyssey, solid forays into the tough territories charted by August Wilson and Athol Fugard, and rousing takes on Zora Neale Hurston's *Spunk* and Endesha Ida Mae Holland's *From the*

Mississippi Delta – it's all in a season's work (or maybe two) for this decade-old outfit devoted to the African-American experience, which often produces fine theatre on a tight budget. A lacerating look at Fugard's *Blood Knot* and a fine, snappy staging of *The Story* (a fictionalised take on an '80s *Washington Post* scandal involving a black reporter and a made-up story) have perhaps been the company's finest hours so far.

GALA Hispanic Theatre

3333 14th Street, NW, between Park Street & Monroe Street, Columbia Heights (1-202 234 7174/ www.galatheatre.org). Columbia Heights Metro. **Tickets** $28. **Credit** AmEx, MC, V. **Map** p250 H1.
Newly ensconced in the rehabilitated Tivoli Theatre, Teatro GALA stages Spanish-language classics like Calderón de la Barca's *La Dama Duende* and García Lorca's *Blood Wedding*, plus modern plays by writers such as Venezuela's Gustavo Ott (*Evangélicas, Divorciadas y Vegetarianas*) and the occasional Latin-flavoured musical. Performances are generally in Spanish with a supertitled translation.

Rorschach Theatre

Information: 1421 Columbia Road, NW, #303 (1-202 452 5538/www.rorschachtheatre.com). **Tickets** $12. **No credit cards.**
The rambunctious Rorschach company finds interesting plays and intriguing spaces, and applies its nervy vision to both. For the most part, it's a success; the company serves up everything from Serbian wunderkind Biljana Srbljanovic (*Family Stories: A Slapstick Tragedy*) to the sprightly Amy Freed (*The Beard of Avon*). Recent outings have included a solid staging of Tony Kushner's Nazi-era fever-dream *A Bright Room Called Day* and a smart take on *The Arabian Nights*, the sexy, swoony fable by German playwright Roland Schimmelpfennig.

Theater Alliance

H Street Playhouse, 1365 H Street, NE (www.theater alliance.com). Gallery Place/Chinatown Metro, then X2 bus.
From a playfully kinetic pass at Salman Rushdie's *Haroun and the Sea of Stories* to a clean, stylish interpretation of Moises Kaufman's *Gross Indecency: The Three Trials of Oscar Wilde* to the DC area's introduction to the hugely ambitious writer Naomi Wallace (2003's gob-smackingly bold *Slaughter City*), the Theater Alliance represents one of Washington theatre's shining hopes. The company has taken more risks and staged more breath-catching moments in five short seasons than most manage in a lifetime: its 2006-7 season, to cite just one move, kicked off with a world premiere from a 17-year-old writer at a Michigan arts academy. **Photo** *p199*.

Washington Shakespeare Company

Clark Street Playhouse, 601 South Clark Street, at Sixth Street South, Arlington, VA (1-703 418 4808/ www.washingtonshakespeare.org). Crystal City Metro. **Tickets** $10-$35. **Credit** AmEx, MC, V.
Not to be confused with the deep-pocketed Shakespeare Theatre, this highbrow-on-a-shoestring troupe has 16 seasons of the Bard – not to mention Beckett, Marlowe, Stoppard, Albee and more – under its scruffy belt. It's sometimes quite good (a 2004 *Waiting for Godot* unearthed all the prodigious tenderness in that bleak play) and always ambitious: what company with a bare-bones budget tackles *The Royal Hunt of the Sun* and *Death and the King's Horseman* within a twelvemonth?

Washington Stage Guild

Arena Stage at 14th & T, 1901 14th Street, NW, at T Street, Shaw: U Street/14th Street Corridor (1-240 582 0050/www.stageguild.org). U Street/African-American Civil War Memorial/Cardozo Metro. **Tickets** $20-$28. **No credit cards.** **Map** p250 H3.
Forced out of its longtime lodgings several years ago by DC's rocketing rents, this respected 20-year-old ensemble still draws a loyal crowd with smart stagings of Shaw (a politically well-timed *On the Rocks* was a 2004 high point, and 2006 saw a pert production of *Fanny's First Play*) along with other literary-minded fare. Playwrights featured recently have included Ferenc Molnar, TS Eliot, and Steve Martin – yes, that Steve Martin.

Dance

The emergence of a company steered by ballet icon Suzanne Farrell and the MacArthur Foundation's 'genius grant' to DC dance guru Liz Lerman were two culture-news headlines trumpeting what cognoscenti already knew: that Washington boasts a healthy and diverse dance scene. Larger venues bring in world-renowned companies, from domestic powerhouses such as Dance Theatre of Harlem and the American Ballet Theatre to young-turk outfits like Matthew Bourne's New Adventures and international legends like the Kirov and the Hamburg ballets.

The home-grown **Washington Ballet** was hamstrung by a bitter labour dispute in late 2005, alas, and the longterm effects of the showdown between dancers and artistic director Septime Webre have yet to play out – though Webre and resident choreographer Trey McIntyre have pushed ahead with new and intriguing dance ventures, including their Bach/Beatles Project, choreographed to the *Goldberg Variations* and music of the Fab Four. Meanwhile the newest DC-based big-time outfit – the **Suzanne Farrell Ballet**, launched at the Kennedy Center in 2000 by George Balanchine's celebrated protégée and muse – draws rhapsodic notices for its excursions into the Balanchine catalogue and explores work by Jerome Robbins, Maurice Béjart and more.

At smaller spaces, vibrant and sometimes surprisingly accomplished local troupes flourish. Modern dance specialist **CityDance**

Ensemble (www.citydance.net, 1-301 581 5204) tours Eastern Europe and commissions work from choreographers from Poland to Paris. The **Joy of Motion** studios are home to five troupes including **Dana Tai Soon Burgess & Co** (www.movingforwarddance.com), critically acclaimed for Burgess's fluid fusion of pan-Asian and Western dance forms.

Carla Perlo and Deborah Riley lead eponymous companies based at **Dance Place**, DC's pre-eminent space for modern classes and avant-garde performance. The venue (also home to the West African-oriented **Coyaba Dance Theatre**) stages the **DanceAfrica DC festival** (*see p162*) each June. The George Washington University dance department (1-202 994 8072) hosts an international festival of improvised dance every December as well as occasional workshops and master classes by visiting artists. Howard University also offers occasional masterclasses (1-202 806 7050), as does the Kennedy Center. And dozens of smaller companies pop into these venues to stage concerts three or four times a year: one example is Pakistan-born choreographer **Tehreema Mitha** (www.tehreemamitha-dancecompany.org), whose multicultural company fuses classical barathanatyam with modern influences.

Companies & venues

Phone for schedules of dance classes at the venues below.

Dance Place

3225 Eighth Street, NE, between Kearney & Monroe Streets, Northeast (1-202 269 1600/www.dance place.org). Brookland-CUA Metro. **Tickets** $16. **Credit** AmEx, MC, V. **Map** p251 M2.
DC's 'hub of dance activity' (according to the *Washington Post*) offers morning and evening classes in modern and African dance, and doubles as a performance space, often featuring emerging artists. A recent season included the KanKouran West African Dance Company, Elevator Repair Service, and the Cleveland Contemporary Dance Theatre, among many others. Dance Place is home for several companies, and the organisation conducts a host of community projects throughout the District.

DC Dance Collective

4908 Wisconsin Avenue, NW, near Ellicott Street, Upper Northwest (1-202 362 7244/www.dcdance collective.com). Friendship Heights or Tenleytown-AU Metro. **Tickets** $10. **Credit** MC, V.
Home to the Ancient Rhythms belly-dance troupe; also hosts performances and offers various kinds of classes, ranging from ballet and bhangra to break dancing and capoeira. Bakaari Wilder, pop star Mya, and tap great Dianne Walker turned up here for a 2004 tribute to the late Gregory Hines.

Joy of Motion

1643 Connecticut Avenue, NW, at R Street, Dupont Circle (1-202 387 0911/www.joyofmotion.org). Dupont Circle Metro. **Tickets** $10-$15. **Credit** AmEx, MC, V. **Map** p250 G4.
Joy of Motion offers a wide range of classes, including jazz, modern, swing, Pilates, yoga, belly dance and flamenco. Resident companies include the CrossCurrents ensemble (www.crosscurrents-dance.org), Middle Eastern dance troupe Silk Road Dance Company and Dana Tai Soon Burgess & Co. **Other locations**: 1333 H Street NE, H Street Corridor (1-202 399 6763); 5207 Wisconsin Avenue, NW, Friendship Heights, Upper Northwest (1-202 362 3042); 7315 Wisconsin Avenue, Suite 180E, Bethesda, MD (1-301 986 0016).

KanKouran West African Dance Company

1-202 528 1213/www.kankouran.org.
Among the strongest of the area's many African dance outfits. Classes in West African dance and drumming are offered throughout the week.

Liz Lerman Dance Exchange

7117 Maple Avenue, near Carroll Avenue, Takoma Park, MD (1-301 270 6700/www.danceexchange. org). Takoma Park Metro. **Tickets** $12. **Credit** MC, V.
Alterna-dance legend Lerman founded this multi-cultural, multi-generational company (the largest and best-known in DC) in 1976, before such adjectives had become clichés. She still creates some of the most innovative work in the area, and several company members, particularly artistic director Peter DiMuro, are impressive choreographers in their own right. The company's studio offers classes focused primarily on modern technique.

Suzanne Farrell Ballet

1-202 416 8029/www.suzannefarrell.org.
An outgrowth initially of master classes taught by the famed ballerina at the centre, Farrell's company now tours the US and the world, and serves as an anchor on the centre's ballet season. The troupe flirts shamelessly with the (homo)sexy work of French-born boundary-pusher Maurice Béjart, but specialises, naturally, in Balanchine – the familiar along with rarities like *Don Quixote* and *Contrapuntal Blues pas de deux*, set to music by Benny Goodman.

Washington Ballet

3515 Wisconsin, Avenue, NW (1-202 362 3606/ www.washingtonballet.org). **Tickets** $25-$85. **Credit** Disc, MC, V.
The Washington Ballet presents a solid season of contemporary and classic ballets from October to May, in addition to an annual *Nutcracker* (re-imagined as a 19th-century Washington fable) around Christmas time. The company tours internationally; local performances tend to be held at the Kennedy Center or at the larger venues downtown. Classes (from beginner to advanced) are offered to the public during the week.

Trips Out of Town

Charlottesville. *See p213.*

Day Trips

Get out of town.

From strip to ship: two different faces of **Baltimore**.

In nearly every direction from Washington there's something worth seeing. To the north is **Baltimore**, a city where redevelopment has made a mark on a gritty reputation, and which is host to a number of first-class museums. To the south are **Shenandoah Valley** and the **Blue Ridge Mountains**, where the natural beauty is staggering and outdoor activities abound. And to the east is **Chesapeake Bay**, America's sailing capital and, at 7,000 square miles, the largest estuary in the United States. Shenandoah and Chesapeake especially offer relief from the summer humidity and hectic pace of urban life. This chapter offers a guide to the best sights in those three destinations – plus, for the history buffs, reviews of the area's collection of historic homes that were once owned by America's Founding Fathers (*see p212* **Presidential seats**).

TRANSPORT

The best (and just about only) way to visit Shenandoah and Chesapeake Bay is by car. Traffic can be extremely heavy during commuting hours or when Washingtonians flee the city at weekends, especially on I-66 or the Beltway that circles the city. The national car rental companies all have chains in Washington, both in the city and at major airports (*see p224*). Baltimore is more friendly to people without cars; trains depart daily from Union Station (50 Massachusetts Avenue, NE, at North Capitol Street). For more information, *see p214* **Getting there**.

Spirit of Washington Cruises (Pier 4, Water Street, SW, at Sixth Street, Southwest, 1-202 554 8000, 1-866 211 3811, www.spiritofwashington. com) operates boat trips from the city to Mount Vernon, site of George Washington's historic

Trips Out of Town

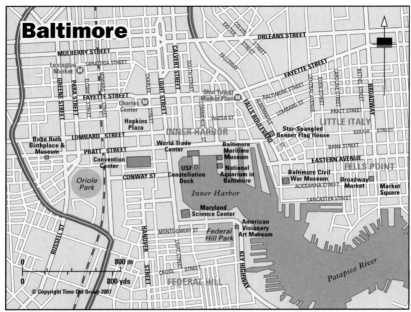

home. Departure is at 8.30am and the trip takes about five and a half hours, including three and a half hours to tour Mount Vernon ($38, $31-$36 concessions, free under-6s, price includes the admission to Mount Vernon).

Baltimore

Baltimore is one of the earliest true cities in America, a thriving port from the very beginning of the country and later an important manufacturing centre. It was even briefly the seat of government of the fledgling nation. Things went wrong, however, and not so long ago it was known mostly for crime and post-industrial grit, and lived very much in the shadow of the nation's capital 40 miles to the south. But since the 1980s, the 'Charm City', as Mayor William Donald Schaefer dubbed it back in the 1970s, has been undergoing a resurgence. Washingtonians not only visit Baltimore for its many attractions; many have made the Charm City their home, commuting each day to jobs in the nation's capital.

INNER HARBOR

Baltimore's revitalisation is nowhere more apparent than around the Inner Harbor. No longer a depressing urban jungle of rundown factories and warehouses, the Inner Harbor has been transformed into Harborplace, a lively civic centre bursting with interesting shops and restaurants. Glass-walled offices in the new high-rise business district form a bright, modern backdrop. For a view of the city from above, take the lift to the 27th-floor observation deck of the **World Trade Center** (aka The Top of the World); at 423 feet it's the world's tallest pentagonal building (401 East Pratt Street, 1-410 837 8439).

For a trip in the opposite direction visit the world-class **National Aquarium in Baltimore**, with aquatic delights including a daily dolphin show (501 East Pratt Street, 1-410 576 3800, www.aqua.org).

The **Baltimore Maritime Museum** (Pier 3, East Pratt Street, 1-410 396 3453, www.balto maritimemuseum.org) is the mooring place for two veterans of World War II, the Coast Guard cutter *Taney*, the last survivor of Pearl Harbor, and the USS *Torsk*, the submarine that fired the last torpedo of the conflict.

The USS *Constellation* (Pier 1, 301 East Pratt Street, 1-410 539 1797, www.constellation.org) is the last Civil War-era vessel still afloat. It patrolled the African coast near the mouth of the Congo River between 1859 and 1861 and intercepted ships that were illegally engaged in the slave trade (the US declared the importation of slaves illegal in 1808).

Trips Out of Town

Time Out
Travel Guides

USA

Time Out
Boston

Time Out
California

Time Out
Chicago

Time Out
Las Vegas

Time Out
Los Angeles

Time Out
Miami
& the Florida Keys

Time Out
New York

Time Out
San Francisco

Time Out
Washington, DC

**Available at all good bookshops
and at timeout.com/shop**

Time Out
Guides

AMERICANA

Baseball is the national pastime, and no one looms larger in the history of the game than the legendary Babe Ruth. The **Babe Ruth Birthplace & Museum** (216 Emory Street, 1-410 727 1539, www.baberuthmuseum.com) is a cramped rowhouse in the scruffy neighbourhood that was home to the young 'Sultan of Swat', a hero to American men and boys during the 1920s and '30s for his home run-hitting prowess on the field. (He was a legendary boozer and lecher off it.) The museum is slated to undergo renovations in autumn 2006 and will be reopened to the public in spring 2007. It sits in the shadow of Camden Yards, a beautiful Major League baseball stadium where the Baltimore Orioles play their home games. The museum stays open until 7.30pm on game days.

For the history behind the American national anthem, which kicks off every baseball game, visit **Fort McHenry** (end of East Fort Avenue, 1-410 962 4290, www.nps.gov/fomc). During the War of 1812, Americans fought off the British attempt to take the fort, which guards the entrance to Baltimore harbour. Bombarded throughout the day and night of 14 September 1814, the fort held out and the British ships eventually withdrew. Francis Scott Key, a young lawyer who happened to be aboard one of the British ships to negotiate the release of a captured friend, was inspired by the sight of his country's badly torn flag still flying at dawn on the 14th and wrote the lyrics of 'The Star-Spangled Banner'. The expanded fort now on the site dates from the Civil War.

It was Mary Pickersgill who stitched the stars and the stripes on to the huge flag that flew tattered over Fort McHenry during the 1814 British bombardment. Her 1793 home is now the **Star-Spangled Banner Flag House** (844 East Pratt Street, 1-410 837 1793, www.flaghouse.org). There are guided tours of the house, furnished with appropriate Federal-period antiques and a museum. The actual banner underwent painstaking restoration at Washington's Smithsonian Institution before it was returned to public display at the National Museum of American History in 2006.

While not the birthplace (Boston was), Baltimore is the burial site of **Edgar Allan Poe**, the master of the macabre who first won national acclaim with his poem *The Raven*. He died in 1849 at age 40. His final resting place is Westminster Hall & Burying Ground, the cemetery of the First Presbyterian Church (West Fayette Street & Greene Street). Visit the churchyard on your own, or call for a guided tour of the catacombs (1-410 706 2072, www.eapoe.org/balt/poegrave.htm).

Camden Yards, home of the Orioles.

The **Reginald F Lewis Museum of Maryland African American History & Culture** (830 East Pratt Street, 1-443 263 1800, www.africanamericanculture.org, closed Mon) is the largest African-American museum on the East Coast. The exhibits are divided into three major areas: community; slavery and labour; and art and intellect. Call or visit the website for information about special exhibitions.

Exhibits at the **Baltimore Civil War Museum** (601 President Street, 1-410 385 5188, www.mdhs.org/explore/baltcivilwar.html) highlight the city's ambivalent role in the bitter 1861-65 struggle between North and South. Baltimore was a station on the 'underground railroad' by which fugitive slaves escaped to the North, but it was also home to many Confederate sympathisers. There were riots when Union troops passed through the city.

ART ATTACK

The **Walters Art Gallery** (600 North Charles Street, 1-410 547 9000, www.thewalters.org, closed Mon, Tue) is one of the best fine art museums in the US, with a collection including medieval, Renaissance, 18th- and 19th-century, Islamic and Asian art. Works on show include Raphael's *Madonna of the Candelabra*, Bernini's statue of the *Risen Christ* and El Greco's depiction of *St Francis Receiving the*

Trips Out of Town

Stigmata. The **Baltimore Museum of Art** (10 Art Museum Drive, 1-443 573 1700, www.artbma.org, closed Mon, Tue) has a notable collection of modern paintings and sculpture from Van Gogh to Warhol and Rodin to Nevelson. At the **American Visionary Art Museum** (800 Key Highway, 1-410 244 1900, www.avam.org, closed Mon) across the harbour in South Baltimore, the focus is on untrained but inspired artists working outside the norms.

Where to eat & drink

Phillips (301 Light Street, 1-410 685 6600, www.phillipsseafood.com, main courses $24-$28) is a large and popular restaurant with a great harbour view, terrace dining in season and seafood. **Rusty Scupper** (402 Key Highway, 1-410 727 3678, main courses $20-$38), across Inner Harbor from Harborplace, also does seafood, plus prime rib and such.

Presidential seats

Monticello.

The Washington area arguably has the greatest concentration of historic homes in the US, headlined by those owned by former presidents (four of the first five US presidents were Virginians). Thomas Jefferson's **Monticello** (State Route 53, 1-434 984 9822, www.monticello.org, open Mar-Oct 8am-5pm daily, Nov-Feb 9am-4.30pm daily) is a two-and-a-half hour drive from Washington, but worth the journey. To understand Jefferson – the author of the Declaration of Independence and third president (1801-1809) – you must first understand Monticello, or so the saying goes. Jefferson was a Renaissance man, an architect and inventor who dabbled in archaeology, paleontology and astronomy. All of his pursuits are on display here. Jefferson designed and oversaw the construction of the house, a neo-classical gem befitting a Founding Father. He selected all the furnishings, many of which he

purchased while serving as a diplomat in France. Tours of the three-storey, 21-room house are conducted continuously each day, in groups no larger than 25 (advance reservations can be made on Monticello's website). In the entrance hall, Jefferson created a mini-museum of European art and artefacts from explorers Lewis and Clark's celebrated Western expedition, which he commissioned as president. Tours also include Jefferson's sitting room, book room, bedroom, dining room and a guest bedroom. Visitors can wander through the wine and beer cellars in the basement on their own.

Tours of Monticello's African-American past address the paradox that lies at the heart of Jefferson as a historical figure: that he both owned approximately 600 slaves during his life and yet was the drafter of the Declaration of Independence, with its confident assertion that 'all men are created equal'. Tours depart

Joy America Café in the American Visionary Art Museum (800 Key Highway, 1-410 244 6500, closed Mon) offers a creative organic menu. Though in a rather bleak location, **Della Notte** (801 Eastern Avenue, 1-410 837 5500, $17-$39) is highly rated for its house-baked breads and extensive wine list. Finally, the area of **Fells Point** is known not only for its antiques shops but its drinking establishments. Head to the funky point for a drink or dinner.

Resources

Hospital
Johns Hopkins, 600 North Wolfe Street (1-410 955 5000/www.hopkinsmedicine.org). **Open** *Accident & Emergency* 24hrs daily.

Internet
Port City Java, 666 East Fort Avenue (1-410 986 0366). **Open** 6.30am-6pm Mon-Thur; 6.30am-8pm Sat; 8am-6pm Sun.

every hour from the front of the museum shop (10am-3pm daily, Apr-Oct).

'No occupation is so delightful to me as the culture of the earth, and no culture comparable to that of the garden,' wrote Jefferson. His flower and vegetable gardens, grove and orchards have been restored and are indeed a delight. Tours depart from the West Lawn behind the house once an hour (9.15am-4.15pm daily, Apr-Oct).

In summer 2006, tours were offered for the first time of Montalto, the hill that rises 410 feet above Monticello and affords views of Jefferson's plantation and grounds, as well as Charlottesville and the Blue Ridge Mountains (tours 1pm and 3pm daily May-Oct).

If you visit Monticello, be sure to drop in on Jefferson's former neighbours. **Montpelier** (11407 Constitution Highway, State Route 20, 1-540 672 2728, www.montpelier.org) is the former home of James Madison, the fourth president. Also designed by Jefferson, the house embodied his classical vision. Later owners, including the immensely wealthy Du Pont family, expanded and significantly altered the original structure. An extensive restoration that began in 2003 seeks to restore the house to its original size and Federal-period appearance. Parts of the house will remain open to visitors, and tours will highlight the progress of the restoration that is scheduled for completion in 2007.

James Monroe, the fifth US president (1817-1825), owned **Ash Lawn-Highland** plantation (Route 795, 1-434 293 9539, www.ashlawnhighland.org). Though without the size or scope of Monticello, it too has breathtaking views.

Just 14 miles south of DC along the George Washington Memorial Parkway (which ends at the visitors' entrance), **Mount Vernon** (1-703 780 2000, www.mountvernon.org, open Apr-Aug 8am-5pm daily, Mar, Sept, Oct 9am-5pm daily, Nov-Feb 9am-4pm daily) is the most celebrated and visited historic home in the country. George Washington has gone down in history as a soldier and statesman, but he devoted the greater part of his life to improving the estate he had inherited from an older half-brother, seeking to recreate an English manor house on the banks of the Potomac. The faithfully restored plantation house contains original furniture and many of the first First Family's belongings. The gardens have been planted in colonial style. A major project in recent years has been the re-creation of a colonial-era farm where crops of Washington's day are raised using the simple implements of the time. It includes an ingenious octagonal threshing barn he devised, revealing him as a true agricultural innovator. The opening in October 2006 of a new orientation centre and museum, tactfully concealed under a meadow, further fleshes out Washington – literally, in the case of a forensically reconstructed statue of him at age 19. Traditional treasures shine alongside, notably Jean-Antoine Houdon's terracotta bust from life – the most accurate likeness of Washington ever created.

There are a couple of appealing ways to reach the estate: by car down the elegant George Washington Parkway (which set the scenic-drive standard in 1932); or by traditional excursion boat, with regular departures from Washington and Alexandria (*see p208*). An alternative route is by Huntington Metro station and then Fairfax Connector bus 101 or 102.

Mount Vernon and Monticello especially are jammed with tour groups during the spring and summer; if you are visiting at this time, go first thing in the morning or in late afternoon when the crowds are not at their peak. Autumn, when the weather is mostly glorious, is an easier time to visit.

Trips Out of Town

Police station

601 East Fayette Street (1-410 396 2525).

Post office

900 East Fayette Street (1-410 347 4202).

Tourist information

Baltimore Area Convention & Visitors Association, 401 Light Street (1-877 225 8466, www. baltimore.org). **Open** 9am-6pm daily.

Getting there

By car

Baltimore is about an hour's drive from Washington. Take I-95 north to I-395, exit 53, which quickly becomes Howard Street (take care not to shoot off to the left on Martin Luther King Jr Boulevard). Continue north on Howard a short distance (a football stadium and the Camden Yards baseball stadium are on your left) to Pratt Street. Turn right and continue past Charles and Light Streets to Harborplace.

By train

Amtrak (1-800 872 7245, www.amtrak.com) and Marc (1-800 325 7245, www.mtamaryland.com/ services/marc) both run services to Baltimore from Washington's Union Station. Amtrak trains to Baltimore's Penn Station take 35-45mins and run until after midnight (most last trains depart Penn Station at 12.40am); Marc trains run into Penn Station and Camden Station, and take a little over an hour. Last trains are at 10.45pm; there is no service at weekends.

Shenandoah

More than a million people pass through **Shenandoah National Park** (1-540 999 3500, www.nps.gov/shen) and the surrounding area each year, making it the undisputed outdoor playground for Washingtonians. Straddling Virginia's **Blue Ridge Mountains** for more than 100 miles, the park takes its name from the valley and river just to its west. Skyline Drive follows the crest of the mountain range for the entire length of the park. There are 75 overlooks where motorists can take in the valley views.

The crowds begin to descend on the park in the spring, as the azaleas and dogwoods bloom. By summer, Skyline Drive can begin to feel like a clogged freeway. But the busiest time may be in the final weeks of October, when the changing foliage adorns the park in a resplendent display of colour. Current accessible areas and other information can be picked up at park entrances and several visitors' centres along Skyline Drive.

TAKING TO THE TRAILS

A visit to Shenandoah is not complete without setting foot on one of the national park's 500 miles of trails. Trail maps published by the Potomac Appalachian Trail Club can be

purchased ($6) when entering the park. (Some maps can be downloaded at www.nps.gov/ shen/2b.htm.) From Skyline Drive, there are an endless number of hikes. Many include sections of the Appalachian Trail, an idea first conceived by a conservationist named Benton MacKaye as an antidote to the rapid urbanisation and hectic pace of life in the northeastern US. Completed in 1937, the trail extends 2,174 miles from Maine to Georgia. Of these 101 run through Shenandoah National Park.

Waterfalls are Shenandoah's feature attraction. The challenging nine-mile Whiteoak Canyon trail (mile 45.6 off Skyline Drive) passes six of them and is one of the most popular routes. For a shorter hike, try the four-mile Rose River loop (mile 49.4), which runs past a waterfall that drops more than 60 feet.

Vistas are another reason to take to the trails. The Mary's Rock (mile 31.6) trail climbs 1,210 feet and ends at a rock outcropping with a view of Thornton Gap. Legend has it that Mary Thornton, a 15-year-old former park resident, hiked the two miles to the top and returned with a bear cub under each arm. For a shorter hike with a big payoff, try Stony Man (mile 41.7). It's less than a mile to the 4,011-foot summit, the second highest in the park. If you can, take in the valley at sunset.

Shenandoah's most popular hike is Old Rag Mountain. At 3,200 feet it offers a breathtaking view of the valley. Near the summit of the mountain, the trail gives way to massive boulders. Scaling these rocks (or sliding between or under them) requires a sturdy pair of hiking books and, on occasion, a friend's helping hand. The non-adventurous need not apply. Be forewarned: arrive at sunrise on weekends. Parking spaces fill up quickly, and in some cases you may need to hike before you even reach the trail.

To avoid the crowds, nearby **George Washington National Forest** (1-888 265 0019, www.fs.fed.us/r8/gwj/) is less visited but has great scenery and hundreds of miles of trails. Signal Knob trail leads to the top of a mountain that Confederate forces used to send messages during the Civil War. There are two overlooks before the summit – Buzzard Rock and Fort Valley. The ten-mile loop marked with yellow blazes starts just north of Elizabeth Furnace Campground off State Road 678. A shorter option is the Big Schloss trail, which starts at Wolf Gap Campground off State Road 675. The hike is about two miles one way and leads to a rock outcropping, which offers a panoramic view of the forest below. Peregrine falcons have been released in the wild here. Go to www.fs.fed.us/r8/gwj/lee/recreation/hiking/ popular_hikes.shtml for directions.

Shenandoah National Park.

GOING UNDERGROUND

Shenandoah is home to hundreds of caves, where summer temperatures hover around a cool 55 degrees – a great way to beat the heat. Many are accessible to the public. **Luray Caverns** (970 US Highway 211 West, 1-540 743 6551, www.luraycaverns.com) has paved, well-lit walkways and a Disney World feel. Its main feature is a stalacpipe organ. Outside the caverns is a garden maze where the children can have fun getting lost ($6, $5 concessions, free under-6s).

Crystal Caverns offers a more authentic underground experience (33231 Old Valley Pike, Strasburg, 1-540 465 5884, www.waysideofva. com/crystalcaverns). Artificial light is scarce and tours are by the light of a lantern. Other options include **Endless Caverns** (1800 Endless Caverns Road, New Market, 1-800 544 2283, www.endlesscaverns.com), where the fossilised tooth of a woolly mammoth was found in 1996, and **Shenandoah Caverns** (261 Shenandoah Caverns Road, Shenandoah Caverns, 1-540 477 3115, www.shenandoah caverns.com), which has a calcite crystal formation called the Diamond Cascade.

Civil War soldiers during a break in the fighting autographed the walls of **Grand Caverns** (Grand Caverns Drive, Grottoes, 1-888 430 2283/uvrpa.org), and locals hosted dances in a 5,000-square-foot chamber called the Grand Ballroom. **Skyline Caverns** (10344 Stonewall Jackson Highway, Front Royal, 1-800 296 4545, www.skylinecaverns.com) has rare white-spiked ceiling formations called anthodites.

REEL TALK

Herbert Hoover, the nation's 31st president (1928-32), was one of the first Washingtonians to flee the humidity of the nation's capital for Shenandoah. He chose for his presidential retreat a spot along the Rapidan river, largely because he loved to relax with rod and reel. Fishing, he wrote, 'is the chance to wash one's soul with pure air, with the rush of a brook, or with the shimmer of the sun on the blue water'.

Hoover had 13 cabins, three of which have been restored to their former glory, including the president's grand abode. Hike two miles down to the cabins along the Mill and Laurel Prong loop (mile 52.7) and meet up with a tour, or catch a van from the Harry F Byrd visitor centre at Big Meadows. Tours are three hours long and have a 13-person limit. Check the schedule and make reservations by phone on 1-540 999 3283 or in person at the Byrd Visitor Center. There is also a small self-guided exhibit.

If Hoover inspires you, grab a reel and rod yourself (the president loved trout, particularly with bacon and eggs for breakfast). Brook trout, smallmouth bass, brown trout; fly-fishing or conventional fishing; the options are well-nigh limitless. Guides provide equipment and can find the best holes. Harry Murray of **Murray's Fly Shop** (121 Main Street, Edinburg, 1-540 436 3964, www.murraysflyshop.com) and his son Jeff grew up fishing Stoney Creek, which flows by his store in the valley and into the North Fork of the Shenandoah River. Billy Kingsley of **Blue Ridge Angler** (1756 South Main Street, Harrisonburg, 1-540 574 3474,

Enough fish for all at **Sandy Point**. *See p218.*

www.blueridgeangler.com, closed Sun) attended nearby James Madison University and lived in Montana before returning to Virginia. You'll need a Virginia fishing licence, which you can purchase and print out online (www.dgif. virginia.gov/buy_license.asp). It's $16 for a five-day freshwater licence.

RIDING THE RIVER
Take your pick – canoe, kayak, raft or tube – numerous outfitters are ready to set you up for a whitewater adventure or a leisurely float. Reservations are essential; trips can fill up quickly. Front Royal bills itself as the 'Canoe Capital of Virginia'. Head to **Front Royal Canoe Company** (8567 Stonewall Jackson Highway, 1-800 270 8808, www.frontroyal canoe.com). In Luray, try **Shenandoah River Outfitters** (6502 South Page Valley Road, 1-540 743 4159, www.shenandoah-river.com). And in Bentonville, there is **Downriver Canoe Company** (884 Indian Hollow Road, 1-800 338 1963, www.downriver.com).

Where to eat

Thornton River Grille (3710 Sperryville Pike, Sperryville, 1-540 987 8790, www. thorntonrivergrille.com, closed Mon, mains $9-$28) can fill up quickly for dinner thanks to its delicious burgers and crab cakes. Make a reservation. The **Joshua Wilton House** (412 South Main Street, Harrisonburg, 1-888 294 5866, www.joshuawilton.com, closed Sun, Mon, mains $18-$30) is more upscale. The outdoor patio is a good place to wind down a day of outdoor fun. The menu is seasonal and reservations are recommended. To stock up on a few treats before hiking, head to **Cranberry's Grocery & Eatery** (7 South New Street, Staunton, 1-540 885 4755).

Where to stay

Skyland Resort (Mile 41.7 Skyline Drive, 1-800 778 2851, doubles $64-$184) is located at the highest point (3,680 feet) on Skyline Drive. It has lodge suites, rustic cabins, a decent restaurant and spectacular views. **Big Meadows Lodge** (Mile 51.2 Skyline Drive, 1-800 778 2851, doubles $69-$160) has 25 rooms in the beautifully panelled main lodge and another 72 in multi-unit lodges and rustic cabins; it, too, has a restaurant. **Lewis Mountain Cabins** (Mile 57.5 Skyline Drive, 1-800 778 2851, doubles $74-$119) is a more outdoorsy option.

Resources

Tourist information
Shenandoah County Tourism *600 North Main Street, Suite 101, Woodstock (1-540 459 6227, 1-888 367 3965/www.shenandoahtravel.org).* **Open** 8.30am-5pm Mon-Fri.

Shenandoah Valley Travel Association
277 West Old Cross Road, (PO Box 1040), New Market (1-540 740 3132). **Open** 9am-5pm daily.
George Washington National Forest – Lee Ranger Forest District
109 Molineu Road, Edinburg (1-540 984 4101, 1-540 933 6171). **Open** 8am-4.30pm Mon-Fri.

Getting there

By car

Of the several entrances to the park, the most convenient from Washington is at its northern tip, 90 mins or less via I-66 to exit 6, then south three miles on US 340 to Front Royal.

Chesapeake

Sailboats dotting the bay, gentle bay breezes, life at a languid pace. There is no shortage of reasons to visit picturesque **Chesapeake Bay** and embark on a vacation from your vacation. **Annapolis** is the jewel of the Chesapeake and has been Maryland's capital since 1695. A modern city has grown up around the colonial core, but the historic city is largely preserved. The narrow streets surrounding the old harbour are lined with what is claimed to be the largest concentration of Georgian houses in the country. Annapolis is no longer the busy port it once was, but the sea remains very much part of its identity. Marinas, sailing schools and charter services make it a recreational centre. Several tours, self-guided and otherwise, of the whole Annapolis historic area are also available. Check at the City Dock information booth for details.

South of Annapolis, the Chesapeake's less publicised West Shore stretches more than 100 miles to Point Lookout, where the Potomac river flows into the bay. Cross over the Bay Bridge from Annapolis to reach the Chesapeake's Eastern Shore.

NAVAL GAZING
Annapolis is the home port of the **US Naval Academy**, which was founded in 1845 and educates future naval and marine officers. It is a must-see for those with a yearning for all things maritime. The academy appeared in *Patriot Games*, the 1992 movie that starred Harrison Ford as professor Jack Ryan. The 4,000 students (or midshipmen, as they're known) stride around town conspicuously in their white uniforms. Despite heightened security at military installations since 9/11, the academy remains open to the public. Picture identification is required to enter the campus for anyone over 16. Visiting hours are generally 9am-5pm. Visitors may observe the noon formation of midshipmen held Monday to

Friday, weather permitting, during the academic year. Guided tours are available at the **Armel-Leftwich Visitor Center** (52 King George Street, 1-410 263 6933). The visitor center also has naval and astronautical memorabilia, such as the *Freedom 7* space capsule and an exhibit on John Paul Jones.

Jones is America's preeminent naval hero from the Revolutionary War, best known for the words he uttered on 23 September 1779. As Jones fought the HMS *Serapis* on the North Sea off Flamborough Head, his ship, the *Bonhomme Richard*, came under fire and began to sink. When the opposing captain called for Jones to surrender, he allegedly responded, 'I have not yet begun to fight!' Jones then proceeded to board the *Serapis* and captured it. In 1792, Jones died in Paris. But in 1905, his remains were unearthed, and he was re-buried in a crypt in the basement of the Naval Academy's chapel. Today, the crypt is surrounded by artefacts from Jones's life, such as the gold medal Congress awarded him in 1787.

A collection of 108 ship models is one of the highlights of the **United States Naval Academy Museum** (Preble Hall, 1-410 293 2108). The museum also has artefacts from the USS *Constitution* and other ships, art work depicting naval battles and memorabilia from significant naval figures.

BAY BREEZES
Annapolis has been called the 'sailing capital of the world', which should be incentive enough to take to the water. Call ahead for reservations and prices. Two-hour cruises usually run for around $30 per person. The *Woodwind* (1-410 263 7837, www.schoonerwoodwind.com), a 74-foot schooner, departs from the Annapolis Marriott Waterfront Hotel and offers two-hour rides. On Tuesdays, the captain offers up a selection of beer from microbreweries for tasting. He'll even let you take the wheel or help hoist the sails. If power boating is more your speed, **Watermark Cruises** (1-410 268 7601, www.watermarkcruises.com) has 90-minute and full-day tours. Full-day tours head to St Michaels or the fishing village of Rock Hall. Ninety minutes will get you to Thomas Point Lighthouse, a National Historic Landmark, among other destinations.

Chesapeake Bay was once filled with so many oysters that Maryland and Virginia fishermen actually resorted to violence as they argued over where the rightful boundary was between the two states. To revisit the bay when the oyster was king, set sail for a two-hour cruise on the *Rebecca T Ruark* (1-410 829 3976, www.skipjack.org), built in 1886 and currently the bay's oldest working skipjack. Captain

Wade Murphy will demonstrate how skipjacks dredged for oysters before he does some dredging of his own.

Captain Ed Farley offers two-hour cruises on skipjack *HM Krenz* (1-410 745 6080, www.oystercatcher.com). Farley helped author James Michener in his research for *Chesapeake*, the epic historical novel about the bay.

JUST BEACHY

Chesapeake's strands may not rival Miami's South Beach or Southern California's Laguna Beach, but they do attract a faithful following because of the many different activities on offer. More than a million visitors each year descend on Annapolis's **Sandy Point State Park** (1100 East College Parkway, 1-410 974 2149, www.dnr.state.md.us/publiclands/southern/sadypoint.html). The site of a pre-Civil War resort, the park boasts a mile-long beach and the chance to swim (although there were problems with high bacteria levels in summer 2006), fish, go crabbing, rent a rowboat or motorboat (call the marina for prices and availability, 1-410 974 2772), have a picnic, or hike along nature trails. But maybe the best attraction is watching traffic back up on the Bay Bridge. For those not interested in this perverse pleasure, there are sailing regattas and sea-bound ships to ogle.

Calvert Cliffs State Park (Lusby, 1-301 743 7613, www.dnr.state.md.us/publiclands/southern/calvertcliffs.html) features 100-foot cliffs that loom over a small beach. More than 600 species of fossils have been discovered on the beach and cliffs, including the teeth of various sharks. From the parking lot, the hike to the beach is about two miles. **Point Lookout State Park** (11175 Point Lookout Road, Scotland, 1-301 872 5688, www.dnr.state.md.us/publiclands/southern/pointlookout.html) is nothing if not picturesque. A beach three-quarters of a mile long overlooks the point where the Potomac River flows into Chesapeake Bay. Rent motorboats or canoes, go fishing, hiking, or swimming. A museum explains the park's history as a Civil War prison camp for more than 50,000 Confederate soldiers.

GETTING CRABBY

Forget fancy napkins, highbrow wine lists and a maitre d' in tails. Maryland crab houses are all about the crab. The tables are paper-covered and the utensil of choice is a wooden mallet. No trip to Chesapeake is complete without tasting the local delicacy, but be forewarned: this isn't fast food. There's lots of labour necessary to get at the succulent meat.

Maryland's blue crabs spawn in southern Chesapeake Bay once the brackish water starts to warm in June, moving up the bay and its 150 tributaries, periodically shedding their shells as they grow. A crab caught during the first few hours between shedding its old shell and growing a new one is called 'softshell', capable of being cooked and devoured in its entirety. 'Hardshells' over the legal minimum size are a decidedly different dish. The cycle ends in late autumn. Don't be afraid to ask for a tutorial in how to open and slice up your crab, but whatever you do, don't eat its organs! Most crab shacks also offer a selection of shrimp, clams, mussels, calamari and fish, for those who are not crab crazy.

Jimmy Cantler's Riverside Inn (458 Forest Beach Road, 1-410 757 1311, www.cantlers.com) is a short drive from downtown Annapolis and the local favourite. Set against Mill Creek, Cantler's has outdoor seating. For another local favourite visit **Mike's Bar and Crab House** (3030 Riva Road, Riva, 1-410 956 2784, www.mikescrabhouse.com, mains $14-$30). Established in 1958, Mike's has a deck with views of the South River. **Cheshire Crab Restaurant** (1701 Poplar Ridge Road, Pasadena, 1-410 360 2220, www.pleasurecovemarina.com/CHESHIRE, closed Mon Jan-Mar, mains $15-$26) has an outdoor deck that overlooks the Pleasure Cove marina, where watermen can tie up and head inside for a quick bite to eat before returning to the waves. On the east side of the Bay Bridge is **Harris Crab House** (433 Kent Narrows Way N, Grasonville, 1-410 827 9500, www.harriscrabhouse.com, mains $13-$26), which has a rooftop deck with a view of the Kent Narrows. Housed in an 1830s building first used as an oyster shucking shed (check out the authentic bar ceiling joints), **St Michaels Crab House** (305 Mulberry Street, St Michaels, 1-410 745 3737, www.stmichaelscrabhouse.com, mains $15-$25) has a waterfront patio overlooking a marina off the Miles River. Finally, **Waterman's Crab House** (Sharp Street Wharf in Rock Hall, 1-410 639 2261, www.rockhallmd.com/watermans) has a deck that overlooks Rock Hall Harbor and the Bay Bridge. Sunsets can be spectacular.

Resources

Tourist information

Annapolis & Anne Arundel County Conference & Visitors Bureau *26 West Street, Annapolis (1-888 302 2852/www.visit-annapolis.org).* **Open** 9am-5pm daily.

Maryland Department of Natural Resources *580 Taylor Avenue, Annapolis (1-410-260-8367/www.dnr.state.md.us).* **Open** 9am-5pm Mon-Fri. Hiking, camping and fishing information.

Directory

Features

Masonic House of the Temple.
See p93.

Directory

Getting Around

By air

Three airports serve Washington. **Washington Dulles International Airport**, 25 miles out in the suburbs of Virginia, handles the longer flights into the region, including most international flights. **Baltimore-Washington International Airport** (or BWI) is a lot closer to the first half of its name but easily accessible from Washington by public transport, and is popular for its cheaper fares and more bearable traffic. **Ronald Reagan Washington National Airport** (most people still use the old name 'National') is the closest to DC, located just across the Potomac River from downtown, and gives a great view of the monuments as you fly in; it's used mostly for short- and medium-haul flights within the US and Canada.

The airports have their own official websites, but for general information, including ground transportation, shops and services, hotels and maps, go to www.quickaid.com or www.metwashairports.com.

Super Shuttle

1-800 258 3826/1-202 296 6662/ www.supershuttle.com.
Offers door-to-door shared van service between all three airports and anywhere in the area. Prices run from $15 to $30 for the first passenger and from as little as $8 for each additional passenger going to the same place. It's helpful to know the zip code of your final destination.

MAJOR AIRLINE CONTACT DETAILS

Note that most airlines now offer cheaper fares through their websites.

Air Canada *1-888 247 2262/ www.aircanada.com.*
American Airlines *1-800 433 7300/www.aa.com.*
British Airways *1-800 247 9297/ www.britishairways.com.*
Continental Airlines *Domestic 1-800 523 3273/international 1-800 231 0856/www.continental.com.*
Delta Air Lines *1-800 221 1212/ www.delta.com.*
Northwest Airlines *1-800 225 2525/www.nwa.com.*
Southwest Airlines *1-800 435 9792/www.southwest.com.*
United Airlines *1-800 241 6522/ www.united.com.*
US Airways *1-800 428 4322/ www.usair.com.*
Virgin Atlantic *1-800 862 8621/ www.virgin-atlantic.com.*

To & from Dulles Airport

1-703 572 2700/ www.metwashairports.com.
The quickest and cheapest way to downtown DC is by getting the **Washington Flyer Bus** (1-888 927 4359/www.washfly.com), which operates between Dulles and the West Falls Church Metro stop (20 to 30-minute ride) at the western end of the Orange Line. It costs $9 one way, $16 round trip, and runs at least every half hour (from 5.45am to 10.15pm Mon-Fri, and between 7.45am and 10.15pm at weekends). From here you can continue your journey into the city on the Metro.

The **Washington Flyer Taxi Service** (1-703 661 6655) has the sole concession to operate out of Dulles (unless incoming passengers have a prearranged pick-up with another cab company). A ride from Dulles to downtown DC costs about $42 plus tip. All Washington Flyer cabs take credit cards.

To & from BWI

1-800 435 9294/1-410 859 7111/ www.bwiairport.com.
Getting to Washington from BWI can often be expensive, a hassle, or both. A cheap combination (best if you have little to haul) to downtown DC is the shuttle-train-Metro option. Take the free shuttle bus (marked **BWI Rail**, 1-410 672 6169) from the BWI terminal to the train station about a mile away, then catch a Marc ($5 one way) or Amtrak (from $20) train (www.mtmaryland.com) south

25 minutes to Union Station, from where you can get on the Metro.

BWI is also served by cabs, private car companies and the **Super Shuttle** (*see above*), but beware of the long waits for the latter. You can get complete BWI ground transport information from the booth in Pier C or by calling 1-800 435 9294. A cab from BWI to downtown Washington costs about $60 plus tip.

To & from Reagan National Airport

1-703 417 8000/ www.metwashairports.com.
National Airport is served by the Metro subway system (Yellow and Blue lines). It's about a 20-minute ride to downtown. Going by cab is another option: signs outside each baggage claim area will direct you to the taxi stand. The taxi stand operator will point you to a particular cab depending on whether you're going to DC, Virginia or Maryland. Virginia-licensed cabs can take you anywhere; DC- and Maryland-licensed cabs can't serve Virginia. The fare is determined by meter in Maryland and Virginia cabs, by mileage in DC cabs. All pick-ups from National Airport add a $1.75 surcharge. A cab to downtown Washington costs about $14 plus tip.

By rail

A train from New York City (Penn Station) to Washington takes roughly three hours and costs about $85 each way for an unreserved ticket and $125 each way for a reserved seat. For more information on trains, call Amtrak on 1-800 872 7245 or go to www.amtrak.com. All trains to DC arrive at Union Station, which has its own Metro station.

By bus

You can also catch the bus from New York to DC. The journey takes longer (about five hours), but it's really cheap – around $42 each way. Greyhound buses (1-800 231 2222, www.greyhound.com) leave from a terminal in a grimmish area north of Union Station, and arrive at the Port Authority Bus Station in New York.

By car

Washington is served by several major highways, including Interstates 270, 66 and 95. At Washington, the 95 splits into the 495-95 and 95, looping the metropolitan area as the Capital Beltway. A useful resource when planning a car journey is www.map quest.com. If you type in your address (it only works in mainland USA) and the address in Washington you want to drive to, Mapquest will provide directions, complete with maps and the distance between turns.

Navigation

DC's western border is the Potomac River. It is surrounded by Maryland on all other sides. The border is more significant for administrative reasons than geographical: the metro sprawls into the neighbouring states.

The city is divided into four quadrants – NW, NE, SE and SW – which meet at the US Capitol, the geographical centre of Washington before the 1846 land retrocession to Virginia. North, South and East Capitol Streets, and the National Mall to the west, radiate out from the Capitol and serve as quadrant dividing lines. On one level, the District is completely rational in its layout. Numbered streets run north and south on both sides of the Capitol, with intersecting lettered streets and a few named streets tossed in, running east to west, for about 50 square blocks. The higher the number, and the further on in the alphabet the letter, the further away the street is from the Capitol. This grid system fades when the alphabet ends

(when words beginning with A through Z replace the lone letters). But as straightforward as this seems, there is a crucial nuance. Because the naming system radiates from a central point, there are two First Streets (and Second, etc), one on either side of North/South Capitol Street – and ditto for lettered streets, one north and one south of the Mall (aside from A and B Streets, which don't appear in all four quadrants). This means that there can therefore be four different places – one in each quadrant – where, say, a Fourth Street and a G Street intersect, so you need to know which quadrant you're aiming for. This is why we have given the quadrant after every address in our listings, and this is also how you should give directions to a taxi driver (say 'Northwest' not 'NW'). Northwest is by far the biggest quadrant.

Street numbers correspond to cross streets; thus 800 C Street will be on C Street at Eighth Street (or rather, the eighth block from the US Capitol); 890 C Street will be on the 800 block but closer to Ninth Street. For addresses on numbered streets, you can also work out the location. For instance, 400 Eighth Street will be at the fourth block from the US Capitol. In practice this means you can count up the alphabet – ie 400 Eighth Street will be at D Street. There are some exceptions to this rule, however: the letter 'B' (or, strictly speaking, the 200 block) is counted even though there are no B Streets in central Washington (there are named streets in their places – Constitution Avenue in NE and NW and Independence Avenue in SE and SW). Note also that there is no J Street, so it's ignored. For locating yourself, it's useful to remember that E Street is at 500, K is 1000, P is 1500, and U is 2000. Above W Street, the counting depends

on the number of blocks, regardless of what the streets are named, although they are generally in alphabetical order. Woven into the grid of lettered and numbered streets are diagonal avenues, all named after American states – Pennsylvania Avenue, Massachusetts Avenue, and so on – that can easily cause drivers and walkers severe disorientation. Some diagonals can be a fast way across town, but most hit confusing traffic circles designed more for horse-and-buggy contraptions than modern travel, or run into parks or important buildings (such as the White House) that cause them to dogleg disconcertingly. Note that I Street is often written 'Eye' Street in order to avoid confusion with 1st/First Street.

Most hotels provide adequate tourist maps, but much better is the ADC Washington DC Visitor's Map, which helpfully shows the shapes of the buildings on the Mall and subway entrances. It's very good for central DC, but shows almost nothing of the NE or SE quadrants, and does not include Arlington. Most bookstores stock maps, and gas stations have large-scale driving maps. Or visit the terrific ADC Map & Travel Store (see p145).

You don't really need a car in DC. It's a pedestrian-friendly city and most of the main monuments and museums are well served by public transport. Taxis are reasonably priced and easily flagged down in the centre. Parking in downtown DC and near popular nightspots is often a hassle. And while a car can be the best way to get out of town, beware: rush-hour traffic is hell.

Public transport

The **Washington Metropolitan Area Transit Authority** runs the entire

Directory

timeout.com

Over 50 of the world's greatest
cities reviewed in one site.

DC-area public transport network. For information on the Metrorail subway system and buses, call 1-202 637 7000 (hours of operation: 6am-10.30pm Mon-Thur; 6am-11.30pm Fri; 7am-11.30pm Sat; 7am-10.30pm Sun) or go to its website at www.wmata.com, which features real-time scrolling alerts on delays.

Metro

The **Metrorail** (or, more commonly, Metro) subway system is a clean, safe and reliable public transport system. Trains run from 5am Monday to Friday and from 7am on Saturday and Sunday. The system closes at midnight Sunday to Thursday and at 3am on Saturday and Sunday mornings, but the last trains from the suburbs may depart before that. Holiday schedules vary. At busy times, trains come as often as two minutes apart. But even if everything is running on time, the scheduled waits at nights and weekends can be up to 20 minutes. Most signs and announcements use the line's final station as the identifier for platforms and trains – though not all trains go as far as the last station, so you need to know which direction you're heading.

You'll find a Metrorail map on page 256; also use the handy TripPlanner on the Metro website (www.wmata.com), or pick up the *Metro Pocket Guide*, which usefully lists the nearest Metro station to the monuments and other points of interest. Station entrances are marked on the street by square columns with a big white 'M' on top.

Throughout this guide, we've listed the Metro stop nearest to each destination. If the Metro station is some distance away, a bus number is also listed, but in practice, and in the daytime at least, it's usually nicer to walk the last part of the journey.

Metro lines can run deep and the escalators can be very long. The network is, however, wheelchair-accessible via elevators. If the elevators are broken at a particular station, a bus service will run from a nearby station. Check at the information kiosk before boarding for the latest information on elevator breakdowns.

Fares & passes

The minimum price of a Metro trip is $1.35 but fares depend on when and how far you travel – and can almost double for some rides during rush hours. Fares are printed on a big board on the information kiosk in

each station. Up to two under-4s travel free with a full fare-paying adult; each additional child must pay full fare.

Payment is by Farecard: you put up to $20 or your credit card into a machine, which pops out a flimsy card with a magnetic stripe on the front. Use the card to enter and exit the Metro turnstiles. The price of each trip is subtracted and the remaining amount printed on the card until there's not enough value left to go anywhere. You can then transfer the remaining amount to a new card using the same machines you buy cards from. You can't get into the Metro without at least $1.35 on your card. If you don't have enough to get out at a particular station, use the ExitFare machines just before the exit turnstiles, which take only $1 or $5 bills.

A particular bargain is the $6.50 one-day pass for unlimited trips (valid after 9.30am Mon-Fri, and all day at weekends). They are sold at some hotels, major grocery stores, most Metro stations and online at www.wmata.com. If your visit is going to last longer than a week, look into Metrochecks, which are available in denominations of $1, $5, $10, $20 and $30. These vouchers are accepted by more than 100 different transportation services – trains, buses and van pools – throughout the region. Check www.wmata.com/riding/passes.cfm for full details.

The lines

Red Line: serves the Maryland suburbs north of DC and runs through the downtown business district. The Zoo, Union Station and UDC (University of the District of Columbia) are on this line.
Green Line: serves Anacostia, the U Street district, Howard University and the eastern Mall area.
Blue Line: serves Arlington, Alexandria, National Airport, the RFK Stadium and most downtown memorials and museums. It parallels much of the Orange Line and some of the Yellow.
Yellow Line: serves Fairfax County (Virginia) via Alexandria to the Mall. Includes National Airport.
Orange Line: serves the suburbs from western Virginia to eastern Maryland. Parallels the Blue Line through most major tourist sights.

Buses

The bus system, also run by the Washington Metropolitan Area Transit Authority, covers the city well and is heavily used by locals, especially for commuting.

Metrobuses cost $1.25, or 35¢ with a subway transfer (get one after you

enter the Metro but before you get on the train – look for a machine near the top of the escalators to the platform). You need exact change; dollar bills are accepted. Bus stops are marked by three horizontal stripes in blue, white and red. Metrorail passes are not valid on the bus, with the exception of certain weekly deals. A regional one-day pass costs $3 and is good for an entire day of bus trips (and covers $1.25 of the $3.00 fare on Express bus routes). A good timetable and route tool is available on the Metro website (www.wmata.com/timetables/default.cfm).

The greater Washington area is served by different local bus systems. Alexandria and Fairfax Counties in Virginia and Montgomery, Prince George's and Prince William Counties in Maryland each run their own public transport or ride-share systems. To reach these services, call Metro (1-202 637 7000) for phone numbers and information.

Useful bus routes

One popular area served better by bus than Metro is Georgetown: catch a 30, 32, 34, 35 or 36 bus marked 'Friendship Heights' running west on Pennsylvania Avenue. The same buses serve the Upper Northwest area along Wisconsin Avenue, parts of which are far from any Metro stop. For Adams Morgan, including busy 18th Street, take the 90, 92 or 93 (U Street/Garfield line) bus from Woodley Park-Zoo/Adams Morgan Metro, or the 42 (Mount Pleasant line) bus from Dupont Circle Metro. (Adams Morgan is also within walking distance of Columbia Heights Metro).

Trains

Both Amtrak and Marc (Maryland Rail Commuter Service) operate out of DC's Union Station. Amtrak connects with cities all over the US, including Baltimore, and also has stops at Alexandria in Virginia and at Rockville and New Carrollton in Maryland. There are several trains daily to New York, Philadelphia and Boston, including Metroliner services, on which you're allowed to reserve seats. Marc is a commuter train running from Union Station to parts of West Virginia and Maryland (including Baltimore). The Penn line goes to Baltimore's northern suburbs and runs from 4.45am to 11.40pm on weekdays (every 30 minutes during rush hour, every hour otherwise). It does not run at weekends. The Camden line stops at Camden Yards (Baltimore's baseball stadium) and runs only during morning and evening rush hours (6.42-8.05am and 4.13-7.35pm). Marc stops at some Metro stations in Maryland. Fares between DC and Baltimore are $7 one-way, $15 round trip. Both Amtrak and Marc serve the BWI Airport station, from where you take a free shuttle bus for the short journey to the terminal.

Union Station
50 Massachusetts Avenue, NE, at North Capitol Street, Union Station & around (Amtrak 1-800 872 7245/ www.amtrak.com/Marc 1-866 743 3682/www.mtamaryland.com). Map p253 L6.

Taxis

As elsewhere in the States, driving a taxi is a typical job for recent immigrants, so it's not uncommon to get a driver who needs directions.

There are no taxi ranks but you can usually find cabs outside hotels and it's easy to flag down a DC-licensed cab around most central parts of the city. Cabs for hire have a light on top and the company name on the door. To call a cab in the District, try **Diamond** (1-202 387 2221) or **Yellow Cab** (1-202 544 1212). Cab fares are based on how many zones you travel through (maps should be displayed in every cab), plus extra charges for additional passengers, rush-hour travel, calling for a cab and travelling during designated snow emergencies. Baggage charges are usually 50¢ for each largeish, grocery-sized handbag after the first one and $2 for each big bag. In reality, some cabbies charge, some don't, depending, it seems, on their mood. The minimum fare possible under the zone system (for one person, flagging the cab, no bags, not at rush hour or in the snow) is $5 plus tip. That will get you from Capitol Hill to Dupont Circle – and it seems to be this trip that brings the smouldering resentment about the zone system into the open. Most cabbies can't wait to see the congressionally mandated zones disappear.

In Maryland and Virginia, cabs run on meters. Cabs licensed for these areas can legally only pick up fares in DC on a pre-arranged basis – and only take them to the jurisdiction in which they are licensed. That might be why, no matter how hard you're waving on a DC street, that empty cab goes right on by.

Driving

The Washington area (especially between DC and Virginia) is not a great place to drive. The traffic circles are confusing and some streets, notably Rock Creek Parkway, change direction in rush hours. Read carefully the times posted in the middle of 'Do Not Enter' and 'No Turns' signs; at other times, entrance is allowed. Unless there's a sign saying otherwise, you can make a right turn when the lights are red.

Parking

There are plenty of off-street pay parking lots around town: **Monument Parking** (1-202 833 9357) has seven locations; **Parking Management Incorporated** (PMI, 1-202 785 9191) has many more. Street parking ranges from difficult to impossible, especially near the Mall, downtown and in popular nightlife areas such as Georgetown and Adams Morgan. The parking police are notoriously pedantic. Add to this the regular street shutdowns for presidential motorcades and you'll see why nearly a third of District residents don't own a car.

For up-to-the-minute traffic conditions, check the live cameras on www.trafficland.com. Tune to WTOP (103.5 FM) for traffic reports every ten minutes.

Vehicle hire

For getting right out of town, driving is often the best option. Most major car rental companies have offices in and around DC. Almost every rental agency will require a credit card and matching driving licence, and few will rent to anyone under 25. The price quoted won't include tax, liability insurance or collision damage waiver (CDW). If you already have an insured car in the US, your own liability insurance may cover the rental. Ask about discounts, available to members of the AAA (as well as British AA members), AARP (American Association of Retired Persons) and

other organisations. Zip Car (1-202 737 4900/www.zipcar.com) does hourly and daily rentals in many locations around the city.

The following are national car rental companies with DC locations:
Alamo *1-800 462 5266/ www.alamo.com.*
Avis *1-800 331 1212/www.avis.com.*
Budget *1-800 527 0700/ www.budget.com.*
Dollar *1-800 800 4000/ www.dollarcar.com.*
Hertz *1-800 654 3131/ www.hertz.com.*
National *1-800 227 7368/ www.nationalcar.com.*
Thrifty *1-800 847 4389/ www.thrifty.com.*

Cycling

DC is a great place to cycle. Much of the city, including most of the Mall and downtown, is flat (though there's Capitol Hill at the eastern end of the Mall). And if you don't mind a less-than-direct route, you can avoid the hillier parts of Washington (in particular, north of Florida Avenue – both NE and NW – and Upper Northwest). A web of bike paths can take you to out-of-centre spots, and riding from museum to monument will save your feet hours of ache (though you'll have to lock your bike to a signpost or railings). For more information on biking in and around DC, get in touch with the **Washington Area Bicyclist Association** (1-202 518 0936, www.waba.org).

Walking

Dawdlers beware! Washington has its fair share of aggressive walkers. Drivers can also be a hazard, cutting up pedestrians even when the traffic lights are in their favour. Walking is a great way to get around, but remember that summers are hot and muggy, and while the Mall might like look like a nice gentle stroll, it's actually two miles long, with a hill at the Capitol end.

Resources A-Z

Addresses

See p221 **Navigation**.

Age restrictions

You have to be 21 to drink alcohol in DC, Maryland and Virginia. Note that the law is very strictly enforced, with severe penalties. Be sure to carry ID with you (*see p227*).

Attitude & etiquette

Washington is unquestionably a major tourist destination, so if you wear jeans, trainers and carry a small rucksack you should feel right at home. It is also, of course, a major business centre, and walking around downtown you'll see lawyers in suits and other members of a well-dressed workforce.

DC residents usually inhabit their own little niches. They read the *Washington Post* on the Metro, mind their business on the sidewalk and get upset when tourists stand on the left side of the escalator instead of the right. But if you do stop someone on the street to ask for directions, they will generally be happy to oblige.

Business

There was a time, not that long ago, when the business scene in Washington could pretty much be covered in one word: government. Not only was the federal presence far and away the dominant industry, but dealing with it was the primary purpose of most private-sector activity. Government is still the 800lb gorilla of the DC jungle, but a number of A-list corporations have their headquarters in the Washington area. A high-tech industry has established itself along the so-called Dulles Corridor, turning the expressway linking the city with Dulles International Airport in the Virginia suburbs into something of a Silicon Valley East (AOL Time Warner has a headquarters here, and some Virginians' car tags bear the business bureau catchphrase 'internet capitol'). The business epicentre is downtown's K Street, lined with glassy office buildings. DC now has more office space than any other American city aside from New York.

That said, while Washington may have made the big time, standard operating procedures are lower-key than in comparable cities. There are similarities, such as the ubiquitous power lunch, but the overall style is less frenetic. In fact, as viewed from the vantage of New York, Washingtonians have no style. The idea is to dress down: dark (preferably blue) suits, and ties with a touch of red. In summer, when the heat and humidity threaten to reach meltdown levels, light-hued poplin and seersucker suits are almost a uniform. Year-round, by far the preferred accessory is a neck chain from which dangles a photo-ID card – it's virtually a badge of belonging.

Conventions

Washington Convention Center

801 Mount Vernon Place, NW, between Seventh & Ninth Streets, Downtown (1-202 249 3000/www. dcconvention.com). **Map** p253 J5. The largest single building in the city, this new centre opened in 2003 to rave reviews and booming business. Its 52,000sq ft ballroom and $4-million art collection make it worth a peek for casual visitors, many of whom stop in at the restaurants and retail outlets on-site.

Couriers

All the major international couriers, in addition to several locally based enterprises, are active in DC. For other outfits, check the *Yellow Pages* under 'Air Cargo & Package Express Service', 'Delivery Service', or, for local deliveries, 'Messenger Services'.

Federal Express *1-800 463 3339/ www.fedex.com.* **Credit** AmEx, DC, Disc, MC, V.

Skynet Worldwide Courier *1-703 759 6381/www.skynet.net.* **No credit cards.**

United Parcel Service *1-800 742 5877/www.ups.com.* **Credit** AmEx, MC, V.

Publications

The top domestic business papers are readily available in Washington, while foreign publications can be

---

Travel advice

For current information on travel to a specific country – including the latest news on health issues, safety and security, local laws and customs – contact your home country's government department of foreign affairs. Most have websites with useful advice for would-be travellers.

Australia
www.smartraveller.gov.au

Canada
www.voyage.gc.ca

New Zealand
www.safetravel.govt.nz

Republic of Ireland
http://foreignaffairs.gov.ie

UK
www.fco.gov.uk/travel

USA
http://travel.state.gov

found at larger newsstands. Local journals worth a look include the weekly *Washington Business Journal* (http://washington.bizjournals.com/washington). For more on the local media scene, *see p228*.

Useful organisations

For details of the Washington DC Convention & Tourism Corporation, *see p234*. For the US Customs Service, *see p226*.

District of Columbia Chamber of Commerce *First floor, 1213 K Street, NW, at 12th Street, Downtown (1-202 347 7201/www.dcchamber. org). McPherson Square Metro.* **Open** 8.30am-5.30pm Mon-Fri. **Map** p252 H5.

Greater Washington Board of Trade *Suite 200, 1725 I Street, NW, between 17th & 18th Streets, Downtown (1-202 857 5900/www. bot.org). Farragut North or Farragut West Metro.* **Map** p252 G5.
The Board of Trade functions as a regional co-ordinating organisation for DC, northern Virginia and suburban Maryland.

US Department of Commerce *14th Street & Constitution Avenue, NW, The Federal Triangle (1-202 482 2000/www.doc.gov). Federal Triangle Metro.* **Open** 8am-5.30pm Mon-Fri. **Map** p252 H6.

Consumer

Whenever possible, pay with a major credit card so you can cancel payment or get reimbursed if there is a problem (be sure to keep receipts or a form of documentation). Consider travel insurance that includes default coverage to protect yourself against financial loss.

Customs

A visa waiver form (I-94W) is generally provided by the airline during check-in or on the plane and must be presented to Immigration at the airport of entry to the US. International visitors should allow about an hour in the airport to clear Immigration. For more on visas, *see p235*.

A customs declaration form (6059B) is also provided on international flights into the US; this must be filled out and

handed to a customs official after Immigration (keep it handy). Current US regulations allow foreign visitors to import the following duty-free: 200 cigarettes or 50 cigars (Cuban cigars are generally not allowed), 1 litre of wine or spirits (over-21s only), and a maximum of $100 in gifts. You can take up to $10,000 in cash, travellers' cheques or endorsed bank drafts in or out of the country. Anything above that you must declare on a customs form, or it risks seizure. It is illegal to transport most perishable foods and plants across international borders. If you are carrying prescription drugs, make sure they are labelled, and keep a copy of your prescription with you. The Customs and Border Patrol website (www.cbp.gov) contains information.

US Citizenship and Immigration Services *2675 Prosperity Avenue, Fairfax, VA 22031 (1-800 375 5283/www.uscis.gov). Dunn Loring Metro.* **Open** 8am-3.30pm Mon-Wed; 8am-11am Thur.

US Customs Service *1300 Pennsylvania Avenue, NW, at 13th Street, Penn Quarter (1-202 354 1000/www.customs.gov). Federal Triangle Metro.* **Open** 8.30am-5pm Mon-Fri. **Map** p252 H6.

Disabled

Washington is good at providing facilities for all types of tourists, including the disabled and elderly. Most museums, monuments and memorials are accessible to visitors using wheelchairs and many have other facilities to help disabled travellers. Nearly all streets in the downtown area have wide sidewalks with kerb cuts for greater accessibility. The Metro has excellent facilities for visitors with visual and auditory impairments, or mobility problems. All stations are theoretically wheelchair-accessible, although lifts are not always in service. *See also p223.*

Information

An extremely useful website is **www.disabilityguide.org**, which rates DC's hotels, restaurants, malls and sights according to accessibility. It's run by Access Information (1-301 528 8664). The Washington DC Convention & Tourism Corporation (*see p234*) also has information and a free brochure on city accessibility. The New York-based Society for Accessible Travel & Hospitality (1-212 447 7284, www.sath.org) offers advice for disabled travellers throughout the US.

Tours

Sprout, in New York City (1-212 222 9575, 1-888 222 9575, www.go sprout.org) offers tours for the disabled, while Melwood (1-301 599 8000, www.melwood.com) is a useful local resource for disabled travellers.

Drugs

Hard and soft drugs are illegal in Washington, as in the rest of the US. In practice, however, arresting people for the possession of small amounts of soft drugs is not a high priority for DC police.

Electricity

The US electricity supply is 110-120 volt, 60-cycle AC, rather than the 220-240 volt, 50-cycle AC used in Europe. Plugs are standard two-pins. An adaptor and, in some cases, a voltage converter (available at airport shops and hardware stores) are necessary to use foreign appliances. Check www. voltagevalet.com for answers to electricity questions.

Embassies & consulates

Note that most visa services keep shorter hours than the business hours listed. For other embassies/consulates, consult the *Yellow Pages*.

Australia *1601 Massachusetts Avenue, NW, at 16th Street, Dupont Circle (1-202 797 3000/www.aust emb.org). Dupont Circle Metro.* **Open** 8.30am-5pm Mon-Fri. **Map** p250 H4.

Canada *501 Pennsylvania Avenue, NW, at Sixth Street, Penn Quarter (1-202 682 1740/www.canadian embassy.org). Archives-Navy Memorial or Judiciary Square Metro.* **Open** varies. **Map** p252 J6.

Ireland *2234 Massachusetts Avenue, NW, at Sheridan Circle, Dupont Circle (1-202 462 3939/ www.irelandemb.org). Dupont Circle Metro.* **Open** 9am-1pm, 2-4pm Mon-Fri. **Map** p250 F4.

New Zealand *37 Observatory Circle, NW, at Massachusetts Avenue, Upper Northwest (1-202 328 4800/www.nzembassy.com). Dupont Circle Metro.* **Open** 8.30am-12.30pm, 1.30-5pm Mon-Fri. **Map** p249 E3.

United Kingdom *3100 Massachusetts Avenue, NW, at Whitehaven Street, Upper Northwest (1-202 588 6500/www.britain usa.com). Dupont Circle Metro then N2, N4, N6 bus.* **Open** 9am-5.30pm Mon-Fri. **Map** p250 F3.

Emergencies

The number to call for fire, police, ambulance and other emergencies is **911** (free from public and cellular phones).

Gay & lesbian

Washington is home to a thriving, well-established gay and lesbian community. For information about groups and what's on, consult the *Washington Blade* (their excellent website is www.washblade.com).

The bookshop Lambda Rising (*see p147*) is a fine gay and lesbian resource centre. For further information on the local scene, *see pp177-81*.

Health

Accident & emergency

Emergency treatment in the United States is provided on receipt of hard cash. It is often rumoured that many emergency rooms won't even see you unless you show them a credit card first. This is, in fact, illegal: emergency rooms are only allowed to turn you away if your injury is not considered an emergency, though they will likely do all they can to make you pay up. Taking

out full medical cover is still imperative, ideally with a large and reputable company that will pay upfront rather than reimburse you later. The hospitals listed all have 24-hour emergency rooms.

Contraception & abortion

Several branches of the CVS chain (*see p158*; or call 1-888 607 4287) are open 24 hours a day. Like other pharmacies, they sell condoms and can fill out prescriptions for other contraceptives. If you need advice about abortion, call Planned Parenthood on 1-800 230 7526 or go to its website, www.planned parenthood.org.

Dentists

DC Dental Society

1-202 547 7613/www.dcdental.org. The DC Dental Society can refer you to a local dentist for treatment.

Doctors

Doctors Referral

1-800 362 8677/ www.1800doctors.com. Can recommend a local doctor.

HIV & AIDS

Elizabeth Taylor Medical Center

1701 14th Street, NW, between R Street & Riggs Place, Shaw: Logan Circle (1-202 745 7000/www. wwc.org). McPherson Square Metro. **Open** 8am-10pm Mon-Fri. **Map** p250 H4.
Part of the Whitman Walker Clinic – a pioneering institution offering many services to people with HIV and other sexually transmitted diseases – the Elizabeth Taylor Medical Center provides counselling to AIDS patients and their families. The excellent website contains a wealth of useful information.

National HIV/ AIDS Hotline

1-800 342 2437.

Hospitals

Children's National Medical Center

111 Michigan Avenue, NW, at First Street, Shaw (1-202 884 5000/ www.cnmc.org). Brookland-CUA Metro then H2, H4 bus. **Map** p251 K2.

Georgetown University Hospital

3800 Reservoir Road, NW, between 38th & 39th Streets, Georgetown (1-202 444 2000/www.georgetown universityhospital.org). Dupont Circle Metro then D6 bus. **Map** p249 E4.

George Washington University Hospital

900 23rd Street, NW, between I Street & Washington Circle, Foggy Bottom (1-202 715 4000/www. gwhospital.com). Foggy Bottom Metro. **Map** p252 G5.

Pharmacies

See p158.

Helplines

Alcoholics Anonymous
1-202 966 9115/www.aa-dc.org.
Auto Impound
1-202 727 5000.
Dental Emergency
1-800 362 8677.
Mental Health Crisis Hotline
1-703 527 4077.
Non-emergency Metropolitan Police
311/www.mpdc.dc.gov.
Poison Center
1-800 222 1222.
Rape Crisis Center
1-202 232 0789.
Substance Abuse Hotline
1-800 234 0402.
Suicide Prevention Center
1-800 784 2433.
US Capitol Police
1-202 228 2800.
US Park Police
1-202 619 7300/www.nps.gov/uspp.

ID

Unless you're driving or drinking alcohol, there isn't any law that says you must carry identification with you, but it makes sense to do so. Keeping your passport with you is risky, but a driver's licence is usually a good idea, as everyone under the age of 40 seems to get carded – for entry to nightclubs, in particular – in DC.

Insurance

Non-nationals should arrange baggage, trip-cancellation and medical insurance before they

Directory

leave home (but first check what your existing home and medical insurance covers). Medical centres will ask for details of your insurance company and policy number if you require treatment, so keep this information with you.

Internet

Libraries (*see below*) are a good bet if you need a local place to go online for the web or to pick up email.

There are also many internet cafés and some shops have internet access. Online guide www.cybercafes.com is useful for finding cybercafés. In addition, your existing ISP may have a Point of Presence (POP) that will let you connect to the internet at local call rates. Alternatively, setting up an account with Compuserve (www.compuserve.com) or AOL (www.aol.com) gives you access to local POPs through the US. If all you want to do is access your email while in Washington, but don't want the hassle of setting up a new ISP account, you can set up the 'POP [Post Office Protocol] Mail' feature of Microsoft's free Hotmail (www.hotmail.com) service to fetch your mail instead. You can then access your mail from any computer with an internet connection. Many hotels now have net access (for facilities at individual hotels, see the Where to Stay chapter on pp40-55). For a list of useful websites, *see p236. See also p229* **WiFi Washington**.

Left luggage

All three of the area's major airports have effectively done away with luggage storage at their facilities in light of the US Homeland Security Department's new regulations following 9/11. The airport may be able to advise you on other facilities available.

Legal help

In the legal capital of the country, more than one person in seven is a lawyer. If you can't afford a local lawyer, stop by the Legal Aid Society of the District of Columbia, where legal aid lawyers can provide free legal assistance.

Legal Aid Society *Suite 800, 666 11th Street, NW, at G Street, Downtown (1-202 628 1161/www.legalaiddc.org). Metro Center Metro.* **Open** 9am-7pm Mon; 9am-3pm Tue, Thur. **Map** p252 J6.

Libraries

Washington is home to a range of sites from the endless shelves of the Library of Congress to specialised libraries in each of the Smithsonian museums. Many national and international organisations also have their headquarters in DC, complete with archives. The universities all have excellent libraries, and the public library system has 27 branches, many close to Metro stops.

Library of Congress

First Street & Independence Avenue, SE, The Capitol & around (operator 1-202 707 5000/visitor information 1-202 707 8000/www.loc.gov). Capitol South Metro. **Open** varies. **Map** p253 L7.
As the central library for the US, the Library of Congress makes it its business to have a copy of almost everything printed. However, it may take a very long time to find one small book among the nearly 100 million items on 535 miles of shelves, even when the staff do the search for you. The library is open to the public, but you must first wait in line for a library card and an extensive security check. Take at least one photo ID. Note that opening times vary for the different buildings within the complex. *See also p77.*

Martin Luther King Jr Memorial Library

901 G Street, NW, at 9th Street, Downtown (1-202 727 0321/www.dclibrary.org/mlk). Gallery Place-Chinatown Metro. **Open** 9.30am-9pm Mon-Thur; 9.30am-5.30pm Fri, Sat; 1-5pm Sun. **Map** p253 J6.

University libraries

Opening times for the following vary, so check before setting off.

American University Bender Library

4400 Massachusetts Avenue, NW, at Nebraska Avenue, Upper Northwest (1-202 885 3200/www.library.american.edu). Tenleytown-AU Metro then M4 bus. **Map** p248 C1.
Full-service university library, good for international affairs, social sciences, art, science and technology, among other subjects.

Catholic University of America Law Library

3600 John McCormack Road, NE, at Michigan Avenue, Northeast (1-202 319 5156/www.law.cua.edu/library). Brookland-CUA Metro. **Map** p251 L1.
Outstanding legal research library.

Georgetown University Lauinger Memorial Library

1421 37th Street, NW, at L Street, Georgetown (1-202 687 7452/http://gulib.lausun.georgetown.edu). Dupont Circle Metro then G2 bus. **Map** p249 D4.
Comprehensive collections include colonial and American Catholic history, and intelligence and covert activities. A medical library and law library are also on the campus. Photo ID is required.

University of Maryland-College Park Libraries

College Park Campus, Baltimore Avenue, College Park, MD (1-301 405 0800/www.lib.umd.edu). College Park Metro then C2, C8 bus.
The University of Maryland has six libraries, with special collections, including historic preservation, National Public Broadcasting archives and an East Asia collection.

Lost property

If you leave something on the bus or subway, the chances are you won't see it again, but it's worth giving the Washington Metro Transit Authority Lost & Found on 1-202 962 1195 or submitting a claim online at www.wmata.com. It's also worth checking at the nearest police station to see if it's been handed in.

WiFi Washington

As in most American cities, WiFi is slowly creeping across the nation's capital. And, like many other locales, service is great (and free) in some places, poor (and expensive) in others – ubiquitous Starbucks charges by the hour, while equally plentiful Panera locales offer free access. WiFi guides and locators on JWire (www.jwire.com) and WiFi Freespot (www.wififreespot.com) are great places to start – supplying frequently updated lists of WiFi hosts, technical FAQs and common sense tips. Most importantly: don't conduct secure transactions in public – security controls are often turned off to increase accessibility. Many places will require that you register (first and last names and a password) before logging on for the first time. That said, here are a few free, reliable (and lively) WiFi hubs:

Busboys and Poets
See p126.

Dupont Circle.
A local IT company has set up the entire area of Dupont Circle as a WiFi spot – great for pleasant afternoons.

Murky Coffee
See p132.

Tryst
See p123.

Warehouse Cafe
1017 Seventh Street, NW (1-202 783 3933/ www.warehousetheatre.com). Mount Vernon Square-7th Street-Convention Center Metro. **Open** 5-11pm Mon-Fri; 10am-midnight Sat; noon-6pm Sun. **Map** p253 J5.

Media

Washington is the one American city where many people actually watch the political chat shows run every Sunday by the main television networks and offered every day by the growing ranks of cable news channels – notably, the abrasive Fox News cable channel, which has been winning viewers at the expense of such polite operations as CNN (now part of Washington's multimedia superpower AOL Time Warner). There's even a local radio station that carries an audio version of the C-SPAN cable channel's Congressional coverage (WCSP, 90.1 FM). With all the major American news organisations and many foreign ones in residence in DC, news crews are a common sight around town. Newsmakers frequently appear at the National Press Club (13th Floor, 529 14th Street, NW, 1 202 662 7500, http://press.org), although only some of these events are open to the public.

Newspapers & magazines

Dailies
The Godzilla of local print journalism is the *Washington Post*, whose clout is the object of some awe and much resentment. Nonetheless, the *Post* has the highest market penetration of any major US daily, although its executives fret, with reason, that its power is waning with younger Washingtonians. The *Post's* coverage exemplifies the inside-the-Beltway mentality, with heavy emphasis on politics and policy, and a poorly concealed scepticism that anything else really matters. By the standards of US newspapers, international coverage is strong, and over recent years the paper has greatly expanded its online presence as well as coverage of business and technology because of the local high-tech sector's rapid growth. By contrast, genuinely local news and the arts are often treated with indifference. On Fridays, however, the *Post* publishes its 'Weekend' section, with extensive arts and entertainment listings.

This, along with the *Washington City Paper* (*see below*), is what most Washingtonians turn to for current entertainment information.

Owned by cronies of the Rev Sun Myung Moon, the *Washington Times* offers a right-wing view of events, with front-page stories that are often amusingly partisan. Although some commend its sports coverage, the paper is read principally by paleo-conservatives and people who really, really hate the *Post*. A local edition of the syndicated *Examiner* paper has also turned up recently, accounting for a small, occasionally interesting third voice. Although it offers little specifically for Washingtonians, the *New York Times* has a significant DC readership. The paper is most popular on Sundays, when its arts and feature writing trounces the *Post's*. Most large US newspapers are available in local street boxes, but only the *Los Angeles Times* prints a special daily DC edition. *USA Today*, the country's only national general-interest daily, is produced at Tysons Corner, Virginia, but its terse stories, graphics-heavy presentation and middle-American mindset are not much to local taste.

Weeklies
Geographical or cultural subdivisions of the metropolitan area are served by many weekly tabloids, including some suburban ones owned by the *Post*, but the only such weekly of regional significance is *Washington City Paper* (www.washingtoncitypaper.com). Founded in 1981 and owned by the *Chicago Reader*, this 'alternative' free weekly has softened its approach in recent years. Although it covers local politics, the paper is read mostly for its arts coverage, listings and adverts. The *New Republic*, a longtime liberal journal that in the 1980s became 'neo-liberal', has shifted a bit back towards the left recently. Its most recognisable voice, however, is that of British-born gay

Directory

conservative Andrew Sullivan. His feisty blog, the Daily Dish – well worth a look – can be found at http://time.blogs.com/daily_dish/. *Roll Call* and *The Hill* compete for the small but influential readership that makes national policy in the Capitol and its adjacent office buildings. These tabloids occasionally break major stories, but to outsiders most of the coverage will seem arcane.

The District's gay community is served by the weekly *Washington Blade*, which is a good source of local and national news. *MW* (*Metro Weekly*, www.metroweekly.com), includes listings for bars, clubs, guest DJ spots and parties. It also takes a more gossipy, dishy tone than the *Blade*. Both are free and readily available.

Monthlies

The *Washingtonian* is professional but seldom provocative, except in its coverage of the *Post*. It specialises in service journalism and tepid profiles, pitched to an overwhelmingly suburban readership. Two locally published magazines with global agendas are *National Geographic* and *Smithsonian*, which are circulated to members of their respective organisations and are also sold at newsstands. Their articles on science, history and other subjects of enduring importance – and *National Geographic*'s exceptional photography – exemplify the side of DC that is not consumed by the latest poll numbers.

A pioneering 'neo-liberal' policy journal, the *Washington Monthly* was once known as much for grooming young journalists as for anticipating Washington policy shifts, but these days it is little-read. Among the monthlies devoted to arts and entertainment, *One* covers dance clubs, fashion and upscale dining; the *Washington Diplomat* chronicles the international set, and the free *On Tap* – though intoxicated by beer and places to drink it – provides decent local entertainment ads and listings.

Outlets

Washington has more newspaper and magazine outlets than you might at first think. Many large office buildings have newsstands, often concealed in their lobbies so that only workers and regular visitors are aware of them. Outdoor newsstands (along with sidewalk cafés) were illegal in Washington for much of the 20th century, and since the ban was lifted in the 1960s most attempts to establish them have failed – which explains why the sidewalks at major intersections are overwhelmed by newspaper vending machines. Among the larger newsstands – and

the ones with the best selection of foreign publications – are the Newsroom (1803 Connecticut Avenue, NW), News World (1001 Connecticut Avenue, NW) and Metro News Center (1200 G Street, NW). The city's numerous Borders and Barnes & Noble outlets (*see p145*) have extensive periodical selections; Tower Records (2000 Pennsylvania Avenue, NW, Foggy Bottom, 1-202 331 2400) has a wide selection of music and youth-culture titles.

Television

Washington's airwaves carry all the usual suspects: **NBC** (WRC, Channel 4); **Fox** (WTTG, Channel 5); **ABC** (WJLA, Channel 7); **CBS** (WUSA, Channel 9) and the WB and UPN - merged **CW Network**. These offer the familiar sitcoms, cop and hospital dramas, and growing numbers (because they're cheap to produce) of news magazine shows. The local news programmes on Washington's commercial TV outlets are supposedly just lurid than in most American cities, although that's hard to imagine. There are also three local public TV stations featuring the customary line-up of *Sesame Street*, British drawing-room dramas and highlights from *Riverdance*: **WMPT** (Channel 22), **WETA** (Channel 26) and **WHUT** (Channel 32). The latter also runs some Spanish-language shows, while a fourth public station, **WNVC** (Channel 56), along with the local cable network **MHZ**, specialise in international programming, from classic Japanese films to the day's news in Mandarin, Polish and French. On cable, the fare is also commonplace, although it varies sightly among local jurisdictions. National channels based in Washington include **BET** (Black Entertainment Television) and the **Discovery Channel**, as well as the latter's documentary offspring – **Animal Planet**, the **Learning Channel** and the **History Channel**. Washingtonians watch more **C-SPAN** and **C-SPAN 2** (with live coverage of Congress and other public affairs programming) than most Americans; channels seen only locally include the extensive local news coverage of **NewsChannel 8**.

Radio

World events can change Washington's daily climate rapidly, so visitors would be well advised to keep on top of daily headlines via the city's excellent all-news station, **WTOP** (103.5FM), which also offers traffic and weather updates every ten minutes. Beyond that, the city

is upscale, urban and has a large African-American population, so local radio stations play more classical and hip hop, and less country music than in most parts of the US. Since the Federal Communication Commission weakened regulations restricting the number of stations that could be owned by large corporations, however, regional diversity in US radio programming is dwindling. Increasingly, stations are tightly formatted to attract a chosen demographic, often with a carefully test-marketed subset of oldies: 'classic rock' (**WARW**, 94.7 FM), 'classic hits' (**WBIG**, 100.3 FM) and 'urban adult contemporary' (**WMMJ**, 102.3 FM). **WWDC** (101.1 FM) is the area's only 'alternative' station left. 'Urban contemporary' (hip hop and soul) music is heard on **WKYS** (93.9 FM), **WPGC** (95.5 FM) and **WHUR** (96.3 FM). Of the three, WPGC is the rowdiest, while WHUR goes for a somewhat older audience. The leading Top 40 station is **WIHT** (99.5 FM). **WGMS** (104.1 FM) is the city's commercial classical station. The top two public radio stations, **WETA** (90.9 FM) and **WAMU** (88.5 FM), broadcast much of the news and arts programming of Washington-based **National Public Radio (NPR)**. The former also plays classical music; the latter offers public-affairs talk shows and weekend folk and bluegrass music. The once-radical **WPFW** (89.3 FM) still mixes jazz and politics, but has become tamer. The *Washington Post* has started a station (107.7FM) that mixes in-depth stories, feedback from writers and Washington Nationals baseball broadcasts. College radio, a free-form catalyst in many markets, is insignificant here; the University of Maryland's **WMUC** (88.1 FM) can be received only in the north-eastern suburbs. Washington is also the home of **XM**, the country's first digital satellite radio service. It broadcasts 100 channels of CD-quality music programming for those who have purchased the special receivers.

Money

As elsewhere in the US, credit cards are virtually a necessity in Washington. If you want to rent a car or book a ticket over the phone, you will need a major credit card. They are accepted almost universally in hotels, restaurants and shops, though occasionally you will find a gas station, small store or cinema that only takes cash.

New passport regulations

People of all ages (children included) who enter the US on the Visa Waiver Progam are now required to carry their own machine-readable passport, or MRP. MRPs are recognisable by the double row of characters along the foot of the data page. All currently valid burgundy EU and EU-lookalike passports issued in the UK since 1991 (ie all that are still valid) should be machine readable. But some of those issued abroad may not be; in this case, holders should get a replacement even if the passport has not expired.

The US's requirement for passports to contain a 'biometric' chip applies only to those issued from 26 October 2006. By then, all new and replacement UK passports should be compliant, following a gradual phase-in. The biometric chip contains a facial scan and biographical data.

There is no current requirement for UK passports to contain fingerprint or iris data. The application process remains as it was, except for new guidelines that ensure that the photograph you submit can be used to generate the facial scan in the chip.

Further information for UK citizens is available by calling 0870 521 0410 or by logging on to www.passport.gov.uk. Always check the above advice still stands before travelling. Nationals of other countries should check well in advance whether their passport meets the requirements for the time of their trip, at http://travel.state.gov/visa and with the issuing authorities of their home country.

Visa and MasterCard are the most widely accepted cards, with American Express a distant third. Credit cards are also useful for extracting instantaneous cash advances from ATMs and banks. However, where US account holders pay a flat service charge for getting cash this way, UK companies' charges vary – and you pay interest, of course. Debit cards are increasingly accepted at many shops, grocers and eateries. The cost of a holiday in DC compares favourably with other US destinations because there are few admission charges to pay at museums and galleries. Out of season, accommodation can be cheap.

ATMs

Automated Teller Machines are located outside nearly all banks, inside all malls and major shopping areas, and now in many bars and restaurants. They are the most convenient and often the most cost-effective way of obtaining cash – but remember that most charge at least a $2 service fee on top of any charges levied by your home bank. All you need is an ATM card (credit or debit) – and your usual PIN number. Check with your bank before leaving home to find out if they are linked to any DC banks and what the fees will be.

Banks

Bank of America

1501 Pennsylvania Avenue, NW, at 15th Street, White House & around (1-202 624 4253). McPherson Square Metro. **Open** 9am-5pm Mon-Thur; 9am-6pm Fri. **Map** p252 H6.

PNC Bank

1503 Pennsylvania Avenue, NW, at 15th Street, White House & around (1-202 762 2265). McPherson Square Metro. **Open** 9am-6pm Mon- Fri; 9am-4pm Sat. **Map** p252 H6.
The best branch for foreign exchange.

Currency

The United States' monetary system is decimal-based: the US dollar ($) is divided into 100 cents (¢). Coins and dollars are stamped with the faces of US presidents and statesmen. Coin denominations are the penny (1¢ – Abraham Lincoln on a copper-coloured coin); nickel (5¢ – Thomas Jefferson); dime (10¢ – Franklin D Roosevelt); quarter (25¢ – George Washington); the less common half-dollar (50¢ – John F Kennedy) and the 'golden' dollar (depicting Sacagawea, a Native American woman who acted as a guide to 19th-century explorers Lewis and Clark). You may also come across the smaller 'Susan B Anthony' dollar coin, a failed attempt to introduce dollar coins.

Bills, or notes, are all the same size and come in $1 (George Washington); $5 (Abraham Lincoln); $10 (Alexander Hamilton); $20 (Andrew Jackson); $50 (Ulysses S Grant); and $100 (Benjamin Franklin) denominations.

The US Mint recently changed the look of the bills; both old and new bills are in circulation and are valid. Older bills have smaller portraits, while newer ones have bigger, more cartoonish portraits.

Exchange

Some – but not many – banks will exchange cash or travellers' cheques in major foreign currencies. The most convenient place to exchange money is at the airport when you arrive – but banks often give better rates. Travelex, American Express and Thomas Cook (5335 Wisconsin Avenue, NW, 1-202 237-2229) also exchange currency and sell travellers' cheques. Most hotel desks will do the same – handy if you're stuck late at night without any cash. You can also use travellers' cheques as payment in shops and restaurants, which seldom ask for ID (though banks and exchange offices generally do).

American Express

1150 Connecticut Avenue NW, between L & M Streets, Downtown (1-202 457 1300). Farragut North Metro. **Open** 9am-5.30pm Mon-Fri.
Map p252 G5.
Call 1-800 721 9768 for purchase or refund of travellers' cheques.

Travelex

1800 K Street, NW, at 18th Street, Foggy Bottom (1-202 872 1428/ www.travelex.com). Farragut North Metro. **Open** 9am-5pm Mon-Fri. **Map** p284 G5.

Directory

Travelex also has branches at Union Station; at the corner of 14th and I Streets; and Dulles and National airports. The central number is 1-800 287 7362.

International networks

Cirrus/MasterCard (1-800 424 7787) and **Plus/Visa** (1-800 843 7587) are also linked, respectively, to Maestro and Delta, which let the card function as a debit card to pay for goods and services. Credit and debit cards can be used in ATMs (call the above numbers to find out your nearest), but only debit cards can be used to get cash back when making a purchase.

Lost/stolen

In the event of a lost or stolen card, call the company immediately to deactivate it and also to request a replacement. Travellers' cheques can be replaced via a local office.

American Express cards
1-800 992 3404.
American Express travellers' cheques
1-888 412 6945.
Diners Club
1-800 234 6377.
Discover
1-800 347 2683.
MasterCard
1-800 622 7747.
Thomas Cook travellers' cheques
1-800 223 7373.
Visa
1-800 847 2911.

Tax

The general consumer DC sales tax is 5.75 per cent; it's five per cent in Maryland and Virginia. The tax on restaurant meals is ten per cent and is added later to the advertised menu price, while the tax on hotel and motel rooms is 14.5 per cent.

Opening hours

Business hours in DC are 9am to 5pm Monday to Friday. Most shops are open 10am to 5 or 6pm Monday to Saturday and noon to 6pm on Sunday. Even in the business-heavy downtown area, most shops are open at the weekend. From Monday to Saturday, mall stores usually stay open until 9pm. On the whole, banks open at 9am and close at about 3pm on weekdays only. Restaurants

are usually open for lunch from 11am to 2pm and for dinner from 5 to 10pm, but many are open all day. In Adams Morgan, Georgetown and Dupont Circle, some bars and eateries don't close until 2 or 3am.

Police

There are three main phone numbers you should know in case you need to reach the police. The first number, **911**, is used in cases of emergencies: if a crime is in progress or has just occurred, or if you see a fire or medical emergency or a major vehicle crash; it is also the number for violent crimes.

The police non-emergency number, **311**, is for minor vehicle crashes, property crimes that are no longer in progress, and animal control problems. If you have a need for any other city service, call **1-202 727 1000**. A good resource is http://dc.gov.

Postal services

Call 1-202 635 5300 or check the phone book to find your nearest post office. They are usually open 8am-5pm on weekdays; some open for limited hours on Saturdays. Mail can be sent from any of the big blue mailboxes on street corners, but if you are sending a package overseas that is heavier than 16oz, it must be sent directly from a post office and accompanied by a customs form. Thomas Cook and American Express (for both, *see p231*) provide a postal service for their clients.

General Mail Facility

900 Brentwood Road, NE, at New York Avenue, NE (1-202 635 5300). Rhode Island Avenue Metro. **Open** 8am-8pm Mon-Fri; 8am-6pm Sat; 10.30am-6pm Sun. **Credit** AmEx, MC, V.
The main postal facility, but quite a way from downtown. A letter sent Poste Restante will end up here; better to have it sent to a specific post office (you'll need the zip code). Mail is held 30 days.

National Capitol Station Post Office

City Post Office Building, North Capitol Street & Massachusetts Avenue, NE, Union Station & around (1-202 523 2628). Union Station Metro. **Open** 7am-midnight Mon-Fri; 7am-8pm Sat, Sun. **Credit** AmEx, MC, V. **Map** p253 K6.

Religion

Adas Israel Congregation

2850 Quebec Street, NW, Cleveland Park (1-202 362 4433/www.adas israel.org). Cleveland Park Metro. **Map** p250 F1.
Conservative Jewish.

Basilica of the National Shrine of the Immaculate Conception

400 Michigan Avenue, NE, at Fourth Street, NE (1-202 526 8300/www. nationalshrine.com). Brookland-CUA Metro. **Map** p251 L1.
The biggest Catholic church in the western hemisphere.

Foundry Methodist Church

1500 16th Street, NW, at P Street, Dupont Circle (1-202 332 4010/ www.foundryumc.org). Dupont Circle Metro. **Map** p250 H4.

Islamic Center

2551 Massachusetts Avenue, NW, at Belmont Road, Adams Morgan (1-202 332 8343/www.theislamic center.com). Dupont Circle Metro then N2, N4, N6 bus. **Map** p250 F3.

New York Avenue Presbyterian Church

1313 New York Avenue, NW, between 13th & 14th Streets, Downtown (1-202 393 3700/ www.nyapc.org). McPherson Square Metro. **Map** p252 H5.

St John's Episcopal Church

1525 H Street, NW, at Lafayette Square, White House & around (1-202 347 8766/www.stjohns-dc.org). McPherson Square Metro. **Map** p252 H5.

Washington Hebrew Congregation

3935 Macomb Street, NW, at Massachusetts Avenue, Cleveland Park (1-202 362 7100/www.whc temple.org). Cleveland Park Metro. **Map** p249 D1.
Reformed Jewish.

Washington National Cathedral

Massachusetts & Wisconsin Avenues, NW, Upper Northwest (1-202 537 6200/www.cathedral.org/ cathedral). Bus 30, 32, 34, 35, 36. **Map** *p249 E2.*
Episcopal.

Safety & security

Apart from the large-scale security concerns and restrictions that come from being the capital of the United States, the areas of DC that are notorious for crime are parts of the Southeast and Northeast quadrants plus pockets of the Northwest, mostly east of 16th Street and north of Columbia Road, far from the main (and even most of the secondary) tourist sights. The threat of crime near the major visitor destinations is generally small.

The area around the Capitol is very heavily policed, and Metro trains and stations are also well-patrolled and virtually crime-free. Adams Morgan and the U Street/ 14th Street Corridor are much too heavy with traffic to be considered dangerous (the panhandlers are mostly harmless; feel free to ignore them), but the sidestreets surrounding them can be dodgy after dark, as can some streets near Union Station and around Capitol Hill. Stick to the heavily populated, well-lit thoroughfares when walking in these areas at night.

Generally, as in any big city, you should take the usual security precautions. Be wary of pickpockets, especially in crowds. Look like you know what you're doing and where you're going – even if you don't. Use common sense and follow your intuition about people and situations. If someone does approach you for money in a threatening manner, don't resist. Hand over your wallet, then dial 911 or hail a cab and ask the driver to take you to the nearest police station where you can report the theft and get a reference number to claim insurance and travellers' cheque refunds.

Smoking

Fewer and fewer people in the US smoke, and DC is no exception. It is illegal to smoke on public transport, in public buildings, theatres, cinemas, restaurants (except in designated smoking areas) and most shops. If you want to smoke, best go outside. The City Council passed a law in January 2006 that will make virtually all indoor places smoke free by 2007.

Study

While not a full-blown university town like Boston, DC does have its share of colleges and universities. The major ones are listed below, but there are many smaller institutions, branch universities and schools in suburban Virginia and Maryland. Most of these schools conduct summer courses in politics, international relations and other programmes directly relating to the city's weighty political scene.

For Washington's libraries, *see p228.*

American University

4400 Massachusetts Avenue, NW, at Nebraska Avenue, Upper Northwest (1-202 885 1000/www. american.edu). Tenleytown-AU Metro then M4 bus. **Map** *p248 C1.*
Over 11,000 students attend this university in residential Washington. It has strong arts and sciences programmes, and a law library.

Catholic University of America

620 Michigan Avenue, NE, at Harewood Road, Northeast (1-202 319 5000/www.cua.edu). Brookland-CUA Metro. **Map** *p251 L1.*
Catholic University received a papal charter in 1887. Its diverse programmes include architecture, engineering and law.

Georgetown University

37th & O Streets, NW, Georgetown (1-202 687 0100/www.george town.edu). Dupont Circle Metro then G2 bus. **Map** *p249 D4.*
Georgetown attracts students from all over the world to its prestigious international relations, business, medical and law schools.

George Washington University

I & 22nd Streets, NW, Foggy Bottom (1-202 994 1000/www. gwu.edu). Foggy Bottom-GWU Metro. **Map** *p252 G5.*
GWU houses law and medical schools, and has strong programmes in politics and international affairs.

Howard University

2400 Sixth Street, NW, at Georgia Avenue, Shaw (1-202 806 6100/ www.howard.edu). Shaw-Howard University Metro. **Map** *p251 J2.*
About 10,000 students attend this predominantly African American university, studying medicine, engineering, dentistry, social work and communications.

University of the District of Columbia

4200 Connecticut Avenue, NW, at Van Ness Street, Upper Northwest (1-202 274 5000/www.udc.edu). Van Ness-UDC Metro.
UDC was formed in 1974 as a land-grant institution with an open admissions policy. Not as prestigious as most of its neighbours, it nonetheless has a variety of programmes, including arts, sciences and law.

Telephones

Dialling & codes

The area code for DC is 202. To make a call within the District, you need only dial the seven-digit local number, not the 202 area code. Maryland and Virginia are more complicated. The area codes for the city of Alexandria and the counties of Arlington and Fairfax in Virginia are 1-703 and 1-571. In Maryland, Prince George's County and Montgomery County both use 1-301 and 1-240 area codes. Calls from any one of these area codes to another, as well as within one area code, are classed as local, but you must dial the area code, even if you're dialling from DC. Some calls are treated as local, others long distance. Non-Washingtonians will probably not know which is which, but you will always get through by dialling the '1' first, and if it is a local call you will only be charged for a local rate. For this reason we have included the 1 prefix before all numbers.

Numbers to other parts of the US always require the 1 prefix before the area code. This is also the case for numbers beginning 1-800, 1-888 and 1-877, which are all toll free within the US, though note that your hotel may still bill you a flat fee. Most are also accessible from outside DC and – at the usual international rates – from outside the US.

Public phones

Yes, even in an age when it's not possible to go a block without seeing someone with a mobile phone pressed to their ear, there are still public pay phones in DC. To use a public phone, pick up the receiver, listen for a dial tone and feed it change (35¢ for a local call). The operator is free, as is directory assistance on a Verizon phone (other companies may charge 35¢). If you use a payphone for long distance or international calls, use a phonecard (available at supermarkets, drugstores and convenience stores everywhere) or calling card. Otherwise, you will need a lot of change – a quarter is the highest denomination a payphone will accept. After you dial the number a recorded voice will tell you how much you need to put in. Some payphones, especially at airports and big hotels, accept credit cards.

Most hotels charge a flat fee for telephone calls which can quickly add up. You can get round this at some hotels by using a house phone and asking the operator to connect you to your number. Alternatively, look for payphones, usually located in the lobby or near the restrooms. If you need to make a long-distance or international call, you will often have to leave a cash deposit or credit card at the hotel desk. But the rates will be high, so you are better off using a phonecard.

Operators & assistance

For local directory assistance within the DC metro area, dial 411. For national long-distance enquiries, dial 1 + [area code] + 555 1212 (if you don't know the area code, dial 0 for the operator). For international calls, dial 011 then the country code (UK 44; New Zealand 64; Australia 61 – see the phone book for others). For collect (reverse charge) calls, dial 0 for the operator. If you use voicemail, note that the pound key is the one marked # and the star key is *. On automated answering systems, 0 often gets you through to a real-life operator.

Mobile phones

US readers with mobile phones should contact their mobile phone operators about using their phone in Washington. All five UK mobile phone operators have roaming agreements with major US operators, so you should be able to use your mobile in Washington – as long as your phone is a tri-band (and modern phones generally are). All you need do is ensure that the roaming facility is set up before you travel.

Time

Washington, DC, operates on Eastern Standard Time (the same time zone as New York and Miami), which is five hours behind Greenwich Mean Time (London) and three hours ahead of Pacific Standard Time (Los Angeles). Clocks go forward one hour on the first Sunday in April to daylight saving time and back one hour on the last Sunday in October. To find out the exact time, call 1-202 844 2525.

Tipping

Cab drivers and waiters are generally tipped 20 per cent – more for exceptionally good service. Bartenders expect 50¢-$1 per drink. Hairdressers get ten per cent, bellhops $1 per bag and hotel maids $1-$2 per day.

Toilets

Malls, museums, bookstores and even some grocery stores have toilets; clothes shops almost always do not. In restaurants you may have to buy a drink in order to use them.

Tourist information

British visitors can call the Washington DC Convention & Tourism Corporation's London outpost on 020 8877 4521 for an information pack, or the Capital Region Brochure Line on 01234 767928. Like other US cities, Washington employs street cleaners who are also versed in essential information for visitors – they are highly visible in their red or gold jackets.

DC Chamber of Commerce Visitor Information Center

Ronald Reagan Building & International Trade Center, 1300 Pennsylvania Avenue, NW, between 13th & 14th Streets, The Federal Triangle (1-866 324 7386/ www.dcvisit.com). Federal Triangle Metro. **Open** *Apr-Sept* 8.30am-5.30pm Mon-Fri; 9am-4pm Sat. *Oct-Mar* 9am-4.30pm Mon-Fri . **Map** p252 H6.
Tons of information and advice.

International Visitors Information Service

Meridian International Center, 1630 Crescent Place, NW, at 16th Street, Adams Morgan (1-202 939 5544/ www.meridian.org). U Street/ African-Amer Civil War Memorial/ Cardozo Metro. **Open** 9am-5pm Mon-Fri. **Map** p250 H3.
Brochures, maps and resources for international visitors, including a 'language bank' (for translations) with 42 languages (1-202 939 5587) and a helpful information desk at Dulles International Airport.

Local weather
1-202 936 1212.

National Park Service
1-202 208-6843/www.nps.gov.

Smithsonian information
1-202 633 1000/www.si.edu/visit.
Information on all the Smithsonian's museums.

Traveler's Aid
1-703 546 1127/ www.travelersaid.org.
Network of travel support, with locations at Union Station, and National and Dulles airports.

Washington DC Convention & Tourism Corporation

4th Floor, 901 Seventh Street, NW, at I Street, Downtown (1-202 789 7000/www.washington.org). Metro Center Metro. **Open** 9am-5pm Mon-Fri. **Map** p253 J5.
A good starting point for general information. on the city.

Visas & immigration

If you are a citizen of the United Kingdom, the Republic of Ireland, Australia, New Zealand, Japan or most western European countries (check with your local US embassy or consulate for the exact status of your nation), have proof of intent to leave (such as a return plane ticket) and are visiting the US for less than 90 days, you need only a valid passport and visa waiver form (*see p231*) to enter the country. Canadians and Mexicans do not need visas but must have legal proof of their residency and valid identification. Citizens of other countries or people who are staying for longer than 90 days or who need a work or study visa should contact their nearest US consulate or embassy well before the date of travel (note that visitors requiring visas will also have to submit biometric data). The US embassy in London has a service (020 7499 9000) for all general visa enquiries. The website (www.usembassy.org.uk) also has information. Another useful resource is www.visafaqs.com.

When to go

The best time to visit Washington is autumn, avoiding the humidity and heat of summer and the colder winter weather. April is, in theory, a lovely time to come – early in the month, the cherry blossoms are in flower at the Tidal Basin. However, it's also one of DC's busiest months for tourism. In autumn, the trees turn brilliant shades of orange, red and yellow, and the weather is pleasant. Perhaps most importantly, tourists are scarcer in autumn than in mid summer. If you do visit in summer, be sure to drink plenty of water so you don't get dehydrated, and start sightseeing early to avoid long lines. Daytime summer temperatures average 86°F (30.2°C) but feel much hotter because of the high humidity; aim to be inside an air-conditioned building at midday. Winters are fairly mild, but even a light snowfall can still bring the city to a halt. Don't be surprised if there are long periods of bitter weather. Otherwise, winter days can be bright and clear.

If you want to see government in action, remember that in addition to Christmas and Easter breaks, Congress is in recess during August and the Supreme Court from May to September.

National holidays

New Year's Day (1 January); **Martin Luther King Jr Day** (third Monday in January); **Presidents Day** (third Monday in February); **Memorial Day** (last Monday in May); **Independence Day** (4 July); **Labor Day** (first Monday in September); **Columbus Day** (second Monday in October); **Election Day** (first Tuesday in November); **Veterans Day** (11 November); **Thanksgiving Day** (fourth Thursday in November); **Christmas Day** (25 December).

Women

Women travelling alone inevitably face more safety concerns than men or women in groups. Washington is no different from any other big city so take the usual precautions.

Local contacts

National Organization for Women

3rd Floor, 1100 H Street, NW, Downtown (1-202 628 8669/www. now.org). McPherson Square Metro. **Open** 9am-5pm Mon-Fri. **Map** p252 H5.
Can refer women to rape crisis centres and counselling services and provide lists of feminist events.

Average monthly climate

Month	Max (°F/°C)	Min (°F/°C)	Rainfall In/cm	Humidity %
Jan	42/5.6	26/–3.4	2.7/6.9	62
Feb	45/7.3	27/–2.8	2.7/6.9	60
Mar	56/13.4	37/2.8	3.2/8.1	59
Apr	66/19	46/7.8	2.7/6.9	58
May	76/24.6	56/13.4	3.7/9.4	64
Jun	84/29.1	66/19	3.8/9.6	66
July	88/31.3	71/25.2	3.8/9.6	67
Aug	86/30.2	70/21.2	3.9/9.9	69
Sep	80/26.9	62/16.8	3.3/8.4	70
Oct	69/20.7	50/10.1	3.0/7.6	67
Nov	58/14.5	41/5	3.1/7.9	65
Dec	47/8.4	31/–0.56	3.1/7.9	64

Directory

Further Reference

Books

Non-fiction

All the President's Men
Carl Bernstein & Bob Woodward
The story behind the Watergate scandal.

The Beat
Kip Lornell & Charles Stephenson, Jr
Go-go's fusion of funk and hip hop, DC's music.

Dance of Days
Mark Andersen & Mark Jenkins
Two decades of punk in DC.

Dream City: Race, Power and the Decline of Washington, DC
Harry Jaffe & Tom Sherwood
An in-depth look at how race and power-lust corrupted local politics.

George W Bushisms: The Slate Book of the Accidental Wit and Wisdom of Our 43nd President
Jacob Weisberg
Self-explanatory.

Godless: The Church of Liberalism
Ann Coulter
The conservative poster girl and scourge of the left sticks it to the liberal establishment – again.

Parliament of Whores
PJ O'Rourke
America's most scabrous commentator gets to grips with the US political system, as practised in Washington.

Personal History: Katherine Graham's Washington
Katherine Graham
The autobiography of the erstwhile publisher of the *Washington Post*.

Plan of Attack
Bob Woodward
The inside story of the George W Bush administration's planning for the 2003 invasion of Iraq, by the famous reporter.

Ronald Reagan
Dinesh D'Souza
A view from the right: Dinesh D'Souza puts the case for viewing Ronald Reagan's presidency in a more favourable light.

Shadow: Five Presidents & the Legacy of Watergate
Bob Woodward
Thought-provoking bestseller on how the Watergate affair affected subsequent presidential scandals.

The Truth (With Jokes)
Al Franken
This writer and political commentator continues to be George W Bush's worst nightmare.

Washington Goes to War
David Brinkley
The history of Washington during World War II.

Fiction

Drum-Taps
Walt Whitman
Whitman's war poems were directly influenced by his work in Civil War hospitals in Washington.

Echo House
Ward Just
The story of three generations of a powerful Washington family, written by a former *Washington Post* reporter.

Empire
Gore Vidal
A historical novel based on Theodore Roosevelt's Washington, Vidal's epic brings America during the Gilded Age into vivid focus.

King Suckerman
George P Pelecanos
Murder, drugs and the coolest music in this homage to blaxploitation.

Murder in the Map Room (and other titles)
Elliott Roosevelt
Series of White House murder mysteries written by FDR's son, with First Lady Eleanor Roosevelt as the problem-solving sleuth.

Primary Colors
Anonymous
Guess who's who in this fictionalised retelling of Bill Clinton's run for the presidency.

The Tenth Justice
Brad Meltzer
Bestselling thriller based on the travails of an ambitious young clerk to a Supreme Court justice.

Thank You for Smoking
Christopher Buckley
Send-up of TV pundits and political special-interest groups.

Reference

AIA Guide to the Architecture of Washington, DC
Christopher Weeks
Concise descriptions and photos of DC's most notable structures, including 100 built since the mid 1970s.

Buildings of the District of Columbia
Pamela Scott & Antoinette J Lee
Detailed architectural history of DC, from the Revolutionary War to post-World War II, with photos, drawings and maps.

The Guide to Black Washington
Sandra Fitzpatrick & Maria R Goodwin
Places and events of significance to DC's African-American heritage.

Websites

Listed below are some useful stand-alone websites. Many tourist information services, museums and attractions have their own sites, which are given in the listings of their respective entries elsewhere in this guide.

Washington Post
www.washingtonpost.com.
The Post makes every word it prints available online, although the stories are moved after two weeks to the archives, access to which requires the payment of a fee.

Washington City Paper
www.washingtoncitypaper.com.
Much of this paper's content is not available online, but its listings and classifieds are there, however, in a searchable form.

WTOP News
www.wtopnews.com.
The city's leading all-news radio station's excellent website includes breaking news and helpful links to weather and traffic reports, as well as a listen-live option.

DCist
www.dcist.com.
Daily digest for the blog generation, committed to 'documenting the nation's capital and all its quirks, one small detail at a time'.

Craigslist
www.washingtondc.craigslist.org.
More than ten million people visit this exhaustive community clearing house of jobs, housing, products and information each month.

DC Watch
www.dcwatch.com.
For outsiders seeking a sense of the passion and perplexity of civic affairs in America's 'last colony', this site gives an exhaustive introduction.

Congress
http://thomas.loc.gov.
Links to lots of useful Congressional information, including days-in-session for the House and Senate, full text of the bills that are being considered and a listing of how congressmen and -women have voted on specific issues in the past.

Index

Note Page numbers in **bold** indicate section(s) giving key information on a topic; *italics* indicate photographs.

accident & emergency 227
Accommodation 40-55
  best 41
  by price budget 48, 51, 52-53, 55; *expensive* 41, 42, 45-47, 47, 49-51, 52, 55; *moderate* 41-42, 42, 47, 47-48, 48, 51, 53-54, 55; *very expensive* 41, 42, 45, 47, 48-49, 51-52, 54
  hotel bars 138
  rates & services 40
  youth hostels 40, 48
Actors Theatre of Washington 203
Adams Morgan 96
  accommodation 51-53
  bars 137-139
  restaurants 121-125
Adams Morgan Day 163
Adams, John 12-13, 29, 75
addresses 225
Adventure Theatre 167
AFI Silver Theatre & Cultural Center 170
age restrictions 134, 225
AIDS & HIV 177, 227
Air Force Memorial 109
airports 220
Alexandria 107-109, *107*
Alexandria Black History Museum 108
American Century Theater 203
American football 198
American Visionary Art Museum 212
Anacostia 106
Anacostia Community Museum for African American History & Culture 106
Anderson House 35
Annapolis 217
Annual High Heel Race 164
Annual White House Easter Egg Roll 160
antiques shops 144
aquariums *see* zoos & aquariums
Architecture 32-37
  see also individual

buildings and architects, listed by name
Arena Stage 106, **200**
Arlington & Alexandria (VA) 107-110, *107*
  accommodation 55
  map 108
Arlington House 33, **110**
Arlington National Cemetery 109-110, *110*
Armel-Leftwich Visitor Center 217
Army-Navy Club 37
Arthur M Sackler Gallery **62, 63**, 166-167
  shop 144
Arts & Industries Building 62, 90
Arts Club of Washington 84
Ash Lawn-Highland 213
Atlas Performing Arts Center 104
ATMs 231
attitude & etiquette 225
Avalon cinema 168, **169**, *169*

Babe Ruth 211
Babe Ruth Birthplace & Museum 211
babysitting services 165
bakeries 153-154
Baltimore 208, *208*, **209-213**
Baltimore Civil War Museum 211
Baltimore Maritime Museum 209
Baltimore Museum of Art 212
Baltimore Orioles 211
Baltimore Ravens 198
Baltimore-Washington International Airport 220
banks 231
barbers 156-158
Barry, Marion 20, 24
Bars 134-140
  best 135
  hotel bars 138
  politicians' hangouts 129
baseball 196, 211
Basilica of the National Shrine of the Immaculate Conception 104, 189

basketball 198
beauty shops 154-155
bicycles & cycling 195-197, 224
  rentals & tours 197
  shops 149
  trails 195-197
Bill of Rights 29, 31
Black Family Reunion 163
Black History Month 164
Black Pride 161
Blair House 71
Blowoff 177, **178**
Blue Ridge Mountains 208, 214
  boat trips 208-209, 216, 217-218
  boating 195, 208, 216, 217, 218
Bodisco House 97
Bohemian Caverns 187
books 236
book fair 164
bookshops 145-147
boutiques 147-148
Boy Scout Memorial 62
Bureau of Engraving & Printing 82
buses 223
Bush, George W 27, 29, 31
business 225

C&O Canal Towpath 196
cabaret 194
cafés & coffeehouses 117, 119, 123, 126, 127, 132-133
  gay & lesbian 180-181
Calvary Baptist Church 90
Calvert Cliffs State Park 218
Camden Yards 211, *211*
camera shops & film processing 147
Canadian Embassy *91*, 92
canoeing *see* boating
Capital Fringe festival 199
Capital Jazz Fest 161
Capital Pride 161
Capitol & around, The 32, 33, *33*, **62**, *68-69*, **76, 78**
  accommodation 41-42
  bars 134-135
Capitol Hill 105-106
  bars 140
Capitol Hill United Methodist Church 93
Caribbean Festival 162
Carlyle House 33, 107, **108**

cars & driving 224
trips out of town 208
Catholic University of America 104
Catoctin Mountain Park 197
caves 215
CD & record shops 158
Central Washington 61-82
Cherokees 29
Cherry Blossom Festival 160
Chesapeake Bay 208, **217-218**
Children 165-167
  babysitting 165
  clothes shops 148
  entertainment 165-167
Chinatown *84-85*, 87
Chinese New Year 164
Choral Arts Society 188
Christ Church, Alexandria 33, 107, **108**
Christmas 164
churches & cathedrals 34, 71, 93, 97, 99,102, 107, 145, 163, **232-233**
  as music venues 189
cinemas 168
  foreign & independent films 169
  IMAX 69
  mainstream films 168-169
  repertory 169-170
CityDance Ensemble 206
Civil War **14**, 29, 92, 97, 107, 211, 215, 218
  museum 211
Claris Smith Performing Arts Center 190
classical music 188-190
Cleveland Park 103
  bars 140
climate 235
clothes shops 147-150
clubs & lounges 191-194
Cluss, Adolf 90
comedy 194
Congressional Cemetery 93, *98*, **105**
Constitution *see* US Constitution
consumer services 225-226
contraception 227
conventions, business 225
Coolidge Auditorium, Library of Congress 190

Index

Advertisers' Index

Please refer to the relevant pages for contact details

Place of interest	
University	
Railway station	
Park or forest	
Area used in this guide	SHAW
Historic homes	🏠
Great outdoors	🌳
US Federal highway	(50)
US Interstate	495
State and provincial road	(4)
Airport	✈
DC quadrant	NE
Metro station	Ⓜ
Hotels	❶
Restaurants	❶
Bars	❶

Maps

OUR CLIMATE NEEDS
A HELPING HAND TODAY

Be a smart traveller. Help to offset your carbon emissions
from your trip by pledging Carbon Trees with Trees for Cities.

All the Carbon Trees that you donate through Trees for Cities
are genuinely planted as additional trees in our projects.

Trees for Cities is an independent charity working with local
communities on tree planting projects.

www.treesforcities.org   Tel 020 7587 1320

Trees for Cities
Charity registration number 1032154

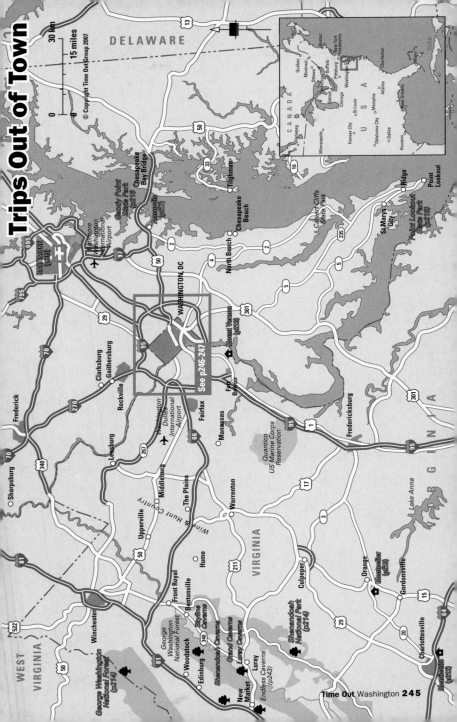

Trips Out of Town

DELAWARE

© Copyright Time Out Group 2007

30 km
15 miles

BALTIMORE (p248)

Baltimore Washington International Airport

Sandy Point State Park (p218)

Chesapeake Bay Bridge

Annapolis (p217)

Tilghman

Chesapeake Beach

North Beach

Calvert Cliffs State Park

St Mary's City

Ridge

Point Lookout

Point Lookout State Park (p219)

WASHINGTON DC

See p246-247

Mount Vernon (p250)

Fort Belvoir

Frederick

Clarksburg
Gaithersburg

Rockville

Washington Dulles International Airport

Fairfax

Manassas

Quantico US Marine Corps Reservation

Fredericksburg

Sharpsburg

Leesburg

Middleburg

The Plains

Warrenton

Lake Anna

Upperville

Winchester's Hunt Country

Hume

WEST VIRGINIA

Winchester

Front Royal

Bentonville

Skyline Caverns

New Market

Woodstock

Edinburg

Shenandoah Caverns

Grand Caverns

Luray

Luray Caverns (p243)

Endless Caverns

George Washington National Forest (p214)

George Washington National Forest

Shenandoah National Park (p214)

VIRGINIA

Orange

Montpelier (p252)

Gordonsville

Culpeper

Charlottesville

Monticello

DC Overview

270
270

RIVER RD

WISCONSIN AVE

M A R Y L A N D

BETHESDA

CHEVY CHASE

GLEN ECHO

RIVER RD

FRIENDSHIP HEIGHTS

Rock Creek Park

495

MASSACHUSETTS AVE

UPPER NORTHWEST

GEORGETOWN PIKE

LANGLEY

CONNECTICUT AVE

WISCONSIN AVE

See p248

See p249

See p250

NW

MADISON BLVD

To Dulles Airport

DOLLEY

MCLEAN

DOMINION DR

ADAMS MORGAN

Naval Observatory

GEORGETOWN

Dupont Circle

See p252

DULLES INT AIRPORT RD

CANAL RD

GEORGE WASHINGTON MEMORIAL PKWY

White House

LEESBURG PIKE

LEE HWY

NORTH GLEBE RD

WILSON BLVD

ROSSLYN

Theodore Roosevelt Island

West Potomac Park

Potomac R.

FALLS CHURCH

66

Arlington National Cemetery

LEE HWY

ARLINGTON BLVD

50

ARLINGTON BLVD

ARLINGTON

COLUMBIA PIKE

The Pentagon

Pentagon City

Ronald Reagan Washington National Airport

V I R G I N I A

LEESBURG PIKE

CRYSTAL CITY

S GLEBE RD

1

CAPITAL BELTWAY

395

SHIRLEY MEMORIAL HWY

VAN DORN ST N

KING ST

VAN DORN ST S

WASHINGTON ST

George Washington Masonic National Memorial

DUKE ST

OLD TOWN ALEXANDRIA

See p108

495 95

CAPITAL BELTWAY

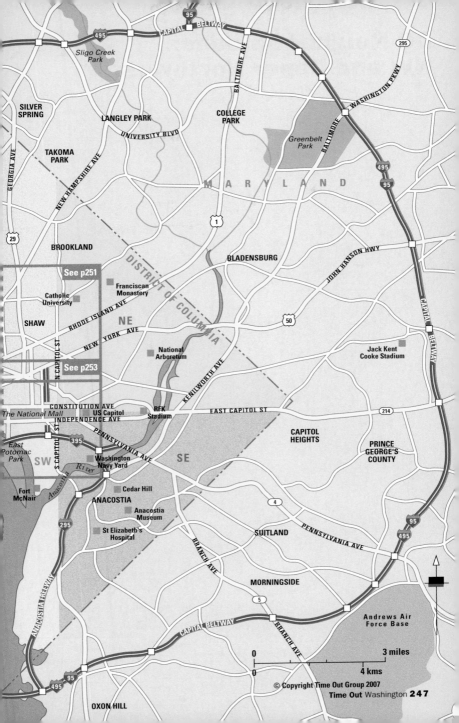

SILVER SPRING

LANGLEY PARK

COLLEGE PARK

95

495

CAPITAL BELTWAY

295

Sligo Creek Park

BALTIMORE AVE

WASHINGTON PKWY

M A R Y L A N D

Greenbelt Park

BALTIMORE

495

95

UNIVERSITY BLVD

GEORGIA AVE

NEW HAMPSHIRE AVE

TAKOMA PARK

1

29

BROOKLAND

BLADENSBURG

JOHN HANSON HWY

CAPITAL BELTWAY

D I S T R I C T   O F   C O L U M B I A

See p251

Franciscan Monastery

Catholic University

RHODE ISLAND AVE

NEW YORK AVE

50

SHAW

NE

National Arboretum

Jack Kent Cooke Stadium

N CAPITOL ST

KENILWORTH AVE

See p253

214

CONSTITUTION AVE

US Capitol

INDEPENDENCE AVE

RFK Stadium

EAST CAPITOL ST

The National Mall

395

PENNSYLVANIA AVE

CAPITOL HEIGHTS

PRINCE GEORGE'S COUNTY

East Potomac Park

SW

Washington Navy Yard

SE

S CAPITOL ST

River

Anacostia

Fort McNair

Cedar Hill

4

295

ANACOSTIA

Anacostia Museum

SUITLAND

PENNSYLVANIA AVE

St Elizabeth's Hospital

95

495

BRANCH AVE

MORNINGSIDE

ANACOSTIA FREEWAY

5

Andrews Air Force Base

CAPITAL BELTWAY

BRANCH AVE

0   3 miles

0   4 kms

© Copyright Time Out Group 2007

495

95

OXON HILL

DC Neighbourhoods:
NW and Upper Northwest

DC Neighbourhoods:
NW and NE

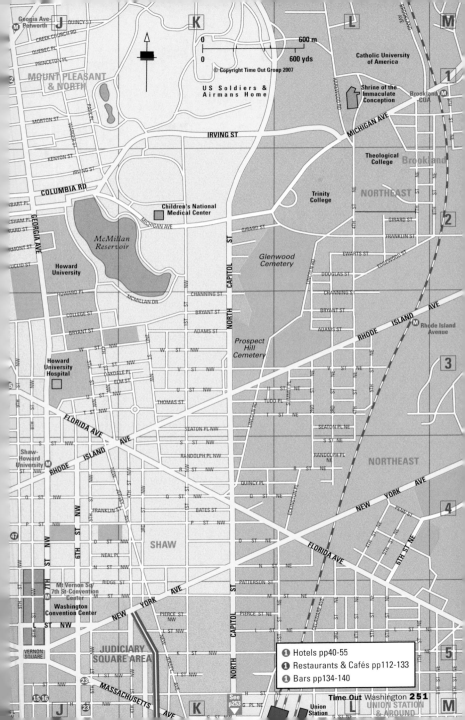

© Copyright Time Out Group 2007

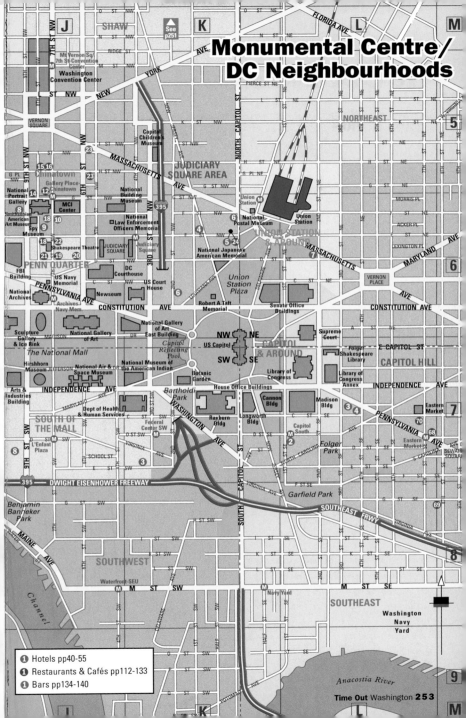

Monumental Centre/ DC Neighbourhoods

❶ Hotels pp40-55
❶ Restaurants & Cafés pp112-133
❶ Bars pp134-140

Street Index

System Map

Legend

● Red Line • Glenmont to Shady Grove
● Orange Line • New Carrollton to Vienna/Fairfax-GMU
● Blue Line • Franconia-Springfield to Largo Town Center
● Green Line • Branch Avenue to Greenbelt
● Yellow Line • Huntington to Mt Vernon Sq/7th St-Convention Center

Commuter Rail
Virginia Railway Express
Station in Service
Transfer Station
Banking
Parking
Planned Station

No Smoking

No Eating or Drinking

No Animals (except service animals)

No Audio or Video Devices (without earphones)

No Litter or Spitting

No Dangerous or Flammable Items